Syria and the Palestinians

Copyright 2001 by Ghada Hashem Talhami. This work is licensed under a modified Creative Commons Attribution-Noncommercial-No Derivative Works 3.0 Unported License. To view a copy of this license, visit *http://creativecommons.org/licenses/by-nc-nd/3.0/*. You are free to electronically copy, distribute, and transmit this work if you attribute authorship. *However, all printing rights are reserved by the University Press of Florida (http://www.upf.com). Please contact UPF for information about how to obtain copies of the work for print distribution.* You must attribute the work in the manner specified by the author or licensor (but not in any way that suggests that they endorse you or your use of the work). For any reuse or distribution, you must make clear to others the license terms of this work. Any of the above conditions can be waived if you get permission from the University Press of Florida. Nothing in this license impairs or restricts the author's moral rights.

Florida A&M University, Tallahassee
Florida Atlantic University, Boca Raton
Florida Gulf Coast University, Ft. Myers
Florida International University, Miami
Florida State University, Tallahassee
University of Central Florida, Orlando
University of Florida, Gainesville
University of North Florida, Jacksonville
University of South Florida, Tampa
University of West Florida, Pensacola

Syria and the Palestinians
The Clash of Nationalisms

Ghada Hashem Talhami

University Press of Florida
Gainesville · Tallahassee · Tampa · Boca Raton
Pensacola · Orlando · Miami · Jacksonville · Ft. Myers

Copyright 2001 by Ghada Hashem Talhami

All rights reserved

06 05 04 03 02 01   6 5 4 3 2 1

Library of Congress Cataloging-in-Publication Data
Talhami, Ghada Hashem.
Syria and the Palestinians: the clash of nationalisms / Ghada Hashem
Talhami.
p. cm.
Includes bibliographical references and index.
ISBN 0-8130-2063-8
1. Syria—Relations—Palestine. 2. Palestine—Relations—Syria.
3. Palestinian Arabs—Politics and government—20th century.
4. Nationalism—Arab countries—History—20th century.
5. Arab countries—Politics and government—20th century. I. Title.
DS95.6.P19 T35 2001
320.54'089927—dc21   00-051052

The University Press of Florida is the scholarly publishing agency for the State University System of Florida, comprising Florida A&M University, Florida Atlantic University, Florida Gulf Coast University, Florida International University, Florida State University, University of Central Florida, University of Florida, University of North Florida, University of South Florida, and University of West Florida.

University Press of Florida
15 Northwest 15th Street
Gainesville, FL 32611-2079
http://www.upf.com

Contents

Preface   vii

1. The Struggle for Geographic Coherence:
   Reclaiming Southern Syria   1

2. The Earthquake of the 1948 Palestine War   25

3. The Political Co-optation of the Palestinians   47

4. The Guerrilla Factor and Syria's Vulnerability   78

5. When Brothers Collide: The Confrontation over Lebanon   112

6. The Clash of Nationalisms   154

7. Peace or Pax Americana?   195

8. The Search for a Unified Strategy   212

Notes   221

Bibliography   233

Index   241

Preface

Western scholarship on pan-Arabism has tacitly accepted Fouad Ajami's thesis heralding the demise of this ideology. First articulated in his *Foreign Affairs* article "The Death of Pan-Arabism" (Winter 1978–79), this development was blamed for the resurgence of inter-Arab clashes, Israeli-inflicted defeat, and the replacement of the paper independence of Arab states by the steady growth of neocolonialism. A new reality emerged from this transformation, namely, a collection of individual Arab states that are steadily winning the hearts and loyalties of their citizens through their distributive capacity and monopoly over the resources of the nation. Ajami called on scholars to acknowledge the emergence of what he termed "raison d'état," which has replaced the grandiose objectives of the pan-Arabists.

No better refutation of this sweeping thesis can be found than in a careful reading of Syria's recent history. It is here that one begins to recognize the wisdom of Moshe Ma'oz and Avner Yaniv, who reminded us in *Syria under Assad* (St. Martin's Press, 1986) that the dissolution of the grand pan-Arabist idea was only partial. Both stated, based on the work of Gabriel Dor, that individual states have yet to be fully legitimized as distinctly different from the larger conceptualized and unified Arab entity. Arab states, they argued, have indeed emerged, but only against the enduring concept of a single Arab nation.

Clearly, we have just begun to study the implications of this assessment of the changing reality of the pan-Arabist idea, particularly as it relates to Palestinian-Syrian relations. We still lack a full and comprehensive study of the dilemma of Palestine in the Arab context, particularly as this Arab fragment sought to define its position vis-à-vis the pervasive notion that Palestine is fated to remain the ward of the Arab states. Although most would argue that the creation of Israel was the factor most responsible for the decline of pan-Arabism, few have analyzed other than in military and economic terms the reasons for this phenomenon. The few studies on Jordan's secret relationship with Israel, for instance, such as Avi Shlaim's *Collusion across the Jordan* (Oxford University Press, 1987), do shed some light on the consequences of fragmenting the anti-Israel struggle. Yet little is learned about the Palestinian and Arab dilemmas as they, the pseudostate and the full states, attempted to reconstruct their relations in the twilight of the pan-Arab idea.

Even the latest effort to articulate and propagate pan-Arabism—that of the Ba'th—failed to anticipate the problem of subsuming Palestinian nationalism under its finely tuned ideology. Ba'thist nationalism, as Albert Hourani reminded us in *A History of the Arab Peoples* (Harvard University Press, 1991), turned out to be but one strand of nationalism vying with such newly emergent ideas as the "Third World" for a position in the postcolonial world of the Arabs. Michel 'Aflaq, the Ba'th's original ideologue, was preoccupied with the problem of reconciling secular nationalism and the Arabs' historical experience of Third World revolutions as the inspiration for their own struggle. As Hourani has indicated, Fateh in particular determined to remain independent of Arab regimes after the 1967 failure to protect the remaining Arab parts of Palestine. Yet the survival of pan-Arabism became, in Hourani's words, "a pretext for the interference of one state in the affairs of others." When Syria's Ba'th regime attempted to interfere in the affairs of the Palestinian guerrillas in order to contain them, differences between Palestinian particularism and Arab nationalism loomed on the horizon.

The Palestinians' mistake, as will be illustrated here, was the failure to recognize when to move with the Arab tide and when to balk. This was partly due to their illusion of absolute independence from the Arab states. According to Bassam Tibi's interpretation in *Arab Nationalism: A Critical Inquiry* (St. Martin's Press, 1971), this illusion was fostered by the Fanonesque idea of an emerging nationalism that is born in the process of the anticolonial struggle. But unlike the classic Third World revolutions, such as those of Cuba and Vietnam, which the Palestinian Liberation Organization (PLO) took as its model, the PLO and particularly Fateh lacked some of the important elements of a mass revolution. As Samir Amin stated in his classic work *The Arab Nation: Nationalism and Class Struggles* (Zed Press, 1983), the PLO defined the armed struggle in military terms only, having missed the social revolution entirely.

This book brings home the message elucidated even in the literature of the Arab League of States—namely, that its members constituted several states but only one nation. Thus, all the league's members who were sovereign states, with the exception of the Palestinians, coexisted in this mythical framework of equal representation and rights. This structure inevitably encouraged the interjection of each member in the affairs of the other in the name of common nationhood. But along the way, as the Palestinians' struggle took them from one Arab theater to the next, absence of a clear view of Arab nationalism and Palestinian particularism led to the tragic battles of Amman, Beirut, and Tripoli. This book offers a modest explanation of this loss of vision on the part of Syrians and Palestinians alike.

Several agencies and individuals contributed to the completion of this research. I am first and foremost indebted to the International Fulbright Commission for granting me a semester of study, the fall of 1997, in Syria. Without that opportunity I would not have been able to approach this subject with any confidence. This grant enabled me to lecture at the Syrian University at Damascus and to learn through lengthy contacts with people in all walks of life of the persistent centrality of the Palestine issue to Syria's self-image in the Arab world. My thanks go especially to Professor Sadek al-ʿAzm, noted Syrian philosopher and critic, who facilitated many of my contacts at the university. Emeritus professor of history Najda al-Khamash also was of great help in making possible my contacts with the university. While in Syria, I benefited from the support extended by the staff of the Institut Français des Études Arabes à Damas (IFEAD) and the Syrian National Archives (Markaz al-Watha'iq al-Tarikhiyyah). My greatest thanks go to Dr. Daʿad Hakim, the director of the archives, whose gracious support and remarkable understanding of the needs of visiting scholars made my research so much easier. The staff of al-Thahiriyah Library were also very helpful. I would like to thank, in addition, scores among the leadership and elite of Syria's Palestinian community, inside and outside of the Yarmouk refugee suburb of Damascus, who contributed valuable and surprising insight into the nature of the Syrian-Palestinian relationship. The American Cultural Center of Damascus and its director, Dr. Evelyn Early, opened many doors that would otherwise have been difficult to penetrate, even for a Palestinian-American expatriate scholar like myself.

In the United States, special thanks go to Professor Fred Donner of the Oriental Institute of the University of Chicago, who put me in touch with several prominent Syrian scholars. Finally, this book would not have been possible without the serious commitment of Lake Forest College to scholarly research. I owe many thanks to the administration of the college for being supportive of my efforts to follow the politics of the Arab World and to enhance my scholarship in this field. It should be noted, however, that none of these individuals or groups bear any responsibility for the views expressed in this book; they are mine alone. As in any writing adventure, a work of this length quickly takes on a life of its own and develops into a mosaic of analyses and information, shaped and framed by the author alone.

1

The Struggle for Geographic Coherence
Reclaiming Southern Syria

The area extending from the Taurus Mountains in the north to the northern fringes of the Sinai Desert in the south, and from western Iraq to the eastern shores of the Mediterranean Sea, was always perceived as one territorial unit. The Arabs called it *Cham*, but gradually it became known as Syria.[1] Anton Sa'adeh, the founder of the Syrian Social National Party (SSNP), reflected on the origin of the term *Syria* by emphasizing its distinctness from the term *'Araba*, denoting the birthplace of Arabs. Syrians, on the other hand, inhabit something called Syria because the name derives from *Assuria* (Ashur), the city-state on the upper Tigris River that gave rise to the Assyrian Empire, which at one point dominated this part of the world. Syrian Canaanites who were Arabized also predominated in the Arabian Peninsula in ancient times, and may have been greater in number than the pure Arabs who entered Syria over time and became Syrianized. The point Sa'adeh was making is that Arabs and Syrians were not the same and that Syrians enjoyed a common geographic bond that distinguished them even from those with whom they shared linguistic and religious ties. Arabs, he concluded, were not a race but the inhabitants of a common domicile. Thus it is geography that determines national roots and origins, and the Syrians were no exception to this general rule.[2]

Sa'adeh was clearly arguing his specific political program, but his point was not exaggerated. Syria was regarded as an integral territorial unit by various Arab empire builders, the most recent being Muhammad 'Ali Pasha of Egypt. Following his Arabian campaigns in the name of Sultan Mahmoud II, Muhammad 'Ali discovered the strategic value of the Syrian territory and contemplated using it as a springboard for his imperial ambition. After conquering Syria in 1833, his son and field commander, Ibrahim Pasha, at first declined a request by the clergy to invoke his father's name during the Friday prayers, an honor customarily reserved for the sultan. But after conquering Aleppo, Ibrahim took a similar proposal to his father, also suggesting that currency be minted in the Egyptian ruler's name. Both ideas were declined in order to avoid alarming the great powers. But the Syrian province continued to be the centerpiece of Muhammad 'Ali's dream of an independent Arab kingdom. This entity was to be totally free of its Ottoman shackles; it would be anchored in Egypt but extend westward to Tunisia. Muhammad 'Ali was thus the first modern Arabized ruler to appreciate Syria's strategic value to his dreams of Egyptian sovereignty and independence.[3]

In addition, the Syrian province attracted Muhammad 'Ali's attention because of its natural resources. Coal from the Mountain of Lebanon was central to Egypt's industrialization plans, and the timber of the Syrian coast would be valuable for building Muhammad 'Ali's military and commercial fleets. Also, Syria beckoned with its silk products, olives, and soaps, as well as its animal skins and horses. Then there was the indisputable religious significance of Jerusalem and Damascus, which would enable Muhammad 'Ali to fortify his claims of religious legitimacy as a contender for the Ottoman throne.[4]

This Ottoman province was originally organized into the pashaliks of Aleppo, Damascus, and Tripoli. The Damascus pashalik (a territory ruled by a pasha) included within its boundaries the districts (Liwa') of Jerusalem, Damascus, Gaza, Nablus, Safad, 'Ajloun, Sidon, Beirut, and al-Shobak. The Tripoli pashalik included the districts of Tripoli, Homs, Sulaimiya, and Jabala. By 1660 two new pashaliks were added, those of Acre and Sidon. Some of the districts originally administered by the pashaliks of Damascus and Tripoli were shifted to the control of the Acre and Sidon pashaliks, and the Mount of Lebanon was accorded autonomous rule under its own local princes. With the onset of the Egyptian period, new changes were introduced and administrative boundaries were redrawn to enhance the contact of major Syrian ports with European traders. Damascus was made the seat of the Egyptian governor, the first being one Sherif Bey, the governor of Upper Egypt. His new title was the governor (hukumdar) of Arabistan. Most of the other administrative posts were assigned to heads of influential local Syrian families who did not oppose Egyptian rule. The Egyptian period in Syria, therefore, eliminated the heavy-handed rule of Ottoman military officials while Ibrahim Pasha prevented Syria from being inundated with Egyptian administrators. Syrians were heavily involved in administering their own homeland. A consultative assembly made up of notables helped the Egyptian administration. Damascus, often referred to as Cham, was the first to enjoy the innovation of a consultative assembly in 1832. This assembly of 22 members included a Jewish and a Christian representative. Members of this assembly were entrusted with judicial tasks. Every major city of 20,000 or more had an assembly with an elected chief and a membership of 12 to 21. Enjoying great freedom, these assemblies dealt with issues referred to it by the governor, while the final decision on all issues rested with Ibrahim Pasha.[5]

The Egyptian period, though modernizing and innovative, did not spell the end of rebellions against established authority. Some of these were direct acts of resistance to the centralizing and modernizing efforts of the new administration. The first took place in 1834 in Palestine, where local feudal families, such as the Abu-Ghosh, were accustomed to exercising a lawless authority by extracting illegal tributes from visiting pilgrims, particularly in the Jerusalem area. A rebellion in the Gaza area was inspired by Bedouin resistance to any kind of centralized rule. In the Nablus area a major rebellion was sparked by the institution of a military draft. In Hebron rebels managed to destroy water-storage tanks. The intensity of the rebellion of Palestinian towns and villages required the personal military intervention of Ibrahim Pasha before law and order were restored. The Nablus uprising, however, recurred and was put down more ruthlessly the second time around. The uprising in Safad targeted Jews and their properties. Eventually, the rebellion spread to Nuseiriyah and Latakia, where Christian and government properties were attacked. Only the Druze rebellion, in reaction to attempts to disarm and draft them, rivaled the Palestinian rebellion in intensity.[6]

The end of Egyptian rule in Syria reinforced the sense of national separateness and distinctiveness among the population of the Syrian province. The return of Ottoman rule plunged the area once again into murderous intrigues, local uprisings, and generally anarchic conditions. The province, however, retained its geographic character as a single integral unit that included—even in the eyes of outside diplomats such as Qostantin Mickaelovich Basily—modern Syria, Lebanon, and Palestine. Basily, serving as the Russian consul at Beirut from 1839 to 1853, provided an informal eyewitness account of the province's most turbulent years. While recording the development of Beirut as an international port, he also faithfully documented the distinct character that set Syria apart from both Egypt and the Ottoman lands. He emphasized not only the religious mosaic that is Syria but also its long and painful slide into civil dissolution and socioeconomic anarchy. Toward the end of the Egyptian era, Palestine—more so than other parts of Syria—fell victim to the total anarchy caused by the revival of tribal rivalries and peasant seizure of wealthy monasteries and churches. Departing Egyptian troops were often followed by marauding peasants who threatened Jerusalem and Jaffa.[7]

The restoration of Ottoman rule following Ibrahim Pasha's withdrawal in 1841 was the last major shift in Syria's international fortunes before the First World War. The immediate losers were the Christians, who suffered from the reprisals of advancing Turkish troops and vengeful attacks by the long-suffering local Muslim majority. The other losers were the Damascene merchants, whose chances of benefiting from trade with India were lost forever as a result of rising Bedouin attacks on the rich eastern caravan trade. Ottoman control, however, remained tenuous throughout the second half of the nineteenth century.[8]

Syrian secret societies proliferated as early as the 1880s, plotting independence and an end to Ottoman rule. These societies conspired to place Prince 'Abd al-Qader al-Jaza'iri, an Algerian exile living in Damascus, on the throne of a future Syria. Innocuous societies that were formed in Constantinople in 1909, such as Jam'iyat al-Ikha' al-'Arabi, helped coalesce the Syrian elite into nationalist groups bent on achieving independence. By 1913 a conference was convened in Paris by Arab literary and political figures from Syria, Iraq, Egypt, and Constantinople; participants called for either a decentralized political system for the Arab territories or total independence. The conferees demanded that the Ottoman government make specific reforms, as well as grant political rights to the Arabs and make Arabic the official language in the Ottoman National Assembly and throughout the Arab provinces. The ruling Committee of Union and Progress (CUP) threatened the Arab conveners with reprisals and accused them of maintaining foreign contacts inimical to the interests of the Ottoman state. A year later, the Unionists abolished all Arab political parties and exiled 490 military officers from the Ottoman capital in order to prevent a second conference from taking place.[9]

The Unionists finally had an opportunity to intimidate the Syrians by assigning the rebellious province to Jamal Pasha and his troops as the notorious "butcher of Syria" was heading to a 1915 confrontation with the British in Egypt. Headquartered in Jerusalem, the new Turkish military leader made it his mission to prosecute and incarcerate Syrian nationalists, whom he accused of treason. He also placed a land and naval siege around Syria in order to prevent its seizure by the British. The blockade resulted in mass starvation in several parts of the region.[10]

Ahmad Jamal Pasha, the Turkish leader, was one of the three-member Committee of Union and Progress, which also included Tal'at and Anwar

Pashas. The committee displayed great intolerance toward rebellious nationalities within the empire, particularly the Arabs and Armenians. Espousing the Turkification of the empire, Tal'at and Jamal carried out a massive removal of these two nationalities from their homeland. Jamal also engaged in well-executed acts of deception by befriending famous Syrian nationalists and journalists such as 'Abd al-Rahman Shahbandar, Muhammad Kurd 'Ali, and 'Abd al-Ghani al-'Arisi and then suddenly turning against them. Arab nationalists became particularly suspicious of the CUP later on because of published accounts detailing Sultan 'Abd al-Hamid's indictment of the Unionists as facilitators of Zionist settlement in Palestine.[11]

Syrian nationalists soon found a future leader and unifier in the person of Prince Faisal of the Hijaz. After establishing secret contacts with Al-'Arabiyah al-Fatah underground society, Faisal began to favor the idea of total rebellion against the Ottomans. His views influenced Sherif Hussein of Mecca, his father, especially after Faisal failed to secure the release of several prominent Syrian nationalists from Jamal Pasha's jails.[12] As the Hijazi ruler continued to intercede on the side of the Syrian nationalists, Jamal Pasha grew increasingly concerned over the sherif's intentions and his ability to influence the Syrians. In consequence, most Arab officers in the Ottoman army were dispersed to various fighting fronts, and Hussein was subjected to a campaign of propaganda and harassment accusing him of plotting to create a dynastic kingdom in the Hijaz.[13]

Many Syrian patriots experienced torture at the hands of Jamal Pasha and his officers at the infamous Khan al-Pasha, the caravansary of a former governor of Damascus. Their main crime was, in Jamal's eyes, suspicion of plotting to facilitate the revolt of the Hijaz. Among his first victims, executed in 1915 after the worst mock trials in the history of the empire, were 'Abd al-Karim Khalil, head of the society of Al-Muntada al-'Arabi, and Salim al-Ahmad 'Abd al-Hadi, brother of the Nablus delegate to the Ottoman parliament Amin Bey 'Abd al-Hadi. Others receiving death sentences in absentia included several prominent Palestinians, such as Hafiz Bey al-Sa'id, the Jaffa delegate to the Ottoman parliament, Sheikh Sa'id al-Karim, the mufti (archbishop) of Toulkarm, and Hassan Hamad of Nablus. In the 'Aleh trial in Lebanon, Jamal Pasha's victims included Riadh al-Solh, the future Prime Minister of Lebanon, and his father, Ridha al-Solh. Faris al-Khouri, the future Syrian Prime Minister, also experienced interrogation and imprisonment. Syria's future president, Shukri al-Quwatli, attempted suicide after experiencing torture when his affiliation with Al-'Arabiyah al-Fatah became known. In time, Jamal Pasha's police ferreted out information about such secret societies as Al-Qahtaniyah, Hizb al-Lamarkaziyah, and Hizb al-'Ahd. After spending three years in Syria, Jamal Pasha evacuated his troops in 1917 and departed laden with looted treasure. He met his end at the hands of an Armenian assassin at Tiflis in 1921.[14]

The Arabs Face the Mandates

The end of the Ottoman era opened a wide window for the empire's suppressed Arab population. In the period before the French and British mandates were established in the former Ottoman territories, there was great diplomatic activity on the part of Sherif Hussein's son Prince Faisal and his team of Arab and British advisors. Among Faisal's closest aides during those uncertain years was 'Awni 'Abd al-Hadi, a French-educated Palestinian lawyer who participated in Faisal's fruitless efforts to prevent the detachment of Palestine from the Syrian homeland. 'Abd al-Hadi, who began his legal studies in Paris in 1908, was among the founders of Al-'Arabiyah al-Fatah society in 1911, and one of the conveners of the 1913 Arab conference in Paris. After meeting Syrian journalist 'Abd al-Ghani al-'Arisi, 'Abd al-Hadi was converted to the ideas of al-Lamarkaziyah, the secret society advocating decentralization and reforms for the Arab territories within the Ottoman system of government. While in Paris, he came face to face with the intrigues of Lawrence of Arabia to compel Faisal to sign the Faisal-Weizmann Agreement without understanding its English-language text.[15]

Although 'Abd al-Hadi referred to his country at the beginning of 1914 as Syria, he later clarified that Syria was then an appropriate term since it included Palestine and Transjordan. But he was also pulled in the direction of his Palestinian birthplace in reaction to the Zionist intrigue he witnessed during Faisal's participation in the 1919 Paris peace talks. His Palestinian contacts in the Arab nationalist movement were constantly keeping him informed of developments in Palestine. Rafiq al-Tamimi, a fellow Arab nationalist from 'Abd al-Hadi's hometown of Nablus and an official on Faisal's team at Damascus, wrote in 1919 that Palestinian Christians and Muslims were determined to resist British-Zionist plans. He added that on the eve of the King-Crane commission's visit, Palestinians were united in their desire to be part of Syria, both politically and economically, and to seek total independence. When 'Abd al-Hadi returned to Damascus with Faisal in 1920, he was placed in charge of foreign affairs. The creation of the Arab kingdom of Syria on March 8, 1920, however, did not stop the European powers from moving to implement the San Remo agreement. 'Abd al-Hadi not only witnessed the battle of Maysaloun on July 24, 1920, and the massive defeat of Arab forces at the hands of the French commander General Henri Gouraud, he was also involved in a futile, last-minute effort by Faisal to convince French authorities to keep him in Syria while promising to cooperate with the new mandate government. When the French refused this offer of cooperation and ordered Faisal to leave, the Arab leader departed Damascus by train on July 25.[16]

The dismemberment of Syria into French and British mandates, 'Abd al-Hadi soon realized, began to drive a wedge between various communities of the Arab Syrian province. As a transitional figure who straddled the Ottoman and mandate eras, he was fully cognizant of the specific dangers surrounding his Palestinian homeland, but he never anticipated that European-imposed divisions would eventually breed divergent interests. 'Adel Areslan, a Syrian nationalist, complained to 'Abd al-Hadi that the Palestine Congress, meeting at Haifa on January 13, 1920, had proclaimed that the French mandate system was preferable to the British system and that Syrians were much better off than their Palestinian brethren. Areslan even intimated that the fact that the Haifa congress could have been convened at all, and that Palestinians were able to criticize the British government publicly, indicated that the very opposite of these contentions was true. When Syrians read these Palestinian statements, Areslan wrote, they might believe that they were less miserable than they really were. This could not be beneficial to the Palestinians. Why, Areslan asked, was the congress not satisfied with tackling purely Palestinian issues, such as demanding immediate independence and an end to Zionist immigration?[17]

Friction also developed between Faisal and 'Abdullah, the two sons of Sherif Hussein, over who owned the rightful title to Iraq. Faisal reported to 'Abd al-Hadi, after his acceptance of the Iraqi throne, that when he was first approached about this by the British foreign minister, Lord Curzon, Faisal had protested strongly. He reminded Curzon that the Iraqi delegates to the Syrian congress that convened in 1920 in Damascus had chosen 'Abdullah to be their monarch. Curzon replied that the decision to offer Iraq to Faisal was not his alone but had the support of the British and French governments. Curzon added that placing Faisal on the Iraqi throne was Britain's way of reassuring France that Faisal would not attack Syria. The British and French determination not to place 'Abdullah over Iraq apparently prompted Faisal to accept the British offer lest they move in the direction of a non-Hashimite choice. Faisal also became critical of Syrian nationalists who demanded the independence of all of Syria, including

Palestine, without any regard to their own weaknesses and disorganization. The Palestinians themselves, however, adopted during their first congress at Jerusalem in 1919 a Palestinian national charter rejecting the Balfour Declaration, the mandate, and Zionist immigration, and they coined the term *Southern Syria* for Palestine.[18]

Resolutions of popular congresses were not rejected by Faisal while he was a contender for the Syrian throne. Before his ejection from Syria, the reassertion of the territorial integrity of Ottoman Syria seemed as legitimate as his right to lead the Arab revolt. The Syrian congress of March 7, 1920, specifically called for the independence of Syria according to its natural boundaries, which included Syria, Lebanon, and Palestine, and it named Faisal as its choice for constitutional monarch. The only qualification attached to this blueprint was a call for recognition of the wishes of the Lebanese people for autonomous rule. The congress, however, rejected any plan to make of Palestine a national home for the Jews. By March 15 the European powers rejected this resolution and all others by the Syrian congress and declared their intent to reach a peace settlement at San Remo. The creation of the mandate system resulted from this conference, and French forces quickly began to threaten Faisal and his government.[19] The Syrian congress gave life to an executive committee representing various Syrians, Lebanese, and Palestinians, which met at Geneva, Switzerland, and continued until the 1930s to agitate for the reconstitution of all of Syria.[20]

Several prominent future Arab leaders participated in Faisal's Syrian regime. Iraq was represented by Taha al-Hashimi, later to hold the post of Iraqi Minister of Defense. Al-Hashimi was a member of Al-'Ahd underground society and was stationed in Syria at one time as part of the Fifth Ottoman Army. He returned to Syria in 1920 and joined Faisal's government there as director of general security. Following the Arab defeat at Maysaloun, he returned to Turkey as the chief of the military-history division in the General Staff office. He resigned in 1921 and joined Faisal's government in Iraq.[21] Jordanian leaders who served in Faisal's Syrian administration included Ibrahim Hashem, future Jordanian Prime Minister, who was appointed to the newly opened College of Law at Damascus.[22]

This interlocking Arab elite, though dispersed after Syria's takeover by the French, continued to cling to the nationalist territorial program of the secret societies of the Ottoman period. Refusing to accept the demise of Faisal's Arab kingdom, they gave their loyalty to various Levantine Arab governments as if they were one and the same. One of the beneficiaries of this trend was Transjordan, which appointed a series of Prime Ministers of

Syrian origin. These political exiles included Rasheed Taleeʿ, who served as the governor of Aleppo during Faisal's administration; ʿAli Ridha al-Rikabi, who was Syria's first Prime Minister under Faisal; and Hassan Khaled Abu al-Huda, one-time Prime Minister to Sultan ʿAbd al-Hamid. By 1923, however, Palestinians had replaced expatriate Syrians in most of the Jordanian ministries.[23]

Syrians continued to cling to the shattered nationalist territorial program in various and surprising ways. One of these demonstrations of commitment was the proliferation of political parties that evolved from the secret societies of the final Ottoman decades. Al-ʿArabiyah al-Fatah gave rise to the Istiqlal Party, whose branches in Jordan and Iraq (and later in Palestine) continued to espouse the objectives of total independence and Arab unity. The Syrian congress, which had proclaimed Syria's independence in its natural boundaries, eventually gave rise to the Taqqadum (Progress) Party as a parliamentary formation representing Al-ʿArabiyah al-Fatah. The Democratic Party came into being to represent the landowning elite opposed to French rule and al-Fatah. Al-Lamarkaziyah society also gave rise to a political group that participated in Faisal's government and joined hands with al-Fatah deputies. Some accounts claim that as many as 25 political parties developed in Syria between 1928 and 1934, all of which proclaimed the goal of independence as their main platform.[24]

Another Syrian effort to preserve their nationalist program involved resisting British plans to impose an unfavorable border settlement in the south, which benefited the Zionists. This battle was fought by the French as Syria's Mandate power. Syrian-Palestinian boundaries were fixed in the Paulet-Newcombe agreement, signed in Paris in February 1922, and later elaborated in a protocol defining the boundary from the Mediterranean to al-Himmah that was signed in Paris in March 1923.[25] This was not the first time that Syrians came face to face with Zionist ambitions and plans and with Jewish settlement schemes. As early as 1838, soon after the Egyptian occupation of Syria, a member of the Montefiori family of British financiers approached Muhammad ʿAli Pasha and asked to rent some one to two hundred Syrian villages for a fifty-year period. These villages were to be in northern Palestine, in the vicinity of Safad and Tiberias. The scheme was never realized, however, although the idea of acquiring land in the Golan area lingered on.[26]

By 1917 the strategic vision of Zionist planners had again focused on the Golan area. The Golan Heights were viewed as a shield for the Megiddo Plain in Palestine and a forward fortress of the British empire. Thus, a Zionist delegation attended the 1919 Paris peace conference in order to secure international acceptance for the Balfour Declaration and its attachment to the Paris peace agreement, as well as to the charter of the League of Nations. The Zionist delegation was also determined to disrupt any plans to internationalize Palestine or attach it to a neighboring Arab state. This plan entailed a broad attack on the extension of the right of self-determination to the Palestinian population and supported the imposition of British rule over this area. The Zionists expressed their backing for British designs in the form of a memorandum on February 27, 1919, demanding certain land concessions in the north. They called for adding territory that began at Sidon on the Mediterranean and extended in a line running between the eastern and western slopes of Mount Hermon and then followed the northern shoreline of the Litani River eastward to the Hijaz Railroad. These boundaries would have given British Palestine a swath of southern Lebanon, as well as control over sources of the Jordan River within modern Syria.

After extensive discussions, the French insisted on accepting only the boundaries specified in the earlier Sykes-Picot agreement. They eventually agreed to give up control over the districts of Mettula and Banias, but refused to cede control either of Sidon or Tyre, or the southern shoreline of the Litani River and the sources of the Jordan. The French also rejected demands to surrender the eastern shoreline of Lake Tiberias, the Golan, or the Yarmouk River. Only a few miles along the western shores of the Yarmouk tributary before it emptied into the Jordan were given up. The Zionists continued to articulate their case, however, through a 1920 resolution of the predominantly Jewish city council of Jerusalem addressed to the British High Commission. The resolution claimed that a majority of the Palestinian population demanded the inclusion of the northern and southern shores of the Litani River, as well as the Jordan Valley with all of its tributaries, into British Palestine. The French were adamant about their claims, however, emphasizing that the Litani River in particular should remain within Lebanese boundaries since its source and entire course are found within that country.[27]

When the Paulet-Newcombe agreement was drawn up in 1922, therefore, French Syria was accorded permanent rights in the waters of Lakes Tiberias and Houleh, as well as in the waters of the Jordan River. The agreement spelled out guarantees for the navigation and fishing rights of Syrians and Lebanese in these three bodies of water.[28] Zionist plans for the development of the water resources of the Jordan and its tributaries, however, were not constrained by the loss of much border territory to the French mandate in Syria and Lebanon. The failure to secure access to the lower Yarmouk Valley did not deter the new Israeli settlers from launching an electrification project, known as the Palestine Electric Works, to facilitate more settlement on the land. This project was initiated by Pinchas Rutenberg to supply all Palestine with electricity; in 1921 he had received an exclusive concession from Winston Churchill. Churchill was then Secretary of the Colonies, before the mandate government was established. The concession was for 70 years and granted exclusive rights for the exploitation of the Jordan and Yarmouk Rivers and all of their tributaries. Rutenberg was licensed to build an electrical power station at Jisr al-Majame'i and a dam to raise the level of the waters of Lake Tiberias. The concession permitted the diversion of the Yarmouk River in the direction of Lake Tiberias and the acquisition of any land necessary for the project. The broad and sweeping privileges granted by the Rutenberg concession covered territory later demarcated within the Syrian border since the Zionists and the British were hopeful of monopolizing these significant water resources. The fact that the project had to be curtailed after the signing of the mandate agreements in Syria and Palestine did not end these ambitions. In 1956 the Israeli authorities began their 10-year development plan to dam Lake Houleh upriver from Tiberias and divert its waters westward inside of Israel. The plan also called for the diversion of a section of the Jordan near Jisr Banat Ya'qoub. Water tensions have continued to plague the Syrian-Palestinian-Jordanian border since that time.[29]

Syria also suffered dismemberment and partitioning at the hands of the French beyond the divisions created by the European mandate system. Great territorial concessions were granted to the republic of Turkey at the expense of the Syrians. Beginning in March 1921, Cilicia was surrendered to Turkey and the Turkish minority in Alexandretta were given a special administrative system. The status of Turkish was elevated to that of Arabic and French. By October of that same year, a new Turkish-French agreement was signed giving the population of Alexandretta and Antioch the right to raise the Turkish colors. The Alexandretta province and the important Christian Syrian seat of Antioch were finally ceded to the Turks in June 1939. Lebanon was detached by Gouraud in 1920 and was systematically enlarged at Syria's expense over the next twenty years. Gouraud also established an 'Alawite state in the north and a Druze state in the south. This divide-and-rule policy led to rebellions, the most severe occurring in 1925–26.[30]

A new French high commissioner, Henri Ponsot, attempted to pacify Syria by calling for the election of an assembly in 1928 and the drafting of a democratic constitution. Under the leadership of Hashem al-Atassi, the assembly drafted a constitution faithfully reflecting the dashed nationalist hopes of the Arab revolt. Article 2 of the new document maintained "that the Syrian lands which are detached from the Ottoman State constitute a single and indivisible unit. Any divisions which took place within this unit since the end of the First World War are not recognized."[31] Ponsot rejected six articles, placing Article 2 at the top of his list. The other five contained provisions to limit the constitutional authority of the future president and to expand the role of parliament. When the assembly refused to yield to the high commissioner's warnings to choose a realistic course, Ponsot intervened in this constitutional impasse by dismissing the newly elected assembly in May 1930. He then issued a new constitution, which amended Article 2 to read, "Syria is an indivisible political unit."[32] A new article was added, Article 116, which stipulated that the assembly could not issue laws to contravene the international commitments of France, particularly those pertaining to the League of Nations. Thus, the French were adamant about preserving the mandate arrangement and the new sectarian statelets created for the Druze and 'Alawites. Waves of protest spread all over Syria as the battle for independence revived the vision of a united Syrian province. Even French promises to sign a treaty with the Syrians, along the lines of the Anglo-Iraqi agreement of 1930, did not put Syrian fears and suspicions to rest. Each of the new Syrian movements and quasi-parties that emerged in the new constitutional climate vociferously expressed a preference for the reconstitution of the old Syrian province.

The nationalist bloc, for instance, adopted a platform that called for liberating the Syrian lands that had been separated from the Ottoman state and bringing them to total sovereignty and independence. It also called for unifying all the dismembered lands of the province in one state, enjoying one government, and working toward unity with all the Arab states. The nationalist bloc included an array of Syria's future leadership, such as Hashem Atassi, Ibrahim Hanano, Sa'id al-Allah al-Jabri, Jameel Mardam Bayk, Shukri al-Quwatli, 'Abd al-Rahman al-Kayyali, and Faris al-Khouri.[33] When Hizb al-Sha'b (the People's Party) had coalesced from within the nationalist bloc, its internal constitution, first revealed at the party's inauguration at Damascus in 1925, also called for the reconstitution of greater Syria. In Faris al-Khouri's words,

> the party called for the unity of the Syrian land in its natural boundaries. Since the current policy has succeeded in dividing and dismembering Syria, slicing off a large section in the south [reference to Palestine] and placing it under different rule, if these divisions persist

one generation after the next, then all ties between this one people will be severed. This will be in addition to the material damage which will affect this nation as a result of the obstacles created by the partition. The People's Party feels that the Syrian land should re-emerge within its natural boundaries, and include its unified population, which is tied together by the bonds of race, language, and social custom.[34]

Syrian opposition to French rule, thus, was a continuation of the struggle against the Ottomans before and during the First World War. The term "the nationalists" was at first applied in the press and in private letters to all those opposed to French rule. Leaders who were actually founders of the People's Party, such as al-Khouri, Lufti al-Haffar, and Husni al-Barazi, were at first identified as nationalists even though they were more accurately representative of Hizb al-Sha'b. In the pro-French Syrian press, however, all the nationalists were referred to as "the monopolizers of politics." For a while the nationalist bloc even attempted to create a joint Lebanese-Syrian front against the French-mandate government in both countries by inviting delegates from Beirut and Tripoli to its Beirut convention of 1927. The meeting called specifically for uniting the Syrian-Lebanese effort to face the French mandate system and directing a lengthy report to the Syrian and Lebanese press.[35]

Syrians and Iraqis Aid the Palestinians

Although Palestinian nationalists who were actively involved in Faisal's Syrian Arab kingdom were now separated from their Syrian brothers by the boundaries of the San Remo agreement, they continued to adhere to the pledges of the wartime secret societies. During the Islamic conference of 1931, which sought to mobilize international Islamic opinion against Jewish encroachment on the Wailing Wall, there was a parallel meeting at 'Awni 'Abd al-Hadi's house of some veterans of the Arab nationalist movement who opposed the Turkification projects of the interwar years. The meeting included non-Palestinians such as Kheir al-Din al-Zarkali and As'ad Dagher. The meeting resulted in the creation the following year of Hizb al-Istiqlal (the Independence Party), which included in the executive committee, besides 'Abd al-Hadi, such prominent Palestinian figures as Mu'een al-Madhi, 'Izzat Darwaza, Subhi al Khadhra, Akram Zu'ayter, Fahmi al-'Abboushi, 'Ajaj Nuwayhedh, and Hamdi al-Husseini.[36]

The first statement of the Istiqlal, composed by ʿAbd al-Hadi, decried Western designs to exploit the resources of the Arabian Peninsula and to continue imposing their rule on much of the Arab world. The statement also reiterated the Palestinian call for resistance to Zionism and the exclusive right of the Arab nation to determine its own future. ʿAbd al-Hadi's gaze, however, was fixed on Iraq in the lingering hope that Faisal might still come to the rescue of the Palestinians. Satiʿ al-Husri, the renowned Syrian educator and nationalist, was enlisted to intercede with Faisal. But Husri reported back pessimistically in June 1933 that Iraq's reputation in the Arab world was greatly exaggerated. Husri added that if Iraq's political situation (its proximity to independence) had existed in Syria, or if Syria's culture had been present in Iraq, an Arab state would have emerged. He blamed the Iraqi situation on the absence of real men capable of exploiting their political situation to advantage. ʿAbd al-Hadi and the Istiqlal Party thus turned their attention to staging demonstrations in various Palestinian cities, during one of which (Jaffa, in 1933) he and Darwaza were summarily imprisoned. Following the turbulent years of 1933, new Palestinian parties emerged, such as al-ʿArabi, al-Islah, al-Kutlah, and al-Difaaʿ. The Istiqlal, though quickly losing its influence, was the only direct descendant of al-ʿArabiyah al-Fatah. Clearly, ʿAwni ʿAbd al-Hadi's tortured quest for a legitimate Arab leader to lead the struggle against the European and Zionist colonizers, and to resurrect the political program of the Arab revolt, was evidence of the powerful hold of the pan-Arab secret societies of Greater Syria. With a leg in each world, ʿAbd al-Hadi and some of his associates clung to that vision even as it led them into the service of the other Hashimite claimant to a unified Arab kingdom, King ʿAbdullah of Transjordan.[37]

Syrian commitment to the liberation and reattachment of its southern territory was not limited to the nationalist elite of the interwar years. Evidence shows that the fate of Palestine constantly inflamed the imagination of ordinary Syrians. The heroics of the Syrians succeeded in stoking the fires of the Arab nationalist ideology for a long time. Thus, Palestinians were not surprised to see the name of a legendary Syrian patriot, Sheikh ʿIzz al-Din al-Qassam, invoked in the second bulletin of the *intifada* on August 1, 1988. The bulletin, issued by the unified command of that early phase of the uprising, addressed Palestinian rebels as "the nation of martyrs and the descendants of al-Qassam."[38] The sheikh led a Palestinian rebellion against British authorities in Palestine the year before the Palestinian revolt and boycott movement of 1936. With a message easily grasped by the residents of Palestinian towns and villages, al-

Qassam defied the official nationalist leadership and carried out his militant campaign on his own. His Palestinian exploits, however, were easily explainable in light of his unusual life and pan-Arab, pan-Islamic career.

Al-Qassam was born in 1882 in the small town of Jablah on the Syrian coast, and he died a martyr in the forests surrounding the Palestinian town of Ya'bad near Jinin, in November 1935. His nationalist years began as a rebellion against the Turkish authority along the Syrian coast, where it appears that he participated in guerrilla campaigns of the 'Alawite rebel Saleh al-'Ali. The famed 'Alawite leader, who was considered aligned with the Arab revolt, waged successful campaigns to disrupt Ottoman supply routes between Tartous and Hama.[39] Al-'Ali and his men also gained notoriety in 1919 as fierce fighters against the French.[40] Al-Qassam, evidence has it, also participated in the battle of Maysaloun in 1920, after which the French sentenced him to death in absentia.[41] With a price on his head, the sheikh departed to Acre in Palestine by boat, and from there he and some fighters took a boat to Haifa, probably arriving there in November 1920.[42]

The life and martyrdom of al-Qassam point not only to the commitment of Syrians to the liberation of southern Syria but also to the rich tapestry of the Palestinian nationalist ideology. Al-Qassam's nationalist philosophy apparently fed on the Arab ideology of Ibrahim Hanano, with whom he was once associated, as well as the pan-Islamic ideas current at the turn of the century. Having received his religious training at al-Azhar Islamic University of Cairo, he was also instructed there by such famed Islamic reformers as Imam Muhammad 'Abduh and fellow Syrian Muhammad Rashid Ridha. A firm believer in the jihad as a sacred Muslim duty against invaders, al-Qassam was greatly influenced by the writings of Jamal al-Din al-Afghani. Knowing no contradiction between Arab and Islamic reformist nationalism, al-Qassam seems to have read 'Abd al-Rahman al-Kawakibi's works on political absolutism and the early expressions of modern Arab nationalism. Thus, he was greatly influenced by the great Egyptian and Syrian nationalist figures and their call for reform. A central principle of the Islamic reformist school called for a jihad against absolutism and foreign colonial rule. The reformists emphasized the eternal bonds between Arabism and Islam and the need to clear Islam of all its impurities and sectarianism. Al-Qassam's ideological makeup prompted him to attempt to lead a relief mission to Libya in 1911, but he was turned back by Ottoman authorities.[43]

Palestine, it seems, offered a perfect field for the application of these ideas. Al-Qassam quickly won the support and affection of the religious dignitaries of Haifa, a port city teaming with labor and political unrest. His appointment in 1925 as the imam of al-Istiqlal mosque gained him wide fame as an eloquent and impassioned preacher. Soon he acquired a following among the unlettered and poor as well as among various sectors of the middle class, whom he served as a teacher and patriotic leader. Never attaining high office, he remained confined to northern Palestine, where he gained the respect of Muslims and Christians alike. Some of his unusual activities turned out to include training others in the use of firearms.[44]

Qassam often spoke bitterly about the tragic ending of Syria, Palestine, and all its Arab lands. He began to organize a secret group of dedicated men known variously as Qassam's clique, the followers of Qassam, and the Qassamis. These names, never used in his lifetime, became honorific epithets for those who lived his message after his death. He began to organize secret and militant cells of fighting groups soon after the Young Men's Muslim Associations spread into Palestine from Egypt, which facilitated his work. The Young Men's Muslim Association of Haifa played a role similar to al-Muntada al-'Arabi in Constantinople, becoming a magnet for young men destined to join the secret societies. Al-Qassam chose members of his cells, ranging from five to nine members each, from the Haifa association. Most of his followers were drawn from the ranks of workers and the Muslim clergy, and never exceeded two hundred. Those who volunteered for military operations reached eight hundred during the sheikh's lifetime. The Qassamis rose in number during the 1936 Arab revolt in Palestine, and in later years specialized in eliminating spies with the approval of a mufti. During their military operations each fighter purchased his own gun.[45]

The Qassamis began their military operations in reaction to the Wailing Wall incident of 1929. Angered by Jewish intransigence and attempts to widen their customary rights within the vicinity of the wall, the Arab population rioted and forced the British government to take the question of the Wailing Wall's ownership to international adjudication. While the mainstream Palestinian nationalist movement under the leadership of the mufti of Jerusalem, Amin Husseini, sought to mobilize international Islamic opinion in support of Arab religious rights, Sheikh al-Qassam swung into direct action against Jewish settlers. Beginning in 1931, he and his followers attacked Jewish settlements in the Galilee, using guns and homemade explosives. Without as much as a single leaflet announcing his revolt, al-Qassam departed Haifa with his followers and went to the hills. He wrote to a friend that he expected the echo of his scream to travel in every direction.⁴⁶ He was killed in the battle of Ya'bad, near Jinin, after battling a British force on November 20, 1935. Badly outnumbered, his group of barely twenty fighters suffered great losses but produced an unusual trio of martyrs. Al-Qassam was buried following a huge funeral procession in Haifa, next to two other martyrs of the battle of Ya'bad, an Egyptian, Hanafi 'Attiyah, and a Palestinian, Yousef al-Zibawi.⁴⁷

The saga of al-Qassam and his Arab volunteers is now considered a prelude to the great revolt of 1936. The revolt was sparked by followers of al-Qassam who, under the leadership of Sheikh Farhan al-Sa'di, attacked a Jewish convoy near 'Anabta in the vicinity of Nablus, on April 5, 1936. This attack was apparently a protest against the willingness of Palestinian parties and officials to negotiate with British authorities. Just like the intifada of 1987, the 1936 revolt began spontaneously in a highly charged nationalist climate, this one generated by news of al-Qassam's unconditional commitment to Palestine's liberation. Leadership of the 1936 revolt initially devolved on the leader of the Supreme Muslim Council, Amin Husseini, and one of his rivals, Ragheb al-Nashashibi, who came together in the Arab Higher Committee. But the revolt, just like the intifada, which began as a spontaneous event, was later taken over by the official Palestinian leadership. Although al-Qassam inspired the 1936 Revolt, he was never admitted to the ranks of Palestinian nationalist circles. His fame remained limited to the local vicinity of Haifa. Partly due to his desire to maintain a cloak of secrecy over his operations, al-Qassam was also predisposed against official and empty gestures, such as the Islamic conference of 1928 that convened to protect the al-Aqsa Mosque. Neither did he attend the 1931 international Islamic conference to mobilize support following the Wailing Wall disturbances.⁴⁸

To understand the significance of al-Qassam's contribution to the Palestinian ideology of struggle, it is essential to analyze his relationship with the mufti. Al-Qassam sent a messenger to the mufti calling upon him to declare a jihad in 1935, promising to undertake all military operations in the north if the mufti was willing to direct operations in the south. Al-Qassam himself departed Haifa for a week to meet the mufti, only to be told that the time for a general jihad had not yet arrived. The mufti, it appears, feared the independent and hugely popular appeal of the sheikh's message and disapproved of his jihadist tactics and philosophy. It was reported that even Palestinian Christians adopted the philosophy of the jihad and were inspired by al-Qassam's leadership. Sources in Haifa indicated that one of al-Qassam's faithful financial contributors was Bishop Gregorius Hajjar.⁴⁹ Greek Orthodox parochial schools developed an anthem celebrating the jihad.⁵⁰ Clearly, al-Qassam could have been viewed as a potential rival to al-Husseini.

Al-Qassam's heroic struggle resonated particularly with the generation of Faisal's revolt in al-Istiqlal Party. According to veteran Palestinian nationalist 'Izzat Darwaza, al-Istiqlal Party, founded in 1931, was the only Palestinian party to call for overturning the partitioning of Syria and to insist that Palestine was an indivisible part of Syria. The party called for the cancellation of the Balfour Declaration and was not surprised to learn later of al-Qassam's success in recruiting the recently proletarianized Palestinian peasantry of Haifa. Darwaza insisted that al-Qassam was affiliated with al-Istiqlal.⁵¹ The jihad movement, however, did not disappear following al-Qassam's death; it reemerged during the 1936 revolt. When Palestine erupted against the British mandate and Jewish settlers, Arab volunteers flooded Palestine, particularly the Syrians. Of these, Sheikh Muhammad al-Ashmar reprised al-Qassam's role by calling for a jihad. A famed military leader, Sa'id al-'As, also hailed from Syria.⁵²

'Izzat Darwaza led an effort from his residence in Damascus to recruit Syrian volunteers and collect donations. The greatest military support for the Palestinian rebellion, however, came from Iraq. The Lebanese commander Fawzi al-Qawuqji, who was to figure prominently in the 1948 Palestine War, was outfitted by Iraq but came to Palestine at the head of a mixed Arab volunteer army dominated by Syrians.⁵³ Like al-Qassam, he considered Palestine to be partly the responsibility of the generation of the original Arab revolt, and he believed in the effectiveness of a people's war. British-French rivalry also contributed to the ease with which Syrian volunteers crossed into Palestine. In a 1974 interview, Darwaza stated to Palestinian historian Bayan Nuwayhedh al-Hout that he headed a "Central Committee of the Jihad" at Damascus in 1936, along with several Syrians, under the tolerant gaze of the French mandatory authority. The latter sought to avenge earlier complicity in supporting the Druze rebellion of Sultan Pasha al-Atrash. Palestinian support for the Druze of Syria in the 1920s was headed by the mufti, who called his effort the Central Committee for the Assistance of the Syrian Victims.⁵⁴

Syrian nationalists were still weak and did not sign their treaty with the French mandatory power until September 1936. Iraq, on the other hand, was marching toward independence after signing the British-Iraqi treaty of June 1930. Even though the British high commissioner remained dominant, a core of Iraqi army officers harbored strong pan-Arabist sentiments and could be counted upon to assist the Palestinians. By the 1930s, the Palestinian national leadership, represented by the mufti, was beginning to seek wider Arab support and to experience the potentials and pitfalls of joint Arab action. Even though Amin Husseini preferred to deal with Arab nationalist forces, he inevitably confronted the emerging national interests represented by the newly created states. The revolt of 1936 proved to be the first major Palestinian event to test the limits of the Arab commitment to Palestine.

Anti-British sentiment in Iraq also led to greater clandestine Iraqi involvement against the British in Palestine. Hundreds of Iraqis fought side by side with the Palestinian rebels of 1936. The military coup of Baker Sidqi in October 1936 led to Hikmat Suleiman's and Yassin al-Hashimi's governments, which tolerated the dispatching of a steady flow of weapons to Palestine. The flow was interrupted only after Sidqi's death in 1937.[55] But many high-ranking Iraqi officers, such as Col. Salah al-Din al-Sabbagh, who later figured prominently in Kaylani's revolt, acknowledged handing arms and military supplies directly to Palestinian agents in Iraq, such as 'Izz al-Din al-Shawwa. Even the Iraqi Minister of Defense, Taha al-Hashimi, was aware of the operation. Palestinian fighters also received military training secretly at the Rashid base.[56]

Qawuqji, for his part, sought to secure the financial and military support of the Saudi regime. He was to discover that pro-Palestinian sentiments did not always translate into action. Having advocated as early as 1929 the use of Transjordan as a base from which to stage operations inside Palestine, he explained to the mufti that this country offered the best possibility for storing weapons and military supplies. The mufti approached Prince Faisal of Saudi Arabia with this idea, hoping that the latter country would provide weapons and supplies for this operation. Following his consultation with the Saudi monarch, Faisal came back with the idea that the operation should be led by a Najdi prince. King 'Abd al-'Aziz, it was reported, was hoping to instigate a rebellion in Transjordan leading to the death of King 'Abdullah. The Saudis were thus the earliest to attempt to put the Palestine crisis to their own dynastic use. Their scheme, if realized, would have resulted in the Saudi annexation of Transjordan, as well as the Muslim parts of Palestine, leaving the rest of that country to the Jews.[57]

When the Iraqi revolt of Rashid 'Ali al-Kaylani broke out in 1941, coordination between the Iraqi government and the military officers known as the Golden Square (Salah al-Din al-Sabbagh, Fahmi Sa'id, Mahmoud Salman, and Kamel Shabib) had great relevance to the Palestinian struggle.[58] After intervention by Arab governments, the 1936 Palestinian revolt died down and the mufti fled to Lebanon, only to leave it for

Iraq in October 1939. Fearful of being betrayed by his French hosts, he sought a friendlier climate among his Iraqi friends in Baghdad.⁵⁹

Al-Kaylani soon became involved in assessing official German and Italian attitudes toward the Arabs. According to Taha al-Hashimi's memoirs, al-Kaylani was told by Fritz von Grobba, Germany's envoy to Baghdad, that Iraq should not involve itself with Syria and Palestine since these were in the Italian sphere of influence.⁶⁰ The mufti's personal secretary, 'Uthman Kamal Haddad, nevertheless, met secretly with Franz von Papen, Germany's representative to Turkey, and other German officials in various parts of Europe. In his meeting with von Grobba, Haddad reported that he represented an Arab coordination committee that was headed by the mufti and included Iraqi, Syrian, and Saudi officials. Haddad asked for an official German statement recognizing the independence of those Arab countries currently occupied by Britain and France and declaring the disinterest of the Axis powers in supplanting these mandates. His demands also included recognition of the Arabs' right to resolve their dispute with the Jews on their own terms. Germany and Italy were asked to renounce any intention of occupying Egypt or the Sudan. Haddad pledged several things in return, including instigating a great revolt in Palestine and Transjordan. Syria was to be the supply center of the revolt.⁶¹

Palestinian participation in Kaylani's revolt was a natural corollary to this history of broad-based Iraqi-Palestinian cooperation. Future Palestinian military leader 'Abd al-Qadir al-Husseini, as well as many Palestinian exiles in Iraq, were imprisoned by the British.⁶² When this power gained the upper hand in Iraq, as a result of the belated and half-hearted German-Italian military effort on behalf of the Iraqis in 1941, the mufti, along with Kaylani and the Golden Square officers, fled to Tehran.⁶³

The Syrian nationalist desire to overthrow the French suffered from the contradictory interests of Iraqi and Palestinian nationalists. When the Vichy regime took control of the French mandatory government in both Syria and Lebanon, the Axis powers pressured the Iraqis against supporting an uprising by their Arab brothers. In 1940 Jameel Mardam Bayk and Sa'ad al-Allah al-Jabri were dispatched to Baghdad by the emerging leader of the Syrian nationalist movement, Shukri al-Quwatli, to coordinate plans with Iraqi leaders. The Syrians were equally alarmed by Italy's desire to resurrect the ancient Roman empire of the Mediterranean basin and by the brutal British suppression of Palestinian and Iraqi nationalists. Although Germany's victory over the French during World War II aroused the admiration of ordinary Syrians, this could not be translated into an actual advantage. As it turned out, Mardam Bayk was supported in his effort to coordinate Arab plans during the war years by King ʿAbd al-ʿAziz of Saudi Arabia. The king, who naturally was not displeased with the potential demise of the Iraqi Hashimites, counseled Kaylani against a total break with the British. But Mardam Bayk was unable to persuade Iraq and Saudi Arabia to exert pressure against the French government, particularly as the nationalists were losing power in Iraq.[64] The Egyptian government of ʿAli Maher, for its part, was torn between declaring war on the Axis powers or remaining neutral, and finally adopted the posture of a defensive war.[65]

As the Palestinian situation continued to deteriorate, the Egyptian premier, Mustafa al-Nahaas, visited Palestine in 1943 for discussions with what remained of its leadership. This was the first official involvement of an Egyptian government in the Palestine issue, signifying the adoption by the Wafd government of a pan-Arab policy. By contrast, during the 1937 Bludan Arab conference convened in Syria specifically to deal with the Palestine issue, Egypt was unofficially represented by veteran pro-Palestinian statesman ʿAli ʿAloubah and by ʿAbd al-Hamid Saʿid, founder of the Young Men's Muslim Association. One reason for the Wafd's shift in policy was to coordinate plans with other Arab states on the eve of the creation of the Arab League of States. Another reason was related to Egyptian apprehension toward Nuri al-Saʿid's promotion of the 1943 Fertile Crescent project, which proposed unity between Iraq, Syria, Lebanon, Palestine, and Transjordan.[66]

Three years before that, ʿAbdullah of Jordan proposed to the British the Greater Syria scheme, which would include all the above-mentioned countries except Iraq. Anthony Eden's Arab League plan, first revealed on May 19, 1941, opened the way for the coalescing of these proposed unification schemes during talks leading to the creation of the league.[67] Al-Nahaas met Syrian and Lebanese officials on this same trip and pronounced the Palestine question to be the main reason for seeking to unify the Arab world. He also discussed with Palestinian leaders the best method of achieving Palestinian representation in the proposed new body. Nahaas's trip, the first of its kind by an Egyptian Prime Minister, facilitated the choice of Alexandria as the site of the prepatory talks leading to the creation of the league.[68]

On the eve of Syrian independence, Syrians were perturbed by Jordan's call for the creation of Greater Syria and emphasized their attachment to the republican form of government.[69] Not yet fully independent, Syria was struggling to maintain its territory against rival neighbors and at the same time to remain the focal point of inter-Arab coordination. The Syrians performed a valuable service, however, during the second session of the 1945 Arab League's council meetings at Cairo. The league was faced with the problem of designating a formal Palestinian delegation since the flight of the mufti had left the Palestinian national leadership in shambles. The last Palestinian nationalist body, the Arab Higher Committee, had been dissolved and had not been replaced by a formal body. The remaining Palestinian parties had designated Musa al-'Alami as their representative, but he later resigned. The Syrian delegate, Jameel Mardam Bayk, was authorized by the six Palestinian parties to name a Palestinian committee to choose a new delegation. A broadly representative committee was finally put together; it was made up of such figures as Ragheb al-Nashashibi, 'Awni 'Abd al-Hadi, Hussein al-Khalidi, Ya'qub al-Ghussein, Musa al-'Alami, and Emile al-Ghoury. This committee then chose a delegation to attend the remainder of the sessions. Thus, the problem of Palestinian representation, which was to plague all future participation in inter-Arab and international meetings, was temporarily resolved.

Palestinian rifts, however, were not permanently healed. During the 1946 Bludan conference, which was convened by the Arab League in response to the publication of the Anglo-American Committee's report on Palestine, further Palestinian divisions emerged. The greater part of the meeting was devoted to criticism of the activities of Musa al-'Alami and Jamal al-Husseini.[70]

Syrians, in addition, managed to impact Palestinian development on the Arab and world stage through their long-standing association with some prominent Palestinian figures. The future leader of the first Palestine Liberation Organization, Ahmad Shuqeiri, was summoned for consultations by President Shukri al-Quwatli at the Anshas Arab League meeting of May 1946. Quwatli shared with Shuqeiri sections pertaining to the Palestine question in the meeting's final report, which failed to list the Soviet Union as a friend of the Arabs. Shuqeiri objected, but the Syrian president claimed that there was no consensus on this point. During the October 1946 league meeting, Shuqeiri was in constant touch with the Syrian delegation and later prepared legal briefs for its use. He acted as legal advisor to the Syrians at the 'Aleh meeting of the league's council in 1947, from which sprung an Arab military committee. Shuqeiri was also given the use of a private office in the Syrian Foreign Ministry.[71] When the Arab League charter was finalized and signed by Jameel Mardam Bayk and Faris al-Khouri on behalf of Syria, all the Arabs held high hopes. Unanimity was considered feasible since the league's membership did not exceed seven. What led to the evaporation of this unity was the polarization of league members into the Iraqi or the Hashimite camp (which included Jordan) and the Saudi camp (which included Egypt, Yemen, Syria, and Lebanon).[72]

Conclusion

Thus the fate of Palestine and Syria's independence began as one indivisible question, namely, the right of the Arab people to independence and self-determination. A whole generation of military officers, journalists, and statesmen shared the bitter experiences of the Arab revolt, the dismantling of Faisal's Syrian Arab kingdom, and the imposition of two systems of alien rule in place of the unified but oppressive pattern of the Ottoman empire. By the end of the First World War, only Iraq enjoyed a semblance of sovereignty and independence. Yet Iraq's tight domination by Britain cancelled its other economic and military advantages. The mirage of Iraq's independence was finally dissipated with the crushing defeat of al-Kaylani's revolt and the violence inflicted on the country's ultra-nationalist officers. Although historians continue to debate the degree of pan-Arab commitment of these officers, their attachment to the Arab nationalist ideology managed to stir the imagination of the other Arab countries.

Not unlike the Iraqis, the Syrian generation of Faisal's campaigns held tenaciously to Sherif Hussein's essential dream. Though disillusioned by British ties to the defeated Hashimites and their descendants, the beacon of a united Arab state continued to shine brightly. Syria's subsequent history, however, diverged from that of Iraq. Clinging to the forms of parliamentary rule and suffering greater territorial amputations than Iraq, a diminutive and weak Syria continued to defy the French and insist on resurrecting the boundaries of the Syrian Ottoman province. The dedication of ordinary Syrians to that program saw expression in Sheikh 'Izz al-Din al-Qassam's populist campaign on behalf of the Palestinian struggle against British rule and Zionist immigration. Al-Qassam's movement, more importantly, gave birth to a pan-Arab populist ideology centered around the fate of Palestine. The Syrian national movement, however, suffered a tremendous blow to its hitherto unchallenged status as the heart of Arabism. As political ideology gave way to new territorial realities, Iraq supplanted Syria as the focal point of Arab nationalist sentiments. Syria suffered additional blows in the mid 1940s, when both royalist Iraq and Transjordan began to spin new schemes of forced unification and state enlargement.

The Palestinians continued to cling to the original ideology of Arab nationalism until the realities of the new state system impinged on their struggle during the revolt of 1936. The Istiqlal Party, one of six Palestinian groupings in the 1930s, maintained ties to Syria's patriots. The new Palestinian leadership represented by the mufti, Amin al-Husseini, and later the Arab Higher Committee, became disillusioned with Syria's support. Instead, Iraq attracted the mufti's attention as he sought military weapons and volunteers. Ejected from one Arab capital after another, Husseini tried residence in Beirut, Baghdad, and Cairo, and appealed for help to various governments. His flight from Palestine following the 1936 revolt created the first Palestinian leadership crisis in recent memory, as independent personalities and political parties sought to fill the resulting leadership vacuum. The lesson absorbed by Husseini was not dissimilar to the reactions of later Palestinian leaders. Instead of working toward Arab unity, he began exploiting Arab divisions, for Palestine had also acquired distinct "state" interests of its own. Angry at Syria for failing to secure French support for his repatriation to Palestine, Husseini declined to thank Faris al-Khouri for eloquently defending the rights of Palestinians at the United Nations.[73] Oblivious to the interlocking fate of Palestine and the Arabs, the mufti's strategy manipulated one Arab actor after the other. The outbreak of the 1948 Arab-Jewish war naturally spelled disaster for Palestine and its Arab neighbors, particularly for Syria.

2

The Earthquake of the 1948 Palestine War

Although historians commonly point to Egypt as the country that suffered the greatest fallout of the first Palestine war, it was Syria that shook to its foundations. Syria suffered massive and prolonged destabilization because of its recent experience with independence, its geographic location midway between the Mediterranean coast and the Iraqi and Saudi oil fields, and its solid attachment to different strands of the Arab nationalist ideology. The negative effects of Egypt's decaying political system and the utter unpreparedness of its military forces were mitigated by the country's stable geographic identity and relative insularity vis-à-vis radical Arab ideologies. Egypt may have provided the most powerful example of the new phenomenon of military regimes following that war, but Syria demonstrated the havoc wreaked by a military junta on a fledgling parliamentary system.

By the time of Syria's independence, Iraqi oil was flowing in two pipeline systems, one terminating at Haditha in northwest Iraq, the other taking the much longer westward route across Syria and terminating at Tripoli in Lebanon. Until the 1948 Arab-Jewish hostilities, a stretch of pipeline branched off to Haifa in Palestine. These installations were part of the Iraq Petroleum Company (IPC) but generated substantial revenue for the Syrian government. Syria's location, therefore, increased Iraq's strategic vulnerability after the discovery of petroleum. It also increased Syria's susceptibility to foreign intrigue whenever a Syrian regime was toppled by a new junta.[1] In Saudi Arabia, in addition, the Arabian-American Oil Company (ARAMCO) began lobbying the Syrians for a pipeline from Saudi Arabia to the Mediterranean and succeeded in inaugurating this line in February 1950. Owned and operated by a specially constituted company known as Tapline, this pipeline heightened Saudi Arabia's interest in Syria's neutrality.[2] Granting concessions for these pipelines often aggravated relations with Lebanon and Jordan, who were normally more anxious to conclude these lucrative agreements than Syria.[3]

Whether British or American controlled, the oil industries of Iraq and Saudi Arabia suffered the consequences of Syrian hostility as a result of the Palestine War. The oil situation generated enormous economic instability for Syria and sometimes even political turmoil. Additionally, inter-Hashimite rivalries made Syria more vulnerable than ever before and dampened its desire for a greater share of the oil windfall. Notwithstanding these threatening developments, Syria could not ignore rising Zionist threats to its south. Syria's involvement in the activities of the Arab League was symptomatic of that country's insecurities, as well as of its inability to bypass public sentiment on behalf of the Palestinians.

As the final report of the 1947 'Aleh meeting of the Arab League was issued, in response to the work of the United Nations Special Committee on Palestine (UNSCOP), Syria's share of the Palestinian burden increased. The Arab League reacted to news of the impending withdrawal of British troops from Palestine, which would leave the unprotected Palestinian population at the mercy of the Jewish underground, by calling for the coordination of Arab military plans. The league specifically called on states adjacent to Palestine not to impede the military activities of other Arab states. This recommendation opened the door to the stationing of Arab troops along Palestine's borders, mainly in Syria and Lebanon. The Arab member states were urged to provide moral and material support to the people of Palestine in order to enable them to defend themselves. A military committee was organized to supervise the imminent war. The committee was composed of Lt. Gen. Isma'il Safwat (Iraq), Lt. Col. Mahmoud Hindi (Syria), Lt. Col. Shawkat Shqeir (Lebanon), and 'Izzet Darwaza (Palestine), who was later replaced by Subhi al-Khadhra. Egypt, Jordan, Yemen, and Saudi Arabia declined to send any of their military officers to this committee.

The committee's first secret report, issued on October 9, 1947, made a series of recommendations to the council of the Arab League, including the immediate recruitment and military training of volunteers. The first training camp for these volunteers was founded at Qatana, near Damascus. A thousand Palestinians were the first to volunteer for military duty; they were later joined by Arab civilian recruits and military officers. This batch of volunteers was the core of what later became known as Jaysh al-Inqath (the Salvation Army), numbering around four thousand. The army consisted of eight battalions, one of which was led by the famed Palestinian commander from Jaffa, Michel 'Issa. Each battalion was named after a historical Arab battle, and the Yarmouk battalion was led by future Syrian strongman and instigator of the third coup, Adib al-

Shishakly.⁴ Other future Syrian leaders who took part in the first Palestine war included noted Ba'thist and king-maker Akram Hourani, member of the Syrian General Staff Col. 'Adnan al-Malki, the first and second military dictators of Syria, Husni al-Za'im and Sami Hinnawi, as well as former Prime Minister Fawzi Silo.

Syria contributed to the 1948 War in two ways: by participating with its formal army and by coordinating the volunteer army and providing it with training space. It was in this latter capacity that Fawzi al-Qawuqji, Tripoli born but a long-time resident of Syria, left his mark on the Palestine campaign of 1948 and on Syria alike. Al-Qawuqji had already proved his pan-Arabist dedication by leading bands of Iraqi, Druze, and Syrian volunteers in the 1936 Palestinian revolt. Always referring to Palestine as southern Syria, Qawuqji was a man of all causes, as welcome in Iraq as he was in Syria.⁵ To most Arabs, he was a Syrian because of his leadership of the 1926 Syrian uprising against the French, which rose in support of the Druze revolt of Sultan Pasha al-Atrash. Qawuqji led an attack against the French at Hama in order to divert French troops from Jabal al-'Arab, the Druze area. The revolt also spread to Damascus and its surroundings. Qawuqji became a legend in Hama because of his military valor and his austere lifestyle.⁶

Qawuqji's heroic exploits were noted as early as 1917, by German officers serving in the Ottoman army. In a document prepared by the German head of the Ottoman cavalry, Qawuqji was described as extremely intelligent, a man who mastered German in a matter of months when he was 23 years old. Qawuqji served as von Layser's assistant and was highly lauded by his commanding officer.⁷ A 1926 British newspaper article expressed apprehension about Qawuqji's participation in Palestinian disturbances. The Syrian commander, the article stated, was an expert in revolutionary warfare who had already executed surprising maneuvers against British forces.⁸ From 1928 until 1932, Qawuqji commanded and trained Saudi Arabian troops and was asked to continue in his Saudi service.⁹ He left the Saudis in order to lead the volunteer troops against the British during the 1936 Palestine revolt. His first experience in the Palestinian campaigns turned out to be his main introduction to inter-Arab strife.

During that period, Qawuqji maintained cordial relations with Prince 'Abdullah of Transjordan as a man whose territory was a crucial crossing point into Palestine. 'Abdullah began to apply pressure to the Syrian commander in order to persuade him of the futility of taking on Britain's superior troops. 'Abdullah also tried to imply to Qawuqji that the Palestinian leadership, exemplified by the Arab Higher Committee, was well meaning but ill informed. ʿAbdullah counseled immediate negotiations. Qawuqji responded in the only way he knew to be appropriate, namely, by suggesting that a Jordanian jihad on behalf of Palestine would grant the monarch the joint crown of Transjordan and Palestine.[10]

While still on the battlefield, Qawuqji read newspaper reports regarding the appeals of Arab heads of state to the rebels to lay down their arms and end the strike. Qawuqji made inquiries regarding the sincerity of the British and whether it was advisable to believe their promises. His concern was for the safety of his fighters, and he suggested that a special area should be set aside for them while an armistice was being negotiated. He added that at least three hundred men should remain under arms and the possibility of continuing the rebellion from Transjordan should be considered.[11] Qawuqji's populist view of the Palestine revolt reverberated through a communiqué that he issued calling for a cease-fire. The Palestinian revolution, the communiqué read, was defended in the first instance by the poor people, some of whom had provided their own provisions and weapons. Let the British high commissioner know, he pronounced, that Qawuqji was not a stranger here but dwelt among his own people.[12] His military successes against the British were detailed in communiqué no. 17, in which he called on people to continue their total boycott of Jewish settlers. He signed it as "The General Commander of the Arab Revolt in Southern Syria (Palestine)."[13]

To gain some insight into Qawuqji's Arab nationalist views before the 1948 Palestine War, one needs to read the rebel leader's own summary of his life. Around 1936 he wrote that while he served in the Ottoman army he used to despise the Arab fighter and his military abilities. All this changed when he heard of the heroic feats of the Riff Moroccan rebels. Then came the Druze and Hama rebellions. These impressed him with the genius of the Arab nation and its glorious history, but he remained obsessed with the tragedies of Syria and Palestine, unable to decide which of the two deserved his immediate attention. He also continued to shuttle between various Arab capitals seeking material assistance for his revolutionary efforts.[14]

When the 1948 War began, Qawuqji enjoyed a reputation as the champion of Arab nationalist causes. It was generally expected that he would be entrusted with the general command of the Salvation Army. Led by Syrian, Iraqi, and Palestinian officers, the army was officially organized by January 1948 and included, beside the Arabs, a number of Turkish and Yugoslav nationals. A serious dispute over leadership of the army soon erupted between the military committee of the league and the mufti Amin al-Husseini. The mufti vehemently opposed entrusting the general command to Qawuqji, whom he considered to be lacking in field experience. Instead, the mufti favored the appointment of his cousin, ʿAbd al-Qadir al-Husseini, the commander of the recently formed Palestinian force known as the Sacred Jihad. The Palestinian force, the mufti argued, was capable of undertaking responsibility for the war if adequately supplied. In order to resolve this impasse, the military committee opted for dividing the theater of war among the two armies, assigning northern Palestine (Galilee and Samaria) to the Salvation Army while giving central Palestine to the Sacred Jihad forces. The latter area, which included Jerusalem and its surroundings, was divided into an eastern zone under Husseini's command and a western zone under the command of Sheikh Hassan Salamah.[15]

The mufti apparently had begun waging a vilification campaign against Qawuqji as early as 1947, while remaining cordial to him in person. Some of the criticism went beyond the mufti's aspersions on the commander's field experience. In his contacts with Quwatli, the Syrian president, the mufti expressed doubts regarding Qawuqji's military credentials, only to be reminded by Quwatli that the commander was experienced in guerrilla warfare. The mufti then played on Quwatli's Syrian insecurities by alleging that Qawuqji was the favored choice of Iraq and Transjordan. Quwatli, who was apprehensive about the speed with which Transjordan had dispatched its Arab Legion to Palestine, feared a British plot to annex the Arab part of Palestine to Transjordan. In his view, this eventuality would be a prelude to the creation of Greater Syria, which under this scenario would take shape first in the south. Quwatli's fears of Transjordan were so acute that he even suggested at one point bypassing Qawuqji and Husseini altogether and importing military officers from Pakistan. This idea was mentioned to Quwatli by Faris al-Khouri, Syrian representative to the UN, who was extremely moved by a speech of Muhammad ʿAli Jinnah, the founder of Pakistan, in support of the Palestinians. The mufti also expressed fears of Qawuqji's rising popularity by sharing a leaflet with Taha al-Hashimi, the Iraqi Defense Minister, in which Qawuqji was lauded as the League-appointed general commander who called on Palestinians to rally around his banner.[16]

There is no indication in Qawuqji's 1950 memoir that he at first reciprocated the mufti's ill will. Qawuqji began to assess the potential for a general popular mobilization on behalf of the Palestine War when he resided in Lebanon in 1946. He then sent a letter to the mufti in which he described the possibility of mobilizing all the previous Arab revolutionary cadres for the sake of mounting a popular war in Palestine. Although delivered through his friend from the Iraqi days, 'Izz al-Din al-Shawwa, the letter to the mufti was never answered. Qawuqji was told later that the mufti had his own secret Palestinian formations, which he calls "cells," and that no such Arab effort was needed. The only support the mufti asked for was in the form of weapons and financial assistance. Qawuqji disagreed with this approach and advocated a transnational Arab effort similar to the one being mounted by the Zionists. He was to discover that the Syrian president was also lukewarm to his ideas, apparently because of suspicions regarding collusion between Qawuqji and the Transjordanian monarch. But the Arab League considered Qawuqji's past experience to be perfectly suited to the upcoming campaign, and people like the league's secretary-general, 'Abd al-Rahman 'Azzam, sought his advice. Qawuqji makes the claim that it was his idea to organize a pan-Arab, but especially Palestinian, force of volunteers, and to station Arab armies along Palestine's borders. The formal armies, he advised, should not enter Palestine except in extreme necessity and only after Arab irregulars had facilitated the armies' operations.[17]

Qawuqji's supporters within the Arab League also included Muhammad 'Ali 'Aloubah, who directed much of Egypt's pro-Palestinian effort. The mufti, on the other hand, was resented not only by 'Azzam but also by Jordan and Iraq. In 1947 the mufti was just returning from his exile and requested reports from various Arab and Palestinian military commanders. Quwatli was finally persuaded to provide the Qatana base for training, and 'Izzet Darwaza consented to undertaking the task of organizing contribution committees and registering the volunteers. But the propaganda war against Qawuqji accelerated, with the mufti's office circulating rumors of his secret cooperation with the British during the Second World War. Qawuqji in turn threatened to reveal information regarding the mufti's secret wartime cooperation with the Axis powers and their promises to appoint him to the caliphate. The war of words was finally fought on the pages of the Egyptian press, with the mufti issuing hot denials.[18]

Quwatli eventually expressed Syria's fears of Arab mobilization to Qawuqji directly. Would King 'Abdullah use the Palestine campaign to achieve his dream of Greater Syria? What about Iraqi troops crossing into Jordan? Would they side with the Jordanians in annexing Arab Palestine? Qawuqji sought to allay the Syrian president's fears by indicating that the army of Arab irregulars, the Salvation Army, could be counted upon to intervene against the intrigues of other states and would not be used to topple the weaker Syrian regime. When the Saudis asked Jordan to assign them some territory for the stationing of their troops, Qawuqji reported, the Jordanian monarch balked at this suggestion, fearing a Saudi plot to invade his country. The Jordanians were apparently fearful of a Saudi-Syrian plot to divide Jordan's territory between them, especially in view of the Saudis' long-standing claims on 'Aqaba. Egypt promised to assist the Saudis and Syrians. After the Salvation Army was founded, Qawuqji had to request supplies and equipment from Taha al-Hashimi, who was appointed the general inspector of the irregular force. Qawuqji suspected, however, that this appointment was made in order to have Hashimi keep an eye on him lest he go along with 'Abdullah's Greater Syria scheme. These suspicions were confirmed by the Syrian Minister of Defense, Ahmad al-Sharabati, in conversations with Qawuqji. Despite all this, Syria contributed its quota of weapons to the irregular force, as well as many officers.[19]

When Qawuqji's troops finally entered Palestine they faced two serious handicaps: a shortage of weapons, and leaflets calling on Palestinians not to cooperate with the irregulars and to fight instead under the banner of the Arab Higher Committee. Qawuqji also confronted a British withdrawal plan that tactically favored an Israeli takeover of major Palestinian towns. As the situation deteriorated in Jaffa and Jerusalem, the general command of the Salvation Army asked Qawuqji to assist in defending central Palestine. It sent him two companies of troops, but they lacked any armored cars or cannons. When major cities in the north, such as Haifa and Tiberias, were threatened by Jewish fighters, Qawuqji was promised relief as soon as the regular Arab forces joined the battle.[20]

The entry of formal Arab armies to Palestine, Qawuqji believed, was orchestrated in such a manner as to obstruct King 'Abdullah's Greater Syria scheme. Most of these troops rushed into Palestine on May 15, 1948, upon the withdrawal of the British, simply in order to set up a Palestinian government headed by the mufti. But no one cared to discuss the future of the Salvation Army with Qawuqji or whether it should conclude its mission and depart, given that the Arab states had finally joined the war. Qawuqji began to wonder aloud to whom he should transfer the areas that had been liberated by his troops. When he visited John Glubb Pasha, the British commander of Jordan's Arab Legion, at Amman and indicated that plans called for a withdrawal over a period of three days beginning on May 17, Glubb asked him to change or at least delay his plans. But the Syrian president insisted to the Salvation Army's Damascus headquarters that a speedy withdrawal should be ordered soon. Qawuqji interpreted this Syrian pressure to stem from Quwatli's fear that King 'Abdullah would seize the Salvation Army and direct it for his own purposes. If this were to happen, the Syrian president feared the realization of the Greater Syria scheme. Qawuqji preferred to remain at his position and to contribute to the effort of the regular forces, particularly if his troops were to be supplied with weapons. He was to realize quickly, however, that despite the existence of a unified command, each Arab army responded to its own government and suspected the others of intrigues. Qawuqji's troops finally evacuated the Palestinian central region and left it under the control of Jordanian troops. After meeting with military and civilian officials at Damascus, Qawuqji directed his irregulars to proceed to Lebanon and to assist the Lebanese army upon Riadh al-Solh's request.[21]

Qawuqji was able to benefit from hindsight and summarize the Palestinian-Arab problem succinctly. The Arabs needed a catastrophe before they could rise to greatness, and that catastrophe turned out to be the loss of Palestine. The mufti may have contributed to the defeat because of his insistence on being considered by the Arab states as the head of the Palestinian state. The Arabs, however, considered the Palestine issue to be their joint concern. Tragically, Arab armies entered Palestine in a spontaneous manner, reprising their pattern of advance throughout the different stages of the Arab national struggle over the previous thirty years.[22] But at least Qawuqji survived the war, albeit with his military reputation in shreds. The two Sacred Jihad commanders, 'Abd al-Qadir al-Husseini and Sheikh Hassan Salamah, perished along with many other Palestinian and Syrian casualties of this war.[23]

Inter-Arab Dissension and Intrigue

Another elaborate view of inter-Arab rivalries emerges from the memoir of Muhsin Barazi, chief of staff of President Quwatli during the Palestine War. The Syrian-Jordanian dispute, which began in the summer of 1947, destabilized relations between these two countries on the eve of the Palestine War. King 'Abdullah openly called for the convening of an organization to work toward the unification of Iraq and Syria. 'Abdullah sent a letter to that effect to Quwatli via his chief of staff, Muhammad Shuraiqi. The Syrian president considered the letter a personal challenge and immediately appealed to Kings 'Abd al-'Aziz and Farouq for assistance. Barazi carried 'Abdullah's letter to Egypt and Saudi Arabia for consultations and took with him the Jordanian communiqués distributed to the Jordanian and Syrian press. Quwatli told the two monarchs that his appeals to Britain's representatives to dissuade 'Abdullah from going ahead with the Greater Syrian scheme had failed to achieve any results. Although the British declared their displeasure with this development, they considered it the concern of Syria and its Arab neighbors. To keep Saudi Arabia on his side, Quwatli suggested the possibility of ceding 'Aqaba and Ma'an to the Saudis if Syria succeeded in annexing Transjordan. Saudi Arabian and Syrian apprehension at the sight of Jordanian troop movement into Palestine, and Iraqi troop movement into Transjordan on their way to Palestine, was apparently justified. In addition, Saudi and Syrian suspicion that Transjordan planned to seize the Arab portion of Palestine prompted the Saudis to donate large quanities of arms and money to the mufti. Despite widely circulating rumors regarding the mufti's corruption, the Saudis agreed to supply him generously in order to stiffen his back against Jordanian forces.[24]

The Syrians also schemed with Farouq against the mufti. The Egyptian head of state was made aware of the mufti's rejection of the authority of the Arab Military Committee created by the Arab League. Barazi pleaded with the Egyptians not to transfer any more funds to the mufti, claiming that Qawuqji was much more trustworthy. But if the mufti was unreliable, he was the best suited to act as a barrier to 'Abdullah's Palestinian plans. When the Government of All Palestine (Hukumat 'Umum Falastin) was announced in 1948, under the leadership of Ahmad Hilmi 'Abd al-Baqi, an associate of the mufti and a member of the Arab Higher Committee, Syrians immediately decided to recognize it. The Syrians, Egyptians, and Iraqis made this decision on the basis of the recommendation of the Arab League's political committee. At the same time, they discouraged the mufti from publicly associating himself with the Ahmad Hilmi government. The new Palestine government was also a response to the Falke Bernadotte plan, which placed the weight of the United Nations behind the cession of the Arab part of Palestine to Transjordan. Clearly, the Arab states viewed the Bernadotte plan as contributing to the realization of the Greater Syria scheme. The Government of All Palestine was actually proposed as early as October 1947, when it was opposed by Transjordan and Iraq. The Jordanian monarch had withdrawn his recognition of the Arab Higher Committee when Jordanian troops entered Palestine on May 15, 1948. This was viewed as a blow to Palestinian aspirations, as well as an additional indication of 'Abdullah's expansionist ambitions.[25]

Whether or not the mufti was acceptable to the Syrian government, Transjordan's Palestinian policy during the Palestine War viewed the Arab

Higher Committee and its successor, the Government of All Palestine, in the same light. At the time, Syrians were acutely conscious of their military weakness and lack of preparedness, which heightened their fear of Jordan as well as of the new Jewish state. No one was more concerned than Khaled al-'Azm over the issue of acquiring modern weapons for the Syrian army on the eve of the Palestine War. Al-'Azm was serving at that time as Minister Plenipotentiary at the Syrian legation in Paris. After reaching a tentative agreement with the French Department of the Navy to purchase a large amount of weapons, al-'Azm saw the deal fall through when Jewish ministers in the French cabinet threatened to resign. Al-'Azm finally persuaded the French government to sell him arms in order to prevent the Jordanian monarch from occupying Syria. Al-'Azm never tired of warning the French of their potential loss of influence, and the possible expansion of British control in the region, if the Jordanian army, which was vastly superior to that of the Syrians, was allowed to occupy Syria. The difficulty of obtaining foreign weapons was also visible in the amount of rusted and ancient weapons that were seen at the time around Damascus.[26]

The Syrian-Saudi friendship during the war, however, did not compel the Syrians to look favorably on Saudi Arabian oil projects. As early as February 1948, and even before the formal involvement of Arab armies in the Palestine War, the political committee of the Arab League of States adopted a resolution calling on all member states to use the oil weapon as a means of maintaining pressure on the United States and other Western countries. The resolution did not recommend threatening existing oil concessions granted to these foreign governments, but it did advise against concluding pipeline agreements across Arab countries, especially with the Western governments that voted in the United Nations for partitioning Palestine. Syria was among those countries voting in favor of the Arab League's resolution, along with Egypt, Iraq, Jordan, and Lebanon. Saudi Arabia opposed the resolution and warned against the adoption of any measures inimical to the interests of Anglo-American oil companies, which had military backing by their respective governments that was quite capable of defeating the Arabs.[27] Moreover, Syria was under extreme pressure from Jordan and Saudi Arabia to sign such an agreement, but it held out since the majority of Syrian deputies opposed it. The government of Jameel Mardam Bayk refused to sign an agreement with the Tapline Company, which proposed building the oil pipeline across Syria. Lebanon adopted the same position against the American pipeline company in sympathy with the Syrian stand. At times the Tapline Company threatened to extend the pipeline through other countries.[28] Even King 'Abd al-Aziz's personal approach to Quwatli urging him to sign the Tapline agreement failed since the Syrian president insisted on standing behind the decision of his government, stating that "the national interest is always above the economic interest."[29]

The government of Jameel Mardam Bayk faced additional crises and was forced to resign after news emerged that a shipment of arms had been diverted to the Zionists. At the center of this story was a military officer named Fu'ad Mardam Bayk, who was a relative of the Prime Minister. Apparently a shipment of arms originating in Europe was diverted to an Israeli port instead of Latakia, causing an uproar and a demand for the Syrian officer's imprisonment. The incident triggered public protests and disturbances leading to the fall of the Mardam Bayk cabinet. This led Quwatli to recall Syria's Minister Plenipotentiary at Paris, Khaled al-'Azm, and to ask him to form a new cabinet. Al-'Azm's government signed an agreement with the Tapline Company in February 1949, allowing for the transport of Saudi oil to Tripoli in Lebanon. But the deputies of the People's Party, as well as those of the Muslim Brotherhood, attacked the government severely in parliament and refused to ratify it. The agreement, they claimed, would only open the way for further American influence.[30]

Another negative consequence of the Palestine War resulted from the signing of the armistice agreement leading to the cessation of Syrian-Israeli hostilities. When Khaled al-'Azm assumed the premiership at the end of 1948, fighting between the Arab armies and the Israelis had stopped on all fronts. The United Nations was already holding face-to-face meetings between each set of combatants to facilitate the signing of agreements, which it hoped would lead to the recognition of the new Israeli state. The UN was committed to upholding the partition plan of Palestine even though Israel had expanded beyond the boundaries of the partition resolution of November 29, 1947. The Arab combatants, who had already rejected the partition idea, were further embittered at the end of the war by the Israeli takeover of the triangle area in northern Palestine and the Negev in the south. Arab public opinion did not permit the signing of permanent peace, however, and only armistice agreements were possible.

Egypt, as it turned out, was the first to accept the principle of a permanent armistice with no time limitations. Egyptian delegates proceeded to Rhodes, the site of the negotiations, without any prior consultations with other members of the Arab League of States. A new wave of bitterness developed as Egypt's unilateral action pressured other Arab states to seek a similar arrangement. Egypt's willingness to abandon the war effort, however, was attributed by the Egyptians to the Jordanian and Iraqi conduct of the war. Iraq was blamed for failing to occupy Tel Aviv when the city came within shooting range of Iraqi guns. The Egyptians criticized King 'Abdullah for withdrawing from the triangle area (which included Nablus, Lyddah, and Toulkarm), in compliance with the UN partition resolution, which placed that section outside the designated Arab area. Mahmoud Fahmi al-Nuqrashi, Egypt's premier, was among the most embittered, accusing Iraq and Jordan of being British and U.S. lackeys. Egypt's poor military performance on the southern Palestine front made a cessation of hostilities seem to be Egypt's only option. As soon as Egypt signed an armistice agreement, Jordan and Lebanon followed suit. Iraq and Saudi Arabia rejected the notion of signing such agreements because of the absence of a common border between their territories and Israel. Of all the countries bordering Israel, only Syria continued to resist.[31]

The Beginning of Military Interventions

The seriousness of this situation forced al-'Azm to request a secret session of parliament convened by the Prime Minister, Faris al-Khouri. The president emphasized to the deputies Syria's inability to save Palestine single-handedly and its increasing vulnerability to Israeli border attacks. He recommended joining Egypt, Lebanon, and Jordan in the negotiations at Rhodes. Farid Zein al-Din was designated to lead the negotiating team and was instructed by al-'Azm, the Foreign Minister, to place the armistice lines at the current troop positions in order not to surrender territory won during the recent fighting. This territory, it was emphasized, was necessary to safeguard the future defense needs of Syria. The armistice lines, added al-'Azm, should run in the middle of all bodies of water, such as Lake Tiberias. During the first round of talks, UN mediator Ralph Bunche agreed to these demands. But the coup of Husni al-Za'im on March 30, 1949, changed all that. Under the new Za'im regime, Syria agreed to pull out from all territory seized during the war. Syria also ended its earlier insistence on placing the armistice lines in the middle of bodies of water. As a result, the Israelis increased their territory at the expense of the Syrians and were protected by a stretch of no-man's-land that was in actuality Palestinian territory. As a result, all the land overlooking Lake Tiberias was now demilitarized. Al-Za'im, it was rumored, was backed by the United States, which sought the signing of the Tapline agreement as well as the conclusion of a peace deal with Israel.[32] The Tapline contract, the monetary agreement with France, and the armistice agreement were signed by the new dictator after the Syrian parliament had been dismissed.³³

By 1954 Akram Hourani, a rising star of the Arab Socialist Party, was still critical of the signing of the first armistice agreement with Israel. In a parliamentary speech that year, he charged that the armistice was responsible for destroying any possibility of Arab unity. This agreement, he added, was the last nail hammered in the coffin of the Palestine question and the main reason that Palestine had been lost to the Zionists.³⁴

Although Za'im's coup was generally perceived as Western instigated (a claim given credence by Miles Copland's account in *The Game of Nations: The Amorality of Power* [1969]), Syrian accounts attribute the coup to fallout over the Palestine War. As chief of the armed forces, Za'im came under heavy attack in parliament for failure to wage a successful war and for corruption in the army involving tainted provisions and defective weapons. The most vicious attacks were mounted by Faisal al-'Assali, a deputy from a minor party known as the Socialist Cooperative Party (al-Hizb al-Ta'awuni al-Ishtiraki). In one violent session on March 17, 1949, al-Za'im was accused of conspiring with King 'Abdullah. Al-'Assali said that al-Za'im should be tried on charges of treason. Al-'Assali then accused al-Za'im of attempting to firebomb his house. When Khaled al-'Azm's government began to investigate the issue of defective weapons, al-Za'im feared the worst. When al-Za'im began to arouse the fears of army officers about impending forced retirements and trials, a coup became imminent. Army officers held a meeting at Quneitra and called for the arrest and trial of deputy 'Assali.³⁵ When the coup took place, most Syrians remained relatively unperturbed because of the damaged legitimacy of the previous civilian governments.

Al-Za'im lasted in office barely four months and was executed, along with his respected Prime Minister, Muhsin al-Barazi, on August 14, 1949. What is of great significance here is that al-Za'im's coup not only triggered a series of coups but also inaugurated the insertion of the Syrian army into politics. The first attempt to politicize the army was made by Akram Hourani, who took upon himself the task of writing several of the early populist and progressive communiqués of the new regime. Among these were announcements granting women the right to vote, promising to fight unemployment, calling for the redistribution of land, and renewing Syria's commitment to the Arab League charter.³⁶ Hourani, the deputy from Hama at the time of the coup, was a member of the parliamentary committee charged with investigating the Syrian debacle during the Palestine

War. This assignment brought him in contact with Za'im, who Hourani claimed had summoned him to police headquarters after the coup had taken place. Other deputies were present as Za'im began explaining his case. Hourani always disclaimed any responsibility for Za'im's coup, but he did admit playing the role of advisor and speechwriter. Hourani also felt confident enough to level occasional criticism at the new strongman because the Hama deputy was well-supported by the army ranks. But after three weeks, Hourani returned to Hama and his links to al-Za'im were dissolved.[37] Hourani, nevertheless, was strongly inspired by the first Syrian coup, seeing it as a fulfillment of his own revolutionary and nationalist aspirations. Contemporaries often recalled that Hourani repeatedly used the word "coup" (*inqilab*) before al-Za'im took over, suggesting that the latter may have been inspired by Hourani's rhetoric.[38] Viewing himself as another Ataturk, al-Za'im benefited from the aftermath of the Palestine War. Although his brief tenure in office did not turn violent, his coup opened the way for further military intervention. The general public never forgave the violent blow that he dealt to democratic rule.

Once al-Za'im seized power, the Israelis, fearing expansionist moves in their direction, issued several threats. Al-Za'im responded by warning Ralph Bunche, the UN mediator, that any Israeli attempt to seize areas held by Syrian forces would force the Syrians to resume fighting. Since the Syrian-Israeli front was not yet subject to an armistice agreement, the Syrian body politic began to experience the familiar pangs of insecurity. It was at this juncture that Nouri al-Sa'id, the Iraqi premier, landed suddenly in Damascus and held a long meeting with al-Za'im in which the prospect of an immediate Iraqi-Syrian union was discussed. The Iraqi communiqué that followed this meeting referred to the Palestine issue as the major reason for these plans. The Iraqis assured the Syrians that any Zionist attack on their territory would be repulsed by Iraq. Al-Sa'id had indeed broached the subject of a Syrian-Iraqi union as a necessary step to ward off Israeli attacks along Syria's borders. The cool reception of the Syrians to the Hashemite idea of the "Fertile Crescent" union triggered a campaign of mutual recrimination in the Syrian and the Iraqi press. Iraq's hostility forced Za'im to turn to Egypt for support against the Iraqi regent's ambition to grab the Syrian throne. A trip to Cairo by al-Za'im and a private meeting with King Farouq produced joint Egyptian-Saudi pledges of support. From that point on, Syrian relations with Iraq and Jordan deteriorated perceptibly to the extent that al-Za'im at one point threatened King 'Abdullah with public hanging.[39]

Prospects for an Iraqi-Syrian union revived as a result of the second

Syrian coup, which took place on August 14, 1949. By that time, al-Zaʿim had lost much of his appeal and the signing of the Syrian-Israeli armistice agreement fostered the impression of softness toward Israel. Al-Zaʿim had also lost much public support because of his handling of the Anton Saʿadeh case. The founder of the Syrian Social National Party (SSNP), charged with plotting the overthrow of the Lebanese government, was handed over to Lebanese authorities after he had been granted asylum in Syria. His summary execution embittered many of his followers in Syria, and the majority of Syrians felt repulsed by the gross violation of the rules of Arab hospitality. After Saʿadeh's death, the new coup leader turned out to be a military man who had taken part in the Palestine War. General Sami al-Hinnawi immediately ingratiated himself to the old ruling elite by promising a speedy return to democratic rule.[40]

Former President Hashem al-Atassi was asked to form the new cabinet, which included veteran statesmen such as Khaled al-ʿAzm and Nathem al-Qudsi as well as rising socialist stars Michel ʿAflaq for the Ministry of Education and Akram Hourani for the Ministry of Agriculture.[41] Hourani offered his resignation after two months, largely because of his opposition to any declaration of unity between Syria and Iraq. Like many of his generation, he saw this union as a threat to Syria's independence and a blow to its republican form of government. Hourani was also wary of the Hashimite royal family in Iraq and its designs on Syria. Added to this, most Syrians shared a strong loathing for Britain, which dominated Iraq's government at the time and which Syrians held responsible for the loss of Palestine. Houraniʾa views on this recurring threat to Syria's sovereignty and independence were particularly important in light of his far-reaching influence in civilian and military circles. The Iraqi unification project, moreover, seemed more threatening than ʿAbdullah's Greater Syria plan because of the availability of the Iraqi regent to sit on the Syrian throne. The prospect of such a union seemed very real in 1949 as the People's Party came out in support of the Iraqi Hashimites. Hourani declared publicly that while he might favor Arab unity, he would not accept a British or American form of Arabism. He added that he might also be in favor of Arab socialism, but he did not favor communist socialism.[42]

The Hinnawi coup, according to one author, had the thumbprints of Britain all over it. Syria went back to its subordinate position in the Hashimite and Saudi axis. Although described as having limited intelligience, Hinnawi supposedly knew how to play his role. He quickly took the army out of politics and handed civilian leadership to those, like Premier Atassi, who favored taking Syria out of the Egyptian-Saudi axis. The traditional leadership of the People's Party, headed by Rushdi al-Kikhya, pushed openly for the Iraqi union as a means of checking any Israeli push toward the east. The Nationalist Party, on the other hand, was determined to prevent linking Syria to a British-dominated Iraq. Other political parties also chose sides. France, seeing the possibility of increased British influence in the Middle East, expressed its displeasure. Egypt and Saudi Arabia opposed this union strongly.[43]

Syrians became even more apprehensive when King 'Abdullah pursued his intrigues, and the Greater Syria project ran in a dead heat with that of the Iraqis.[44] The People's Party emerged as the arbiter of politics at this time but could not reconcile the various parties or achieve total dominance in the political arena. At first the Syrian army was divided over this issue, with one faction supporting the union that was led by two officers, 'Alam al-Din Qawwas and Muhammad Ma'rouf. A large faction led by the future leader of the third coup, Col. Adib Shishakly, vehemently and vocally opposed the union. Both Rushdi al-Kikhya and Nathem al-Qudsi, respectively Minister of the Interior and Minister of Foreign Affairs in Atassi's cabinet, proceeded with great caution to negotiate with the Iraqis. But the Ba'th and the Muslim Brotherhood continued to oppose the union until the Nationalist Party, represented by Sabri al-'Assali as its secretary, changed its position and welcomed the Iraqi regent to Damascus. But in the meantime the Syrian army began to exercise genuine authority in the country, and Akram Hourani emerged as its political voice.[45] Al-'Azm claimed in retrospect that al-Kikhya saw in the union Syria's only hope of curbing the power of the army. The Iraqi army, the larger of the two, was expected to swallow its Syrian counterpart and keep it in check.[46]

But the Syrian army finally intervened on December 19, 1949, by seizing power and removing al-Hinnawi from office. Akram Hourani's role as the instigator of this coup was widely acknowledged, if for no other reason than his long friendship with Adib Shishakly.[47] Both Shishakly and Hourani were from the town of Hama, attended elementary school together, and joined the SSNP at the same time. Their friendship was strengthened when Hourani returned from Iraq, after the defeat of Kaylani's revolt, with a vigorous hatred of the Hashimites, and when both fought in the Palestine War. Hourani, by 1949, was also a firm believer in the army's indispensability to any movement for social change. Hourani, not surprisingly, was assigned the Ministry of Defense during Khaled al-'Azm's first cabinet after Shishakly's coup. Hourani began to encourage peasant youths, particularly those from Hama, to join the military academy in order to politicize the armed forces further. Upon resigning from this position a short while later, Hourani announced the formation of the Arab Socialist Party.[48]

Plagued with assassination attempts and acts of civilian resistance, Shishekli started a slow decline as he became one of the most brutal of Syria's modern dictators. At first his stated objective was to restore Syria to its civilian rulers. Continued interparty strife eventually alarmed the military, particularly Shishakly, who decided to come out from the shadows of power. In a blow to the government of the People's Party, the Syrian strongman moved to incarcerate President Hashem al-Atassi and the entire cabinet. This took place on December 2, 1951, in what was referred to as Syria's fourth coup. Fawzi Silo, a military man and Minister of Defense, was named head of state, while Shishekli became Prime Minister. By 1953 Silo was removed from office and Shishekli was elected president. The fourth coup lasted until February 25, 1954, thus allowing Syria the longest period under the same rule.

By that date, the dual government of civilians and military authorities had dissolved into a pure military dictatorship. One reason for the survival of this particular dictatorship is that it was supported by all the leftist parties, which derived a certain advantage from the suspension of democracy and the old established parties. This was true in the case of the Ba'th Party, which was unable to monopolize politics under the old democratic rules and which extended its support to Shishekli until the fourth coup. But when Shishekli created his own organization, the Arab Liberation Movement (Harakat al-Tahrir al-'Arabi), and began to siphon off recruits from the familiar Ba'th pool of students, youths, and white-collar workers, the Ba'th was alarmed. With this new party, the Syrian strongman dealt a blow to both the traditional and radical parties. He began to draw the support of young Syrian nationalists around the theme of retrieving Palestine, which he called "the second Andalus." Shishekli's liberal economic policies also alarmed the socialist Ba'thists. Finally, the combined effort of all the opposition forces produced a massive rebellion in Jabal al-'Arab, or the Druze area.[49]

The Druze rebellion would not have been viewed with great alarm were it not for its suspected links to the Hashimites of Iraq and Jordan. The 1951 government of Hassan al-Hakim had already shown indications of tilting in that direction. Its dispute with the People's Party over the Western-inspired defense pact already rejected by Egypt aggravated interparty relations and drew the ire of the military.[50] Hakim, like most members of the old establishment, had advocated union with Iraq on the basis of the new reality of Israel.[51] Pro-unity voices like Ihsan al-Jabri saw Israel as the reality "which imperialism has planted in the heart of the Arab countries." There was no way of excising the Zionist threat, Jabri added, except through a total Arab union, military readiness, and a stringent economic boycott against Israel. The ideal solution was a total Arab union, but if this was impossible, unity should start with a dual, tripartite, or quadruple union. The door should be left open for other Arab states to join.[52] Along with the first step of partial unity involving one or more of the surrounding countries, Hakim recommended a Turkish alliance and a tilt to the West. In his view, this was the only way of resolving the Palestine question.[53]

The Druze rebellion, which erupted in 1953, was seen as the initial phase of a larger rebellion that involved all the opposition forces in Syria. Shishekli viewed it primarily as a Hashimite plot. It was reported that the ruthlessness with which the rebellion of Jabal al-'Arab was crushed was meant to convey a message to the nearby Jordanian Hashimites. Shishakly's Egyptian-Saudi ties permitted this military demonstration along the Jordanian border.[54] But Shishakly also never overlooked the indigenous character of this rebellion, stating privately that, "My enemies resemble a snake, whose head lies at Jabal al-'Arab, its stomach at Homs, and its tail at Aleppo. If the head is crushed the snake will perish."[55]

The end for Shishakly came on February 25, 1954, when an army rebellion led by a junior officer, Captain (al-Naqib) Mustafa Hamdoun, broke out at Aleppo. The rebellion was quickly joined by civilian groups all over the country, forcing Shishakly to resign and go into exile the following day. Shishakly's reluctance to confront this small rebellion militarily surprised everyone but was later interpreted in light of a developing confrontation with Israel. The regime's insecurities and declining public support soon caught Israel's attention. Israel was among the first of the neighboring states to emphasize the sectarian nature of Shishakly's attack on the Druze. Since Israel was constituted along sectarian lines, it has always noted the potential for communal breakdown in the Arab countries. Israel's own Druze community was always singled out for favorable treatment in a clear case of "divide and rule." Thus, Shishakly's onslaught on the Druze of Jabal al-'Arab presented a tremendous propaganda opportunity for Israel. The latter, additionally, anticipated the imminent fall of the Syrian regime and planned to reap some advantage from Syria's recurring troubles.[56]

The question remaining today is why Shishakly yielded power to an obscure junior military officer and declined a military confrontation he probably could have won? Even though the military uprising quickly spread to Homs, Latakia, and Deir al-Zour, he could easily have crushed it with the remaining military power at his disposal. But genuine fear of an imminent Iraqi intervention gripped the Syrian leader.[57] Since the rebellion started among disaffected and exiled Druze officers in the Deir al-Zour area, according to some observers, Shishakly feared the worst. Led by an officer named Muhammed al-Atrash, the uprising then linked up with the Aleppo military camp.[58] The proximity of the Deir al-Zour Druze officers to Iraq (about 50 percent of whom were Druze) would have made it easy for them to seek Iraqi military assistance. Had the Iraqis intervened, the American ambassador warned Shishakly on the day of the Aleppo uprising, then surely Israel would mount a severe attack.[59]

Israel, according to Moshe Dayan, would have a golden opportunity to intervene in Syria if Iraqi troops invaded that country. Dayan felt at the time that Israel needed to teach the Syrians a lesson so they would not interfere with Israeli fishing practices in Lake Tiberias. An invasion of southern Syria would also improve Israel's strategic position along its northern boundary. Another Israeli hawk, Pinchas Lavon, weighed in on the side of Dayan's suggestion. He strongly urged Moshe Sharett, Israel's Prime Minister in 1954–55, to use this opportunity by going beyond the demilitarized zone separating the two countries. Argued Lavon, the Minister of the Police, "This is the right moment to act—this is the time to move forward and occupy the Syrian border positions beyond the Demilitarized Zone. Syria is disintegrating. A state with whom we signed an armistice agreement exists no more. Its government is about to fall and there is no other power in view. Moreover, Iraq has practically moved into Syria. This is a historical opportunity, we shouldn't miss it."[60]

Sharett hesitated, however, not feeling that what he characterized as a "disastrous adventure" was justifiable. Iraq's invasion of Syria was merely a possibility, not a reality, and even Shishakly's fall from power was still within the realm of conjecture. After Shishakly's removal from office, Sharett reminded his hawkish colleagues that such an adventure would certainly elicit the condemnation of the UN Security Council. The hawkish members of his cabinet insisted that the Iraqi threat to Syria provided a perfect excuse for intervention. They only desisted when the Iraqis failed to act. When Hashem al-Atassi took over at Damascus as the new president, the Israeli cabinet rejected the invasion scheme altogether.

The Israeli hawks, however, continued to seek new forms of confrontation with Syria despite the fact that Israel continued its transgression on Arab farming lands along that border. On December 12, 1954, for instance, a Syrian civilian plane was forced to land at Lydda airport on the pretext that it threatened Israeli sovereignty. Sharett, however, called this an act of aerial piracy and his disapproval, as well as international outrage, forced the release of the passengers after two days of interrogations. Apparently, this Israeli provocation was a response to the capture, on the day before the hijacking incident, of an Israeli spy ring operating in Syria. The Israelis refused to take any responsibility for this botched operation, claiming that the Syrians had kidnapped the five Israelis and taken them to Syria. When one of the Israeli captives committed suicide, the Israeli press published charges of torture. Sharett wrote in his diary that "our soldiers have not been kidnapped in Israeli territory by Syrian invaders as the army spokesman announced. . . . They penetrated into Syria and not accidentally but in order to take care of a wiretapping installation that was connected to a Syrian telephone line."[61]

Confirmation of rumored Iraqi collusion with Syrian opposition forces during Adib Shishekli's years in office came later from the pen of one-time Iraqi Foreign Minister and Prime Minister, Dr. Fadhel al-Jamali. Commenting on revelations in the newly opened British archives in the 1980s, al-Jamali confirmed that prominent Syrian leaders had asked for Iraq's assistance in ending Shishekli's rule. The Iraqi government refrained from taking any action, he wrote, fearing the implications of pushing the Iraqi army into this situation. Iraqi assistance was limited to offering material and moral support to the liberal forces of Syria. Requests for Iraq's support came from such eminent figures as the veteran statesman Hashem al-Atassi and former Prime Minister Ma'rouf al-Dawalibi. The latter visited Baghdad secretly and asked for Iraqi troops to be placed under his command in order to return to Syria at the head of a conquering army. But again the Iraqis balked at the prospect of a military intervention that was certain to have serious international repercussions. It was later revealed that the head of the Nationalist Party, Sabri al-'Assali, received sums of money from the Iraqi regime during Shishekli's rule.[62]

Adib al-Shishekli made another attempt to recapture the presidency in 1956, from his exile in Europe. This attempt, by a man known for his skill in staging coups, was seen as a natural development. Syrians felt that he had given up power willingly in order to avoid unnecessary bloodshed as well as the destruction of the armed forces and most of their equipment. His quick departure in 1954 was seen as a strategic retreat meant to allow him time to gather his forces and pounce on his enemies. Significantly, Shishakly's attempted return to power was made with the help of the United States. By 1956 the American motivation for meddling in Syrian affairs was related to the rising tide of radicalism in the Arab world. The

United States would have been satisfied to have Syria under Iraq's wing in order to stem the pro-Soviet Arab tide. But British-dominated Iraq failed to achieve this objective, and Syria drifted gradually into the Egyptian orbit. Even France supported the return of Shishakly, fearing a Syrian-Egyptian alliance harmful to its interests in Lebanon and Algeria. Most of the information related to this phase of Shishekli's career came from the testimony of Lt. Gen. Ghazi Daghastani, deputy chief of the Iraqi armed forces, before the revolutionary court in Iraq. Apparently some Iraqi officials during that time received messages from Shishakly at his Swiss place of residence, requesting Iraq's financial assistance and promising a change in his policy toward the neighboring state. After Shishakly arrived at Beirut, he made contact not only with Iraqis but with former Syrian supporters and American and British diplomatic representatives. Shishakly, fearing failure and inadequate funds, preferred to abort the conspiracy and leave. When the Syrians uncovered the plot and its foreign aspects, three Damascus-based American diplomats were expelled. The United States retaliated by expelling Syria's ambassador to Washington, Farid Zein al-Din. Some units of the U.S. Mediterranean-based Sixth Fleet also approached Syrian territorial waters. Shishakly received a life sentence in absentia, and his co-conspirators were given prison sentences of various lengths.[63]

Conclusion

Syria's unusual record of instability and the political ascendancy of the military were undoubtedly the result of its involvement in the first Palestine War. The war, which could neither be avoided nor prevented, exposed all the weaknesses of the young Syrian democracy. Perhaps Syria's greatest weakness at this stage was its unprotected boundaries, which exposed it to Arab and Israeli threats alike. Syria's vulnerability, however, was not limited to its geographic location but extended to its pan-Arab ideology. The earnestness with which Syrian statesmen and military officers approached the Palestine War revealed for the first time the new conflicting interests of various segments of the great Syrian province. Both the mufti's intransigence and obduracy, as well as the unabashed territorial ambitions of the Iraqi and Jordanian Hashimites, revealed the disintegration of the old pan-Arab dream. By 1948 there were new conflicting state interests, including those of Arab Palestine, which took the Syrian nationalist elite by surprise. Nothing illustrates the despair and shock resulting from these changed realities better than the Palestinian career of Fawzi al-Qawuqji. A veteran of several Arab liberation wars, Qawuqji found himself caught between the new jealousies and rivalries unleashed by the Palestine War.

Failure to coordinate with other Arab governments finally caused the Syrians to lose not only the battle for Palestine but also the battle for a decent, if temporary peace. Israel's success in forcing the signing of unilateral armistice agreements drove a powerful wedge between different members of the Arab League of States. Furthermore, Israel's menacing moves along the Syrian border provided a convenient justification for Iraqi and Jordanian Arab-unity plots focusing on Syria. Each Hashimite scheme to force a union on Syria claimed to be doing so in the interest of defending Arab lands against Israeli attacks. This argument heightened Syrian insecurities regarding friend and foe alike. Additionally, Syria's anti-American and anti-British mood following the Palestine War prevented the newly independent republic from concluding normal economic agreements with the oil interests of Saudi Arabia and Iraq. Western pressure to extract economic concessions from Syria acted to widen the gulf between the country's civilian and military wings of government.

Finally, it is clear that the Arab debacle of 1948 facilitated the unusual military dominance of civilian politics. Not only did mutual recriminations regarding responsibility for losing the war polarize the civilian and military establishments, the accusations also exposed the inadequacies of both. The resultant mutual loss of trust encouraged one military faction after the other to attempt the restructuring of Syrian politics. As is clear from the career of Akram Hourani, the military emerged as a potential instrument of social justice but could not delegitimize civilian politics entirely. Becoming increasingly subject to rising new nationalist ideologies, the military failed to display the ruthlessness of other Arab military regimes. Even Adib Shishakly, who came the closest to achieving a Nasserite style of hegemony over the body politic of Syria, failed to find the right balance between power and civilian politics necessary for the survival of any regime. He also exemplified the typical Arab political operative who was made and unmade by the sheer weight of Israeli threats to his own country. Therefore, Syrians began to realize by 1954 that managing the Palestinian dimension of pan-Arab politics was just as important as managing the Israeli dimension. Lacking any political structure of their own, the Palestinians were still potentially important as actors in the battle against Israel and the struggle against the Hashimites. With the return of civilian politics to Syrian life in the mid 1950s, the official approach to the Palestinian question turned to diplomatic, rather than military, solutions.

3

The Political Co-optation of the Palestinians

Syria's experience with the mufti of Jerusalem was no different from that of any other Arab state. As the representative of the official Palestinian national movement, the mufti attempted to gain a voice in the halls of Arab power equal to that of other heads of state. The only means of achieving this objective were to exploit Arab differences and their conflicting state interests. The mufti developed a somewhat successful strategy along these lines which was based on avoiding dependence on any single Arab country. This turned out to be an elusive goal largely due to the mufti's failure to achieve international recognition of his cause.

With the 1957 death of Ahmad Hilmi 'Abd al-Baqi, the mufti's deputy inside of Palestine, the only Palestinian governmental structure, the Government of All Palestine, faded from existence. But the Palestinian voice was barely audible even before that. Confined to the Egyptian-controlled Gaza Strip, the Government of All Palestine lacked any semblance of genuine sovereignty and exercised only limited authority over the Palestinian residents of that area. Although still residing in Lebanon, the mufti was prevented by Egyptian authorities from returning to Gaza. The Jordanian-held West Bank was also closed to him. Thus, it was possible in the mid 1950s to foster an alternative, tame Palestinian leadership.

Palestinian Statesmen and Revolutionaries

Syria was the first to embrace the Palestine cause anew after the loss of the Palestine War. Always willing to represent the Palestinian point of view in international forums, Syria could be relied on to treat this issue as its own. In 1948, for instance, Syria's representative to the United Nations found himself arguing strongly at the Security Council against an American proposal for an Arab-Israeli cease-fire. The future Prime Minister of Syria, Faris al-Khouri, bristled at the suggestion of the American representative, Warren Austin, that Israel be viewed as a legitimate state since it had been recognized by the United States and other members of the UN. Al-Khouri demanded that the International Court of Justice be given an opportunity to examine the legality of the act of recognition. The United States rejected this suggestion, which was one of many attempts to test the jurisdiction of the UN in this matter.[1]

Later on Al-Khouri was advised in his UN work by Ahmad Shuqeiri, a Palestinian diplomat and international lawyer and a member of the Saudi team. He had been appointed in 1951 as an assistant secretary general at the Arab League of States but was on loan to the Syrian delegation whenever the UN was in session. Shuqeiri continued in this dual role for some time until he was offered the position of Syrian Foreign Minister by strongman Adib al-Shishakly, which he promptly refused. He returned to the Saudi delegation at the UN in 1957. His work there was not confined to the Palestine question but extended to the defense of the Arab states that remained under colonial rule. His first opportunity to elevate the Palestine issue to a higher international level came during the Bandung Conference of 1955.[2] At the invitation of Syria's Foreign Minister, Khaled al-'Azm, Shuqeiri joined the official Syrian delegation, which included two ministers, Fakher al-Kayyali and Dr. Ma'moun al-Kuzbari, as well as Ba'thist founder Salah al-Din al-Bitar. Other Arab delegations to this landmark conference, which inaugurated the Non-Aligned Movement, included Gamal Abdel Nasser, who headed the Egyptian delegation, Prince Faisal for Saudi Arabia, and Sami al-Solh and Charles Malik for Lebanon. Jawaharlal Nehru of India and Zhou Enlai of the People's Republic of China were also in attendance.

Al-'Azm's intent was to give the Palestine question maximum exposure by placing it on the agenda. For China the conference was an opportunity to emerge from international isolation and the limited orbit of the socialist states. Al-'Azm invited Shuqeiri to give the Chinese leader a detailed historical lecture on the Palestine issue in order to win this great state to the Arab viewpoint. Al-'Azm and Shuqeiri also managed to place this question on the agenda against the objections of the Burmese delegation, which pointed to the inappropriateness of this move in the absence of the other party to the dispute. The conference finally called for the application of the 1948 UN resolutions pertaining to the Palestine question and recognition of the legitimate rights of the Arabs. The resolutions in question urged that the Palestinian refugees be returned to their home or compensated for lost properties. The Israelis never promised to comply, and the Arab states themselves, as al-'Azm observed, were loath to see the Palestinians return to an Israeli-ruled Palestine. But the political advantage of utilizing this new international forum was not lost on the Syrians.[3]

As a non-Syrian, Shuqeiri had no problem when drafted by specific Syrian governments for various diplomatic assignments. His qualification for high Syrian office was questioned only once, when he was nominated to be head of the Syrian delegation to the UN. The Syrian president, Hashem al-Atassi, objected to this appointment, claiming that Palestinians who resided in Syria were entitled to all rights and privileges of Syrians except when it came to appointments to high government office. Al-'Azm drafted a law to facilitate such appointments, but the president refused to sign the law in order to bring it to the attention of parliament. Some deputies adopted the proposal and tried to have it passed in parliament but were blocked by the deliberate procrastination of the People's Party. The tortuous course this law followed was indicative of some of the constitutional issues related to the presence of a large Palestinian community in different parts of Syria.[4] By 1956 Shuqeiri was representing the Saudi government at the UN. His relations with the Saudi Foreign Minister, Prince Faisal, soured, however, when Shuqeiri refused to bring the matter of Egypt's support for the Yemeni rebels before the UN. Preferring instead to charge Egypt before the League of Arab States, Shuqeiri lost his position in 1963.[5]

There were other forms of Palestinian agitation in Syria besides the official efforts of Shuqeiri following the first Palestine War. This activity assumed the shape of Arab nationalism rather than Palestinian particularism. In contrast to Shuqeiri's harmonious relations with the Syrian nationalist establishment, members of the revolutionary Palestinian current sought to avenge the loss of Palestine through acts of assassination and sabotage. A new political formation known as Kata'ib al-Fida' al-'Arabi, which included Egyptians and Syrians as well as Palestinians, emerged in Lebanon in the early 1950s. The purpose of this group was to assassinate King 'Abdullah of Jordan, John Glubb Pasha, the chief of the Arab Legion, and the Iraqi Premier, Nuri al-Sa'id. Al-Kata'ib also targeted Adib al-Shishakly, although he was not held responsible for the losses of 1948. The founder of al-Kata'ib, though not necessarily the inspiration for the attempt on Shishakly's life, was George Habash.

Forced to go into hiding following the botched assassination attempts, Habash caught the attention of Syrian authorities. Habash's group was unimpressed by the existing pan-Arabist and pan-Syrian parties, such as the Ba'th and the SSNP, which seemed not to emphasize the Palestine question. The entire Palestinian nationalist infrastructure, it seems, was searching for the right ideology and the right circumstances to begin the process of Palestinian retrieval and national reconstruction. After the departure of the early pan-Arab Palestinian revolutionaries from Syria and Lebanon and their dispersal in various Arab countries, they continued to work toward the creation of a coherent movement. By the time of their first conference in 1956, the early band of revolutionaries had acquired the name of the Arab Nationalist Movement (Harakat al-qawmiyeen al-'Arab). Born of the 1948 Palestinian War, the ANM was joined early on by non-Palestinians who later represented the new revolutionary vanguard in their own countries. The Palestinians included George Habash and Wadi' Haddad. Others came from Kuwait (such as the future opposition leader Ahmad al-Khatib) and from Egypt (such as Hussein Tawfiq, son of a prominent member of the Egyptian cabinet). Hani al-Hindi was an activist from Syria. The Palestine issue thus galvanized the Arab intelligentsia around it just as it found a hearing in Syrian politics.[6]

In the meantime, Syrian-Israeli clashes along the border increased, as did various American attempts to destabilize Syria's radical governments. American alarm at the rising radical tide in Syria was evident in U.S. involvement in several plots to overthrow the Syrian government. The plot to restore former strongman Adib al-Shishakly and Col. Ibrahim al-Husseini to power in 1957, with help from Damascus-based American diplomats and Iraqi funding, was one of the most serious of that decade. Apparently, American participation in the latest Iraqi-Syrian unification plans was due to two recent events: the Soviet-Syrian economic agreement of 1957, and the radicalization of the Syrian armed forces as a result of the appointment of the communist-leaning 'Afif al-Bizreh as chief of staff.[7] The appointment of the latter as head of the military was intended to encourage the Soviets to become a source of economic and military assistance.[8] The assassination of Col. 'Adnan al-Malki on April 22, 1955, was also attributed to his resistance to American approaches. According to some of the testimony during the trial, the murder of the most promising Ba'thist in the military was intended to launch an American-backed coup attempt. The conspirators in this case, all members of the SSNP, were found to be in close contact with American officials at Beirut.[9]

U.S. regional moves to control what it perceived to be an increasingly radicalized Syria finally led to the idea of regional defense pacts. First came the Turkish-Iraqi agreement of February 1955, which was viewed as a prelude to the Baghdad Pact. Then came the 1957 Eisenhower Doctrine, which emphasized American strategic interest in the eastern Mediterranean area. U.S. Cold War tactics frightened both the Syrians and Egyptians and drove them toward greater coordination. Egyptians' desire to work with the Syrians resulted in consultations prior to the convening of the Bandung Conference in order to present a united Arab posture at that important international forum. The signing of the Turkish-Iraqi agreement brought an Egyptian team to Damascus, led by Salah Salem, which succeeded in issuing a joint declaration with Syria against the agreement. The declaration also called for the creation of an Arab defense and economic organization. A Syrian-Egyptian delegation followed this with a visit to Lebanon, Jordan, Saudi Arabia, and Iraq. When Britain joined the Turkish-Iraqi agreement a few months later, giving it the new name of the Baghdad Pact, Egypt and Syria negotiated a military pact in September 1955. A Syrian-Egyptian economic pact was signed by January of the following year. This agreement allowed for the free movement of people, capital, and manufactured goods between the two countries.[10]

There is no question that the Eisenhower Doctrine and the Baghdad Pact were intended to contain radicalism in Syria more than anywhere else. U.S. concern over the so-called Syrian crisis and Syria's perceived imminent fall into communist hands heightened Syria's sense of its own vulnerability. Moreover, the guarantees offered Israel by the Baghdad Pact upset the Syrians, who could not escape the lesson of Israel's 1955 attack on Gaza. Following the conclusion of the pact, Quwatli visited the Soviet Union and received commitments for Soviet weapons.[11] Syria was feeling the pinch of military conspiracies along all of its borders. Egypt's commitment to neutrality, and its recent experience of the British, French, and Israeli attack during the 1956 Suez War, began to drive the two countries closer together.

Having rejected the concept of a "Middle East system" (a term he knew to be the invention of Western military contingencies during World War II), Nasser was anxious to develop an Arab system to ensure the interests and safety of the Arab people. A Middle East system of states would include Turkey, Iran, and Pakistan. It probably would also include Israel, even if indirectly. The proposed Western pacts, like the Baghdad Pact, would also violate basic articles of the Arab League of States. Nasser's opposition to the pact was mainly its threat to the principle of positive neutrality and its restriction of any future anti-Israeli activity. The Egyptian leader's only possible defense against this new encirclement was to take active steps toward the creation of an Arab system.[12] Muhammad Hassanein Haykal, Nasser's trusted advisor and political strategist, had always recognized Syria's geopolitical significance to Egypt and pointed him in that direction. "Palestine, with Syria behind it, were always nothing other than the land bridge connecting Egypt to the East," Haykal wrote.[13] All invaders, whether ancient ones like the Babylonians and Persians or more recent invaders like the Arabs and the Turks, had crossed this land bridge on their way to Egypt. Similarly, Egyptian armies like those of Muhammad ʿAli Pasha had also traveled this road in defense of Egypt. Greater Syria, then, should be considered Egypt's strategic buffer as well as the ancient land route on which international trade traveled. This land bridge, Haykal wrote, was also Egypt's highway to the rest of the Arab world.[14]

Water Disputes and Unity Talks

Syria, for its part, had its own reasons for seeking a union with Egypt. Syrian authorities generally reject the notion that nationalists and Baʿthists in Syria sought a union with Egypt in order to stem a communist takeover of Syria. This interpretation, which originated with Haykal and was repeated by many Western writers, is apparently inaccurate.[15] Khaled al-ʿAzm reminds us that while there is no proof that the United States was behind the union, Washington certainly welcomed this move.[16] Despite the appointment of the communist-leaning ʿAfif al-Bizreh to the top position in the armed forces, two-thirds of the members of parliament were rightists belonging to the Nationalist and People's Parties, as well as to the Muslim Brotherhood. A wing of the People's Party had turned leftward but that did not mean they embraced communism. The National Party was also divided, but most of the deputies were turning away from the West because of its steadfast support of Israel. The memory of French and British collusion with Israel during the recent Suez War was still vivid in people's minds.[17] The fact that only one Communist deputy, Khaled Bakdash, was elected to the Syrian parliament in 1954, and that the Communist base of support never rivaled that of the Baʿth, indicated the absence of a Communist threat.[18] But there were domestic incentives for unity with Egypt, apart from mounting communist influence in the army and in government. For instance, Rushdi al-Kikhya, head of the People's Party, was apprehensive about changes in the Syrian domestic scene and had almost completely withdrawn from political life on the eve of unity with Egypt. When parliament held a special session on February 5, 1958, to discuss the impending unity, Kikhya showed up and voted for the proposal. Many believed that he was glad for this opportunity, which would curb the political influence of the army. Kikhya, nevertheless, was known to be anti-Nasser and a promoter of the failed Iraqi unity scheme. Mahmoud Riadh, Egypt's ambassador in Syria, had assured him that unity would result in the army's retreat from politics. The Muslim Brotherhood shared Kikhya's incentives despite Nasser's recent persecution of their Egyptian ideological comrades. The same could be true of the National Party and other tribesmen. Clearly, fear of the Syrian army's dominance of politics was a strong notivation for unity.[19]

Rising tension on the Syrian-Israeli border also contributed to Syria's interest in linking with a powerful army. Just as all unity schemes in the past were advocated as a solution to Israel's increasing threat in the south, the union with Egypt promised to rid both countries of the same dangerous enemy. Following the signing of the 1949 Syrian-Israeli general armistice agreement, Israel was in the habit of sending heavily fortified farmers to plow the rich Huleh Valley's demilitarized zone. UN observers were prevented from checking and ending these illegal practices. General Carl von Horn of the UN peacekeeping force had repeatedly complained about this, although he admitted that the extremely rich soil was a great temptation and resource for the Israelis, who had built a maze of canals and irrigation works in this area. These illegal actions were also intended to push Israel's boundary eastward to the old Palestine border during the British mandate. This plan was based on occupying the demilitarized zone and removing its Arab farmers. Yigal Allon, former Israeli deputy prime minister, admitted in 1948 that he instructed Jewish farmers in the area to spread rumors among the Arabs of the Huleh Valley that Jewish military reinforcements were on the way. This was intended to produce a general flight of the Arab farming population eastward.[20]

The object of Israel's designs was the so-called "Palestinian Golan," which was occupied by Syria during the 1948 War although it was allotted to Israel by the UN partition resolution of 1947. These lands, of course, were Arab lands belonging to the area's Palestinian farmers. Israel was resentful of this, even though it was able as a result of the 1948 War to increase its share of Palestinian territory in the UN partition resolution throughout Palestine by 40 percent. On the Syrian front, Israel lost only four-tenths of one percent of the land allocated to it by the UN. By March 1951, completely revoking the terms of the Syrian-Israeli general armistice agreement, Israel publicly declared its entitlement to the demilitarized zone and expelled two thousand inhabitants of the villages of al-Bakarah, Ghannam, and al-Khouri, which lie within that zone. Israelis then shelled al-Himmeh, which caused the Syrians to retaliate by encroaching on the area where the Jordan River empties into Lake Tiberias.[21] Reports by the UN Truce Supervision Organization (UNTSO) and the UN chairman of the Syrian-Israeli Mixed Armistice Commission (MAC) documented the illegality of Israel's actions. UNTSO's chief of staff, Lt. General E. L. Burns, wrote:

Major differences arose over the legal status of the (demilitarized) zone. Israel claimed sovereignty over all of it; set fortifications in it; and sent well-armed frontier police and some heavy military equipment in it. Not only Syria, but the UN and the United States (including the late Ralph Bunche who helped write the Syrian-Israeli General Armistice Agreement) denied Israel's claim to sovereignty. . . . The Israelis in fact exercised almost complete control over the major portion of the . . . zone through the frontier police. . . . This was directly contrary to Article V of the General Armistice Agreement and the "authoritative interpretation" of it (by Ralph Bunche).[22]

Israel's illegal expansion toward the east at the expense of Palestinian farmers resulted in armed conflict with the Syrian military on the Golan Heights. Israeli fishing activities on Lake Tiberias were also expanded and were accompanied by armored landing craft and police boats. Syrian fishing on the lake completely ceased.[23] On December 11, 1955, an Israeli army raid on Arab villages and front-line positions of the Syrian military adjacent to the demilitarized zone resulted in 56 Syrian deaths, 7 wounded, and 32 unaccounted for. The raid was condemned by the Security Council, which passed Resolution 111.[24] Most Israelis were well aware of the illegal nature of their government's activities in the Golan-Tiberias area. Dovish former Israeli General Mattityahu Peled wrote in *Davar* on April 7, 1972, that Israel's policy of forcibly settling the demilitarized zone was responsible for over 50 percent of the border incidents along the Syrian lines.[25]

The other running dispute with the Israelis concerned the waters of the Jordan River and its tributaries. Israel's need for water caused similar encroachments on the demilitarized zone in Lake Huleh. Despite protests by the UN, Israel succeeded in damming this lake completely between 1953 and 1955. This project, which entailed the construction of an electrical plant and the diversion of the Jordan River between Lakes Huleh and Tiberias, added considerable agricultural land to Israel.[26] U.S. efforts to defuse the Jordan River crisis and to settle claims of the different riparian states failed miserably. The reason for this failure was political rather than technical, specifically the absence of trust and a spirit of cooperation among the parties.

The United States dispatched Eric Johnston, head of the Motion Picture Association, in 1953 to study the situation and make recommendations. The Johnston report, known as the Jordan River Plan, was completed in October 1955 and provided a formula for the distribution of the Jordan and Yarmouk Rivers between the area's major users—namely, Israel, Jordan, Lebanon, and Syria. The Johnston plan was rejected by the Arab League of States but was accepted by the Israelis since it decreed that the majority of the waters of the Jordan River could be used by Israel while the larger portion of the waters of the Yarmouk River could be used by Jordan.[27]

The Johnston plan recommended that Israel be given 375 million cubic meters of water per year from the Jordan, but only 25 million cubic meters from the Yarmouk, even though the latter barely runs along Israeli territory. The Jordanians were given 100 million cubic meters from the Jordan and much more from the Yarmouk (377 million cubic meters), since the latter runs primarily in Jordan. Syria, with land access in the northern area, was permitted the use of 42 million cubic meters from the Jordan and 90 million from the Yarmouk.[28] After the Arab League rejected this plan, Syria began its own project to divert the Jordan in the north before it entered Israel. This could have been feasible, since the two main sources of the Jordan—the Banias and Hasbani—begin in the Syrian and Lebanese highlands. The Yarmouk River, which is the natural boundary between Jordan and Syria, was also considered part of the natural resources of these two states.[29]

What motivated the Syrians to undertake this diversion project was fear of Israel's massive plan to divert the Jordan's waters, which was completed in 1963.[30] This system, known as the National Water Carrier, was composed of a network of pipelines that conveyed the water of the Jordan, Lake Tiberias, and the Yarmouk, beginning near Lake Houleh, to Tel Aviv in the south and from there all the way to the Negev Desert in order to permit the settlement of more Israelis in the area.[31] At first, the Syrians sought a collective Arab military effort to destroy the Israeli installation, but Egypt was opposed. The Arab League's summit meeting in September 1963 refused to go along with the plan and a counterplan was suggested.[32] Egyptian-Syrian differences (the two were united as the United Arab Republic in 1958) over the best response to the Israeli diversion of the river, however, began before the termination of the union in 1961. In a 1959 UAR cabinet meeting, the Egyptians at first suggested requesting the Secretary-General of the UN, Dag Hammarskjöld, to attempt a revival of the Johnston plan, rejected by the Syrians in 1955. Nasser's argument during that meeting was that, based on the Secretary-General's opinion, the Israelis were determined to complete their diversionary plans by 1960, and any Arab action to stop them would be considered an act of aggression. Mahmoud Fawzi, the UAR's Foreign Minister, counseled against bringing the matter before the UN. Nasser then added that the UAR was about to implement a ten-year development plan that was expected to double the republic's gross national product. Any disruption of this plan, he added, was not in the best interest of the UAR, or even the Palestine question. The only way of forcing Israel to cease its diversion plans would be through a war for which the Arab Republic was not prepared and that would result in Western backing for Israel. Moreover, Egypt's strained relations with the Iraqi regime of ʿAbd al-Karim Qasem, as well as with Jordan, Saudi Arabia, and Tunisia, would certainly encourage Israel to retaliate. Nasser emphasized that the Arab states could not be expected to help. He cited the recent examples of Saudi complaints against Israeli shipping in the Gulf of ʿAqaba and Qasem's recent declarations calling for the creation of the Fertile Crescent. Neither of these initiatives had been backed by Arab action and had instead elicited a threatening response from David Ben Gurion.[33]

Nasser reported that Ben Gurion had recently expressed his intention of diverting the river despite the objections of the UAR. Since the Arab Republic was not prepared for war, Nasser argued, Hammarskjöld's mediation offer should be accepted. He was to revive the Johnston plan but without referring to it by its original name. The Secretary-General was to be invited to Cairo in order to discuss, in this context, Egypt's application for a World Bank loan. The issues of the diversion of the river and the Palestine question, Nasser concluded, would be dealt with in the near future, when the UAR gained strength. For now, the UAR should focus on economic development. According to Muhammad Hassanein Haykal, Nasser suggested to the Syrian ministers the alternative plan of building some water projects on the Jordan before it reached the Israeli installations downriver. This plan, he advised, would avoid the need for war and at the same time diminish the value of the Israeli project. Akram Hourani argued in favor of resorting to force as well as pursuing the issue before the Security Council. But Nasser insisted that since the Israeli project fell within Israeli territory, just south of the demilitarized zone, the UAR would not be able to make a legal case for war. Hourani responded that the basic justification for such action was that the river belonged to the Arabs and they could not allow Israel to steal its waters. He explained that once the Arabs stopped the project by force, the Security Council would intervene and the diversion work would cease pending a resolution of the conflict.[34]

In his later accounts of this meeting, Haykal contended that Israel's diversion plans had begun long before the Syrian-Egyptian union. This fact, he felt, would exonerate Egypt from taking action against Israel. Haykal went as far as to write that Israeli plans for waterworks, immigration, and settlement were begun long before Nasser's and his own generation. Syrian historians of this period claim, however, that the idea of developing a diversion of the Jordan upriver from the Israelis did not originate with Nasser but was suggested by Ahmad 'Abd al-Karim, chief of the Syrian delegation to the Mixed Armistice Commission in 1953–54, when the Syrians shelled and stopped a minor Israeli diversion scheme. Karim reported during that same meeting the near completion of the Israeli plan and the urgent need to take collective action. Thus, the Ba'th Party was clearly chafing at Egypt's resistance to an armed confrontation with Israel over the river project. Nasser even alluded during that meeting to the possibility of Damascus being shelled by the Israelis from the air. Amin Nafouri, another Syrian officer, responded that this would not be the first time that Damascus suffered from shelling. Had the French not bombed Damascus? The Syrians pushed on, with Salah al-Din al-Bitar suggesting a complaint to the Security Council and issuing a warning that unless the diversion stopped, war would follow. He also recommended mobilizing the public for the impending battle. A committee was then formed to study the matter from the political, military, and technical angles in order to make recommendations to the Arab League. It was also reported that Anwar Sadat addressed Hourani with these words: "Do you wish to turn the world upside down over a little water?"[35]

Clearly, the Syrian-Egyptian union did not break up solely as a result of their differences over the river diversion. But the matter was serious enough to have precipitated the resignation of some top Ba'thists from the cabinet, including Hourani, Bitar, Mustapha Hamdoun, and 'Abd al-Ghani Qanout. The union was to last until 1961, with the Syrians groaning under the weight of intelligence services, economic exploitation, and marginalization of their political institutions.[36]

The Syrians continued to agitate in the Arab League against Israeli diversion of the Jordan. When the Israeli National Water Carrier was completed in 1963, the league adopted resolutions calling for a canal to be built to the Hasbani and Banias Rivers, the sources of the Jordan River in the Golan Heights. The canal was intended to convey the waters of the Hasbani and Banias, which lie east of the Jordan in Syrian territory, to the Yarmouk River. A dam, the Makhaibah, was to collect these waters and the Yarmouk flow. The plan actually called for building the dam first, which would not have been a threat to Israel since no one disputed Jordan's exclusive rights over the Yarmouk. However, the canal was begun first, in 1965, which would have diverted the Banias River to the Yarmouk for a length of 70 kilometers. The Israelis raided the canal from the air in the spring of 1965, putting an end to this plan. Syrians complained bitterly against Egypt during the Arab League's meeting of May 1965, only to be told that Egypt was not prepared to go to war against Israel because of a few Syrian earthmovers.[37]

When the United Arab Republic dissolved on September 28, 1961, no one was more disheartened than the Palestinians. This was principally due to their faith in pan-Arabism and their conviction that it was the only means of liberating Palestine. The unified Arab state was seen as a pair of pliers squeezing Israel, or occupied Palestine, from two directions. Indeed, it was Ben Gurion who applied the descriptive term "pliers" to the first unified Arab state. Until 1964 Palestinians retained much of their pan-Arabist vision. They had not yet developed any regional or local complexes. Neither did they resent that non-Palestinian Arabs were leading the Palestinian political and military struggle. At that time most Palestinians were enrolled in the Ba'th, Arab Nationalist, Nasserite, and even Communist Parties. Always embracing a wider identity, they were unable to fathom the Syrian, Lebanese, and Iraqi lack of appreciation for Arab unity. Thus when a coup toppled the separatist government of Nathem al-Qudsi, and the reins of government were handed to Salah al-Din al-Bitar, the Palestinians were jubilant.[38]

Khaled al-'Azm wrote that Palestinians and Jordanians were among the most reckless when it came to Nasserite unity plans. In his view, the Palestinians themselves were mostly to blame for the loss of Palestine in 1948, even though many young men died during that war. But their flight to Syria and Jordan resembled a form of escapism or suicide. Rather than work to restore Palestine, they were willing to accept a UN dole and to descend to a lower level of poverty. Their miserable living conditions induced most of them to enroll in the destructive pro-Nasserite organizations within Syria and to take part in the Lebanese revolution. In their enthusiasm for the Nasserite project, Palestinians were willing to be financed by Nasserite forces in order to lay Syria again at Nasser's feet. Al-'Azm saw Palestinians attempt the assassination of Syrian, Lebanese, Iraqi, and Jordanian leaders while declining an opportunity to assassinate the Zionist leaders.[39]

In his own way, al-'Azm was expressing the old generation's impatience with the new tide of radicalism sweeping the Arab world. In the 1960s, this radicalism had two characteristics: it was highly representative of

Palestinians of the Arab diaspora, and it focused on Nasser's pan-Arabist project. But while the old guard of Syria's Arab nationalists quarreled with Nasser over the shape of that unity, desperate Palestinians supported any type of unity. What mattered was that one or two strong Arab states drew closer together, which to the exiled Palestinians meant a step closer to the restoration of Palestine. The same al-'Azm who gave Ahmad Shuqeiri an opportunity to articulate the Palestinian case before Zhou Enlai was still incapable of gauging the depth of Palestinian desperation. He was also oblivious to the inherently popular character of the Palestinian refugee political culture.

Unbeknownst to al-'Azm, many Palestinians, inspired by the successes of the Algerian revolution, had begun to gravitate toward exclusive Palestinian organizations. This was true even among the Palestinian ranks of such wider movements as the Ba'th and the Nasserite Parties. A new Palestinian consciousness was emerging, and Palestinians were demanding their own framework even within these pan-Arabist movements.[40] When Egypt sponsored a new Palestinian organization, no one questioned its eligibility for the role, for who other than Nasser could claim the role of official sponsor and revolutionary creator? By the mid 1960s not even the Syrians had managed to exorcise themselves of the pan-Arabist fever, and Palestinians were that much more susceptible and vulnerable.

By 1963 Ahmad Shuqeiri had moved in the direction of heading an exclusively Palestinian populist formation. When his service with the Saudis ended following a dispute over Egypt's Yemen war, Shuqeiri was approached at his Lebanese residence by many Palestinian delegations calling on him to lead a populist Palestinian effort. At the same time, 'Abd al-Khaleq Hassounah, Secretary-General of the Arab League, summoned him to Cairo to attend the first Arab summit meeting. Egyptian diplomats conveyed Nasser's invitation to Shuqeiri to assume the position of the late Ahmad Hilmi 'Abd al-Baqi, who had represented the last known Palestinian structure, the Government of All Palestine, in the Arab League. Shuqeiri's previous experience with the Arab League, however, induced him to decline until he was persuaded that this time things had really changed. He attended the September 19, 1963, session at Cairo with some trepidation. The Egyptian-dominated league quickly approved his appointment, with the exception of the Saudi and Jordanian delegations and the expressed reservation of the Iraqi delegation. Shuqeiri insisted on a modification of the Palestinian annex in the league's charter to read that he was selected as the Palestinian representative until such a time when the Palestinian people were able to make this choice themselves. Thus began Shuqeiri's struggle to establish an independent Palestinian will and to eliminate Arab patronage of the Palestine question.[41]

Shuqeiri's first assignment was to lead a Palestinian delegation to the UN to represent the Palestinian issue during upcoming discussions of matters concerning Palestinian refugees. Leading a delegation of eighteen, he confronted the unsolvable issue of Palestinian representation at the UN. His difficulty was to speak on behalf of a Palestinian delegation authorized by the league before the creation of a special organization, such as the soon-to-be-created Palestine Liberation Organization for Palestinians. Golda Meir, who led Israel's UN delegation as the country's Foreign Minister, strongly objected. She argued that there were only two states following the Palestinian partition resolution, namely, Jordan and Israel, and that Palestinians could only be allowed to offer testimony as refugees. Shuqeiri, however, inflamed the meeting by presenting the Palestine case as that of a people engaged in an anticolonial liberation struggle.[42]

But this was only the first of Shuqeiri's legal troubles. His greatest challenge was to convince other Arab states of the legitimacy and nonthreatening nature of his new project. Realizing that Egypt embraced Palestinian national aspirations in order to deflect Arab, particularly Syrian, charges of an insufficient defense of Arab riparian rights along the banks of the Jordan, Shuqeiri still plunged ahead. His most delicate task was to obtain Arab approval of a territorial base for this new organization. Since Egypt exercised territorial control over no major Palestinian land with the exception of Gaza, Egypt was not threatened by the territorial dimensions of the new entity. Shuqeiri, thus, faced protocol-related and sovereignty issues right from the start. He soon found that his attendance at the Arab summit of January 13, 1964, specifically convened to discuss the Palestine issue and Israel's encroachment on various Arab border areas, was quite problematic. Denied a seat next to the convening Arab heads of state, he pushed a chair next to the Moroccan king and proceeded to lecture the meeting on the urgency of opening up the entire Palestinian issue, not only the question of the diversion of the Jordan River. In the next session of the league, he seated himself next to the Algerian president, Ahmad Ben Bella, and spoke in favor of arming the Palestinians. He also explained that his new entity would not conflict with Jordanian sovereignty. The league, which had a full plate before it, paid scant attention to the proposed new entity and authorized Shuqeiri to launch his own Arab contacts. The final resolutions of the summit devoted only a few lines to the creation of a new Palestinian organization. These read as follows: "that Mr. Ahmad

Shuqeiri, Palestine's representative to the Arab League of States, undertake contacts with the member states and the Palestinian people in order to create a sound foundation for organizing the Palestinian people enabling it to liberate its land and decide its future."[43]

The only means of making this project a reality was to convert the idea of a new Palestinian entity into a people's movement. Shuqeiri therefore called for the convening of a Palestinian national council, to be held at Jerusalem, in order to develop a charter and a set of by-laws for a new Palestinian Liberation Organization. What he had in mind was the selection of an executive committee that would be eligible to participate in the next Arab summit meeting at Alexandria in the name of the PLO. He did not wish that representation to remain merely at the level of "the representative of Palestine at the Arab League." Although it now seems that the Arab League never intended that the appointment of a Palestinian representative should lead to the creation of a Palestinian entity, Nasser was soon won over to this idea, and eventually King Hussein of Jordan came around, after the whole plan was detailed for him. Hussein's concern was that the new entity might result in the detachment of the West Bank from the Hashimite kingdom or that it might aggravate the East Bank–West Bank rivalries within the country. But it was when Shuqeiri arrived in Damascus to seek Syrian support that he met serious resistance. Before the Syrians could approve such an entity, they demanded guarantees that it would not be a paper organization. Instead, they argued that Jordan and Egypt should give up the West Bank and Gaza and restore them to their people. Only these two steps would guarantee the founding of the nucleus of the new Palestinian entity, Syria felt. Furthermore, for this new structure to be effective, an army would be needed. Perhaps the Arab states could finance this army and could permit the creation of an elected government.[44]

Syrians, unlike the Jordanians, did not fear the new project and its implications for their own national security. They merely doubted its effectiveness. Syrians were calling for more, not less, Palestinian mobilization in order to assist in the ongoing battle against Israel. Nasser's ploy of offering only half measures as a response to Israel's rising aggression, particularly on the Syrian front, was fully transparent. After all, this was the same thing Syria had done during the Quwatli and 'Azm regimes, when diplomacy was substituted for action with regard to the Palestinians. Shuqeiri himself had once played the tame diplomatic role, and nothing in his past would indicate that Egypt's sudden sponsorship of the Palestine issue would transform him into an agent of action and confrontation.

The issue of Arab sponsorship created negative fallout in other quarters. Not all Palestinians, it seemed, welcomed Shuqeiri's project or his designation as the new representative of the Palestinians. Nasser, as well as the other Arab heads of state, preferred to ignore the presence of the old man of the Palestinian national movement, the mufti Haj Amin Husseini, then residing in Beirut. Although devoid of any authority, he was still regarded, at least by the Lebanese leadership, as the representative of the stateless Palestinian refugees in Lebanon's camps. Indeed, in order to move inside or outside of Lebanon, the refugees required the written permission of the mufti, which the Lebanese government readily honored.[45] But the memory of the Arab Higher Committee and the mufti's struggle against the Zionists, the British, and the Arab states could not be easily erased. As late as September 1963, according to some accounts, even Shuqeiri continued to defer to the mufti and seek his advice. But when Shuqeiri, in a moment of weakness, attacked the mufti in the pages of the Egyptian press, accusing him of grand treason, the mufti and his advisors struck back.[46]

The weakest element in Shuqeiri's new project was its dubious legitimacy as the sovereign creation of the Palestinian people, and the mufti's attack hammered on this issue. His spokespersons issued a statement emphasizing that he and the Arab Higher Committee were not opposed in principle to resuscitating the Palestinian structure since this had been their own goal since 1950. What they opposed was the weak and artificial framework created at the Jerusalem meeting. The mufti had not fled Palestine and abandoned the struggle, as Shuqeiri claimed. Rather, he had been driven out in 1937 and, fearing for his life, had lived first in Lebanon, then in Iraq, then Iran, always hoping to return. He did return briefly to Gaza in October 1948, in an attempt to head the Government of All Palestine, but was driven out by the government of Mahmoud Fahmi Nuqrashi Pasha. Shuqeiri must convince the public, the statement added, that his new entity was not indirectly aligned with Israel; Shuqeiri's new assignment, it suggested, might be part of a scheme to crush the old Palestinian leadership. Thus, Shuqeiri stood accused not only of destroying what remained of the legitimate Palestinian movement but also of extinguishing the Palestinian struggle.[47] The attack on Shuqeiri, nevertheless, did not allude to Egypt's role in creating a dependent Palestinian organization. Only Shuqeiri was singled out for the attack.

Shuqeiri's Project Is Challenged

Shuqeiri was opposed not only by the traditional Palestinian leadership but also by the rising radical underground. Perhaps one reason for that was competition for the same recruitment pool. Even though Shuqeiri's greatest appeal was to the Palestinian middle class and professional groups, he too sought legitimacy from residents of the refugee camps.[48] But the refugees of Lebanon, Syria, and Jordan, as well as the Palestinian revolutionary vanguard, were already organized within their own formations. No country showed greater tolerance for these revolutionary Palestinian organizations than Syria.

In the 1950s and 1960s, George Habash, the future leader of the Popular Front for the Liberation of Palestine (PFLP), was one of the pillars of the Arab Nationalist Movement (ANM). But despite its broad boundaries, the ANM was as dedicated to the task of liberating Palestine as it was to the principles of the Arab revolution. As Habash put it later on, "We began as a Palestinian formation with an Arab perspective."[49] The movement's links to Syria were also multiple. Although the base of operation of the ANM shifted to Jordan following the discovery and trial of members of Kata'ib al-Fida' al-'Arabi, the main slogan of the movement became "the road to Tel Aviv goes through 'Amman, Damascus, and Beirut."[50]

Jordan had the advantage of being the nearest area from which to launch attacks on Israel, but Syria was infinitely more hospitable. The main organ of the movement, *al-Ra'i,* was banned in Jordan and moved later to Damascus, where freedom of the press in the 1950s was more tolerated. In time the publication became widely read by students at the University of Damascus. Palestinian creative expression also thrived in Syria, and Palestinian novelist Ghassan Kanafani and journalist Bilal al-Hassan enjoyed the free atmosphere. 'Abd al-Hamid Sarraj, chief of Syrian intelligence and later Nasser's main deputy in the northern province of the UAR, allowed the ANM great latitude during the unity years. Because of the tolerant atmosphere in Syria, the movement was able to penetrate southern Lebanon. Student members of the ANM used their contacts at the University of Damascus in order to recruit Tunisian and Moroccan students. The refugee camps in Syria also provided fertile grounds for recruitment.

In Syria the ANM enjoyed cordial relations with the Ba'thists and Communists as one of the main bona fide nationalist parties. Even after the

Syrian-Egyptian split of 1961, the ANM remained pro-Nasser, and it was one of the few parties calling for the restoration of unity with Egypt. While both the Syrian Ba'thists and Communists abandoned Nasser after 1961, Habash and his group remained loyal. Indeed, the ANM debated whether to discuss publicly an alternate ideology to Nasserism, but opted to remain within the Nasserite camp. The separation period between Syria and Egypt turned out to be a short one, for on March 31, 1962, a rebellion led by Jasem 'Alwan and his Aleppo unit once again raised the banner of the United Arab Republic. Even unity with Iraq turned out to be a perennial theme as pro-Iraqi Syrians, buoyed by the revolution of 'Abd al-Karim Qasem, once again called for unity. Habash claimed that the ANM participated in the tripartite unity talks between Egypt, Syria, and Iraq through Hani al-Hindi, who joined the Syrian negotiating team.[51]

Habash was also encouraged by Nasser to pursue a strategy of armed struggle. Habash was convinced through several direct conversations with Nasser, after the Egyptian-Syrian separation, that the Egyptian leader believed that Palestine could be retrieved by force. But Habash admitted that he and Nasser differed on the timetable of a military confrontation with Israel. Nasser believed that it would be difficult to anticipate and control Israel's reaction. He felt that it was too early to attack Israel.[52]

Fateh, then a newly emerging guerrilla organization, was also unimpressed by Shuqeiri. Yasser Arafat found favor with the mufti when the latter began to discredit the new Shuqeiri framework.[53] Although active in Gaza as early as 1954, pre-Fateh formations did not emerge until 1965, when operations were launched inside Israel because of the river dispute, one at Deir Nakhas and one at Bisan. What pushed Fateh and other Palestinian revolutionaries to undertake the campaign of armed struggle on their own was their conviction that no Arab regime, not even Nasser's, intended to seek a military confrontation with Israel. Arafat, who did not meet Nasser personally until after the June 1967 War, was convinced of Nasser's reluctance to fight the Israelis. He often repeated a comment made by Nasser to a visiting delegation from Gaza, to the effect that he, Nasser, had no specific plan for Palestine and those who said they did were totally dishonest. Arafat used to emphasize that, among all the Arab states, it was Algeria that had extended the greatest support to the early Palestinian guerrillas. But he added that Syria in particular was very supportive of Fateh. The relationship with Syria became a strong one after March 8, 1963, which concluded the turbulent separation from Egypt. The special relationship was mostly with the Ba'th ruling party. Hafiz al-

Assad, apparently, often smuggled arms to Fateh without the knowledge of his military superiors. Syria, furthermore, was the only Arab state to tolerate attacks being launched from its own territory.[54]

But Egypt was the only country capable of orchestrating a Palestinian diplomatic initiative as well as a guerrilla movement targeting Israel. Syria, on the other hand, was well aware of the strength of anti-Nasserite forces at the time. With Amin al-Hafiz as president, the separatist Syrian regime was mistrustful of Shuqeiri because he derived his new mandate specifically from Nasser. Whether selected by the Arab League of States, which was in its most Nasserist-dominated phase, or delegated by Palestinian groups, Shuqeiri did not appear to be an independent Palestinian representative.[55] Thus it was not surprising to see Syria, along with Saudi Arabia, initially decline Shuqeiri's invitation to attend the Jerusalem conference that would launch the new Palestinian organization.[56]

Despite Syria's reservations about this particular Arab project, it did nothing to obstruct Shuqeiri's work. In a meeting attended by King Hussein of Jordan; the Secretary-General of the Arab League, 'Abd al-Khaleq Hassounah; the mayor of Jerusalem, Rouhi al-Khatib; and numerous representatives of the diaspora Palestinians, Shuqeiri was elected president and chair of the executive committee of the new entity called the Palestine Liberation Organization. The May 28, 1964, meeting also adopted a charter that was a testament to Shuqeiri's diplomatic skills. The charter or covenant, as it became known, was authored by Shuqeiri and edited by a special committee. The document expressed Shuqeiri's own efforts to allay the fears of the Jordanian monarch, as well as those of the powerful pan-Arabist and nationalist current sweeping the region at the time. After specifying that the new organization had a flag, a pledge of allegiance, and a national anthem, the charter proceeded to address other issues. Article 24 tackled the matter of Palestinian jurisdiction, stating clearly that the new entity would not exercise territorial sovereignty over the West Bank, Gaza, or the Himmeh area. The latter was the small Palestinian territory that the Syrians occupied as a result of the 1948 Palestine War, but the declaration was principally aimed at Jordan's large Palestinian holdings. The new entity, the charter read, would pursue activities on the national and populist levels and focus on liberationist, organizational, political, and financial endeavors.[57] Shuqeiri elaborated these points quickly in his opening speech at the conference by reminding his audience of the auspicious coincidental creation of the unity between Iraq and the United Arab Republic:

> Unity... is the dearest wish of the Palestinian people... and one of the meanings of this unity is that the creation of the Palestinian entity at Jerusalem does not aim at detaching the West Bank from Jordan, but [rather] the liberation of our beloved land west of the West Bank. We do not confront the Jordanian entity from near or afar since these lands have always been throughout history one homeland and one people. All the obstacles which colonialism created over thirty years are too weak to sever the relationship of the years and the generations. And we shall never forget that the Middle Ages witnessed the battle for Palestine not only from the walls of Acre and Jerusalem, but also the walls of Kerak [Jordan].... We call upon the entire Arab nation, governments and people alike, to consider Jordan the launching site of the liberation of Palestine.[58]

The charter also emphasized the Arab nature of the Palestinian struggle while making a careful distinction between Palestinian and Arab nationalism. The charter began with the words: "We the Palestinian Arab people," then proceeded to elaborate:

> Article 11: The Palestinian people believe in Arab unity, but in order to fulfill their role at this stage of the struggle, they must preserve the Palestinian character and its basic principles....
>
> Article 12: Arab unity and the liberation of Palestine are two complementary goals, any one of which leads to the realization of the other. Arab unity leads to the liberation of Palestine and the liberation of Palestine leads to Arab unity....
>
> Article 13: The destiny and even the existence of the Arab people are subject to the destiny of the Palestine question.... the Palestinian people are merely performing the role of the vanguard in order to achieve this sacred (unity) national goal.[59]

Shuqeiri also expressed in his inaugural speech sorrow over the limited powers of this new creation:

> As I speak of a Palestinian entity, I find myself before a frightening reality. We have used this expression "the Palestinian entity" for many years. It is a strange expression both in Arab and international circles. It is a new expression, unprecedented in the history of nations. All nations which struggled to realize their freedom do not know this expression. The history of the Arab national struggle did not know anything called the Syrian, Egyptian, Iraqi, or Algerian

entity.... But Palestine is a unique tragedy ... and it was inevitable but that its circumstances will be unique and unusual.[60]

Eventually, a Syrian delegation did attend the Jerusalem meeting, but without the presence of President Amin al-Hafiz. The Syrians included the foreign minister, Dr. Hassan Maryoud; Mansour al-Atrash, a member of the president's council; Zuheir Dalati, Syrian ambassador to Jordan; and Shaker Mustafa, head of the political department in the Foreign Office.[61] Among Shuqeiri's lasting achievements was to build the institutions of this new quasi-state. Some of his ideas included levying five *fils* (pennies) on each barrel of oil exported from the Arab countries. Other ideas were more realistic and became concrete institutions, albeit with some difficulty. These included the Palestine Liberation Army, the Palestine National Fund, a Palestinian broadcasting service, and the Palestine Research Center. The latter was easily established in Beirut and was intended to function as a think-tank. It was also hoped that the center would refute the charge of Egyptian dependency. The "voice of Palestine," however, was located in Egypt because the Egyptian government provided a block of six hours of airtime daily for its broadcasts. The most challenging task turned out to be funding for and the creation of a Palestinian army. The director of the Palestinian Fund, veteran Palestinian entrepreneur 'Abd al-Majid Shuman, used to complain that the Arab states were excessively slow in fulfilling their financial obligations. Originally, the second summit meeting of the Arab League at Alexandria approved the idea of collecting a "liberation tax" on all the Palestinians working in Arab countries. Jordan later reneged on this pledge and limited itself to a fixed donation or country assessment to the league. Saudi Arabia also objected to taxing its Palestinian employees. Kuwait was more lenient and pledged a Palestinian tax as well as a country donation.[62]

But clearly the most problematic question was the establishment of a Palestinian army. During the first Arab summit meeting, Shuqeiri had asked for the creation of regular and guerrilla forces. The idea of Palestinian guerrilla forces was particularly objectionable since the organization lacked both territory and sovereignty. Thus these forces would have to be deployed with their weapons on Arab soil. Eventually, Shuqeiri managed to get approval of the heads of state to create an army under the direction of the Unified Arab Command, which was created after the first Arab summit meeting of 1964. But this army would be part of the new Palestinian organization, and be staffed, armed, and trained by it. On the question of where the army would be based, however, the Arab governments had the final say. Thus, Shuqeiri did not get the independent Palestinian army he wanted. Arab concerns over "foreign" armies on their soil were raised by memories of the 1948 Palestine War. Eventually, with much fanfare, a Palestinian committee was chosen to create the army, which was slated to be stationed at Gaza, Syria, and Iraq. Financing for the army was to come from the Unified Arab Military Command. Shuqeiri had also suggested that a military draft be imposed on young Palestinians, but only Gaza's legislative council approved this idea. After Shuqeiri made a tour of the Arab countries, Iraq agreed to accept Palestinian troops on its soil, a force that Shuqeiri named al-Qadisiyah. Syria accepted the so-called Hittin forces, and Gaza named its armed units 'Ein Jalout. The names were those of famed Arab battles.[63]

Despite Shuqeiri's determination to maintain the goodwill of the Arab states, the Palestine Liberation Organization managed to rankle more than one capital. Shuqeiri's fondest wish was to see Palestinian troops stationed in the West Bank and Jordan. He also hoped that a military draft would be imposed on Palestinians wherever they were found. It would be unforgivable, he used to say, to deprive the major remnant of the Palestinian people, who were located in Jordan, of the honor of participating in the task of liberation. But the Jordanians, motivated by internal security considerations, resisted. Shuqeiri's increasingly revolutionary rhetoric finally provoked the king into placing the PLO's Jerusalem offices under siege and arresting some of its officers. This crisis dragged on until a final rupture occurred in July 1966.

The opportunity to advance this idea arrived in the form of Israel's military attack on a borderline and unarmed Palestinian village in the West Bank. The attack on Sumu' in November 1966 prompted Shuqeiri to contact King Hussein of Jordan and call for drafting the sons of the Palestinians, establishing training camps, and providing them with training in guerrilla warfare. The Palestine Liberation Organization, he wrote to Hussein, would be willing to transport units of the Palestine Liberation Army to Palestinian territory at its own expense. But the Jordanians denied his request. In his earlier writings, Shuqeiri had repeatedly expressed his wish to see units of the Palestinian Liberation Army stationed in the West Bank and particularly in Jerusalem. He had anticipated that in the next Arab-Israeli confrontation, the Israelis would attempt to seize Jerusalem, which would then be subjected to street combat. Only units of the Liberation Army, he felt, were capable of undertaking the defense of Jerusalem in that kind of warfare. Shuqeiri's wish to see the PLA become an active force was realized only once. On the eve of the June War in 1967, he succeeded in removing the headquarters of the PLA from Cairo to Gaza, and his units fought bravely, according to his later statements, on the Gazan, Syrian, and Egyptian fronts.[64]

Another major dispute developed with the Saudi government, which came to see Shuqeiri as an agent of Nasser and of world communism. Shuqeiri defended himself against this charge during the 1967 meeting of the Arab League Council, insisting that no state has the right to choose the leadership of the Palestinian people and that the latter strongly rejected the principle of sponsorship. He also refuted the Saudi charge that PLA forces had been sent to fight in Vietnam and not in Palestine. There was also a dispute with Tunisia as a result of President al-Habib Bourguiba's 1965 tour of the West Bank and Jordan and his call for peaceful co-existence with Israel. Bourguiba's call for normalizing relations with the enemy state in the name of realism forced Shuqeiri to hold a special press conference in which he attacked the Tunisian president and called for the removal of Tunisia from the Arab League and for it to be barred from future Arab summit meetings.

A serious rift had also developed with Egypt when Shuqeiri departed from Cairo with a Palestinian delegation to visit the People's Republic of China on March 15, 1965. Received like an important head of state, Shuqeiri moved from one Chinese city to the next. He asked for arms and military training for his troops, and his old acquaintance Zhou Enlai agreed to send a shipload of weapons to Alexandria. China also extended diplomatic recognition to the young organization and permitted it to open an office in Beijing. Nothing exposed the dependent and quasi-legitimate character of Shuqeiri's PLO, however, more than the rift that developed with Egypt following Shuqeiri's China visit. When he returned to Cairo, he held a press conference detailing the gains that he made in China. But none of this information made it to the pages of the Egyptian press. Shuqeiri realized that Nasser was offended since the trip threatened his relationship with the Soviets. Shuqeiri told his Palestinian associates of his readiness to resign in order to heal the rift with Nasser. But Nasser forgave and forgot and made an unexpected personal appearance at the May 1965 meeting of the Palestine National Council (or parliament) at Cairo University.[65]

Syrians did not attack Shuqeiri or his organization officially, but there were negative campaigns by the Syrian Broadcasting Service and print media, which accused him of a lack of revolutionary fervor. Damascus, the only government to tolerate and even encourage Palestinian attacks against Israel in the area of the river, was used to dealing with the rising militant Palestinian guerrilla organizations. But when Shuqeiri needed it, Damascus was not closed to him. As rumors of war circulated in May 1967, Shuqeiri moved to the Syrian capital, where he used to while away his hours reading official reports at the Foreign Office. It was also at Damascus where he met and debated with members of new groups such as Fateh, Heroes of the Return (Abtal al-'Awdah), and the Front for the Liberation of Palestine (Jabhat Tahrir Filastin). These Syrian-based guerrilla organizations, which contributed greatly to Israel's war of nerves against Syria, were not persuaded by Shuqeiri's strategy. He argued in favor of unifying all Palestinian groups under one umbrella and pointed to the dangers of their own operational strategy.[66] Shuqeiri hewed strongly to the position expressed by the Egyptian head of the Unified Arab Military Command, 'Ali 'Ali 'Amer, who disapproved of any confrontation with Israel in the absence of prior Arab coordination and planning. But the new guerrilla organizations argued in favor of creating the conditions for an Arab-Israeli confrontation. This line of thinking was also supported by many in Syria following its separation from Egypt. These same Syrians, including the Ba'th Party, disapproved of Nasser's willingness to station UN troops in the Sharm al-Sheikh and the Gulf of 'Aqaba region. Palestinian radicals often challenged Nasser to match their daring deeds. Shuqeiri's call for a gradualist approach and continued coordination and cooperation with official Arab circles was totally rejected by these groups. This discord continued until the eve of the June 1967 Arab-Israeli war.[67]

Finally, Shuqeiri's main base of support and the organization from which he derived his mandate—namely, the Arab League of States and its summit formula—suffered a great setback. Following the September 1965 Arab summit meeting held at Casablanca, a great fissure developed in the Arab world. Rumors of a new collective effort were circulating in Islamic and international circles. This effort, to be Islamic in nature, was the brainchild of King Faisal of Saudi Arabia, who had begun to float the idea of convening an Islamic conference devoted to a discussion of Muslim issues and questions. The Saudi monarch, who was involved in supporting the traditional Yemeni imamate against Egyptian troops in Southern Yemen, had more than one reason to create a rival structure to the Egyptian-dominated Arab League. Indeed, Nasser attacked this project publicly, declaring in his Suez speech on March 22, 1966, that he no longer believed in the value of unified Arab action if this was to be the result of summit meetings. Nasser also announced that Egypt would not attend any future summits. The Islamic Conference organization that emerged from

Faisal's initiative was Saudi-led and financed and became a rival to the Arab League.

Shuqeiri, in his usual diplomatic way, did not take part in this public and high-level dispute. But in a speech at Alexandria on July 28, 1966, he pledged to stay out of Arab squabbles as long as they did not infringe on the Palestine issue. We will side with all the kings and presidents who side with us, he said, but will not remain in the camp of those who did not support us and were not supported by the Arab nation. Shuqeiri then began to consider the feasibility of entering into bilateral relations with some Arab states. Thus, one year before the outbreak of the 1967 June War, the Palestine Liberation Organization, as well as the Palestine Liberation Army, faced an uncertain future.[68]

The denouement for the first phase of the PLO came at the Khartoum summit meeting of the Arab League, following the massive Arab defeat in June 1967. The meeting was held between August 19 and September 1, 1967. Often referred to as the meeting of the Four Nos (no peace, no coexistence, no negotiations, and no unilateral deals with Israel), the meeting also adopted the slogan of "removing the after-effects of the aggression."[69] The problem of Palestinian representation manifested itself before the meeting, when the Sudanese government deliberately dropped the PLO from its invitation list. Shuqeiri ignored the Sudanese snub and dispatched his aide, Shafiq al-Hout, to represent the PLO and pave the way for his own attendance. But even before the delegates arrived, the new theme that emerged was the enlistment of the oil weapon in the battle, a theme first sounded in Arab League meetings during the first Palestine War. A meeting of the Arab oil ministers was to take place at Baghdad on August 15 of that year, before the summit was to convene. But the PLO, a non-oil-producing entity, was left out of this meeting as well. Denied access to the Khartoum and Baghdad meetings, the PLO was horrified that the people most affected by the war were deliberately excluded. As al-Hout recorded in his recollections of that meeting, it turned out that Tunisia was principally responsible for seeking to keep the PLO out of the Khartoum meeting. Eventually, Shuqeiri did attend and so did a delegation representing Syria, led by the Foreign Minister Dr. Ibrahim Makhous. But it proved impossible to persuade the Syrian president, Nur al-Din al-Atassi, to attend.[70]

Among the many unusual developments during this historic meeting was the signing of a peace treaty by Nasser and King Faisal that put an end to the Yemeni civil war. It was also the first Arab summit to witness a direct clash between the PLO and the unchallenged representative of pan-Arabism. The Palestinians quickly grasped during that meeting the readiness of Arab leaders to make compromises as a result of the loss of what had remained of Arab Palestine. Al-Hout could not escape the observation that it was the loss of holy Jerusalem that finally motivated King Faisal to seek peace with the Egyptians. The loss of Palestinian territory drove home to Nasser the reason for U.S. hostility to the Arabs, namely, the Palestine question. More than ever, Nasser now began to view the task of defending Palestinian and Egyptian rights as one indivisible whole. That was clearly what he meant when he declared that he was not prepared to resolve the Palestine issue in exchange for the return of Sinai. But when King Hussein spoke, he emphasized the danger of encouraging Palestinian guerrilla attacks, as some Arab states had (that is, Syria), which had the potential of creating more dangers. But no one in the audience commented on this speech. The meeting did, however, consider whether Syria was eligible to receive Arab financial assistance despite the absence of its president from the meeting.[71]

When Shuqeiri spoke, he departed from his former diplomatic balancing of Arab and Palestinian interests. For the first time in his career, he emphasized the Palestinian nature of the Palestine question more than its Arab character. The Palestinian people should have the right to determine their own destiny, he averred. He was also enraged at the final outcome of the meeting, whose delegates voted against the resumption of the war, against severing all political and economic ties with countries that assisted in the Israeli aggression, against a total or partial oil embargo, and against withdrawing the Arab reserves from the Sterling and Dollar areas. Shuqeiri called for the strengthening and independence of the PLO and its forces.[72] He also sounded a note similar to the position of the guerrilla groups with whom he had quarreled in the recent past:

> We the people of Palestine are not members in the United Nations. No matter what our situation is, whether in Israel, in our occupied land, or in the Arab countries, this people of ours, this dismembered people, is one in its dreams and aspirations. Although most of these people are captives or refugees, this does not negate their natural right of self determination.... I have said that we are not represented at the UN, and we did not sign an armistice agreement, nor are we obligated to observe all Security Council resolutions. Therefore, all international considerations do not include us and we are not bound by them.[73]

Shuqeiri also expressed his feeling that the summit was proceeding toward an unprofitable conclusion unless certain conditions were met, including support for the Palestinians to undertake a campaign of popular resistance inside Palestine.[74] Shuqeiri and his delegation finally withdrew from the meeting after the delegates rejected two of the PLO's essential demands, specifically, a commitment to a policy of no peace or negotiations with Israel, and a rejection of any unilateral solution by an Arab state. Shuqeiri was relieved of his duties by the executive committee of his organization and was succeeded as chairman by Yahya Hamoudah. Although Shuqeiri subsequently retired from politics, his organization survived. His forced retirement, it seems, was also caused by rising discontent within his own organization over his leadership style. Any criticism from his own lieutenants he took to be personal in nature. He would often change his executive committee for no apparent reason. He also ignored the decisions of the Palestine National Council, the parliament in exile that was formed out of the nucleus of the first PLO conference at Jerusalem. He would fire anyone whose loyalty was not dependable. He even went so far as to stage a coup against his own executive committee in 1966 in order to effect change.[75]

Thus, the first Arab experiment in Palestinian co-optation came to an ignoble ending. The Palestinians, for their part, suffered the experience of Arab sponsorship unwillingly, recognizing all along that the diplomatic solution brokered by Nasser was simply a confirmation of their political powerlessness. No one knew the perils of Arab sponsorship and constraints better than the mufti of Jerusalem, which accounted for his skepticism and later his utter hostility to Shuqeiri's project. This hostility resonated with Palestinians everywhere. Having spent his entire national career seeking to establish the independent Palestinian will, the mufti was appalled by Egypt's sponsorship of the new Palestinian entity. His reflections on the Palestinian situation and his pessimism about its prospects were justified during the Khartoum summit conference. Feeling betrayed and abandoned, members of the Palestinian delegation at Khartoum lashed out at everybody, particularly the Syrian delegation, which was represented at a lower ministerial level than all the others. The Palestinians' anger was finally checked by the Syrian Foreign Minister, Dr. Ibrahim Makhous, who said, "Listen ... you Palestinians have only one choice before you, namely, to rule this entire nation first, and to liberate Palestine later. And if you do not undertake this, they [the Arab states] would pounce on you and liquidate your cause."[76]

This startling statement, which summed up the order of priorities of the extreme Palestinian guerrilla organizations like the Popular Front for the Liberation of Palestine, rang true even as early as 1967. It was certainly expressive of the general Syrian view that the Palestinians were allowing themselves to be pawns in Nasser's grand chess game of pan-Arab politics. But because of his post–Suez War prestige, Nasser could articulate the principles of pan-Arabism without being challenged by doubters and competitors. He was the only Arab leader whose pan-Arabist credentials were still largely unblemished and the one whose national prestige extended beyond his borders.

One way of understanding this turbulent period of Palestinian hope, frustration, and despair is to view the Palestine question against the background of Syrian-Egyptian tension. First, it should be reemphasized that what motivated large segments of the Syrian body politic to opt for unity with Egypt was the Syrian perception of the rising level of Zionist and imperialist intrigue in their region. Syria was vulnerable to these twin and interrelated threats from the time of its independence. Fear of Hashimite designs on the fragile republic and of Israel's desire to push the Syrian armistice boundaries eastward could be said to have produced one military coup after the other. It is also possible to trace the entire distorted civil-military relationship in Syria to the inherently destabilizing after-effects of the first Palestine War.

Conclusion

The creation of the Syrian-Egyptian union of 1958 cannot be attributed totally to ideological factors. Fears of Israeli, Iraqi, and Jordanian threats played a large role. So did the U.S. strategy of isolating radical Arab regimes through the formation of regional military pacts. But Syrian-Israeli clashes over the control of the demilitarized zone and the diversion of the Jordan River also pushed the Syrians to seek military alliances of their own. One of the ironies of the triangular Egyptian-Syrian-Palestinian relationship is that although each phase began with grand designs, it also ended in failure. First came the United Arab Republic, which was greeted with great enthusiasm by the radicalized Palestinian current, members of which were among the most ardent pan-Arabists on the scene. Then came the separation of the northern province from the Arab republic, a separation accelerated partially by Akram Hourani's disillusionment with Nasser's tepid reaction to Israeli water-diversion schemes.

This was followed by Nasser's plan to appoint a replacement to the vacant seat of the Government of All Palestine at the Arab League of States. What was clear from the start was Nasser's unexpressed desire to blunt the rising call to arms swirling around him in the Arab world. By giving the Palestinians a voice in the Arabs' foremost regional organization, he would mollify many of the dissidents and perhaps even deliver a threatening message to Israel. What is not clear is whether he anticipated the results of his own creation. The Palestine Liberation Organization turned out to be as much the handiwork of Palestinian leaders as it was the personal invention of Nasser himself. And no one recognized the potential strength of this Palestinian framework, as well as its inherent weaknesses, better than its first chairman, Ahmad Shuqeiri. But while he lamented the new framework's limited sovereignty and lack of military power and funding, he was hopeful that he might still have the opportunity to transform it into a nonterritorial state with a quasi-government of its own, including an army, a treasury, a broadcasting service, a research center, and even an anthem and a flag. What this entity lacked, however, was exclusive jurisdiction over its own citizens, who were dispersed all over the Arab world. Thus, even conscription of the sons of refugees remained an elusive goal due to the security concerns of most Arab regimes. A semi-independent Palestinian foreign policy turned out to be not only elusive but also hazardous, as evidenced by Shuqeiri's China contacts. Furthermore, the Palestine Liberation Organization's close identification with Nasserite Egypt proved to be not an asset but a liability in certain Arab quarters, such as in Saudi Arabia and Tunisia.

Having quarreled with most of the Arab regimes during his tenure as chairman of the new organization, Shuqeiri felt that he could always rely on the Arab League of States, from which he drew his mandate. But the Nasserite-dominated league was a forum and not a real battlefield. When the last of the great pan-Arab regimes was devastated by the 1967 Arab-Israeli War, the collapse of Nasserite Egypt was all too apparent. And in a fleeting moment of deep anger and despair, the chairman of the PLO, who lacked even the complete support of his own organization, felt he could dictate policy to the vanquished heads of Arab states. But what should be of interest to all those concerned with Shuqeiri's career is that he too was a child of Palestinian history. At Khartoum he began to push for the freeing of Palestinian units from control by the Arab regimes in order to launch a genuine guerrilla campaign inside the occupied West Bank. He even proclaimed the right to ignore UN resolutions because Palestinians enjoyed no status in the international system of states. All those familiar with the twists and turns of Palestinian history recognized his late call for a people's war. This was a call first uttered by 'Izz al-Din al-Qassam and later echoed by Fawzi al-Qawuqji. The prospect of a guerrilla campaign, free from the dictates of Arab states, was even frightening to the mufti, who was particularly apprehensive about the possible alignment of these troops with some untrustworthy Arab states. But as Palestinians alternated between Arab sponsorship and independent action, between a war of regular armies and guerrilla warfare, between diplomatic initiatives and military action, they also began to accumulate a definite historical experience. Perhaps the everlasting legacy of Shuqeiri was a broken trust in Arab regimes.

But the short-lived experiment with Palestinian self-representation and limited participation in the Arab system of states was not without any lasting legacy. The second phase of the PLO, which fell under the control of those committed exclusively to the principle of the armed struggle, inherited most of the institutions put together by Shuqeiri. Among the most significant of these were the Palestine Research Center and the Palestine National Fund. The armies of the first PLO, however, remained under the control of and aligned with the governments that allowed them residence on their soil. The Hittin forces located in Syria came to play a significant role in the later history of Syrian-Palestinian relations. Among the unrecognized legacies of Shuqeiri that found expression in some of Fateh's practices later on was the structural basis of the earlier PLO and an individual style of leadership that followed a thread present in the Palestinian nationalist movement since its inception.

During the same period, Syria's relationship with the Palestinians was, in many ways, as significant as that of Egypt. Unlike Jordan and Lebanon, where no Arab governments attempted to promote the forces of Palestinian nationalism, both Syria and Egypt promoted and often represented the Palestinians at one time or another. By 1967 Syria had participated through its own regular forces and volunteers in the 1936 revolt, in the 1948 Palestine War, and in the Jordan Valley battles of the 1950s and 1960s. The involvement of large volunteer units from Syria in the Arab Salvation Army during the first Palestine War parallels the participation of units of the Muslim Brotherhood from Egypt. Both states sponsored Palestinians diplomatically, Syria by affording Shuqeiri a significant platform at the Bandung Conference and Egypt by briefly backing the government of Palestine at Gaza. But Egypt was the first to initiate and encourage a pseudo-independent organization for the Palestinians, thereby nurturing the submerged Palestinian desire for international legitimacy and statehood. Egypt was also able to support, legitimize, and co-opt the radical Palestinian groups almost simultaneously with its sponsorship of Shuqeiri's PLO.

Syrians were not afforded similar opportunities largely because their policy toward the Palestinians was often dictated by a strict ideology as well as geopolitics. A sense of nationalist obligation and allegiance to the pan-Arabism of a previous era prompted Khaled al-ʿAzm to present Shuqeiri at Bandung. But it is clear the Syrian obligation to the Palestinians was not substantially different from their support for the Algerians and Tunisians in their own anticolonial struggles. It is also clear that the presence of Shuqeiri at al-ʿAzm's side bolstered Syria's position at Moscow, which Syria was beginning to regard as an international ally and a source of arms. Shuqeiri's previous record of diplomatic service with the Syrians assured them of his skills in negotiation and diplomacy, which differed markedly from the cantankerous relationship which the mufti maintained with President Quwatli and Premier Faris al-Khouri. But what should be kept in mind is that both Syria and Egypt chose to resurrect Palestinian claims when these posed no threat to their respective interests. But when Shuqeiri's impatience with the limits of diplomacy threatened Nasser's cautious military approach to Israel, Shuqeiri lost out.

Syrians were well aware of the manipulative aspect of the Egyptian-Palestinian relationship. Syria's dominant Baʿth ideology during the 1950s and 1960s was also compatible with Palestinian aspirations. Syria's support in the early 1960s thus went to Palestinian guerrilla groups and the Palestinian pan-Arabists, such as the Arab National Movement. Syria, however, did not obstruct the diplomatic campaign of Shuqeiri; it merely failed to embrace it. One reason for this was the state of internal turmoil that overtook Syria following the separation from Egypt and that lasted until 1970. But what was clear as the Arab world slid toward the military confrontation of June 1967 is that the aftermath of the splintering of the United Arab Republic and the Baʿth Party alike created a sense of competition with Egypt. In this competition, which was never totally replaced by cooperation, revolutionary Iraq played a role. But the emerging guerrilla organizations never gave up on Egypt completely, which continued to influence Palestinian activities in Gaza as well as in various parts of the Arab world. And as long as Egypt pursued a pan-Arab policy, its indispensability to various Palestinian groups became uncontestable. Egypt's involvement with various Palestinian groups in several parts of the Arab world also made the latter less dependent on Syria. Until the signing of the Camp David agreements and the resultant isolation of Egypt in the Arab world, Palestinians were able to avail themselves of the backing of more than one Arab regime.

4

The Guerrilla Factor and Syria's Vulnerability

Following the defeat of the June 1967 War, the national Ba'th Party convened its ninth emergency session, this one to deal specifically with the aftermath of the war. The conference adopted two significant resolutions, the first of which proclaimed that no state or party could take any steps leading to the liquidation of the Palestine question. The spirit of this resolution matched the position of the other confrontational Arab states, which were determined to overcome the devastating effects of Israel's victory. What is of greater interest here is that Palestinians received no mention as parties to this conflict. The other resolution of the ninth emergency session expressed one of the Ba'th's clearest statements on the need to wage a people's war. A popular war, however, could not be waged without the Palestinians. The resolution, additionally, reflected the general Arab disillusionment with the performance of regular armies. The latest Israeli aggression, stated the resolution, proved that the strategy of Israel and that of imperialism could only be met by a people's war.

General Mustafa Tlas, a member of the Ba'th's innermost military circle, elaborated on the disillusionment with Arab arms by claiming in his book *Al-Kifah al-musalah* (The armed struggle) that a strategy that would mobilize the Arab masses was the only means to overcome the enemy's superiority of arms. Since the United States, Britain, and West Germany were always ready to open their vast armament factories to the enemy, the Arabs' only recourse was a people's war. The adoption of this military strategy, he added, did not mean dispensing with regular armies, for each had a specific role to play.[1]

After citing several examples of successful guerrilla campaigns throughout history, the most recent being in Vietnam and Algeria, Tlas proceeded to elaborate on the proper conduct of such a war. Once the enemy occupied the homeland, the occupied people must develop a guerrilla campaign in order to establish a base of operations within the occupied zone. A regular army could then be brought together within the liberated territory in order to deliver a deadly blow to the enemy in cooperation with the guerrilla forces. These were the tactics followed by General Vo Nguyen Giap in Vietnam and by the FLN in Algeria. As far as the Arabs were concerned, the choice of this type of war was dictated by the fact that a regular war requires advanced heavy weapons and also that it would be difficult to get all the Arabs to agree to a total war of liberation since some maintained common interests with the forces of world imperialism.

Tlas continued by suggesting that it would not be far-fetched to see the superpowers impose Security Council Resolution 242 on all the contending parties, either by force or through the threat of force. This would be because of the international community's perception of an increased level of insecurity among the European states as a result of the Arab-Israeli conflict. Under these circumstances, a Palestinian people's war would become the only security shield for the Arab states. Like it or not, these states could not stand in the way of the guerrillas, who were striving to liberate their own land.

Tlas explained that the Ba'th had adopted this strategy after a lengthy study. In fact, more than 30 meetings of the Ba'th National Command before February 23, 1966, had been dominated by discussions of this strategy. The result was the adoption of a people's war as an essential strategy of the armed struggle inside occupied Palestine. When the 1967 War occurred, it merely confirmed the soundness of the Ba'th Party's thinking. Tlas then argued that the struggle in Palestine could be resolved only under two conditions. First, all the Arab countries surrounding occupied Palestine must unite in order to be able to deliver the first blow to Israel and avoid falling victim to a pre-emptive strike. Second, the Palestinians themselves must wage a war of attrition, which could succeed only if the surrounding Arab fronts provided military bases and material and moral support.[2]

In this seminal work, Tlas also reflected on the future of the Palestinian guerrilla movement, its weaknesses and deficiencies, and on the inevitability of linking the Palestinian armed struggle to the wider Arab revolution. The Palestinians turned to the ideas of self-help and a people's war following the failure of Arab summit meetings to confront Israel during the mid 1960s. The issue at hand during that period, he recalled, was Israel's attempted diversion of the Jordan River. This convinced the Palestinians of the futility of relying on Arab regimes and of the need for self-reliance. But, in truth, the Palestinian resistance movement could not be separated from the current Arab revolution. Any attempt to make this struggle an exclusive Palestinian struggle would only help deviant Arab states in limiting the Palestinians' freedom of action on their own national soil. One way of confirming the Arab nature of this struggle was to recall that other Arab lands were also occupied. This reality alone made the battle a totally Arab one, not unrelated to other Arab regimes in the area.³

Tlas, writing in 1971, had already seen dramatic confrontations between the Syrian regime of Hafiz al-Assad and the Palestinian guerrillas. He felt that the time was right to level serious criticism at the Palestinians on behavioral as well as ideological grounds. Some of the negative actions of the Palestinian resistance, he charged, included parading in guerrilla outfits on the streets of Amman and Beirut and forsaking the battle lines in the Jordan Valley for a life of glamour in various Arab capitals. He also emphasized that it was not proper revolutionary conduct to swagger with Kalishnikovs in public places, or to stop and search other Arab security officials and military officers just to insult them. Neither was it revolutionary to hijack non-Israeli airplanes and hold foreigners hostage. What was especially perplexing was the proliferation of guerrilla units, whose numbers were said to range anywhere from 50 (Arab estimates) to 70 (an Israeli estimate). On a more serious level, Tlas criticized the Palestinian resistance's new slogan. Complaining that it proposed the creation of a regional state called "Democratic Palestine," he suspected that this slogan represented an attempt to appeal to Western public opinion. What was needed, however, was the creation of "Arab Palestine." The battle should always be, he concluded, an all-out battle to liberate the entire Arab nation.⁴

Assad's Rise to Power

Mustafa Tlas, Syria's defense minister in 1997 and a long-time associate of Hafiz Assad, served in the mid-1950s in the Syrian Golan area as the head of the second armored division. He discussed his experiences in that area with Assad when the latter received his first military assignment as a second lieutenant in the air force stationed at al-Mazzah base at Damascus. The two ardent Ba'thists lived through the assassination of Ba'thist 'Adnan al-Malki and developed a great loathing for his assassins in the SSNP. The Ba'thists, though they predominated in the armed forces, did not resort to violence against members of this party and were satisfied with the decision to disband it. Young Ba'thist officers at the time were also incensed at various American schemes to contain Syria and sustain Israel. During Assad's and Tlas's early military careers, most Syrians were antagonistic toward the Johnston plan to devise a water-sharing scheme between Israel and its Arab neighbors, which most felt was favorable to Israel. Talk of unity proposals was also in the air as pro-Iraqi and pro-Egyptian elements swung in opposite directions.[5]

Ba'thist discussion of Palestine always accompanied references to Algeria. But Tlas's reflections on the Palestinian issue demonstrate an awareness of the immediacy of the Palestinian-Israeli conflict, which, to the Ba'thists, was an Arab-Israeli conflict. One of the resolutions to come out of attempts by Hourani's wing of the Ba'th Party to reconstitute itself and reclaim its independence following the union with Egypt called for the creation of an independent and unified Arab state, as well as support for the liberation of Palestine and Algeria. This resolution was adopted by the 'Aflaq-led Ba'th conference at Beirut in September 1959, which condemned the merger of the Syrian Ba'th faction with the only legalized political party in the Northern Province, namely the Socialist Union.

This major split in the ranks of the Ba'th prompted a group of high-ranking Syrian officers stationed at Cairo to organize a secret group, known as the Ba'th Military Committee, to facilitate a quick and unified response to the deteriorating situation in Syria even before 'Aflaq resurrected his Ba'th. Among this group of five were Hafiz al-Assad, Mustafa Tlas, and Salah Jadid. But among the 600 Syrian officers stationed in Egypt at the time, only 60 were considered Ba'thist. Around the same time, Palestinian university students at Cairo organized the General Union of Palestinian Students under Arafat's leadership. Also in 1959 Fateh came to life as an underground group in Kuwait.

Syrians within the Ba'th Party were puzzled and confused by the reaction of the Palestinians to the union, particularly that of the mufti, who a year before unity had asked that Palestine be included within the new Syrian-Egyptian framework. When the separation of the two provinces took place on September 29, 1961, the reaction of the group of five was mixed. Although they were critical of some of Egypt's policies in Syria in the past, they were at the same time opposed to a total and final separation of the two provinces. The group were further alarmed by news of Salah al-Bitar's and Akram Hourani's public endorsement of the act of separation. These independent-minded Ba'thists, as expected, worried the Egyptians. Soon, the Ba'thist officers requested permission to return to Syria in order to repair the Egyptian-Syrian rift but were turned down because of suspicion of their collaboration with Hourani. Most of the Ba'thist officers were eventually imprisoned, including Assad, who served a period of 44 days in the Abu Za'bal jail. Tlas escaped his comrades' fate and departed by sea, after being authorized to negotiate on their behalf with the new powers in Syria. Assad was finally released as part of an exchange agreement between the Syrians and Egyptians.[6] The break-up of the Syrian-Egyptian union thus triggered a decade-long struggle between army factions and diverse ideologies.

The new government in Syria was suspicious of the returned officers and considered them loyal to the Egyptian regime. Most were relieved of their military command, and Assad was given a civilian appointment in the department of naval transport within the Ministry of Economics. Tlas was assigned the position of inspector in the Ministry of Food Supplies. Syria's fluid situation permitted the adoption of another constitution on November 15, 1961. In the following year, Nathem al-Qudsi was elected to the presidency and the moderate Ma'rouf al-Dawalibi was chosen as Prime Minister. Al-Qudsi's constitutional mandate was for five years, and he proceeded to gravitate toward the other pan-Arabist pole, namely, Iraq.

This time it was 'Abd al-Karim Qasem's leftist regime and not the Hashimite monarchy that rejected the plan. Moderate Syrians and most of the anti-Qasem Iraqi Ba'thists opposed the union. Syrian military Ba'thists and Nasserite elements staged another coup on March 28, 1962. Both Tlas and Assad participated in this coup attempt but were compelled by the rules of the military hierarchy to stay in the background. Instead, their military superiors, Brig. Gen. Lu'ay al-Atassi, Col. Jasem 'Alwan, and Lt. Col. Muhammad 'Umran, led the coup attempt. The uprising failed for a number of reasons, including the fact that the party was already badly splintered with Hourani still a member of the sitting cabinet.

The declared intention of the Nasserite conspirators in this group was to restore the unity of Egypt and Syria, while most Ba'thist elements at the time preferred to undertake this experiment after a transitional period of some kind. The Syrian public was still alienated from Egypt due to the bitter union experiment. Assad left Syria ahead of the new government and spent some time in Tripoli before being returned to Syria for another brief jail term at al-Mazzah, along with his Cairo associates, Tlas and Jadid. After his release, Assad plunged into the task of rebuilding the party, a task made easier by his new civilian status.

The Ba'th was still badly divided between the old guard who supported the separation from Egypt and the younger members—like Assad, Tlas, Jadid, and two civilians, 'Abd al-Halim Khaddam and 'Abd Allah al-Ahmar—who were still pushing for some form of union with Egypt. But deeper divisions within the party persisted, with some factions still adamantly opposed to unification with Egypt and others calling for immediate unity. An army clique was dedicated to the principle of unity but anxious to maintain a dialogue with all the other groups. These factions came together in May 1962 at the fifth meeting of the regional congress of the Ba'th Party at the city of Homs. A new provisional regional leadership of the party was elected and was charged with the task of rebuilding the party. The main organ of the party, *al-Ba'th,* reappeared, and Akram Hourani, Egypt's determined foe, was removed along with his followers. The general state of affairs in the country, however, remained unstable and unpredictable.[7]

Assad's climb to power could be said to have started in earnest following the coup of March 8, 1963. That was the day when the civilians previously stripped of their military command, such as Assad, Jadid, and 'Abd al-Karim al-Jundi, resumed their military ranks and, along with some rebellious units at Damascus, staged a coup. Fears arose when the leader of the Syrian-Israeli front, Maj. Gen. Ziad al-Hariri, and his troops arrived at the capital. The confrontation, however, never turned bloody as Hariri was won over at the last minute. The coup succeeded and Assad was named as head of the Seventh Air Force Division at al-Dhameer base. He also held the important position of member of the Revolutionary Command Council.

As a result of this successful coup, Lu'ay al-Atassi headed the Revolutionary Command Council and the old Ba'thist, Salah al-Din al-Bitar, headed the government. Conspiracies continued to be hatched, some inspired by personal ambition and some by genuine ideological differences. Soon Lieutenant General Hariri was removed from the military since he was considered unfriendly to the Ba'thists, and he became a roving ambassador. By July 18, Lu'ay al-Atassi himself led a coup in favor of immediate unification with Egypt. Demonstrations continued throughout the major Syrian cities, and the split between the old guard of the Ba'th and the insurgents intensified. In the midst of this turmoil, the Israelis attacked Syrian positions near Lake Huleh, but the internal struggle for power continued.

A new military figure, Maj. Gen. Amin al-Hafiz, was making his impression on Syria in 1963. His climb to power began as head of the Ministry of the Interior, then as deputy prime minister, then chief of staff, and finally president and head of the Revolutionary Command Council. Al-Hafiz was a newcomer to the Ba'th Party, having joined in 1963. His rival for power turned out to be Maj. Gen. Salah Jadid, who headed the artillery section of the military. Both Jadid and al-Hafiz were also members of the Military Committee and the regional leadership of the party. In the meantime, demonstrations swept the country in reaction to the latest unpopular nationalization measures, which for the first time extended to the banks. Assad's star was also rising, for he had combined, along with his membership in the Revolutionary Command Council, membership in the regional and national leadership of the Ba'th Party. By 1964 he had become a major general in the Air Force, and he began to share with many of his contemporaries a sense of despondency over Israel's increasingly bold attempts to divert the Jordan River.[8]

The party framework itself continued to be a contested arena. By 1965 al-Hafiz was elected as secretary-general. By then, the party was clearly split between the old guard, now headed by al-Hafiz, and the new guard represented by Jadid and Assad. Both the civilian and military establishments were also badly divided, primarily over the issues of a timetable for reunification with Egypt but also over the social revolution at home. The military had almost completed their infiltration of the party, which subjected them to its changing ideological winds. Significantly, the eighth conference of the national command of the party, in April 1965, had finally changed its rules to permit the military to be represented in both the regional and national commands of the party. The same conference removed Michel 'Aflaq from his position as secretary-general of the national command and replaced him with Jordanian regional party leader Munif al-Razaz. For the first time in the history of this coup-saturated country, any leader aspiring to rise to the top position in the state had to control the army, the party, and the civilian apparatus. In this new climate, Amin al-Hafiz found his own situation to be untenable since he lacked a wide base of support in the military.[9]

Assad, in contrast, had broad support in the armed forces. He was also beginning to attract attention because his commitment to the ideals of pan-Arabism was combined with a talent for pragmatic solutions. In discussions with his inner circle over how to handle public displeasure with the radical socialist measures introduced by the government, Assad would always express his willingness to revise some of these edicts. He would say that even in the Quran, later chapters superseded earlier chapters. He also recommended flexibility in foreign policy and convinced the regional party command to select a committee of five and charge them with taking the necessary steps to isolate the right wing of the party, even if this meant armed conflict. This committee consisted of Tlas, Jadid, Assad, 'Abd al-Karim al-Jundi, and Saleem Hatoum.

By February 23, 1966, the group of five succeeded in leading yet another coup during which al-Hafiz and his associates were imprisoned. Michel 'Aflaq, the symbol of the party, was permitted to depart for exile with his dignity intact. Salah al-Bitar, the old Ba'thist, was placed under house arrest and the so-called rightist wing of the Ba'th was no longer operative in Syria. This time, the committee of five entrusted Nur al-Din al-Atassi with the presidency and Yousef Za'een with the premiership. Assad was named Minister of Defense, on top of his old duties as head of the Air Force and a member of the Revolutionary Command Council. When the party held its annual conference that year, it elected Nur al-Din al-Atassi as secretary-general of the regional command of the party and Jadid as his assistant. This repeated the old configuration of al-Hafiz serving the dual position of president and secretary-general of the party, a natural corollary to the militarization of the party and the expansion of military influence over all areas of government. Assad emerged as one of the main arbiters of power in the country.[10]

Some civilians also became part of the innermost circle of the party. The rise of 'Abd al-Halim Khaddam, a lawyer who began as the party representative at the Banias area, and 'Abdullah al-Ahmar, a schoolteacher, date back to this period. Khaddam became the governor of Hama in 1964, then of Quneitra in 1965, and then of Damascus. He was to serve as Foreign Minister and later as vice president under Assad's presidency. Al-Ahmar eventually became the secretary-general of the party. But the party continued to experience significant turmoil. The newly elected regional leadership disbanded the national leadership elected in May 1965, claiming that it lacked legitimacy. After this leadership departed the country, it transformed itself into a new national command under Iraqi sponsorship. Another coup attempt was made by Saleem Hatoum, head of the parachutist command, who later fled to Amman. This took place in September 1966, barely a year before the devastating 1967 June War.[11]

Fissures in the Palestinian Front

Relations between Syrians and the Palestinian refugees have always been cordial, but they were to take a completely different turn when the refugees became guerrilla fighters. Although classified as noncitizens, Palestinians enjoyed the right to serve in Syria's government and in the regular armed forces, and to pursue a free university education. Arafat came to Syria in the 1960s and was attracted by opportunities for staging guerrilla attacks from within Syrian territory. Arafat's was not the first Palestinian faction to appear on the Syrian scene. Others who preceded him operated either as heads of independent and shadowy organizations or as part of the Syrian armed forces. Arafat's early contact with the Syrians, particularly with Assad when he was in charge of the Ministry of Defense, contributed greatly to their later confrontations. Syria's roles in the Jordanian civil war and in Lebanon, both largely determined by Assad, were also conditioned by these early contacts.

Several Palestinian groups, some military and some guerrilla fighters, were active on the Syrian scene by 1964. First there were the fighters of the Hittin units of the Palestine Liberation Army, Shuqeiri's creation, who were amalgamated with the Syrian army. A group known as the Palestinian Liberation Front differed from the PLA in that it espoused a strategy of guerrilla warfare. The PLF was also closely aligned with Syria's Ba'thist regime and was headed by Ahmad Jibril and Yousef al-'Arabi. Both men came through the ranks of the regular Syrian army and were graduates of Syrian military institutes. 'Arabi had attained the rank of captain, and he and Jibril were totally committed to the ideals of pan-Arabism as a solution to the Palestine question. The Ba'th Party's promotion of the strategy of a people's war, both for the Algerian and Palestinian wars of liberation, encouraged Arafat to try to deploy the military units of Fateh, al-'Assifa, along the turbulent Israeli-Syrian border.

Arafat's recruiting grounds were in the Gulf countries, and he was moderately successful in gaining young fighters. Thus the prospect of gaining access to the Palestinian population of a hundred thousand around Damascus seemed particularly attractive. The Syrian guerrillas had ample human resources as well as friendly Syrian military contacts. Upon his 1965 arrival at Damascus, Arafat worked briefly with the PLF but found them to be too competitive. Arafat could only entice new recruits away from Jibril's and 'Arabi's units with the promise of funding and fake Algerian passports. The latter were a great luxury to the stateless refugees, facilitating travel and employment opportunities in other countries. Syrian officials, however, could always be counted upon to provide safe passage and storage facilities for weapons destined for Fateh. Arafat's first shipment of arms from China was made possible through the timely intervention of the head of the Syrian air force, Hafiz al-Assad.[12]

But Syria was not an open territory. Arafat, who was unwilling to submit to the checks and controls of the Syrian intelligence services, soon paid a heavy price for his intransigence and his repeated clashes with other guerrilla groups. Palestinian aggression along the Syrian-Israeli border was also often checked for fear of grave Syrian-Israeli military embroilment. When Fateh and the PLF realized the extent of Syria's limits on their military operations, they smuggled most of their fighting units into Jordan, southern Lebanon, and the Egyptian-held Gaza Strip. The Syrian government was willing to tolerate their presence at the Syrian capital but was not willing to surrender the primary initiative in military matters. But the Syrians did provide weapons, access to storage facilities, and military training to the two dominant Palestinian groups. Fateh's fighters and those of the PLF were apparently permitted to cross into Jordan through the Syrian Golan area. The Syrians hoped that this would facilitate attacks from someone else's territory.

The Syrians offered military help, escorting the Palestinian fighters to the front, but also maintained the right to control the extent of the guerrillas' operations. Occasionally, the Syrians permitted direct Palestinian attacks from their territory as long as the Syrians were in charge. A 1966 raid against Israeli positions in the Houleh area, for example, was led by Yousef al-'Arabi as a member of the Syrian armed forces. In the meantime Arafat was in the habit of claiming credit for some of 'Arabi's operations since this type of activity encouraged financial donations from the Gulf countries. In time Arafat took the bold step of using the Golan as an infiltration point without clearance from the Syrians. All of this activity took place around the time of Assad's appointment to the Ministry of Defense, which made these unplanned clashes his direct responsibility. Arafat's use of several assumed identities, his arrest record in Egypt (where he was suspected of belonging to the Muslim Brotherhood), and his smuggling activities in Syria greatly alarmed Assad. Thus, when Yousef al-'Arabi was found murdered on May 5, 1966, all fingers pointed to Arafat. But the circumstances of 'Arabi's death were unclear. Some claimed that he was assassinated by two of Arafat's operatives, while others claimed 'Arabi was killed in an operation by the Israelis after Arafat betrayed him.[13]

Arafat said in later interviews that 'Arabi intended to kill him first. 'Arabi, according to this account, had been planted inside 'Assifa in order to oust Arafat as head and replace him with Ahmad Jibril with 'Arabi next in command. As evidence, pro-Fateh elements offered printed statements distributed by Jibril accusing Arafat of being in the pay of the Saudis and announcing Jibril's own impending leadership of the soon-to-be-united guerrilla forces. The Israelis attributed the murder to the rivalry of Arafat and 'Arabi for the leadership of al-'Assifa. Whatever the reason, Assad had entertained enough suspicions about Arafat and threw him in al-Mazzah jail for a period of 55 days. This was Arafat's last experience in Syria, from which he was released on the promise never to return. While he was in al-Mazzah, along with other Fateh leaders, Um Jihad, Khalil al-Wazir's wife, held the assets of Fateh and al-'Assifa under her control.

According to her account, Fateh was not devoid of influential Syrian friends, such as Ahmed Sweidani, head of military intelligence, who continued to assist Fateh secretly even after this mysterious incident. Al-'Assifa's raids on Israel from within Syria continued, and some accounts claimed that they numbered 200 from 1965 until 1967.[14]

On the eve of the 1967 June War, Syria's troubled relations with the Palestinian guerrilla units and the continuing struggle between various Ba'th factions both persisted. The newest tension to grip the higher ranks of the newly purged party was that between the old comrades Jadid and Assad. Jadid was becoming more freewheeling and leftist, often pushing the government in the direction of serious confrontations with the public. His uncooperative style dismayed many people, particularly when he, along with Ibrahim Makhous and 'Abd al-Karim al-Jundi, painted a desperate picture of the Israeli threat along the Syrian border to Nasser of Egypt. Assad differed with them completely on this issue, claiming that Syria's lack of military preparedness prevented them from going to war. The three also exaggerated Syria's vulnerability to a massive Israeli attack before Soviet leaders, who pushed Nasser in the direction of a military solution. Assad's quarrel with these three, who felt that any confrontation with Israel was winnable once Egypt activated its defense pact with Syria, was based on his assessment of the Syrian military. As Minister of Defense, he knew the limited capabilities of the military and chafed at the idea that military personnel had to submit to the politicians and bear the burden of war.[15]

As a trained pilot, he had witnessed the increased level of Israeli-Syrian aerial combat in the Golan by early April 1967. Assad revealed in later interviews that he also had no confidence in the ability of the confrontation states to coordinate their military plans. Syria and Egypt were unable to overcome their mistrust of each other until November 1966, when they finally signed a defense pact. The Soviets claimed that Israel has massed fifteen divisions on the Syrian front alone. The Soviets advised caution but did not extend much military assistance, and the bulk of their military aid continued to flow into Egypt, not Syria. Meanwhile, Nasser's public speeches, along with Shuqeiri's fiery oratory about the imminent task of liberating Palestine, heightened the Arabs' warlike mood. Israel began to experience anxieties of its own, particularly after Jordan, with whom it shared the longest border, reached an accommodation with Egypt. The joint Arab command was made more effective by the dispatching of Iraqi units to the Jordanian front. To make matters worse for Assad, reports of the state of Egypt's armed forces provided by Syria's representative to the

Unified Arab Command, Maj. Gen. Yousef Shakour, were less than encouraging. At the same time, events in Israel itself became alarming. By early June of that fateful year, the hawkish Moshe Dayan had been given the defense portfolio.[16]

Assad's inability to reverse the tide of war increased his determination to change the situation at home. And when the war ended, he, along with the rest of the Syrian government establishment, first had to cope with its devastating effects. Because Syria was the last Arab state to accept a cease-fire, it was forced to bear the full brunt of the Israeli armed forces, which focused on capturing the Golan Heights. And to add to the deteriorating morale of Syrian troops, Nasser announced his resignation while they were still engaged in combat on the Syrian front. Syrian losses in this war were massive. Quneitra, the main city of the Golan region with a population of 30,000, had to be evacuated. Several villages were also destroyed, resulting in the evacuation of more than 90 percent of their original population. Only 14,000 people of the original Druze population, estimated at 150,000, remained in their original location. The gravity of the situation was compounded when the Israelis proceeded to settle the fertile Golan area with their own farmers, giving every impression that its loss was irreversible. Israeli takeover of the heights had significant ramifications for the future defense of Damascus itself, which now lay within the range of Israeli gun positions. The anger of one segment of the Syrian leadership was directed at Salah Jadid, who was blamed for dragging Syria into war.[17] In later years, Mustafa Tlas, who became chief of staff of the Syrian armed forces, was to remark, "What dragged Syria into a war for which it was ill-prepared was Saleh Jadid's policy of indulging in verbal violence and challenges to Egypt concerning the Palestinian issue."[18]

The war on the Golan Heights did not end with the cease-fire agreement of 1967. A war of attrition developed on the Syrian front, just as the same kind of war raged along the Suez Canal until the outbreak of the October 1973 War. Aerial engagements with the Israeli Air Force continued all along the new Israeli-Syrian lines and were particularly intense in 1970. Following the cease-fire, Assad began a feverish campaign to strengthen Syria's military capabilities. For instance, Syria had only one military academy prior to 1967, the Homs academy. After the war several academies were established and a modernized military curriculum was put in place. Special services and schools were provided for children of those who lost their lives in combat. The most important step to improve the level of military preparedness came after Assad became president in 1970. One of his first diplomatic forays concluded an arms deal assuring his country of more weapons than it had received since the first Soviet arms agreement in 1955. Syria was given easy terms with payments beginning after ten years and extending over a 20-year period, and an interest rate of just 3 percent.[19]

Following the June War, Syria also undertook significant moves on the Arab front that were not all due to Assad's influence. Nur al-Din al-Atassi's government refused to attend the Arab summit meeting at Khartoum, claiming that the participating regimes were politically regressive. When Dr. Makhous, the Foreign Minister, was finally dispatched to Khartoum, his instructions were that he limit his contacts to progressive heads of state like Nasser and Boumédienne of Algeria. One of Assad's main objections to the Atassi-Jadid Arab line was that it severely limited Syria's ability to influence others and imposed on it a state of isolation that would only benefit Israel. Assad did not fully approve what was happening and feared the consequences of severing relations with the United States, Britain, and West Germany, as well as of rejecting Security Council Resolution 242.

A new Marxism was overtaking the Ba'th. This movement, born out of the 1967 military defeat, began to call for intensifying the Palestinian armed struggle and for permitting Palestinians greater freedom in mounting attacks from Syrian territory. This leftist alignment with the goals of the Palestinian revolution was advanced by 'Abd al-Karim al-Jundi, then the Minister of Agricultural Reform and head of intelligence services. Syria's heightened radicalism also led the government to compromise its own economic well-being. Iraq Petroleum Company and ARAMCO oil pipelines across Syria were sabotaged and their stations were closed.[20] Syria's refusal to participate in the debate at the Khartoum summit removed its eligibility to receive Arab financial assistance. Only Egypt and Jordan received aid from the Arab Gulf countries to rebuild their ravaged armies and economies.[21] As a stream of Syrian war refugees, numbering in the vicinity of a hundred thousand, descended on Damascus, Syrians, and particularly Assad, began to realize that they had become, more than at any other time in the past, "captives of the Palestine question."[22]

The sizeable Palestinian refugee community in Syria in the 1960s, estimated between three and four hundred thousand, finally offered the Minister of Defense a solution to the independent activities of the militant Palestinians. Following the war, the Assad group in the higher echelon of the Ba'th and the government began to emphasize that Syria has waged all of its wars since independence as a result of the Palestinian issue. Furthermore, the Palestine question was evolving into the main focus of Syrian-

Arab relations.²³ Assad and Tlas responded to these new realities by making the armed forces as loyal to them as possible. Assad, in his capacity as Minister of Defense, began transferring officers of dubious loyalty away from the sensitive areas of military command. When Jadid awoke to these developments, his base of support within the military had been demolished. He then asked for an investigation by the party leadership, but found no support in these quarters. The Ba'th Party, with Assad's concurrence, then undertook the crucial step of creating a Syrian-controlled Palestinian fighting force. By early 1968 the Sa'iqa was organized.²⁴ Created through a special draft for the Palestinians in Syria, this army was treated like any other segment of the Syrian armed forces in terms of equipment and supplies.²⁵ Control of the 5,000-man army, however, became a source of contention between Jadid and Assad. On the eve of the Jordanian civil war in 1970, Sa'iqa was almost totally disbanded and confined to the refugee camps.²⁶ Syria thus controlled not only the old Palestine Liberation Army of the Shuqeiri PLO but also the new Sa'iqa.

By 1969 divisions within the Palestinian militia groups continued to multiply, some to Syria's advantage. On December 11, 1967, for instance, the Arab Nationalist Movement created the Popular Front for the Liberation of Palestine (PFLP), a direct result of the Arab defeat in the June War. The new organization included the Palestinian-Jordanian and the Syrian-Lebanese branches of the ANM. The PFLP was joined by two militia groups, Ahmad Jibril's Palestine Liberation Front and the Organization of Arab Palestine led by Ahmad Za'rour, an officer in the Jordanian army. On October 10, 1968, it was announced that a major division had occurred in this radical organization. Both the Organization of Arab Palestine and the Palestine Liberation Front split off, the latter forming the Palestine Liberation Front General Command under Jibril's leadership. The Popular Democratic Front for the Liberation of Palestine (PDFLP) also split off on February 22, 1969, thus forever weakening George Habash's original organization, which represented the major leftist configuration among the Palestinian militia groups. The PDFLP began a series of dialogues with other smaller leftist groups and succeeded in attracting them to its program.

Significantly, the splits and regroupings that developed following the war also prompted former Ba'thist members to return to the Syrian Ba'th. By the time of the convening of the fifth Palestine National Council meeting in 1969, the PDFLP was part of it as well as a member of its new PLO. The Sa'iqa already belonged to the PLO and became, along with Nayef Hawatmah's group (the PDFLP) and a number of independents, a member of the PLO's executive committee. The PFLP remained outside the PLO, proclaiming its rejection of the latter's regressive policies until Habash's group rejoined and became represented within the executive committee in 1971. From that point on, the international media began to refer to Arafat's Fateh, Habash's PFLP, and Hawatmah's PDFLP as the main bodies under the PLO's institutional umbrella. Ideological splits over the adoption of an Arab or Palestinian agenda and over how much violence should be employed against Arab regimes provided a convenient opening from which to infiltrate and influence the PLO. Syrian intelligence also continued to pursue the leftist wing of the militias, as when 'Abd al-Karim al-Jundi, head of the intelligence services in Syria, imprisoned Habash and others on charges of involvement in the assassination of one of their own men.[27]

The PLO Cuts the Apron Strings

The other fundamental change after the 1967 war was the transformation of the PLO from an Arab League organization into a totally independent guerrilla national front. Discussions between Fateh, the largest of the independent Palestinian groups dedicated to the principle of the armed struggle, and other Palestinian groups with the same orientation began with the removal of Ahmad Shuqeiri from office. The question before them was whether to form a national front within the framework of the old PLO or to start a new framework. A meeting of the old Palestine National Council (PNC), a key organ of Shuqeiri's PLO, was convened at Cairo in July 1968 under the chairmanship of 'Abd al-Muhsin al-Qattan, a well-known Palestinian philanthropist. During this meeting, the fourth since the emergence of the PNC, the Palestine national covenant and by-laws were amended. A new executive committee was also selected. These changes persuaded Fateh and other guerrilla groups to join the new revolutionized PLO, and Yasser Arafat, the spokesman of Fateh, was elected chairman of the executive committee. In February 1969 Arafat was chosen as chairman of the PLO, and Fateh became dominant over all of the PLO's constituent parts. Palestinians everywhere recognized that a great event had taken place, an event that finally joined ordinary Palestinian institutions such as women's, workers,' and students' groups to the guerrilla organizations that had been active as early as 1964. Fateh, by virtue of its size, dominated all the other groups but, whether intentionally or not, failed to unify them and bring them under its command. The PLO was destined to remain a loose collection of various ideologies that joined and withdrew from the PLO at will. The PLO and its guerrilla components never became an integrated organization.²⁸

The divisions among the various Palestinian groups continued and were largely centered around personalities, sponsorship by various Arab regimes, organizational issues, and the strategy of the new revolution. The latter question concerned the agenda of the revolutionary groups and whether to pursue the liberation of Palestine ahead of revolutionizing Arab regimes. Fateh, which had always stood for the Palestine war of liberation first and for complete independence from the Arab governments, began to move in Nasser's orbit. Closeness to the foremost pan-Arab regime of the time was dictated by the PLO's need for a secure source of weapons. This turned out to be the Soviet Union, with which Nasser enjoyed the closest relationship. Nasser was the first to introduce Arafat to the Soviets on his trip to Moscow in July 1968.²⁹

By that time Nasser had been considered a sponsor of Habash and the ANM for quite a while. But Nasser's closeness to Habash was because of the latter's strong identification with the ideals of Nasserism and not because of his Palestinian ideology. For instance, in 1964 Habash fled Syria after the failed pro-Nasserite coup attempt of Jasem 'Alwan. The Ba'th wing of the government had assumed that he was one of the prime movers behind the coup.³⁰ Arafat, on the other hand, was historically opposed to any official Arab sponsorship. He said to an interviewer once that he did not approve of the entry of Arab armies into Palestine in 1948, but that had been when he was a junior operative and his opinion carried little weight. But to be a leader of a major guerrilla organization required weapons and international contacts, and these could only come via an Arab sponsor. So Khalil al-Wazir, Abu Jihad, and Arafat visited China in 1964 and met Zhou Enlai. The Chinese contact was facilitated by Algeria, which was the first Arab state to assist Fateh. Fateh always praised the Algerian connection, largely because Algeria, geographically distant from Israel, had no basic strategic conflict with the Palestinians. Egypt offered similar possibilities, but Nasser was initially suspicious of members of Fateh, who were described to him by his intelligence sources as members of the Muslim Brotherhood. Egyptian intelligence had actually pursued Arafat even while he was a volunteer with 'Ali 'Ali 'Amer's troops on the eastern front during the June 1967 War. Relations with Egypt began in earnest after the war, when Nasser could no longer ignore the new emerging leader of the PLO.³¹

The Egyptians, for their part, began to see a natural ally in the Palestinian revolution since the latter posed no security or political risk to Egypt.

This was particularly the case after the loss of Egyptian-controlled Gaza to the Israelis following the June War. The Palestinians, in turn, were beginning to realize how much they needed Egypt because of purely Arab considerations. Since the PLO had developed some friction with Syria and Jordan, an Egyptian alliance was necessary.[32] The Palestinians felt that they shared the general goals of Nasser's Arab strategy. The Egyptians also intimated, according to Nasser's advisor Muhammad Hassanein Haykal, that there would be no sponsorship of the Palestinians as in Shuqeiri's days unless the latter operated within the same broad Arab strategy.[33] The Palestinians in Fateh were confident of this and proclaimed their intention of safeguarding the independence of the Palestinian process of decision making. Salah Khalaf (Abu Iyad), Arafat's most important deputy, put it this way:

> The [old] PLO came into being as a result of an Arab decision, but when the revolution joined it, the revolutionaries wanted to replace that with a Palestinian decision. We used to approach the Arab regimes as Fateh, but since 1969, we approach them as the PLO. . . . Those who oversaw the PLO in the past maintained a relationship of weakness with the regimes. They (the old PLO) were forbidden from contacting Fateh. . . . The PLO's (old) leadership used to quake because of a minor news item in *al-Ahram,* and Shuqeiri himself offered his resignation because a news item left out his name and he realized that he had lost Egypt's approval.[34]

By this act of self-creation, Fateh thus hoped to remain independent of the Arab regimes. Once it took over the leadership of the PLO, Fateh felt that the entire Palestinian organization should now be treated as a quasi-state. The new PLO, after Arafat's rise to the helm, felt independent enough to join Nasser's foreign policy without fearing the loss of its independence; hence Haykal's reference to a common Arab strategy. But at the same time it was evident that Fateh and the PLO were not free from Syrian influence. Fateh assumed, additionally, that its operations in the Jordan Valley and the Syrian-Israeli area would not impact the PLO negatively. By 1969 the PLO had also gotten permission from the Lebanese authorities to bear arms and to have access to hundreds of thousands of Palestinian refugees in the Lebanese camps. Now the PLO could operate simultaneously on three fronts.[35]

Soon the Jordanian front became the most active of the three. This was the result of the guerrillas' newfound confidence after they succeeded in inflicting heavy losses on the Israeli army at the March 1968 battle of

Karamah. When the Palestinians, with the support of units of the Jordanian artillery, forced the Israelis to withdraw from this small refugee town just inside Jordanian territory, the PLO's image was magically transformed. Volunteers streamed to join the Palestinian fighting units, and the PLO became an object of respect and popular enthusiasm. But most important, the strategy of the armed struggle as the only means of waging a war of liberation began to be taken seriously. These developments increased the PLO's responsibilities and added to its burdens. After it had preached the inevitability of the Palestinian revolution for years, the idea became a reality almost overnight. There was a revolution at hand, but it developed over the territory of a host government that began to feel threatened by this new political reality and its revolutionary requirements. Karamah, having taken place at the juncture of the reorganization of the PLO and the rise of Fateh within its leadership core, also reflected some of the confusion surrounding the various revolutionary commands. This confusion was most evident in the various names applied to the new movement and its operations, such as "guerrilla operations," "the armed struggle," "Palestinian resistance," or "the Palestinian revolution." And despite Fateh's public statements disavowing any intention of interfering in the internal affairs of Arab states, the Jordanian regime was full of nervous anticipation.[36]

Guerrilla activities inside Jordan escalated between September 5 and 9, 1970, when the PFLP hijacked three civilian airplanes belonging to Western countries and forced them to land inside of Jordan. This clear violation of Jordanian sovereignty compelled the Jordanian hosts to unleash their military fury against all the PLO units. What came to be known as "Black September" turned out to be an indiscriminate campaign by a well-trained Arab army against all the guerrillas. So intense was this assault that it threatened to turn into an all-Arab battle or even the prelude to another Arab-Israeli war. As soon as the United States offered assistance to the Jordanian monarch, public pressure mounted on some of the progressive Arab regimes to assist the Palestinian guerrillas.

By virtue of their ideological stance, the Syrians were the first to feel the pressure. Since much of their political rhetoric revolved around the historic ties between Syria and Palestine, Syrians began to ponder the implications of the Jordanian situation and their responsibility to the Palestinians. Assad sent an armored division to Jordan to assist the resistance. The Ba'th regional leadership apparently approved this step, and Assad made his headquarters at the Jordanian-Syrian border town of Dar'aa, from which he began to direct battle. Syrian participation in the war did not last long, however. As soon as the Syrian combatants took control of the town of Irbed, they handed it to the Palestinian guerrillas and withdrew. The Syrians claimed that this was intended to avoid a Jordanian-Syrian confrontation, and Tlas emphasized later that Jordanian captives were immediately released and treated like a brotherly force.

After the Palestinian takeover of Irbed, the Syrians determined that no air cover was needed. The Syrian government was actually trying to conceal this action, but public statements by President Nur al-Din al-Atassi gave the Jordanian government the impression of renewed Syrian activity in the north. Divergent views between the president and the Minister of Defense were beginning to emerge, with the latter advising caution and an end to direct military intervention. What worried Assad, apparently, was the beefing up of U.S. naval forces in the eastern Mediterranean and Washington's verbal threats to Syria. Syrians also went to great lengths to defend themselves against the charge of abandoning the Palestinians by claiming that the PLO refused the offer of Syrian parachute units. The Palestinians, in the Syrians' view, were not anxious to convert the Irbed area into a Palestinian zone despite the presence there of ninety thousand Palestinian refugees. Israeli threats added to Assad's apprehensions. When Arab mediation to achieve a cease-fire came down on the side of ending the conflict, Syria feared becoming the odd man out.[37]

Assad withstood a great deal of criticism from the PLO and his opponents within the higher ranks of the Syrian Ba'th Party. Assad's statements before the party's September 1970 meeting revealed a great deal about his view of the Jordanian civil war and the extent of Syria's involvement in it. He argued that it was essential that Syria maintain good relations with Jordan in order to preserve the latter's military for a confrontation with the real enemy, the Israelis. Syria was perfectly justified in not offering to send its air force to assist the Palestinians since this might expand the arena of the Arab-Arab conflict. Assad at this time was a powerful figure within the Ba'th government, with membership in both the regional and national Ba'th leadership. He was also emerging as a leader of a certain faction in the military and the party. This faction intensified its call for a change of government during the Jordanian impasse and could only look to Assad for direction. Assad had already created a crisis in the ranks of the party by suggesting a course of action that would bring the government in line with other Arab states and closer to all divergent currents within the country. The emphasis was on bringing an end to Syria's isolation in Arab affairs. In his final draft of suggestions to the party, Assad recommended that Syria should focus on the battle with Israel and work toward closer cooperation with the Arab states and the Soviet Union.[38]

Those who were close to the center of events during the Jordanian crisis hoped that the president could be persuaded to refrain from taking sides in the brewing Assad-Jadid dispute. But Nur al-Din al-Atassi voted against Assad's position, and when the party appeared to be on the verge of ousting Assad, the latter made his move. By November 13, 1970, Assad and his supporters were ready to seize power. The unexpected arrival of Mu'ammar Qaddhafi in the Syrian capital on November 16, on what seemed to be a conciliatory mission, prompted Assad to move sooner than previously planned. He was able to form his first cabinet as president of Syria on November 21. Dominated by loyal Ba'thists, the cabinet also included Nasserites and Communists who pledged not to meddle with the armed forces. By March 8, 1972, Assad took a giant step toward neutralizing his Ba'thist enemies by creating a broad national coalition in place of the dominant Ba'th Party of the past. The coalition became known as the National Progressive Front and was composed of the major parties of the day, namely, the Ba'th, the Communist Party, the Arab Socialist Union, the Movement of Socialist Unionists, and the Arab Socialist Movement. The platform of the new coalition called for the liberation of all Arab land occupied after June 5, 1967, and made this a top priority of the regime. Other priorities were defined as Arab unity and a solution to the Palestine question. Syria quickly joined the Egyptian-Libyan-Sudanese alliance and appeared ready to reestablish relations with the moderate Arab states. Assad's rise to the top position in the country, however, did not influence events on the Jordanian front. The civil war continued and flared anew in early 1971. Tlas's special mediation effort between the Jordanians and Palestinians in April 1971 failed to achieve an end to the hostilities. In July 1971, in the midst of this worsening situation, the PLO held the ninth annual meeting of the Palestine National Council at Cairo.[39]

The Egyptian role in the Jordanian crisis differed dramatically from that of the Syrians. Nasser never promised assistance to the Palestinians when they battled the Jordanian forces, and they understood that his efforts on their behalf would be directed only toward mediation. But Nasser was appreciated because he never pressured the Palestinians to accept U.S. peace initiatives. Always remembering that they were a revolutionary movement and not a regular state, he refrained from demanding acceptance of Security Council Resolution 242. Egypt could accept that resolution, which promised to remove the aftereffects of the June 1967 War. But the Palestinians were treated in this resolution as refugees devoid of any political rights. Similarly, Nasser accepted the Rogers peace plan, which sought a bilateral Egyptian-Israeli agreement without seeking Palestinian participation in this process. Nasser recognized that the Rogers plan did not promise to grant the Palestinians political independence or the right of return. His acceptance of the American plan, according to an account by his chief of staff, 'Abd al-Magid Farid, was a tactical step designed to allow more time for an Egyptian buildup of missile sites along the Suez Canal.[40]

The PLO Moves to Lebanon

To everyone's surprise, the PLO relocated not to Syria but to Lebanon. The prevailing opinion in Arab nationalist and Palestinian circles at the time was that the Palestinian revolution needed its own Hanoi. The analogy of the Vietnam revolution led Arab nationalists and Palestinians to adopt the logic of a guerrilla war of liberation aided and supported by a nearby leftist regime. Many felt that Damascus or Cairo should play the role of the "Hanoi of the Arabs." Cairo was geographically removed from Israeli borders, however, and only Damascus beckoned as a possible center of radicalized support. The choice of Beirut as the "Hanoi" from which support could be channeled to the southern Lebanese front proved to be an ill-fated choice, however. It did not take long before Israel's punishing blows against defenseless Lebanon exposed the fallacy of the Hanoi analogy. Shafiq al-Hout, for many years head of the PLO's office in Beirut, acknowledged this tragic development when he declared in February 1983, before the sixteenth meeting of the PNC at Algiers, "The Palestinian revolution did not arrive in Lebanon via an official or even a popular invitation. The revolution did not choose Lebanon as against any other Arab country because Lebanon was more Arab or more revolutionary. The revolution landed in Lebanon because it was an unfenced garden."[41] These were bold words for a PLO official, but they accurately reflected the Lebanese-Palestinian reality following the 1982 Israeli invasion of Lebanon.

Other Palestinian militias and armies, such as al-Sa'iqa, remained in Syria because they were the creation of the Ba'th Party. The PLO that relocated to Lebanon was dominated largely by Fateh and its allies. There the weakness of Lebanon's central authority and the factionalized political spectrum promised to provide the PLO with a great deal of maneuverability. The loss of Nasser in 1970, whose diplomatic skills had made possible their armed presence in Lebanon, did not immediately impact on the Palestinians' consciousness. Neither did they absorb any lessons about the limits of state hospitality from their experience in Jordan. The PLO was to pay dearly for both failures, particularly the removal of Nasser from the center of Egyptian and Arab politics.

The experience of the PLO in Jordan did make a difference in one regard only. Because of many defections from the ranks of the professional Jordanian army, the PLO's military apparatus, the 'Assifa, was strengthened by the addition of well-trained Palestinian-Jordanian officers. This led to a reorganization of the PLO's military units, with the creation of the Yarmouk division, now primarily officered by Palestinian-Jordanian professional soldiers. The PLO forces were then reorganized in order to create two more units similar to those of al-Yarmouk in structure and self-sufficiency, each containing its own medical, transport, and supply corps. The two new divisions were called al-Qastal and al-Karamah. Several of these units were invited to undergo training in a number of friendly countries. In place of the previous system, whereby fighters used to receive basic training only, now a military academy was founded to produce officers with special skills. Officers in foreign countries were receiving artillery training and being enrolled in engineering studies. They also received instruction in aerial and naval combat and in parachute flying. A system of military ranking was created, and officers were enrolled in special military leadership and administrative courses. In describing this feat, Sa'ad al-Sayel (Abu al-Walid), chairman of the general command of al-'Assifa, boasted that by 1971, the PLO's army was equal to, if not better than, the military of any recently independent country. He also claimed that the PLO units were now trained to wage a people's war, both by virtue of their recent experiences and their location in the midst of revolutionary population centers such as the refugee camps. Then he added, without noticing any contradiction, that these troops were now capable of waging a limited "regular" war though not a traditional "regular" war.[42]

Despite their relocation to Lebanon, the PLO and their troops remained tied to Syria. All of their weapons, their original Syrian-sponsored leaders and Syrian-created units such as al-Sa'iqa, and some of their original bases remained in Syria. Most PLO officers who received training in the Soviet Union, Eastern Germany, or Bulgaria had to travel to these destinations via Syria. This easy access to Syria and its facilities, moreover, remained open until the deterioration of PLO-Syrian relations beginning in 1975.[43] Syria's willingness to tolerate the PLO and its facilities on its soil led to acts of Israeli retaliation. The PLO's attack on Israeli Olympic athletes at Munich in September 1972, for instance, became the excuse for Israel's raids against Lebanese and Syrian villages. In Syria, Israeli targets included al-Hamah, just outside of Damascus, and positions in the Golan area. In Lebanon, Israeli raids targeted the Rashaya al-Wadi and Nahr al-Bared refugee camps. The Israeli raids resulted in two hundred casualties, most of whom were civilians. Syria retaliated by shelling the Golan Heights. The cycle of terror and counter-terror unleashed by the raid on the Munich Olympic games led to several Israeli assassinations of key PLO figures, such as the Palestinian representatives to Italy and France, Wa'il Zu'ayter and Mahmoud al-Hamshari.[44]

By April 1973, clashes between Palestinian militias and the Lebanese armed forces had escalated and the Lebanese political scene had become more divisive. Syrians began a limited diplomatic effort to defuse the Lebanese situation by organizing committees to look into the Palestinian-Lebanese dispute. By the summer of 1973, the fighting in Lebanon had stopped as a result of pressure by Syria and other Arab countries.[45] Continued Israeli retaliation in southern Lebanon also led to the radicalization of one of the country's most apolitical communities, the Shi'ites. One of the unexpected consequences of transferring the Palestinian revolution into Lebanon was the impossibility of containing the movement's revolutionary climate. Poor and disenfranchised Arabs could not but be influenced by the ideology and operations of the Palestinian refugees in their midst. Imam Musa al-Sadr, the Shi'ite spiritual leader, once explained that this represented the affinity of those who were deprived of a homeland with those who were deprived *within* their homeland.[46] Remarkably, however, the Golan front remained quiet. Apparently, in 1969 the chief of staff, Mustafa Tlas, had been instructed by the then Minister of Defense, Hafiz al-Assad, to "coordinate" with Palestinians lest an unplanned military operation in the Golan provoke an unexpected Israeli response. This restriction was followed by a memorandum detailing permissible Palestinian activities within Syrian population centers. From that date forward, Palestinian guerrillas were prohibited from launching any operation from Syrian territory without prior approval by Syrian military authorities.[47]

Syria's march toward another Arab-Israeli confrontation was not surprising, given the Arab-Israeli tensions on the Lebanese, Syrian, and Egyptian fronts. The greatest motivation, however, was to recover lands lost in the June 1967 War. Assad's determination to "remove the aftereffects of the Israeli aggression" was even expressed in the constitution drafted under his direction and submitted for voter ratification on March 1, 1973. Article 1, section 1, titled "Political Principle," reads as follows: "The

Arab Syrian Republic is a populous, democratic, and socialist entity enjoying its own sovereignty. It is not permissible to give up any piece of its territorry."[48] Assad expressed the same sentiment regarding the Golan in 1982. Having fought another war without retrieving lost Syrian territory, he addressed the fifth session of the executive committee of the Ba'th Party with the following words: "The Golan is not occupied according to an Israeli law, and its liberation will not depend on the absence of such an Israeli legal device. Israel did not acquire the Golan through the use of the law and we will not retrieve the Golan by the use of another law."[49]

Indeed, uncertainty about the Golan's return and ongoing tension along the Syrian-Israeli border pushed the Syrians in the direction of war. Despite Syria's acceptance of Security Council Resolution 242, the Israelis remained unyielding on the peace issue. As Assad saw it, liberating occupied Arab land had to be an all-Arab war. He began to look to Egypt, Syria's foremost ally to the south, for a military solution. The possibility of launching such a war was discussed in meetings of the Higher Military Council, which brought together the Syrian and Egyptian ministers of defense as well as the chiefs of staff of both armies and heads of naval operations and the air force. The meetings also included the heads of the military intelligence services of both countries. Both Minister of Defense Tlas and Maj. Gen. Yousef Shakour represented Syria, and the Egyptian side was represented by Maj. Gen. Sa'ad Shadhly and Chief of the Air Force Husni Mubarak. The Jordanians declined to join this war, pleading the weakness of their air force.

Shakour argued that if the first phase of the war succeeded in liberating Sinai and the Golan but did not liberate the West Bank and Gaza as planned, Syria and Egypt would be subjected to a great deal of blame. He also hoped that if Jordanian armored units made a quick run along the Jerusalem flank, this would relieve some of the pressure of aerial bombardment of the Arab air forces. But the Jordanians resisted despite a visit by a high-powered Syrian delegation to the monarchy. There were also attempts to enlist Iraq in the war by having them dispatch their troops to Jordan, but these balked at the prospect of coming all the way to Jordan without being able to participate in battle. The Iraqis also doubted the Arabs' readiness to wage a winning war before 1978, though eventually they played a minor supporting role. The significance of these military talks was that by 1973 the bitter taste of the 1970 Jordanian civil war had vanished. By October 5, on the eve of the 1973 war, Syria restored its diplomatic relations with Jordan.[50]

After the political and military haggling ended, President Assad met with the executive committee of the PLO. This resulted in an agreement to permit the participation of two PLO military battalions, one on the northern and one on the eastern front. The PLO also pledged to undertake some guerrilla operations inside the occupied territories and did so, particularly in the Nablus and Galilee areas. The PLO attacked Qiryat Shmona from the Lebanese side with its own light rockets, and a helicopter landing in the Golan area was supported by units of the Syrian-controlled Palestine Liberation Army. Although the Syrians performed well initially, they were more vulnerable to Israeli counterattacks and saw their main population centers in Damascus, Latakia, and Homs come under heavy Israeli aerial bombardment.[51] The initial success of Syrian troops in breaking through Israeli positions on the Golan Heights was eventually reversed, even though the Syrians almost reached the Jordan River. As Israeli military writers were to remark later on, had it not been for the "strategic depth" provided by the Golan area acquired in 1967, Syrians might easily have reached Israel's population centers. Israelis estimated later that the Syrians had very limited objectives in this war: specifically, the recapture of the Golan Heights area. The Egyptians, similarly, hoped to retake Sinai only up to the Mitla and Gidi passes. The suddenness and massive dimension of the Syrian and Egyptian attacks suggested that they hoped to be done with their task before the Israelis had a chance to regroup and stage a counterattack. The Syrians and Egyptians also hoped that Western intervention would put an end to the war while they still held the upper hand.[52]

All along, the Syrians fought with the understanding that the two Egyptian and Syrian fronts would remain active at the same time. But the Syrian president received a telegram from Anwar Sadat in the midst of the war declaring his intention to seek Soviet mediation to end the war. Sadat claimed that during the prior ten days the situation had deteriorated on the Egyptian front, and he felt he was fighting the United States, not Israel. He would ask the Soviets to secure the superpowers' guarantee for an Israeli withdrawal from current positions. He would also seek the immediate convening of a UN-sponsored peace conference to facilitate a final settlement. Sadat expressed extreme pain at having to take such a decision and promised to give the Egyptian public the disheartening news. Syrians knew that the Israelis, who were receiving massive military supplies via an American airlift, would now gain the upper hand. Syrians still hoped to convince the Jordanians to commit to the war and asked Sadat to remain on the battlefield. But by that time, the Israelis had already reached the western shore of the Suez Canal and managed to break through Syrian lines in the Golan Heights.

By October 22, the Security Council adopted Resolution 338, which called for a cease-fire and for all combatants to maintain their current positions on the ground. Israel, Egypt, and Jordan immediately accepted these conditions, but the Syrians continued to fight. The Egyptian front flared up again, and the Israelis succeeded in encircling the Third Egyptian Army. Egypt's perception was that U.S. military support for the Israelis never ceased despite U.S. participation in the Soviet-sponsored peace effort in the UN. The Syrians pleaded with the Iraqi president, Ahmad Hassan al-Bakr, to keep his forces on the Syrian front, but to no avail. Syria, feeling abandoned on its southern front, eventually accepted Resolution 338 on October 24. The decision to accept the cease-fire was actually announced by the ruling coalition, the National Progressive Front, which called for Israeli withdrawal from all territory occupied since the June 1967 War and for recognition of the rights of the Palestinian people. Syrians accepted at face value Sadat's statement that the Soviets had assured him of Israel's willingness to withdraw completely from these areas.[53]

Resolution 338 also reaffirmed Resolution 242, which upheld the principle of "land for peace" and called on all the parties to negotiate a lasting peace agreement. Cosponsored by both the United States and the Soviets, Resolution 338 called for an immediate peace conference under the auspices of the United Nations but actually chaired by the two superpowers. This turned out to be the Geneva Conference, which met on December 20, 1973, with Israel and four of its Arab neighbors present but without the participation of the Syrians. Since the Geneva Conference was unproductive, the United States launched its own unilateral peace effort by dispatching Secretary of State Henry Kissinger on his famous shuttle diplomacy to Damascus, Jerusalem, and Cairo. Kissinger's negotiations with the Syrians and the Israelis took almost six months and were far more difficult than his effort to bring about the separation of Egyptian and Israeli forces. The disengagement-of-forces agreement, signed at Geneva on June 5, 1974, finally brought the October War to an end. The territorial status quo ante was restored, and both sides pulled back to their former positions. The Syrians were able to get back Quneitra, the main city of the Golan, which the Israelis had captured during the June 1967 War. A demilitarized zone was established between the two forces and was patrolled by a new creation known as the UN Disengagement Observer Force (UNDOF).[54]

As a consequence of this agreement, diplomatic relations between Syria and the United States were restored. More importantly, Syrians boasted that they had refused to make any legal commitment to curb Palestinian operations originating from their territory. In the words of the official organ of the party, *Al-Ba'th,* Israel did not succeed in including a single item in the agreement restricting the activities of Palestinians.[55] Yet Israeli military expert Avraham Tamir remarked later on that a tremendous change had occurred in the attitude of Arab governments toward Palestinian guerrillas. All those sharing common frontiers with Israel, including Syria on the Golan Heights, had finally recognized that Palestinian operations could escalate into an all-out war. These borders remained largely quiet after 1974, and only Lebanon was not strong enough to patrol its own area.[56]

The bitterest experience of the war for Syria concerned the city of Quneitra. First captured by the Israelis in 1967 with most of its installations and buildings intact, the town was bulldozed by the Israelis before its final return to the Syrians in 1974. There was no apparent military justification for this act, which was preceded by the expulsion of its Christian-Muslim population of about thirty-seven thousand. The Syrians' only positive experience of the war was in the effective use of the oil weapon.[57] Discussed by the Arab League since its creation and vigorously debated by the Egyptian columnist and presidential advisor Muhammad Hassanein Haykal in the late 1940s, the use of the oil weapon became a battle cry of the pan-Arabists and the Palestinians. Finally, the October War demonstrated the vast possibilities of this strategic material.

One of the major developments of the postwar years has been Arab and international recognition of the PLO as the sole legitimate representative of the Palestinian people. Buoyed by the nationalist mood of the Arab states after the war and by the reservoir of public sympathy generated for the Palestinians in the wake of the Jordanian civil war, the PLO succeeded in being recognized by the Rabat summit meeting on October 28, 1974, as the legitimate representative of the Palestinian people. Jordan was the most affected by this resolution and lost its exclusive right of representation over the West Bank. Although the final elimination of Jordan's legal authority over the West Bank was not achieved until the intifada of 1987, the severing of the two banks of the Jordan had begun at Rabat.

Among the most ardent of the PLO's supporters at that conference were Syria and Saudi Arabia. The PLO's transformation from a shadowy guerrilla group into a diplomatic interlocutor took a giant step a month later, when Arafat appeared at the United Nations on November 13 to address the community of nations.[58] These diplomatic victories, some observers began to notice, were already producing a moderating influence on the PLO. Few noticed Arafat's subtle offer to turn away from violence in his statement before the UN General Assembly, when he stated, "I declare before you here as the Chairman of the PLO and as the head of the Palestinian revolution that when we speak of our joint hopes for Palestine of tomorrow we include in this vision all the Jews who are now living in Palestine and who accept to co-exist with us in peace and with no discrimination."[59]

The Camp David Accords

Two challenges faced Syria and the Palestinians in the 1970s: Egypt's slide toward peace and Lebanon's slide toward war. Both of these developments were indisputably the by-products of the continuing Arab-Israeli conflict. Egypt's overtures toward peace, culminating in the 1979 Camp David agreements, created new strategic realties for Syria. No longer would its ally to the south assist Syria in its future confrontations with Israel. The military withdrawal of Egypt from the Arab-Israeli arena was also bound to affect other states besides Syria. As Lebanon began to unravel as a result of its intensified sectarian crisis, the Israelis saw a golden opportunity to crush the Palestinian revolution once and for all. Thus, even though the Camp David agreements were condemned in the usual ideological rhetoric as betraying the principles of pan-Arabism and the foundation of the Arab League, Syrians recognized that the real loss to them and to the rest of the confrontation states was strategic in nature. Egypt had abandoned Syria's war on the Golan Front once before, toward the end of the October War. Egypt's abandonment of Syria was felt more bitterly in Lebanon, especially after the Israelis, followed by the Americans, began to attempt the restructuring of the domestic alignments of Syria's neighbors to the west.

When Egypt embarked on the road to Camp David, the Syrians and Palestinians drew closer together despite their disputes over Lebanon. The PLO began to insist on its exclusive right to negotiate the future of any Palestinian territory. Arafat also began to emphasize the Syrian-Palestinian alliance and to accuse the Egyptians of conspiring against Palestinian and Arab armies in Syria and Lebanon. The Jordanians, feeling left out by the Camp David negotiators, drew closer to Syria.[60] The PLO was able to convert Arab rejection of the Camp David negotiations into a platform of its own. Sadat's deed at Camp David, said Arafat, was an act of aggression against Arab lands and all the Arabs' values and sacred beliefs. He saw this as surrendering Jerusalem, Palestine, and all the national rights of Palestinians in exchange for a handful of sand in Sinai. Camp David was an aggression with the participation of Zionist and imperialist forces. He referred to Sadat as "the Petain of the Arabs," and prophesied that Sadat would not be able to make the Arabs surrender. What the Palestinians were asked to do, he added, was to submit to Begin's conditions and to please Carter in order for the latter to be reelected at the expense of the Palestinian and Arab peoples.[61]

On the other hand, the PLO's foreign policy chief dwelled on the American plan to defer the Palestine question. Kissinger's step-by-step diplomacy, Qaddumi said, was accompanied by secret negotiations that attempted to resolve the Middle East crisis without tackling the Palestinian issue. Kissinger rarely referred to this issue in his statements and concentrated instead on partial solutions in exchange for what the Israelis demanded in the way of security guarantees. Camp David was intended to isolate Egypt from the rest of the Arab world since the Americans often repeated that these agreements stood by themselves. What Qaddumi also lamented was that a new Geneva conference was to be convened during a time period suited only to Americans and Israelis.[62]

An Arab summit meeting devoted to the Egyptian-Israeli agreements was then held at Damascus in 1978. Attended by Algeria's Boumédienne, Libya's Qaddhafi, Yemen's 'Ali Nasser Muhammad, and Arafat, the so-called summit of steadfastness, or *sumud*, adopted important resolutions beginning with a call for recognition of the PLO as the legitimate representative of the Palestinian people. The leaders also called for a general Arab mobilization to prepare for a confrontation with the enemy, a publicity campaign to alert international public opinion to the dangers of these agreements, and a general economic boycott of Egypt. The summit called for support for the Syrian position in Lebanon, which was resisting the partition, the slide toward civil war, and the extinguishing of the Palestine question.

During that same year, Assad flew to Moscow for meetings with Leonid Brezhnev, who declared for the first time that since Arab borders ran close to the Soviet Union and to the Warsaw Pact countries, the Soviet Union had a right to be concerned over events in the region. Syria, added Brezhnev, had now become the first line of defense before this new imperialist thrust. This remarkable statement signified a major shift in Soviet Mideast policy as Syria replaced Egypt in the position of the foremost Soviet ally in the area. The Baghdad summit meeting, following in November 1978, turned into a rejectionist summit. After the signing of the Egyptian-Israeli peace agreement on March 26, 1979, the decisions of the Baghdad summit were carried out. These included the transfer of the headquarters of the Arab League from Cairo to Tunis and the election of the

Tunisian Minister of Information, Al-Shathli al-Qleibi, to the position of secretary-general recently made vacant by the resignations of the Egyptian Mahmoud Riadh and the Lebanese As'ad al-As'ad.[63]

The PLO also made a significant response to the Camp David negotiations, one that was noteworthy in its location. For the first time ever, the PLO decided to hold the fourteenth annual meeting of the Palestine National Council at Damascus. Coming after four years of serious friction and even military clashes with the Syrians in Lebanon, the meeting was a confirmation of Assad's unchallenged control of Lebanon. It was also Arafat's way of buying time until another Arab sponsor could be found. The meeting was convened on January 15, 1979, at the meeting hall of the General Union of Syrian Workers. Under the leadership of the PNC chairperson, Khaled al-Fahoum, this PLO meeting had all the earmarks of Ba'thist sponsorship and approval.

Since all the PLO's meetings were hosted by whoever was deemed to be a friendly state at the time, protocol demanded participation by lead figures of the host country and general expressions of Palestinian support for the foreign policy goals of that country. During the Damascus meeting, the opening session was attended by the Syrian Prime Minister, Muhammad 'Ali al-Halabi, and was formally opened by the Syrian president, who affirmed the historic solidarity of the Syrian and Palestinian people. This session was considered critical enough to be attended by a high-powered Iraqi delegation led by Tareq 'Aziz, a member of the Revolutionary Command Council, as well as delegations from other Arab and non-Arab countries. In this session, which was dedicated to the memory of Houari Boumédienne, Al-Fahoum, one of the PLO officials closest to the Syrian regime, spoke of the former Algerian president's love for Palestine. He added that in the past most of the PNC meetings were held at Cairo, in the days when Cairo was a citadel of steadfastness. But now the Egyptian regime had diverted Cairo from its old objectives and twisted its neck in the direction of surrender.[64]

In closed meetings during this conference, the most urgent task turned out to be the achievement of unity among the various factions within the organization. This proved to be an elusive goal, however. Neither the PLO's recognition by the Arab League of States, nor the sympathy it received at the UN, could hide the factional divisions in its internal structure. The conferees rejected once again proposals for Palestinian autonomy in the West Bank and Gaza while affirming that Palestine had no equal and must remain the historic homeland of the Palestinians. The final political report produced by this meeting contained several important points concerning relations with Arab countries. The PLO expressed support for the independence, unity, and Arab character of Lebanon. The PLO also reiterated its adherence to the Cairo agreement, which regulated its relationship to Lebanon's legal authority. The PLO affirmed the historic bonds between the Palestinian and Jordanian peoples. The organization also emphasized its right to pursue its goals of national resistance across any Arab territory for the sake of liberating Palestine.[65]

Conclusion

The decades of the 1960s and 1970s witnessed the greatest turmoil in the history of Syria due to domestic, ideological, and foreign policy differences. Much of this turmoil must be attributed to the breakup of the United Arab Republic. This succeeded in splitting the regional and national commands of the Ba'th Party into pro-unity and anti-unity factions and encouraged the army to make repeated attempts to infiltrate the party. The breakup of the northern and southern wings of the grand republic tore at the heart of the Ba'th, which held Arab unity to be at the core of its ideological system. Repeated attempts were made during this period to gravitate to the Iraqi pole of pan-Arabism, but the party failed to link up with the turmoil-ridden state to the east. This was also the period in which the military committee of five, dominated by the trio of Assad, Tlas, and Jadid, made its strong imprint on Syria's history. At first more pro-unionist than other wings of the Ba'th, the committee increasingly drifted toward a pragmatic and Syria-first approach to politics.

Assad's rise to power, which began in earnest after 1963, can only be explained against the background of the Arab-Israeli conflict. His years as Minister of Defense exposed him to the ever-present danger of a Syrian-Israeli conflagration because of strategic vulnerability in the Golan area. He was also introduced quite early to the perils of unregulated guerrilla activity operating from Syrian territory. Assad, however, was probably the first Arab leader to exploit the nexus between Arab nationalism and Palestinian revolutionary activity by attempting to create Palestinian military units under the control of Syria's armed forces. The Palestinians on the Syrian front were activated particularly during the October 1973 War. Attempts were also made to enforce a certain kind of military discipline on the guerrillas by demanding that they acquire official Syrian military clearance before launching any operations. The fact that Assad succeeded in banning Palestinian guerrilla activity from the Syrian-Israeli border area following the 1974 Syrian-Israeli disengagement agreement is testimony to the success of his policy.

Assad, however, could neither curb guerrilla activity in Jordan nor alter Syria's geopolitical and ideological vulnerability in the Levant. This reality forced Syrians to confront the pan-Arab impact of Palestinian activity head-on. Palestinians were determined to claim a supra-national right to use any Arab territory to launch their attacks against Israel and, if need be, to provoke the military involvement of any Arab regime with the enemy. The policy of *tawreet* (military involvement with Israel) was forcing its logic even on the least ideological factions of the PLO. This posed a great danger to Syria, as Assad discovered during the Jordanian civil war when the Palestinian-Jordanian conflict threatened to open the door to Israeli and U.S. intervention. Assad's brief foray into the emotionally wrenching Palestinian-Jordanian war confirmed his pragmatist approach to politics and his Syria-first proclivities. But he was also able to use the crisis to the south as an excuse for eliminating his serious rival, Salah Jadid. Syria's foreign policy under Jadid was leading the country into an isolationist trap that, Assad felt, would damage Syrian-Arab relations. Assad's role in the Jordanian war also confirmed Fateh's suspicion of him as potentially the most lethal of Arab enemies, since he could use the rhetoric of pan-Arabism not to assist but to curb their activities. Although other Palestinian guerrilla groups did not share this analysis, Fateh's dominant position within the PLO ensured the persistence of this view. Both the Jordanian episode and Arafat's early experiences in Syria, which included imprisonment at Assad's hands, led to the PLO's fateful decision to relocate not to Syria but to Lebanon. Clearly, had the PLO moved its bases and personnel to Syria after Black September, the history of the Arab world would have been vastly different.

Assad's pragmatism in foreign policy was also demonstrated during the October 1973 War, when Egypt's early abandonment of the war effort and the United States' demonstrated commitment to Israel forced Syria to accept the disengagement agreement. This war, which had very limited Syrian and Egyptian objectives, netted no more than the return of Quneitra to the Syrians. Retrieval of the Golan Heights, ostensibly one of the main reasons for the war, turned out to be unachievable. Assad's Syria had to live with the fact of Israeli occupation of part of its land. Any hope for a speedy return of the Golan through diplomatic or military means was dampened by Kissinger's determined opposition to any undue pressure against Israel. Egypt's withdrawal from the center of Arab politics by virtue of the Camp David agreements also caused Syrian hopes to dim. Egypt's isolation emphasized the importance of Arab coordination. As Lebanon's fragile sectarian and communal arrangements began to unravel, Syria feared Israeli intervention; hence Syria's accelerated push for reconciliation with the Palestinians and for putting the Lebanese house in order.

The 1979 PNC meeting at Damascus, the first ever to be held in Syria, also signaled the PLO's growing awareness of Syria's ability to change the face of Lebanese politics. With the removal of Egypt from Levantine politics, particularly as a guarantor of the PLO armed presence in Lebanon, Syria emerged as the major Arab player. Moving in the Syrian orbit, however, meant expanding the role and responsibility of the pro-Syrian Palestinian factions within the PLO. Thus, a dual dilemma emerged: how to deal with Assad's Syria, and how to live with the strengthened pro-Syrian military units. The PLO's aversion to Assad's brand of Ba'thist pan-Arabism was now growing. Having experienced some of the constraints of the Syria-first policy during the Jordanian civil war and the October 1973 War, when their participation in battle was tightly controlled, the PLO was now apprehensive about what Syria might do on the Lebanese front. Indeed, right from the start, Syria's defense of its own interests in Lebanon contradicted the basic tenets of pan-Arabism and Ba'thist ideology.

The PLO that emerged under Arafat's leadership in 1969 was, on the other hand, the child of the 1967 War. Its transformation from a timid Arab League creation into an independent and multi-factional revolutionary organization could not have been achieved without the devastating impact of that war. The expansion of the PLO could hardly have taken place without the negative popular view of the field performance of regular Arab armies and the mythology of guerrilla invincibility that developed after the battle of Karamah. But no sooner had the PLO risen to the leadership ranks of the dismembered Palestinian community than it had to undergo the Jordanian ordeal by fire. Greatly outmatched by the disciplined and battle-tested units of the Jordanian armed forces, the PLO found themselves fighting a losing war. Although the immediate cause of the war was the freewheeling airplane hijackings of the PFLP, the entire guerrilla organization paid the price. The only thing that stood in their favor was Arab sympathy for the victims of this war, which pitted brother against brother. The defections of Palestinian-Jordanian military officers, who introduced a new military orientation to the guerrilla units, turned out to be a positive development.

Arab sympathy was utilized later on to secure international Arab recognition of the PLO's new status as the sole representative of the Palestinian people. Although the admission of the PLO to the Arab League as a member in full standing did not occur until September 6, 1976, the PLO was a major Arab player beginning in 1969.[66] Being declared the twenty-first member of that body did not change the realities of the Palestinian position in Lebanon; it merely afforded them a new platform. Gaining limited acceptability in the UN, on the other hand, brought new privileges as well as limitations. The greatest influence of the UN was to push the Palestinians in the direction of moderation and nonviolence. The road to a diplomatic solution and dialogue with the international community had actually begun in 1974. The impact of the defections of Palestinian-Jordanian officers was similarly unappreciated in 1970. But as the reorganization of 'Assifa, the military arm of Fateh, proceeded apace, a critical change had overtaken the PLO. From 1970 onward, the Palestinian revolutionary leadership had to contend with the presence of a number of formally trained military officers in its ranks. These did not fully approve of the guerrilla tactics employed during the Lebanese civil war. Much of the officer rebellion within the ranks of the Palestinian movement following its 1982 ejection from Lebanon was caused by the dissatisfaction of a corps of professional soldiers with the guerrilla conduct of war.

Lebanon turned out to be the new arena of the Palestinian-Arab conflict. Indeed, by 1973 the dim outline of another looming Palestinian-Arab struggle was becoming apparent. That this struggle was destined to involve Syria as well should have been no surprise, for all the signs were in place indicating that Syria viewed Lebanon as even closer to its heart and borders than Jordan. Only the Israelis underestimated Syria's perception of its own vulnerability in Lebanon. As they prepared to exploit what they correctly saw as a new chapter in the Palestinian-Arab conflict, the Israelis failed to appreciate Syria's determination to impose a new set of priorities on the Palestinian revolution. And the Palestinians, likewise, did not see at first the perils of involvement in the internal affairs of a seemingly weak and factionalized state.

5

When Brothers Collide

The Confrontation over Lebanon

One can argue that the historic bonds between Syria and Lebanon were even closer than those between Syria and Palestine. Just as the concept of southern Syria was deeply imbedded in the national consciousness of Syrians, Lebanon was always felt to be the twin separated at birth. For instance, Syria has never perceived the need to maintain an embassy in Beirut, while people and goods move between the two countries mostly without interruption. In addition, both nations have always shared the view that developments in one are bound to affect the other. This was particularly true in defense and strategic matters. Separated from Lebanon by the Biqaaʻ Valley, Damascus can be easily threatened by any hostile force in the south of Lebanon, a distance of merely eighteen miles.[1]

The first unexpected result of the PLO's relocation to Lebanon was the apprehension of the Lebanese power structure over Israel's increasingly bold response to Palestinian operations in the south. It did not take long, however, before the Lebanese body politic, already divided over the ideologies of Nasserism, Baʻthism, communism, isolationism, and others, began to display deep strains over the Palestinian question. Lebanon, still unclear about its pan-Arab orientation following the 1958 civil war, was now forced to confront its developing identity and its ties to the larger Arab world. The strain, furthermore, was felt not only in the ʻArqoub region in the south but throughout Lebanon. As the progressive parties of Lebanon rallied to the side of the Palestinians, the pro-Western Maronite Christian community, itself divided, circled their wagons. The Palestinian armed presence in Lebanon, and its struggle against Israel's military might in the south, also triggered a social revolution. The dispossessed of Lebanon, who had suffered for years under the exploitative system of an elitist and privileged alliance that cut across sectarian lines, began to look to the Palestinians like welcome allies. Thus Lebanon simultaneously began to experience a political and a social revolution. Before long, it was also to experience foreign invasion as well as an armed Syrian military intervention.

Maronite Christian attacks against Palestinians began in earnest on April 13, 1975, when a bus loaded with Palestinians on their way to the Tal al-Zaʿatar refugee camp was ambushed. The killing of 17 passengers and the wounding of 19 was apparently punishment for going through the Phalangist-dominated ʿEin al-Rummaneh neighborhood. This attack occurred before the subsequent division of Beirut into a Muslim zone (west Beirut) and a Christian one (east Beirut). Among the casualties were members of the Arab Liberation Front, by now Iraqi dominated and operating under the PLO umbrella. The massacre, which was the first direct attack against the Palestinians, took the PLO by surprise, although it continued to call for limiting Palestinian involvement to the defense of the refugee camps. The response from Lebanese progressive and Muslim elements, such as the Druze leader Kamal Jumblatt, was more vehement and called for removing Phalangist cabinet members from office. Despite the massacre, the PLO continued to voice its unwavering respect for the sovereignty of Lebanon, a theme it sounded for some years. But there were several unruly groups within the PLO who were anxious to respond militarily to the Phalangists. Most were pro-Syrian organizations such as the Syrian-founded guerrilla army, al-Saʿiqa, which at that point came very close to matching Fateh's troops in size. The other guerrilla groups in this category included the PFLP, the PDFLP, and the PFLP General Command led by Jibril.[2] The Palestinian slide toward a total involvement in the Lebanese civil war, however, began after this incident. Critics of Arafat began to accuse him of a lack of restraint since some within his camp were calling for "establishing a national democratic system over all of Lebanon."[3] This was before the PLO's decision to join the Lebanese National Movement in January 1978.[4]

Syria Intervenes in Lebanon

Assad's first response to the deteriorating situation in Lebanon was to persuade his Maronite friend, President Suleiman Frangieh, to deliver a conciliatory message at the UN in 1974, pledging not to spill Arab blood.[5] Palestinians were forced to play a more active role in defending themselves and confronting the Lebanese National Front until the massacre of Tal al-Zaʿatar. After a long siege by the Phalangists, the followers of former president Camille Chamoun, and a militia group founded on January 4, 1976, and known as the Cedar Guards, the camp fell to the Christian forces on August 12. Syria's neutral stand during the shelling of the camp alarmed the Palestinians, who began to note Syria's shift of position in favor of the rightist coalition. Jumblatt announced publicly in a news conference that Syria had actually extended its support to the rightists during the battle for Tal al-Zaʿatar. The Palestinians began to side openly with the Lebanese Muslim coalition by demanding that Frangieh resign from his office, since his term was due to come to a close in September 1976. Syria pressured Frangieh to announce on February 14, 1976, a plan for constitutional changes and the reaffirmation of support for Egyptian agreements sanctioning the Palestinian armed presence in Lebanon (the Cairo and Melkart documents). These changes were expected to bring about the end of the war, but the Palestinians did not voice any support. Al-Saʿiqa, led by Palestinian and Syrian officers, approved this step, an indication of their willingness to toe the Syrian line.[6]

Syrians were motivated by many developments to intervene in the Lebanese crisis. First, there was the failure of the Arab League to mediate the conflict and to defuse such tragic incidents as the siege and massacre of the Tal al-Zaʿatar camp. Syrians also began to fear the partition of Lebanon, something that both the extreme Lebanese right and the extreme PLO left, such as the PFLP, were calling for. The latter was calling specifically for the establishment of a truly democratic republic in Lebanon that would share in the burdens of the Palestinian struggle. The Syrians finally recognized their limited influence over the Palestinians when the latter supported "the television coup" of Brig. Gen. ʿAziz al-Ahdab, head of the Beirut force, against Frangieh. The call for Frangieh's resignation, which was ignored by everyone except the Palestinians, enraged Assad. By March 1976, the PLO joined Ahdab's forces and those of Lt. Ahmad Khatib in a military operation in downtown Beirut. The defection of Khatib from the Lebanese Army, which was beginning to disintegrate, was a blow to Lebanon's sovereignty and to Frangieh's government.[7]

Assad's initial response to Lebanon's divisions was to attempt to convince Frangieh to offer constitutional reforms and the early election of a new president. He refused to go along with the leftists and Palestinians who sought his assistance in capturing significant towns and villages. Upon the request of Lebanon's new president, Elias Sarkis, Syria allowed six thousand troops and two hundred tanks to cross into Lebanon but stopped on the road to Sofer upon the intercession of Libya and Algeria. The Syrians then proceeded to Beirut only after incurring heavy casualties. The emigration of Lebanon's Christian population outside of the country was also accelerating. Western policy makers began to suggest specific solutions for Lebanon, some of which departed drastically from conventional diplomacy. Frangieh was to claim, years after he left the presidency in 1976, that Henry Kissinger once sent him an emissary to suggest that most of Lebanon's Christian population be encouraged to migrate to the United States or Canada. Frangieh understood the suggestion to be indicative of the U.S. interest in relieving pressure on Israel by converting Lebanon into an alternate Palestinian region. At the same time, Syria's military intervention into Lebanon provoked a great deal of sympathy for the Palestinians. Syrians were to remark that international opinion usually sided with the Palestinians whenever they were party to an inter-Arab struggle, more so than when they were under attack by the Israelis. Assad also feared the Lebanese progressive camp's stated objective of seizing power with the help of their Palestinian allies, amending the constitution in their favor, and then allowing Lebanon to become a base of operations for the Palestinians. To him this meant opening Lebanon to a massive Israeli retaliation, which would also spell Syria's doom. He continued to stress Syria's interest in preventing the partitioning of Lebanon and upholding its territorial sovereignty.[8]

He began by accusing the PLO of fighting in Lebanon and in the international arena for goals that were not its own and that did not coincide with the best interests of the Palestinian people. He complained that Arafat had asked him personally to secure Frangieh's resignation five months before the latter's term of office ended. Assad said he refused, although he convinced Frangieh to work toward amending the Lebanese constitution. He would also complain that Jumblatt had requested Syria's permission to discipline the Maronites, who, according to Jumblatt, had imposed their rule over the Druze for over one hundred and forty years. And in a stinging attack on Arafat, Assad said that he told the Palestinian leader that the liberation of Palestine did not have to begin with battles in the north of Lebanon. The PLO must always bear in mind, he added, that Beirut was not the capital of Palestine. Assad also tried to convince Jumblatt that Syria's military help for the Phalangists might be an historic opportunity finally to convince them that help would no longer come from the West.[9]

With Egypt's increasing isolation in the Arab world, it was Saudi Arabia and Kuwait that called for an Arab summit at Riyadh on October 16, 1976, to discuss the Lebanese situation. Attended by Egypt, Lebanon, Syria, and the PLO, the Riyadh conference produced the first confirmation of Syria's interventionist role in the Lebanese conflict. But the PLO managed to remain militarily independent from the Syrians and to prevent the dismantling of its various units. Syrians, however, managed to retain control of areas and supply routes surrounding most of the camps. The PLO was able to maneuver between the different Arab states and to use the influence of its radical factions over members of the rejectionist front, such as Libya, Iraq, and Algeria.[10] Syrians were also asking the PLO to call for a meeting of the PNC and to add new non-Fateh members to the council in order to foreclose any possibility of attacking the Syrian position in Lebanon or expelling Sa'iqa from the PLO.

When the PNC met, its membership increased from 187 to 289, but without any reduction of Fateh's influence. The Sa'iqa, created by the Syrian Ba'th party, had actually joined the Syrian forces in battle during the Lebanese war. The leader of Sa'iqa, Zuhayr Muhsin, who also enjoyed a position on the National Command Council of the Ba'th Party, was removed by the PLO from his role as head of its military department. His main ideological difference with Fateh was that he, as a Ba'thist, did not subscribe to the notion of a separate Palestinian nationalism. He emphasized to a Dutch interviewer at the time that there were no such things as Jordanians, Palestinians, Syrians, and Lebanese since they were all Arabs. Encouraging the growth of Palestinian nationalism, he explained, was simply for the purpose of countering the influence and rise of Zionism. The Palestinian identity was propped up for "tactical reasons," he added.[11]

During 1977 a major split began in the ranks of the PFLP General Command, originating in a dispute over the organization's 1974 political program. Ahmad Jibril, the secretary general of the organization, disagreed with his central council over that program. After Syria's entry into Lebanon, the split became permanent, with Jibril clinging to the Syrian line and retaining the original name of the organization, while Abu al-'Abbas, who led the other faction, aligned with Iraq and took the name of the Palestine Liberation Front, the name of Jibril's first organization until 1967. The PFLP General Command and other pro-Syrian organizations remained Syria's pipeline of influence inside Lebanon's refugee camps.

Another reason for the Syrians' displeasure with the PLO in 1976–77 was the organization's unauthorized contacts with Israeli doves, such as members of the Israeli Council for Israeli-Palestinian Peace. These objections were voiced by Zuhayr Muhsin and Farouq Qaddumi, and were directed at recent meetings between a team headed by Dr. 'Issam Sartawi and an Israeli one headed by Mattityahu Peled. The pro-Syrians argued that these meetings had not been cleared by various PLO bodies and that they contravened the PLO's covenant. The PLO doves claimed that the meetings had been cleared by Arafat. Pro-Syrian elements were to criticize subsequent similar meetings by demanding prior approval of Arab governments. But Syrian-Palestinian relations improved as a result of the signing of the Shtura agreement of July 25, 1977, when both came to have similar views on the growing Israeli peril in southern Lebanon and on their rejection of the Geneva Conference. Assad, however, continued to demand a fundamental change in the PLO structure and threatened to force these changes on the Palestinians. In remarks before a 1977 meeting of the PLO Central Committee in Damascus, he urged that the Palestinians take stock of what had happened in Lebanon in order to avoid problems in the future. Zuhayr Muhsin bluntly called for a change in the entire PLO top leadership.[12]

State alignments in the Arab world continued to change in the late 1970s as a result of the changing face of foreign policy both in post–Camp David Egypt and in Lebanon. A noticeable warming of relations between the PLO and Saudi Arabia was occurring. The Saudis were motivated by a desire to prevent the complete Syrian annexation of the PLO apparatus and to avoid a closer PLO-Soviet relationship. The Saudis had a more important motive, however; in weakening radical elements within the PLO, they hoped to prevent the spread of radicalism to other parts of the region. By achieving this, the Saudis hoped to draw the Palestinians into a gradual relationship with the United States.[13] The PLO continued to swing between its leftist and rightist wings, with Arafat managing to hold on to his central position of leadership. The Saudis confronted the Lebanese civil war at a vulnerable moment in their history. With the death of King Faisal in 1975, they lost the very experienced hand that had deftly directed Saudi foreign policy, particularly inter-Arab policy, for several decades.[14]

At first the Saudis tried to "Arabize" the crisis by calling for a summit under the auspices of the Arab League when it was still based at Cairo. Syria's refusal to participate in a meeting with the Egyptians until they revoked the second Sinai agreement put an end to that effort. The Saudis were also concerned over the much-discussed Syrian proposal to bring Syria, Jordan, Lebanon, and the Palestinians into a federal structure in order to form a northern military front against Israel. This plan, which the Syrians put forth following Egypt's departure from the Arab bloc, was not favored by the Palestinians. The Saudis also objected but began to recognize Syria's paramount role in Lebanon following the rise of the militant Phalangists and their alliance with Israel. But Arafat and his foremost conservative advisor, Khaled al-Hassan, appealed to the Saudis to cease their support to the Syrians, whose presence in Lebanon, particularly if prolonged, would surely strengthen the radical wing of the PLO. But Saudi diplomacy during the late 1970s and culminating at the Riyadh summit was principally directed at ending the friction between Egypt and Syria. When the Syrians finally agreed to attend, Syrian forces already in Lebanon (a mix of Sa'iqa and regular Syrian troops) were legitimized by being made part of the Arab League force.[15]

But despite the Syrian-Lebanese-Palestinian Shtura agreement, fighting continued in Lebanon, largely because of the inflamed southern front. Syria's fears of the deterioration of the Lebanese situation drove it to attempt another unity project with Iraq in June 1979. The attempt failed due to Syrian-Iraqi disagreements that had become prominent after the October 1973 War. These included the problem of the Euphrates waters, ideological factors resulting from the Ba'th Party splits, and Iraq's new Kurdish policies resulting from the 1974 Algiers accords between Iran and Iraq. Syria had very few Arab allies in the 1970s, and the warming of its relations with Jordan (which had recently emerged from its Arab-imposed isolation as a result of warring against the Palestinians) did not add any benefits to its posture in Lebanon. The overtures to Jordan were simply an attempt to prevent it from joining the Camp David accords and the American-directed Middle East peace process. The Jordanians were also publicly supportive of Syria's peacemaking role in Lebanon.[16]

The Israelis Open a New Front

By 1978 the Christian camp in Lebanon underwent significant changes. The murder of Suleiman Frangieh's son and his family at the hands of Israeli-trained Phalangist militias left the rightist camp under the sole military command of Bashir Gemayel. At the same time, growing cooperation between the forces of the renegade Lebanese army officer Sa'ad Haddad and the Israeli defense forces in the south of Lebanon began to foreshadow the growing polarization and division of Lebanon.[17] Initially, Frangieh's militia force was part of the rightist military-political coalition, which included the Phalange Party and troops of the Pierre Gemayel family, the Free Nationalists or Liberal Party of Camille Chamoun's family, and a Maronite religious order led by Cherbel Kassis, who provided an ideological content to the alliance.[18] The death of Frangieh's family forced the ex-president to cede his area in northern Lebanon to the Syrian military forces. This intensified the tempo of fighting between the Christian militias and the Syrians, as well as between the Israelis and the Palestinians in the south.[19]

Israel's slide toward a total confrontation in Lebanon during the early 1980s, according to Israeli experts, resulted from the change of government from Labor to Likud. While Yitzhak Rabin was in office, the Israeli government maintained a strong commitment to Lebanon's rightist camp in order to help them stem the PLO tide. But nothing in that policy indicated a desire to lead an Israeli invasion of Lebanon or to become a party to that country's civil war. When Menachem Begin came to office as the new Prime Minister in 1977, Rabin's noninterventionist approach was continued for a while. This was attributed to the influence of Yigael Yadin, the deputy premier, Moshe Dayan, the Foreign Minister, and Ezer Weizman, the Defense Minister. After the departure of all three from the government, particularly Dayan, Begin took the responsibility of the Defense Ministry but came to rely increasingly on the military experience of Agriculture Minister Ariel Sharon and Chief of Staff Rafael Eitan. These two encouraged the development of closer ties with the Lebanese Christian camp, particularly with the Phalangist leadership, and gave them access to Israel's military stores.[20]

But even when Rabin was still in office, the threat of Israeli intervention hung over Lebanon. Israeli officials were saying publicly that what prevented a Syrian invasion of Lebanon was the possibility of an Israeli military intervention. Rabin sounded a note similar to that of the Israelis during the Jordanian civil war when he threatened to intervene in Lebanon if Syria changed the domestic equation of that country. Israel then unilaterally declared a "red line" zone close to its border with southern Lebanon and running northeast parallel to the Golan Heights. Israel transmitted through U.S. diplomatic channels a warning to Syria against crossing that line. Israel's warning was also directed at Arab peacekeeping troops.[21]

The "red line" agreement was actually a series of understandings about what Israel would and would not tolerate in the way of Syrian maneuvers in Lebanon. First and foremost the Israelis opposed the deployment there of surface-to-air (SAM) missiles. Syrians were also warned against using their air force in the war against the Christian militias. These limitations on Syria's activities lasted until 1981 and were reactivated in 1985.[22] The red-line agreements, however, did not always work. A near-collision between the Israelis and Syrians, which became known as a "missile crisis," occurred in March 1981 when the Phalangists targeted areas close to Syria's borders, including the Biqaaʿ Valley, the Damascus-Beirut highway, and the heights surrounding Beirut and Tripoli. When Bashir Gemayel's forces captured the heights overlooking the main highway to Damascus, he provoked a strong Syrian counterattack in the form of a siege of the town of Zahle. Appeals to the Israelis for help brought the Israeli air force into battle, which in turn brought down two Syrian helicopter loads of soldiers. This attack persuaded the Syrians for the first time to place their SAM missiles inside Lebanon and along the Lebanese-Syrian border. A full-blown confrontation was avoided only when the United States intervened.[23]

The Phalangists were encouraged to maintain their intransigence with the June 1981 appointment of Sharon as Minister of Defense. The immediate impact of this appointment fell on the PLO, whose Lebanese bases were now undergoing heavy and continuous Israeli bombardment. The PLO's response came in the form of a fierce shelling of Israeli border towns and positions. Only the mediation of Philip Habib, President Reagan's envoy, was able to produce a cease-fire. The strength of the PLO response led Israel to resolve to clear southern Lebanon of a large zone of PLO positions as a way of permanently securing the safety of Israeli border towns and villages. Such a move would also have the significant added advantage of eliminating PLO influence over the occupied territories and potentially pacifying the West Bank and Gaza.

This hawkish position, which carried the original Israeli policy of assisting the Phalangists much closer to a total invasion, also coincided with the election of the Reagan administration to office. Unlike the Carter cabinet, which had accepted the premise of Syria's peace-making role in Lebanon, the Reagan team, particularly Secretary of State Alexander Haig, was decidedly more sympathetic to Israel. The Reagan policy favored the withdrawal of all non-Lebanese forces from that country, including the PLO armies and the Israeli forces in southern Lebanon, prior to undertaking a new peace settlement. But neither the Israelis nor the PLO had any intention of complying with this policy. Israel's hawks were strengthened by the Knesset vote on December 14, 1981, which extended Israeli law to the Golan Heights. Viewed as a prelude to full annexation, the law added to Israeli fears of an imminent Syrian retaliation in the Golan area. To prevent that, the Israeli military presence in southern Lebanon would need to be strengthened in prepraration to sending reinforcements to the Golan Heights.[24]

In the following months, Israelis debated the effectiveness of various military plans to eject the PLO from Lebanon. The final consensus settled on a military drive along the coast all the way to Beirut, which would be held under siege until the PLO were persuaded to leave. This plan entailed the destruction of the majority of PLO bases along the coast but did not envisage a total war in central and eastern Lebanon, which would have brought in the Syrians. Neither did the Israeli government and military expect to involve Israeli troops directly in urban warfare. Christian forces would have to do the bulk of direct combat against the Palestinians. Sharon traveled to the Phalangist headquarters in the town of Junieh in January 1982 in order to finalize plans and assess the degree of Christian commitment to the war. Both sides concluded by discussing how much Israel could help if Syria came to the aid of the Progressive Front, particularly in the Beirut area. The Israelis made it clear that they did not intend to engage Syrian forces in battle except if directly attacked. But the possibility of Syrian support for some of the combatants and for their own troops in Beirut remained very real. The Israeli dilemma became, therefore, how to assist the Phalangists in driving the PLO out of Lebanon and gaining mastery over all of the country while avoiding a war with Syria. After all, the Israelis did not view the Syrian presence in Lebanon as a threat to Israel, and the cost of fighting Syrian troops could not be justified. The Israelis continued to experience some anxiety over Syria's breach of the red-line understanding with its missile sites in Lebanon, but the Israelis recognized that only international pressure and the political determination of the newly constituted and victorious Christian-dominated government could force Syria's departure. The Arab League could be persuaded at that point that Lebanon's pacification after the PLO's destruction or forced removal from Beirut and other Lebanese locations eliminated the need for Syria's peace-keeping role. The Israelis, according to their own military experts, had no quarrel with the Syrians except in the Golan area. Israel would not oppose a new set of Lebanese guarantees to the Syrians concerning their security apprehension in Lebanon. All of these Israeli assumptions, of course, rested on the willingness of the Christian faction to abandon the dream of a Christian-dominated Lebanon and accept a return to the pre-war Muslim-Christian coalitions but without the disturbing PLO presence.[25]

Israeli military strategists, however, had to contend with the hawkish Sharon, who decided that an Israeli military sweep across all of Lebanon was necessary. He was no longer satisfied with the limited plan of leading a drive to Beirut along Lebanon's coast. The so-called "Operation Pines" was rejected by the Israeli cabinet because of the threat of a full-blown war with Syria. But Sharon, on a visit to Washington in May 1982, did win the hesitant approval of the United States for an Israeli thrust into Lebanon. The United States implied that Israel would need a serious provocation before undertaking this plan, but the two sides did not agree on the scale of that provocation. In subsequent correspondence the U.S. policymakers also failed to express to the Israelis their fear of a large military attack. They did indicate that presidential envoy Philip Habib would continue diplomatic efforts to bring a peaceful solution to Lebanon. All of this changed drastically when the Israeli ambassador to London, Shlomo Argov, was nearly killed by an unknown assailant. This was the provocation for which Sharon had planned and waited in order to drive the PLO completely out of Lebanon. Israeli forces launched what they still anticipated to be a limited operation on June 6, 1982.[26] Called "Peace for Galilee," this operation turned out to be a complete Israeli invasion of Lebanon that brought in its wake not only the invasion of Beirut but also massacres of Palestinian refugees and entanglement with the Syrians.

According to Muhammad Hassanein Haykal, President Sadat had actually warned the PLO representative at Cairo on February 2, 1981, of a possible large-scale Israeli invasion of Lebanon. He strongly advised that the PLO should pull up its stakes, hand over its weapons to the PLA in Lebanon, and leave. There are indications, in fact, that the PLO received warnings of the Israeli attack from multiple sources. According to Palestinian opposition leaders within the PLO, Assad also knew of the attack because of disclosures in the Lebanese paper *Al-Safir* on January 16, 1982. Nayef Hawatmah of the PDFLP reported to the PLO leadership, after meeting Assad at Damascus, that the Syrian president had promised to assist the Palestinians and Lebanese with all his means. When the conflict began, the Israelis initially insisted they had no wish to fight the Syrians, but the Israeli objective became ousting Syrian forces and the Lebanese progressive front from the field in order to concentrate on the PLO. The Israelis also declared that they were not fighting the forces of Amal, the Shi'ite movement in the south, in order to force these to remain neutral.

For the first five days of fighting, and before the Israelis laid siege to Beirut or threatened the Beirut-Damascus highway, their land, sea, and aerial guns were directed exclusively at the PLO. But soon the PLO's lack of readiness for such an organized campaign became apparent. Early in the war PLO forces on the ground lost the ability to coordinate with their various positions and militia groups when the Palestinian leader of the southern front, Col. Haj Isma'il Jaber, left his position and fled north. Tragically, much of the fighting between Israelis and Palestinians took place in the refugee camps. The "children of the RPG," as they were called, confronted Israeli tanks with their own rocket launchers at such camps as Rashidiyah and 'Ein al-Hilwah. Only when the Israelis reached Beirut and began shelling the Damascus highway did the Lebanese realize that the Israelis intended to follow their earlier and more comprehensive attack plan. A war that pitted guerrilla groups against a regular army, one of the best in the Middle East, was bound to be imbalanced. Yet the Palestinian and Lebanese defense of Beirut did not lack for heroism, despite the swift collapse of the front and second lines of command in the south. Syrian forces in the Biqaʻa area and in the Shuf Mountains east of Beirut held their own, as did the Syrian battalion stationed inside Beirut. Syrian losses in this war were massive, amounting to one hundred planes, nineteen ground-to-air missiles, three hundred tanks, a thousand trucks, and thousands of casualties.[27] Some critics complained that the failure of the Palestinian military leadership was not only one of performance but also in the kind of military technology they had amassed through the years. Despite their embrace of the strategy of guerrilla warfare, the Palestinians had encumbered their forces with heavy weapons, such as heavy artillery, and large unit formations that lacked the necessary logistical support system.[28]

When the siege of Beirut made the Palestinians and their Lebanese allies desperate, they looked in vain to the Arab states for help. The greatest disappointment was Iraq, which was mired in its deadly struggle against Islamic Iran. Only Syria was actively engaged on Lebanon's eastern front. The PLO then sought contact with American envoy Philip Habib in order to work out a reasonable withdrawal plan. The PLO negotiating team consisted of Arafat, Salah Khalaf, Saʻad al-Sayel, and the head of the PDFLP, Nayef Hawatmah. They communicated directly with Lebanese premier Shafiq al-Wazan and his military and political team, which put the Palestinians in touch with Habib. The procedure of going through the Lebanese was apparently Habib's requirement, even though direct PLO-U.S. contacts had been established as early as July 21, 1981, when Philip Habib successfully negotiated the first cease-fire agreement with the Israelis. The Soviets' response to entreaties by some Palestinian factions proved to be fruitless; they preferred to apply pressure on Israel through Washington only. French mediation was more forthcoming and attempted to achieve a diplomatic breakthrough during the siege by linking PLO acceptance of Resolution 242 to an Israeli recognition of the Palestinian right of self-determination. But despite the detailed agreement worked out by Habib and approved by all the Palestinian factions, which contained many guarantees for the safe passage of departing troops and protection for the Beirut refugee camps, lifting the siege resulted in a macabre human accident—the massacres at Sabra and Shatila.[29]

Despite Syria's significant role in the war, its contributions and its military losses were habitually overlooked by the international media. Syrians estimated that during the battle for Beirut alone, 46 percent of the military casualties were Palestinians, 37 percent Lebanese, 10 percent Syrians, and 7 percent combatants of various nationalities serving as volunteers with the PLO. Indeed, the special Syrian military unit that fought to protect Beirut's airport suffered more casualties than the Palestinians. Although the Syrians complied with Habib's plan of "the redeployment of troops," meaning a partial withdrawal of Syrian and Israeli troops in order to lift the siege of Beirut, the Israelis reneged on the plan. Syria's withdrawal from Beirut was interpreted by some Palestinians as an abandonment, although it was part of the general plan worked out by Habib.[30]

As a result of the Beirut evacuations, tensions materialized in the Syrian-PLO front as predicted. Assad criticized the PLO publicly in a speech before the twentieth annual meeting of the General Union of Syrian Workers on November 20, 1982. He defended Syria's military record during the war by stating that the Israeli destruction of Syrian SAM-6 missiles in the Biqaaʿ was not surprising. Syria, as well as the Egyptians, acquired these missiles in 1973, but the Israelis had been able to examine them closely after the signing of the Camp David agreements. When the Israelis laid siege to Beirut, he added, Syrians received several Israeli threats pressuring them to leave Beirut. Assad refused until he was persuaded by Lebanese president Elias Sarkis to redeploy Syrian troops in the Biqaaʿ in order to avoid the destruction of the capital. Assad added vehemently that he asked for a postponement of this decision so as not to leave the burden of defending the city to the beleaguered Palestinian and Lebanese forces. Syria agreed to the proposed redeployment only after the PLO expressed willingness to withdraw from Beirut. He then complained that Syria had not been consulted in the total negotiations concerning Beirut and that the Palestinians currently residing in Damascus knew of this fact. Apparently, in Lebanon, Assad complained, Syrians were fighters but not political partners. Syrians fought side by side with their Lebanese and Palestinian brothers but they were not party to the ongoing negotiations.[31]

The PLO deliberately omitted from its bulletins and announcements any mention of Syrian membership in the general Arab front that resisted the Israeli siege of Beirut.[32] Confirmation of Syria's willingness to stand by the Palestinians in their darkest hour came also from Khaled al-Fahoum, chair of the PNC. He insisted that Syrian units at Beirut, which were led by Brig. Gen. Muhammad Halal, had stood their ground to the bitter end. Halal was the one who conveyed Sarkis's message about withdrawal from Beirut to Assad. Israelis had threatened the Syrians with reprisals if they did not depart within 48 hours. Assad rejected this request and ordered his troops to fight until the Palestinians yielded to Habib's terms. When the time came to leave Beirut, some Palestinian troops were dispersed throughout the Syrian-controlled Biqaaʿ Valley and the Tripoli area, but the bulk of Palestinian fighters relocated to other parts of Syria.[33]

According to Hawatmah, the question of relocating the militias was debated among the PLO leadership. Some insisted they should remain in the confrontational states, while others were willing to accept a wider geographic dispersal. Some of these states had refused to accept the PLO military units on their soil. Egypt refused to take the ʿEin Jalut units that had been stationed along the Suez Canal during the October 1973 War. The Jordanians accepted the Bader division, which was in that country until Israel's invasion of Lebanon. The rest headed to Syria, although Arafat kept insisting that Syria was not disposed toward accepting them. After Hawatmah, Habash, and Jibril sent a letter to Damascus regarding this matter, Syria replied by welcoming the troops and the leadership to its soil. Arafat's own personal relocation plans were kept a secret. He and his closest advisors began to communicate with the United States and certain Arab countries in order to facilitate their departure to Tunisia. Arafat's antipathy toward Syria resulted in the dispersal of Palestinian fighting units to countries as far away as Yemen, Algeria, Sudan, and Iraq. Arafat was apparently unperturbed by the isolating impact of these new locations. As for Tunisia, President al-Habib Bourgiba was to confirm in a meeting with Hawatmah that he had agreed to host the PLO leadership only after the United States provided strong verbal guarantees against Israeli acts of retribution.[34]

Events surrounding the death of Lebanese president Bashir Gemayel in a bombing attack on his headquarters led to the tragic refugee massacres at the Sabra and Shatila refugee camps. A swelling wave of sympathy for the Palestinians, as well as negative publicity for the Israelis who were implicated in the affair, softened the agony of forced evacuation. Before too long, however, the PLO were at the center of another savage inter-Arab armed conflict, one that exceeded the ruthlessness of the Jordanian civil war. Coming on the heels of the Palestinians' bitter experiences in Lebanon, the Syrian-PLO confrontation took everyone by surprise.

If anyone understood the ramifications of the PLO's removal from Lebanon, it was Arafat. Not only did he lose his autonomous quasi-state, which had afforded a natural base from which to launch guerrilla attacks on Israel, he also lost what he called "the free will" of the Palestinians. Once again, the PLO would have to depend on the sufferance, the protection, and good-will of another Arab state. What the Syrians saw as their protective role toward the Palestinians, Arafat interpreted as an imposed "custodial" relationship. Furthermore, lack of Arab state support during the invasion and the Beirut siege became the pretext for anti-Arabism arguments directed at Syria. This was a time when Fateh and its allies buttressed their Palestinian nationalist credo with anti-Arab sentiments.

The dispersal of PLO troops added to the morale problem of Palestinian officers and fighters. With 6,500 fighters in the Biqaa', 1,500 around Tripoli in Lebanon, and 3,000 within Syrian territory, the possibility of mounting a stiff attack within the old theater of war appeared dim. To add to the confusion, the PLO's Fateh-dominated inner circle in the institutional side of the organization—including the executive committee, the Central Council, and the PNC or parliament in exile—were all removed to Tunisia. Even the PLO's major publications took themselves out of Lebanon and shunned Syria. Fateh's *Filastin al-Thawrah* and the PDFLP's *Al-Hurriyah* moved to Cyprus, while only the PFLP's *Al-Hadaf* remained at Damascus.

The PLO by its own admission attempted to maintain some presence in Lebanon for a possible return there in the future. The most important symbolic presence of the PLO was its Beirut office, headed for many years by Shafiq al-Hout, an independent, who remained at his post until the signing of the Lebanese-Israeli peace treaty on May 17, 1983. The PLO could easily justify its continued representation in Beirut on grounds of safeguarding the refugee population in the camps. This was hardly disputed in the wake of the Sabra and Shatila massacres, especially since the Lebanese authorities accepted responsibility for the safety of only the original refugees of 1948 and their families. The PLO, furthermore, explained its departure from Lebanon as a move that would hasten a comparable Israeli withdrawal. But the PLO, assisted by a similar position on the Syrian side, also argued that their presence in Lebanon was the result of legally binding agreements (the Cairo agreement and the Arab League charter).[35]

In December 1982, relations between Syrians and Palestinians worsened when a reconciliation committee organized by the PLO's executive committee and headed by Khaled al-Fahoum, the chair of the PNC, failed to bring peace between the organization's various warring factions. These included Fateh, its two rival groups to the left, the PFLP and the PDFLP, as well as such pro-Syrian militias as the PFLP General Command and al-Sa'iqa. The most serious outcome of Assad's differences with Arafat, however, was a Palestinian officers' rebellion that broke out following a new wave of appointments and promotions in May 1983. Fearing an attack by

Assad, Arafat surrounded himself with loyal officers, some recently elevated to higher positions despite their poor field performance during the recent war. The commanders who were by-passed because they lived in Syria and had showed signs of loyalty to Assad rebelled. The rebellion was begun by two of these Syrian-based commanders, Nimr Salih and Samih Kuwayk. Newer commanders who came to the side of Fateh during the Jordanian war, such as Colonel Sa'id Musa (Abu Musa) and Abu-Khaled al-'Imleh, also rebelled against the new appointments.[36]

The pro-Syrian and pro-Fateh factions within the ranks of the PLO had deep ideological and political roots. The organization was seriously shaken following the October 1973 War, when the PLO began to pursue its policy of "phases," which embraced armed struggle as well as diplomacy in the liberation of Palestine. A debate broke out about the wisdom of going the diplomatic route and ignoring regional factors. Another dispute brewed over Arafat's decision to evacuate Beirut. Nimr Salih, for instance, was forced out of the Central Committee of Fateh a year before the rebellion precisely for voicing such criticism. Abu Musa and others accused Arafat of preparing to recognize Israel and of coming close to concluding an agreement with King Hussein of Jordan. At first, the critics did not demand Arafat's resignation. Accusing him of ideological inconsistency, they merely demanded an open and democratic debate. Arafat attempted to contain the rebellion by meeting with Palestinian rebel leaders, the Soviet ambassador, and Assad's brother Rif'aat at Damascus on June 23, 1983. But while in Syria Arafat took it upon himself to proclaim publicly that Syria was attempting to divide and control the PLO. In return, the Syrians expelled him from the country.

Some of Arafat's undiplomatic behavior can be attributed to an ambush on his convoy from Tripoli to Damascus, which he interpreted as a Syrian plot to eliminate him physically from the organization. Once he returned to his Tunisian headquarters, the war of words between him and the Syrians intensified. For instance, Arafat expressed fears for the safety of Palestinian refugee camps in Lebanon, which were surrounded by Syrian troops. Then Arafat contacted various Arab governments asking them to pressure the Syrians and Libyans against attacking the remaining PLO units in the Biqaa' Valley. This Fateh propaganda offensive was also used as a means of airing some of the PLO's historic gripes against the Ba'thist Syrian regime. Arafat called for an end to Syrian meddling in Palestinian affairs and attempts to subvert the PLO. He said that he looked forward to PLO-Syrian rapprochement in which both sides would stay out of each other's domain. For their part, the Syrians mounted a stiff attack on

Arafat's character and Arab patriotism. Calling him a traitor to the Arab cause, Syrians claimed that the Palestinian question was not Arafat's own preserve but concerned the entire Arab nation.[37]

By July 1983 another conciliation effort was mounted. Khaled al-Fahoum led the attempt one more time and organized a committee made up of six PLO executive committee members, which included independents and representatives of the PFLP and the PDFLP. These met with Fateh representatives and 'Abd al-Halim Khaddam, Syria's Foreign Minister. The committee failed in its task because rather than meet the rebels' demands, the PLO and its main Fateh faction wanted merely to restructure relations with Syria. The one rebel demand Arafat finally accepted was the cancellation of the two recent military appointments of Al-Haj Isma'il and Ghazi 'Attallah, which had caused the rebellion in the first place. But other demands for comprehensive organizational change were rejected, such as the formation of a committee to lead Fateh until elections to the Fateh Congress could be held.

In the meantime, several states and groups representing rightist and leftist perspectives—the Arab League, the Islamic Conference Organization, Algeria, Saudi Arabia, the two Yemens, the Soviet Union, and Cuba—attempted to mediate the dispute. The situation in the Biqaa' worsened, however, when rebel forces engaged Fateh loyalist forces in battle and attempted to drive them northward. Arafat responded by announcing his intention to take up positions in the two sprawling Tripoli refugee camps of Nahr al-Bared and Baddawi. Soon the PLO began to move its offices back to Lebanon, this time in Tripoli, which was populated by a friendly Sunni community. First Khalil al-Wazir, Arafat's deputy, arrived at Tripoli. He was followed by Ahmad 'Abd al-Rahman, who established the offices of WAFA, the PLO news organization, in the camps. The PLO radio, the Voice of Palestine, also began transmission in preparation for Arafat's arrival. As the fighting raged in al-Biqaa', Syria continued to disclaim any interest in setting up a counter Palestinian leadership. The rebels, with Syrian backing, had the upper hand militarily, but there was no sign that Arafat's popularity and legitimacy were weakening, either in Lebanon's camps, in the West Bank and Gaza, or inside Fateh's institutions. Still feeling the sympathy generated by Palestinian suffering in Lebanon, most of the Arab world also sided with Arafat.[38]

But there were some defections from the PLO's political ranks. The PLO executive committee lost the representatives of the PFLP General Command and al-Sa'iqa militia groups. But Ba'thist Farouq Qaddumi, the PLO's foreign affairs expert, and Salah Khalaf, who had often been mildly critical of Arafat in the past, remained loyal. More importantly, the PLO's independent opposition, the PFLP and the PDFLP, remained within the fold. So did the Iraqi-backed PLF, although all three continued to demand genuine reforms. Thus, only the small pro-Syrian groups within the PLO joined the military rebels, which strengthened the pro-Syrian character of the whole rebellion. In the meantime, Arafat visited several Arab countries and spoke before some international conferences to bolster his image as the PLO's uncontested leader. Arafat also floated the idea of setting up a government in exile but was not supported by his close aides, who felt the idea to be dangerous.[39] Assad, however, consistently refrained from calling for a change in the PLO leadership. His standard comment was that the internal institutions of the PLO should determine organizational matters, but that responsibility for responding to developments in the Arab-Israeli conflict belonged to all Arabs.[40]

Around the time of the PLO officers' rebellion, Syria was engaged in the most crucial phase of its surrogateship over Lebanon. This came in response to Lebanon's signing of a peace treaty with Israel on May 17, 1983, during the new presidency of Bashir Gemayel's brother Amin. Having been in office only since September 1982, Amin Gemayel was forced to confront the near-dismemberment of Lebanon with an Israeli buffer zone in the south, PLO entrenchment in the north, and the PLO-Syrian struggle in the east. Designed to facilitate Israel's withdrawal, the treaty came as a shock to most Lebanese by virtue of its humiliating context. The Lebanese viewed the treaty as resulting from direct U.S. pressure. Assad's immediate response was to put together a Lebanese opposition bloc and to collaborate with them in bringing pressure against Gemayel to cancel the agreement. The coalition that eventually emerged consisted of former president Suleiman Frangieh, former premier Rashid Karamah, and Druze leader and head of the Progressive Socialist Party Walid Jumblatt. The continued Israeli presence also led to increased clashes between the two historic enemies, the Druze and the Maronites, in the Lebanese mountains. Israel would not only assist and encourage the Maronites to pursue their hegemonic role, it also turned Maronites against Shi'ites and Amal in the south.[41] Thus, a sizeable sector of the Lebanese body politic wanted not to befriend the Israelis but to expel them.

During the PLO's war against itself, Syria became more involved in rebuilding its armed forces. Reconstructing Syria's strategic posture in the wake of the Israeli invasion of Lebanon could be achieved only with Soviet assistance. It is essential to recall that Syria's military capability was not completely destroyed in that war. Additionally, the end of the Egyptian-

Syrian alliance gave Syria the opportunity to replace Egypt as the Soviets' first ally in the Middle East. Syria first began rebuilding its air force. Soviet officials began to tour and inspect the destroyed SAM-1 and SAM-3 missiles. By January 1983, the Soviets provided Syria with SAM-5 missiles. These had never before been seen by the Western powers and were capable of shattering Israel's Hawkeyes. The Air Defense Command was also expanded and reached 60,000 troops in strength. Syria's tank arsenal was improved. The ground forces, special forces containing parachute and commando regiments, and the artillery units were now reorganized. A special surface-to-surface missile (SSM) unit was also created. Sophisticated models of the MiG and Su planes were not acquired from the Soviets until the late 1980s.

Syria's military-improvement program reached its zenith by the end of 1986, then began to flatten out as a result of the weakening of the Syrian domestic economy. This caused the contraction of some of the ground units. By the end of the 1980s, the Soviets began to restrict Syria's military freedom of action, fearing the impact of Israeli retaliation. As Mikhail Gorbachev came to power and began his opening to the West, the Soviets lost interest in challenging the United States over the Middle East. They began instead to follow the U.S. line by demanding the establishment of diplomatic relations with Israel.[42] The Soviets also began to demand a different payment plan in exchange for their weapons. Syria's ability to exploit East-West tensions to its own advantage thus ended by the late 1980s. But until the Cold War came to a close, Syria's improved military posture made a great difference in Lebanon.

The Battle of Tripoli

By September 1983 Arafat had returned to Tripoli, determined to stand up to his own dissidents and to their Syrian backers.[43] Almost oblivious to the big-power interplay between the Syrians, the Israelis, and the United States, he proceeded to activate the Tripoli front as though it were the good old days of his Lebanese grand strategy. What he failed to notice, of course, was Syria's slow, methodical, and determined effort to establish complete control over Lebanon. This was done by extending support to various small Lebanese militias, through which pressure on Israel was increased. Suicide bombing attacks on the Israelis increased dramatically in Beirut and the southern region and forced the Israelis to recalculate the cost of their Lebanese involvement. An official Israeli military publication, for instance, listed the number of Israeli casualties in Lebanon between

June 5, 1982, and May 31, 1985, as 1,116. The bulk of these were the result of guerrilla attacks by various small Lebanese militia groups assisted by Syria.

The Israeli withdrawal from the Lebanese Shouf Mountains, which signaled their intent to leave all of Lebanon except the southern buffer zone, began in September 1983. The loss of Amin Gemayel's Israeli backers was then compounded by a concerted Syrian-Shi'ite effort to push the United States out of Lebanon as well. Using the same strategy that had driven the Israelis out, the Syrians again strengthened small groups to launch attacks on U.S. Marine positions. The objective was to make the cost of the U.S. presence irreconcilable with the benefits. The Marines had entered Lebanon at the head of a UN multinational force to protect the Palestinian camps following the Sabra and Shatila massacres in September 1982. Stationed mainly around Beirut's airport, they provided a target for the enemies of President Gemayel, who was now widely advised and assisted by a variety of U.S. personnel. Finally, the October 23, 1983, suicide attacks against American and French troops destroyed U.S. interest in pursuing its ill-defined Lebanese mission. American casualties numbered 241, a cost that could not be ignored by an administration that would soon be up for reelection. The fact that the perpetrators of this deed were Shi'ites did not conceal the identity of the backers of this group. The Israelis responded with bombing raids against the Syrians in the Biqaa', but their initial enthusiasm for the Lebanese campaign had dissipated.[44]

When attacks against PLO positions inside the two main Tripoli Palestinian camps intensified, Arafat and his forces entrenched themselves inside the city. In response, Tripoli statesman and former Lebanese premier Rashid Karamah appealed to Arafat to remove himself from the centers of civilian population. Mediation efforts were undertaken by some of the Gulf countries and by the Saudi Foreign Minister, Prince Sa'ud al-Faisal, who interceded with Khaled al-Hassan, conservative PLO executive committee member, and Syrian Foreign Minister Khaddam. By November 25, 1983, the Syrians and the Saudis had worked out a plan to evacuate the PLO. The agreement also called for an immediate cease-fire, the resolution of PLO internal differences through peaceful means, and the departure of PLO fighters from the city within a period of two weeks. Anti-Arafat fighters in Tripoli were led by Ahmad Jibril of the PFLP General Command, but Arafat was shunned by the military factions of Tripoli with the exception of Sheikh Sa'id Sha'ban's Islamic Unification Movement.

At the last moment before the evacuation, the PLO had a change of heart and demanded to return to the Palestinian camps, claiming that these did not fall under the terms of the agreement. But when the Syrians threatened to drive Arafat out and turned their guns on the city on December 2, he prepared to leave. Apparently this had been a stalling tactic in order to discern the health status of the ailing Assad and to seek UN cover for his departure. Greece came to the rescue by providing five ships to transport Arafat's four thousand loyalist troops, and the French government agreed to send naval support. Arafat's troops were dispersed between North Yemen, Tunisia, and Algeria, ending his effort to claim some armed presence in a corner of Lebanon.[45] The departure date was December 19, 1983, and according to Hawatmah, the Palestinians also secured Egyptian guarantees of their safety.[46]

Syrians lamented that in the midst of all the turmoil enveloping Lebanon, only the battle of Tripoli captured the interest of the international media.[47] The PLO independent opposition had a far more serious concern. The resettlement of the PLO leadership and its institutions in Tunisia, they claimed, was a disaster. For one thing, the new location was far removed from such Palestinian population centers as the refugee camps and villages. The day-to-day interaction between the political leadership and its natural constituency vanished. Gone too were the daily contacts between the fighting militias, the military leadership, and the refugees. Now, hospitable Tunisia provided a new political geography that opened the leadership to the pressure and influence of foreign embassies and intelligence services. Prospects for democracy evaporated in Tunisia, particularly when the leadership began to communicate with Palestinians in the camps, those in the occupied homeland, and those residing in the confrontation states via the fax machine.[48] Under these conditions, the PLO found it easy to resort to a selective response to popular demands.

The PLO under Arafat's direction, however, always knew how to dull the sharp edge of defeat through small but spectacular victories. One such incident took place while the Tripoli loyalists and the PLO leaders were still under siege. The release of 5,900 Palestinian and Arab prisoners from Ansar Prison in southern Lebanon, in exchange for 6 Israeli prisoners, was accomplished when Tripoli was in its 22d day of siege. This was an exchange agreement with Israel worked out by the French government of François Mitterand and the International Red Cross (IRC). Arafat called the release of the prisoners a "miracle" in light of the bad times in which the Palestinian revolution found itself. In a press conference at Tripoli, he indicated that another exchange to secure the release of two fighters captured by Jibril was being negotiated. A third exchange was under discussion at the IRC headquarters at Geneva. He described conditions in the camp as Nazi-like and added that among those released from this prison camp, which held PLO fighters captured during the first stage of Israel's sweep through southern Lebanon, were 136 Syrians as well as some Egyptians and members of other nationalities. The head of the Ansar Committee for the Defense of Prisoners, Salah Ta'mari, praised Arafat and said that all the prisoners expressed strong attachment to him and had never wavered in their loyalty to the PLO. They had always rejected views of the dissidents, and their only hope was to see the PLO launch a dialogue between Fateh's legitimate institutions and the organization.[49]

Other small victories occurred during the siege and shelling of Tripoli, most of them concerning Arab support for Arafat and the sympathy elicited by the Palestinian suffering in the camps. Algerian president Chadli Benjedid, when receiving the released prisoners at Algiers, indicated publicly that Algeria supported the Palestinians' political independence. No state, whatever its reasons or its size, he added, could claim to itself the right of custodianship over the Palestinian revolution. In his telephone calls to King Fahd of Saudi Arabia, Arafat emphasized the deterioration of conditions at Tripoli and the two Palestinian camps as a result of 21 days of killing and siege. He stated also that the battle of Tripoli resulted in the flight of more than thirty-five thousand Palestinians and Lebanese.[50]

There was also positive reporting about the siege of Tripoli by the international media. Reuters, for instance, reported being at first prevented from reaching the refugee camps by the forces of Jibril and Abu Musa. But once it reached Nahr al-Bared, Reuters described a network of poor and decaying homes where loyalty to Arafat overlaid everything. The camp residents, made up of young and old men, women, and children, expressed great love for Arafat and spoke of Jibril and Abu Musa in disparaging terms. Some of the young men confessed to being defectors from the dissidents' army. The camp residents claimed that the dissidents were serving the interests of Syria, Libya, Israel, and the United States.[51] The juxtaposition of the prisoner release and the Tripoli siege was used to drive home an important message: while Syria was destroying Palestinian lives, the PLO was saving them. In practical terms, however, the exchange agreement demonstrated the effectiveness of Arafat's international skills even while cornered in the far north of Lebanon.

During the Tripoli siege, the official press of the PLO provided a detailed account of the Syrian-Palestinian conflict, including its historical and ideological background. An editorial in *Filastin al-Thawrah* began by giving a running account of Fateh's early history in Syria. The article acknowledged that Fateh's first training camp was established at al-Hamah, a suburb of Damascus, with the full knowledge of Syrian military authorities. Because Syria was one of the most prominent opponents of Israeli plans to divert the Jordan River, Fateh was allowed to carry out its guerrilla operations from the Syrian-Israeli border. Some experts still contend that the establishment of Fateh within Syria and its subsequent attacks on Israel were among the major contributing causes of the June 1967 War. Al-Sa'iqa was created by the Syrian military in the wake of that war as an expression of Syria's commitment to the principle of armed struggle. But Fateh did not see the need for a guerrilla organization sponsored by Syria, fearing the proliferation of Arab-sponsored guerrilla organizations. Fateh believed that it alone should be the beneficiary of Syrian sponsorship.

The article continued, noting that Fateh's worst nightmare became a reality when, barely a year after it saw the light, the field was inundated with Arab-sponsored organizations, numbering 35 by 1968. Among those who organized a guerrilla group was Wasfi al-Tal, the former Jordanian Prime Minister, who was eventually responsible for decimating the Palestinians during the battle of Black September. But none of these organizations was able to rival Fateh or usurp its leadership role in the Palestinian revolution. Neither did this plurality affect Syria's Palestinian role since al-Sa'iqa occupied the second position after Fateh in the Palestinian arena until 1971. Sa'iqa was represented within the PLO's executive committee by two members. Sa'iqa's founder and leader, Zuhayr Muhsin, occupied the position of deputy chair of the Palestine National Council, although it was evident that Sa'iqa represented Syria on the Palestine front.[52]

Fateh's ability to maintain its leadership role, continued the editorial, was attributable to four reasons. First, Fateh enjoyed an independent Palestinian character. That was always its source of strength among the Palestinian masses, but also its Achilles heel before the Arab regimes and the nationalist pan-Arab parties such as the Ba'th. Fateh was always accused of "regionalism" by the Ba'th, which claimed that the task of liberation was a nationalist task that could not be entrusted to a "regionalist" agency. Second, despite the recognition by the leadership and cadres of al-Ba'th, as well as by the Syrian military and state, that Fateh alone stood for the nationalist aspirations of the Palestinians, the Syrian leadership resorted in 1970 to the creation of official military formations to pursue the armed struggle in the Jordanian arena. Al-Sa'iqa was allowed to expand militarily until it numbered as many fighters as Fateh. Third, Fateh's legitimacy was the result of its liberationist role in the Arab and international fields. By presenting itself as the liberation movement of the Palestinian people, Fateh was able to win wide support as well as Arab and other international recognition. This recognition became a legal and official acceptance of Fateh as the leader of the PLO. This was helped tremendously by Fateh's open independence from the Arab centers of influence. Fateh's independence was further confirmed by the Paris Declaration of 1968, which established the concept of the "secular democratic state" as its guiding philosophy. Fourth, Fateh's success in establishing the Palestinian issue as a legitimate Arab issue led the Arab states to deal with Fateh as a Palestinian movement unconnected to any Arab regime. The fear was that the annexation of the Palestine revolution to an Arab regime would disturb the Arab balance of power.[53]

Fateh's adamant defense of its independence led Syria to accuse the PLO of exploiting Arab differences, the writer continued. Syria had always wished to see Fateh side with it in all Arab disputes. Fateh never joined an Arab alliance against Syria, but it did manage to escape Syrian control, hoping to maintain stable relations with other Arab groups. These differences with Syria saw expression before the October 1973 War, when an effort was mounted at Cairo to declare Zuhayr Muhsin the leader of the PLO in place of Arafat. This move was a joint effort of the Syrians, Egyptians, and Jordanians. Attempts to unify the Palestine revolution and Syria just before the Lebanese civil war faltered because of Khaddam's refusal to reject publicly Security Council Resolution 242. Khaddam announced then that Syria was a state, but that the PLO was a revolution, and the difference between the two was that a state must observe certain international responsibilities. Furthermore, Syria's military intervention in Lebanon in 1976 was ostensibly to protect the Palestinian revolution, whereas in reality Syria's strategy was to contain the Palestinian-Lebanese alliance. Syria feared that a victory over the Israeli-Falangist alliance might take the progressive Lebanese alliance beyond Syria's red-line boundary. Syria intervened militarily to safeguard its own understanding with Israel and the United States. Syria also attempted to tighten the noose around the PLO's neck in the wake of Egypt's signing of the Camp David agreements, fearing being dragged into a war against Israel while most vulnerable militarily.[54]

When it became clear after the evacuation from Lebanon that the PLO would have no other territory on which to build its political and military bases except Syria, the latter made it clear that it did not welcome this development. Instead it returned to its former strategy of containing the PLO and dominating its institutions rather than allowing it to make Syria its new base. But Syria was unable to eliminate the PLO, as had been tried by Jordan and Lebanon. Syria would also never realize its dream of declaring Lebanon to be "northern Syria" and the only base for the liberation of "southern Syria," just as North Vietnam had been a base for the war to liberate South Vietnam. Syria now justified its attempts to contain Fateh as being directed not against the institution but against its leader. In truth, Syria was upset at this leader but declined to acknowledge that fact publicly. Therefore, Syria said that it was not opposed to the Palestinian revolution but merely to the policies of its leadership. This was why Syria had sought a Trojan horse from which to infiltrate and destroy the independence of the PLO, under the pretext that it was only striking at Arafat's inner circle. Fateh has been left with no choice but to struggle against this Syrian strategy, which in the end could only serve Israeli and U.S. imperialist interests.[55]

Arafat Draws Close to Egypt

In one of the most surprising developments arising out of the Tripoli crisis, Arafat demonstrated his Machiavellian skills and his disregard for the democratic process by taking an individual decision to visit post–Camp David Egypt. This proved to be a cause for further dissension within the PLO and a harbinger of things to come. An opportunity to offset his broken ties with Syria by forging new ones with Egypt appeared in the form of a solidarity visit by a team of Egyptian opposition leaders and journalists. The group included Lutfi al-Khuli of al-Tagamuʿ opposition coalition and Ibrahim Shukri of the socialist Labor Party, who visited Tripoli as a gesture of support for the Palestinians besieged in their camps. President Husni Mubarak acknowledged during the siege that he remained in touch with Arafat despite joint Arab action to freeze Egyptian activities in the Arab world. Mubarak also affirmed that Egypt regarded Arafat as the legitimate leader of the Palestinian people, clearly in an attempt to reassert Egypt's voice in Arab affairs. To the great satisfaction of the PLO, this gesture came at a time when Palestinians were struggling with the issue of Syrian sponsorship of their movement.[56]

The visiting Egyptian delegation left Tripoli with a message from Arafat titled "With No Boundaries" in which he was careful to address the Egyptian people rather than the Egyptian regime. The visiting delegation, he said, represented a great country that would always play a leading role in confronting the forces of Zionism and imperialism. Egypt had always brought many exceptional resources to bear on this struggle: its historic depth, its cultural heritage, its demographic weight, and its political, labor, and democratic institutions, as well as its armed forces and international stature.⁵⁷ In a press conference held at Nicosia, the departing Egyptian delegation expressed similar people-to-people sentiments while disclaiming the Egyptian government's role in instigating this visit. Ibrahim Shukri said that the Egyptian public worried greatly about Palestinian suffering at Tripoli. The Egyptian public was deeply concerned over the allegation that the fighting was among Palestinian brothers. Egypt would now be told that the attack was directed at Fateh and Arafat under the pretext of an inter-Palestinian war. Shukri accused Syria and Libya of conspiring against the Palestinians, pointing to the presence of Syrian and Libyan prisoners of war captured by the PLO.⁵⁸

Arafat's decision to stop in Egypt after his removal from Tripoli was a surprise even to his closest advisors. For instance, both Khalil al-Wazir and Hayel 'Abd al-Hamid, who were at Tripoli with Arafat, confessed later on to Hawatmah that they knew nothing about this decision. As evidence of this, they said that they both headed to Yemen after the evacuation and took the Suez Canal–Red Sea route but never landed in Egypt.⁵⁹

Once in Egypt, Arafat met Mubarak under the glare of publicity lights. This was the first such meeting with a member of the League of Arab States, which had voted to ostracize Egypt. Quickly, the PFLP General Command, al-Sa'iqa, the Fateh rebellious officers, and various pro-Syrian Palestinian factions condemned the meeting. There was a strong call for Arafat's resignation since he had ignored repeated PNC resolutions that called for punishing Egypt. The most important development was the defection of the PFLP and PDFLP to the ranks of the rebels. The PFLP dubbed Arafat "the Palestinian Sadat." Even someone as close to Arafat as Salah Khalaf, who was a member of the Central Committee of Fateh, promised to discipline Arafat for ignoring the resolutions of the PNC. When the Central Committee of Fateh met from December 3, 1983, to January 4, 1984, it was reported that Arafat was criticized mercilessly. In his own defense, Arafat claimed that the meeting was a blow at the Camp David agreements and an effort to force Egypt back into the Arab fold. He also emphasized that this visit did not result in the signing of any agreements. He explained to his critics that his visit had actually aggravated Egyptian-Israeli relations.

The final statement of the Central Committee fell short of calling for the chairman's resignation. Instead it expressed disapproval, calling the decision to undertake the visit a personal one that violated institutional decision-making procedures. But Arafat did not recant and extended another favor to Egypt by lobbying to have it readmitted to the Islamic Conference Organization (ICO) during its Casablanca meeting in January

1984. He won readmission for Egypt by reminding the ICO that there were no legally binding resolutions barring the return of Egypt. In this same context, Arafat also began to call for reconciliation with Jordan in order to prevent the latter from pursuing a unilateral course in the occupied territories. Fateh also returned to its original strategy of trying to achieve a relationship of equality and coordination with Syria, only to be told that the price of this rapproachment would be Arafat's removal from office. But Arafat insisted before his colleagues that he was still on friendly terms with Rif'aat al-Assad, the president's influential brother. The desire to restore his good relations with Syria stemmed from anticipating a strong Lebanese reaction to his plan to infiltrate a sizeable number of PLO fighters back into the Lebanese camps.[60]

Clearly, Arafat wanted to offset the tremendous blow that he had suffered in Lebanon and the humiliating attacks while in Tripoli by seeking new Arab allies. Also, the damage to the PLO institutions, which were greatly weakened by the defections of the pro-Syrians, needed to be repaired. A new campaign to rebuild his legitimacy within the PLO's higher councils, Arafat realized, could only be carried out with the mediation of some Arab states. Following his visit to Mubarak, therefore, he set about trying to balance the need for powerful Arab allies with the need to maintain the independence of his organization. As an editorial in the Jerusalem-based *Al-Bayader al-Siyasi* put it, "The PLO views coordination with one Arab government or another as a necessary policy in order to defend the interests of the Palestinian people. But this stand also dictates hanging on to its independence while maintaining an indispensable nationalist perspective. All of this is conditional upon the circumspection of the Arab regimes and their readiness to live with the Palestinian desire for independent decision making."[61] The editorial went on to explain that the PLO wished to see a common Arab front emerge and remained dedicated to this central issue.[62] The paper, reflecting the pro-Fateh current in the occupied territories, was clearly anti-Syrian. Indeed, the more Arab regimes battled against Fateh and the PLO, the more the occupied Palestinian population clung to their PLO representative.

The paralysis of the PLO institutions became clear when the executive committee finally met in January 1984 with 5 of its total quorum of 14 members absent. The PLO split had taken its toll, and the pro-Syrian representatives such as the PFLP General Command and Sa'iqa, as well as the independent opposition such as the PFLP and the PDFLP, were boycotting the meeting. An independent member of the executive committee who resided at Damascus, Zuhdi Nashashibi, was denied permission to attend. The challenge to Fateh and Arafat's loyalists in the wake of the PLO rebellion was how to reconvene a loyalist PNC and executive committee without meddling by Syria. Arafat faced the possibility of operating without the accustomed consensual voting, which now seemed a thing of the past. Some of the PLO factions—particularly the so-called Democratic Alliance made up of the PFLP, the PDFLP, the pro-Iraq PLF, and the Palestine Communist Party—stipulated that their participation in these meetings was conditional upon the PLO's willingness to discipline Arafat because of his Egyptian visit. Though independent from Syria, the groups within this alliance were willing to return if the PLO promised to observe certain internal democratic rules.

After some negotiations and the mediation of Algeria and the People's Democratic Republic of Yemen (PDRY), a document known as the Aden Accords was produced in June 1984 and ratified by July in Algeria. The document initially called for the launching of comprehensive discussions with the National Alliance, or the breakaway warring factions, in order to set the date for the next PNC sometime in the coming September. But the rebels refused to join any discussions until Arafat was removed from office. The other problem was to secure a location for the PNC meeting. Algeria was the favored venue until Assad pressured that country against hosting the meeting. The PLO remained confident of attendance by at least two-thirds of the necessary quorum to convene the PNC, but the Democratic Alliance wished to see a postponement of the meeting until the Syrian dispute was put to rest. The Popular Democratic Front for the Liberation of Palestine, however, argued strongly in favor of avoiding a formal split with the PLO, which would only enable Jordan to speak in the name of the Palestinians. But Habash continued to call for the ouster of Arafat. The National Alliance, or the pro-Syrians, continued to claim that Fateh's insistence on the independence of Palestinian decision-making was no more than a ploy to create a permanent wedge between the Palestinian and Arab people in favor of Palestinian rightists.[63]

The PNC was finally convened at Amman, Jordan, on November 22, 1984, but without the determined opponents of Arafat's leadership present and with the problem of a quorum still unresolved. The seventeenth session of the PNC was pivotal in the history of Palestinian-Syrian relations since it tested Arafat's durability in the face of the Syrian challenge. Originally, three states, along with Jordan, had extended an invitation to the PLO to hold its meeting on their territory. These were Iraq, North Yemen, and Iran. The latter's invitation was rejected unless it agreed to end its war with Iraq. The Democratic Alliance had made its attendance conditional on the venue being moved to Algeria or the PDRY. Worse yet, Syria threatened to prevent them from returning to their Damascus offices if they participated in the PLO meetings.

Stiff opposition to the meeting was also mounted by Khaled al-Fahoum, the pro-Syrian speaker of the PNC. His argument was that the PNC would lack the two-thirds membership attendance needed for a legal quorum. The latest figure for the PNC membership was 384, but since the last meeting of February 1983 six members had died. Thus, the required quorum in 1984 was 252. But when the meeting was finally held and Fateh claimed it had obtained a legal quorum, Fahoum proclaimed that Fateh had changed some names around. He published the names of 168 members whom he said were known not to have joined that session, adding that no new names could be added to the membership except after a legal quorum was attained. Some illegal or at best ambiguous maneuvering had apparently taken place through exploitation of the vague PNC bylaws. It was always possible, for instance, to add or drop members through a process of interfactional dealing. What Arafat did in this case was to replace the absent representatives of the professional unions with others readily available to attend, and claim that new members had been legally elected by their unions.[64]

Among the first steps undertaken by this session in order to undercut Syria's influence was the election of an independent, Sheikh 'Abd al-Hamid al-Sayeh, as speaker of the PNC. Al-Sayeh, who headed the Jerusalem-based Supreme Muslim Council (the mufti's former position), enjoyed great patriotic credentials since he was among the first wave of Palestinian leaders to be expelled by the Israeli occupation forces. The PNC also made Amman its temporary headquarters and the other Damascus-based offices—namely, those of the Palestine National Fund—were moved out of the Syrian capital. The PLO headquarters and those of its executive committee stayed in Tunis. Important internal decisions were also made. Among these was a motion (which was passed) by Salah Khalaf to formally expel Ahmad Jibril and suspend the membership of two of his top assistants, Fadhl Shruru and Riyadh Sa'id, from the organization. Other figures who aided the rebels were also suspended, including Elias Shufani, Samih Abu Kuwayk, and Samir Ghawsha.

Arafat's next move after sanitizing the PNC was to reassert his control over the executive committee, which he normally chaired. In a closed meeting of the political committee of the PNC, he pleaded understanding of the reasons that took him to Egypt. He also offered his and the other members' resignation, indicating that this was more than just a ceremonial gesture. Word of his resignation had gotten out, and members responded with impassioned speeches asking him to reconsider. After the chairman accepted this position, as expected, a completely loyalist executive committee was chosen. Not only were the pro-Syrians excluded but newer, dependable figures also joined this critical body. First there was Muhammad 'Abbas of the PLF (Abu al-'Abbas, later of the Achille Lauro incident) as well as the two exiled mayors of the occupied Palestinian towns of Hebron and Halhoul, Fahed Qawasmah and Muhammad Milhem. The other members were the independents Iliya Khouri (the Anglican bishop of Jerusalem), 'Abd al-Razzaq al-Yahya (a former officer in the Syrian army), Jawid al-Ghussein, Qaddumi, 'Abd al-Rahman Ahmad, and Jamal Sourani. The seats of PFLP and PDFLP members Yasser 'Abd Rabbo and Abu Maher al-Yamani were left vacant. The seat of al-Sa'iqa member Muhammad Khalifa also remained unfilled. The new committee was now made up solely of loyalists.[65]

Syria reacted by claiming that the PNC meeting not only was a gesture of defiance but was a serious departure from the PLO's strategy of armed struggle. By holding the meeting in Amman, in Syria's view, the PLO had placed itself at the disposal of the Jordanian regime, which could only mean participation in yet another U.S. peace plan. When Fahed Qawasmah, the mayor of Hebron, was assassinated at Amman on December 29, 1984, observers felt that Syria was delivering a deadly message. The accusation came from Arafat, who quickly pointed a finger at the Syrians. Khalil al-Wazir openly laid the responsibility for this murder at Assad's feet. The National Alliance also threatened to call for the convening of a substitute PNC, but was prevented from doing so by the reluctance of the Democratic Alliance factions to go along. Had this alternative PNC taken place, a second PLO would have been created. Neither the PFLP and the PDFLP nor Fahoum had ever called for the creation of a rival organization. Instead, they continued to call for serious and fundamental reforms.[66]

The War of the Camps

Perhaps the worst crisis in the history of Syrian-PLO relations was the so-called "war of the camps," which demonstrated the depth of bitterness on both sides of the Greater Syria divide. The crisis once again exposed the destitute Palestinian refugee population to Syrian guns and those of Syria's surrogate. One more time, Arafat was able to garner Arab and international sympathy because of the enormous suffering of his refugee constituency. More importantly, the PLO was destined to sustain a bloody defeat at the hands of a hostile Arab regime. Ever since its negotiated departure from Beirut and its ejection under international escort from Tripoli, the PLO had been searching for another Lebanon, or at best a return to the old Lebanon. Not willing to accept the altered state of Lebanon's political and military landscape, the PLO forged ahead with a plan of re-infiltration of the Palestinian camps. The PLO failed to notice, however, that a new force has risen near the camps—namely, the Shi'ites, who were just as impoverished and ideologically inclined as the Palestinian refugees. Neither did the PLO realize that in Lebanon, old allies can turn into new enemies when abandoned to their own fate. Additionally, Syria's new dominant position in Lebanon had forever changed the country's domestic balance of forces. Yet the PLO saw the potential of reestablishing itself in Lebanon as confirmation of its independence from Syria. Realizing that the impending peace plans being floated in the area by the United States required participation by independent states, the PLO was determined to maintain its independence in order to earn a place at the peace table. Calling for an independent voice for the Palestinians had thus become more of a practical necessity than a matter of ideological preference.

After 1982 the PLO managed to maintain within the Palestinian refugee camps in Lebanon sizeable military stores and trained men belonging to the various factions. Young new recruits and seasoned military men continued to drift back to Beirut and the south through Lebanon's porous borders. One Israeli intelligence account claimed that around two thousand PLO fighters managed to reenter Beirut after 1982. Since the Lebanese situation was far from settled, particularly after the Israeli withdrawal, a great deal of population movement took place under the nose of Lebanon's weak authorities. According to Lebanese reports, the pro-Syrian Palestinian operatives were openly resuming their positions in such camps as Beirut's Sabra, Shatila, and Bourj al-Barajneh, as well as Sidon's 'Ein al-Hilwah and Miyah Miyah. The PLO fighters were returning more quietly. Accounts given for the end of 1984 claimed that returned Palestinian militias were in the vicinity of nine to ten thousand. Arafat's loyalists were also joined at one point with fighters of the Democratic Alliance or the independent opposition. As justification for his men's return, Arafat used to point to the survival of the Israeli zone in South Lebanon. Amal, the Shi'ite movement, however, was beginning to claim credit for most of the attacks against the Israelis.

The return of the PLO forces posed a dilemma for the Palestine National Salvation Front (PNSF), a group formed in Damascus in early 1985 and made up of the Palestinian opposition to Fateh. It was caught between the new rising power, Amal, backed by Syria, and old Palestinian comrades in the PLO. The latter group included PFLP and pro-Syrian dissidents. Any move against the PLO, especially around West Beirut, would have provided an opportunity for Amal to establish dominance over most parts of the city. The PLO then formally appealed to UN peacekeeping forces in southern Lebanon to allow it to take up positions around the camps. But Syria opposed this idea and as soon as the Israelis withdrew, the Phalangist and the South Lebanon armies attacked Palestinian positions in the Sidon region. The Palestinian armed presence in the Beirut area was even more vulnerable, and it was in that area that Syrian forces supported the first major Amal offensive against the refugee camps on May 19, 1985. Beirut was already inundated with Syrian-backed Abu Musa forces, who returned as early as January of that year. But as soon as the fighting against the Palestinians began, most of these forces joined the Palestinian fighters in the camps. The militias of the PFLP and the PDFLP also joined Arafat's forces, and the battle lines became clearly defined as the Palestinians in the camps versus Amal and the Syrians outside the large Palestinian concentrations. With the exception of the Maronite Eighth Brigade of the Lebanese Army, neither the Druze nor the Maronites joined the Syrians and Amal, fearing the war would lead to the ascendancy of the Shi'ites.[67]

Most of the Arab world, as well as the Soviet Union, was harshly critical of Syria's war on the camps via its Shi'ite surrogates. By mid-June of that year, the fighting in Beirut stopped, but not before 650 Palestinian deaths had occurred and the Shi'ites took control of the Sabra camp. Palestinians wounded in that war numbered 2,500. The only military assistance the Palestinians received was provided by the Lebanese Sunni militia known as the Murabitun. The Syrians then tried to broker a peace agreement favorable to their own position in Lebanon. A meeting between the Syrian government, the Lebanese National Democratic Front (which included the Druze Progressive Socialist Party, the Syrian Social National Party, and the Lebanese branch of the Ba'th, as well as Amal), and the Palestine National Salvation Front took place in Damascus. The PLO, however, did not participate in the talks since the Syrians and other Palestinian factions did not recognize it. During the meeting, the PFLP criticized the Syrian government mercilessly, only to see its Damascus-based publications and those of the PNSF closed down. Abu Musa and the PDFLP leadership were almost placed under house arrest for voicing criticism. Finally, a cease-fire was announced on June 17, and the Syrians called on the Shi'ites to withdraw to their former positions. The only Palestinian group that was allowed to stay in the camps was the PNSF, which, along with the Lebanese security force, was charged with maintaining security. The PNSF, however, did not comply with other provisions in the agreement, such as completely disarming the camp residents. This allowed the forces of Fateh to maintain their hostile posture and to refuse to depart from the camps. But despite occasional clashes between Fateh and Amal's forces, the first stage of the war of the camps was over as quickly as it began.[68]

Syria's backing of the Shi'ites had a deep impact on the various participants in this war. First of all, Amal's failure to dislodge Fateh and its refugee supporters from the Beirut camps weakened its bid for leadership over all of the Shi'ite community. Syria's instigation of the Shi'ite attacks on the survivors of the Sabra and Shatila massacres resulted in a substantial amount of Arab and international criticism. Furthermore, Syria's intent to create an alternative Palestinian coalition such as the PNSF fizzled completely when the group joined Fateh's forces in the camps. The "war of the camps" thus produced the opposite effect of helping to reunite the various PLO factions. Even though Fateh's forces were weakened by terms of the Syrian army and by subsequent mass arrests by the Syrian agreement, the Shi'ite onslaught on the camps, particularly on Shatila, continued into 1987. The only gain for Syria was in cementing its relationship with Amal, which, according to some accounts, began when Imam Musa al-Sadr issued a religious legal opinion (a *fatwa*) declaring the 'Alawites, Assad's sect, to be mainstream Muslims.[69] Amal were necessary allies for Syria since they began their bid for recognition and power in Lebanon's fractured political picture.

Following the Damascus agreement, the war moved to the Sidon camps. By July 25 the PNSF and Lebanese security forces were carrying out the instructions of Damascus regarding the elimination of all Arafat sympathizers from the camps. The attacks were supposedly to prevent camp residents from stockpiling weapons. The PNSF militia then engaged in a campaign of kidnapping and assassinations.[70] Fateh, however, began to rebuild its forces inside Lebanon (in Beirut and Sidon) as soon as the opportunity presented itself. In 1986 the return of Fateh's forces became visible when Arafat forged a new understanding with the beleaguered government of his old Phalangist enemy, Amin Gemayel, who felt threatened by the new Syrian-Amal alliance. Gemayel found in the PLO a worthy ally and a determined foe of his two new enemies.

Fateh plotted its return so as to begin in the Sidon area and to be devoid of some of the old PLO names to whom the Phalangists had objected. Sidon was also a friendly territory under the control of the PLO Sunni ally Mustafa Saʿid and his militia. The choice of Sidon was meant to create the impression of preparations to defeat the Israelis. By 1986 the returned Palestinians, according to Israeli papers, numbered four thousand. Palestinians re-infiltrated from Cyprus by boat and then proceeded to Beirut's Khalda Airport, which was under the control of the Druze Progressive Socialist Party. Forged passports, which facilitated their passage through enemy roadblocks, made their return possible. The opening of the Phalangist-controlled Port of Junya in the north also allowed large numbers of Palestinians to rejoin the camps.

In the meantime, Fateh never acknowledged its new contacts with the Gemayel government, even when PLO officials were spotted holding meetings with Gemayel. At one point Qaddumi admitted that the Lebanese authorities had provided the PLO with thousands of blank passports. Arafat himself made a controversial, and probably unauthorized, appearance on the television station of the Lebanese forces, reported in the British newspaper *The Guardian,* where he apologized for the PLO's past behavior in Lebanon. Now Syria is the common enemy, he concluded. But the most credible argument made by Palestinian officials to justify the new alliance was the growing Amal and Israeli threats to the camps. Yet analysts insisted that the greatest force driving Arafat back to Lebanon was Israel's attack on PLO bases in Tunisia in 1985 and the Tunisian government's request that only the PLO's offices be located there.[71]

But Amal continued its war on the camps located in the south, claiming that Palestinians could stay if they renounced their military roles. The PLO, true to form, continued to present any attack on the PLO as an attack on all Palestinians. It also insisted that Syria's intent in this war was to eliminate the PLO altogether, since the role of the PNSF in Lebanon was to police and disarm the camps. The entire world condemned this war not because of the PLO's superior informational campaign, wrote an editorialist, but because of the justice of the Palestinian cause. In the final analysis, the paper wrote, the Palestine issue concerned the entire Arab World, not just Arafat.[72] The PLO then called for an emergency session of the Arab League in order to bring collective Arab pressure to bear on Syria and Amal. A meeting of the League at the Foreign Minister's level was convened on June 8 and 9, 1985, at Tunis, specifically to respond to the war of the camps. Reporters were barred, and the proceedings were not made public until much later. Among those who absented themselves from this meeting were the Lebanese. The Syrian delegation was represented by

Farouq al-Shara', the Foreign Minister, who attempted from the start to separate the Palestine issue from Lebanon's internal affairs. Shara' was incensed when the session was named a special Palestine session and Arafat had the honor of making the opening statement. He claimed that the PLO was totally responsible for events in the camps and that the meeting was unnecessary since hundreds of similar incidents had taken place in Lebanon within the past ten years. Besides, he argued, the League had no jurisdiction over domestic matters and was always supposed to oversee the foreign affairs of its member states. Al-Shara' also emphasized the illegality of discussing an internal Lebanese matter in the absence of a Lebanese representative at the meeting.[73]

More details of the position of Shara' and of the other participants during the secret meeting were leaked to the pro-Fateh press. Al-Shara' fought hard to prevent a special fact-finding commission from going to Lebanon without its consent. This would be tantamount to a breach of Lebanon's sovereignty, he claimed. He questioned the motives behind the latest Palestinian plots at a time when Amal was spearheading a great campaign of resistance against the Israelis. The League could not condemn those who forced the Israelis to pull out of Lebanon at great cost to themselves, such as the Syrians and Amal. Despite their entrenchment in southern Lebanon, the Palestinians were unable to prevent the Israeli onslaught. He complained that instead of stopping the Israelis, PLO forces afforded ready excuses to the enemy to inflict on Lebanon severe suffering, occupation, and population removal. Al-Shara' also said bluntly that there was a national Lebanese indictment against some of the Palestinian leadership for what has befallen Lebanon. He reminded those present that the Lebanese people had suffered the same fate as the Palestinian people, which meant that if the Palestinian cause was sacred, then the Lebanese cause should be sacred also. He asked why, when General Sharon invaded the camps of southern Lebanon, they were devoid of weaponry, whereas today the camps were bristling with weapons. He also accused Arafat of deception, citing a statement by the chairman on Radio Monte Carlo in which he claimed that the Assad Brigade had fought alongside the Palestinians in the camps. How could a Ba'thist brigade fight against Amal, Syria's ally, he inquired?[74]

In response Qaddumi attempted to articulate the Palestinian case by emphasizing the tragedy of the camps. He began by stating with obvious humility that in Lebanon the Palestinians were merely guests. He wished that Lebanon was represented at the meeting in order to participate in discussions relevant to an important question being determined on its soil.

The Amal that was attacking the camps, he insisted, was the same Amal with which the Palestinians had fought side by side against the Israelis. He reminded the audience of the PLO's heroic stand in 1982 by quoting François Mitterand, who had said then that there was a heroic Palestinian army and France must save it. The Palestinians who did fight in Lebanon were expelled from the Biqaaʿ and held under siege at Tripoli. How can we negotiate, he asked, when our women and children are being slaughtered in the camps? The Palestinians wished to see Lebanon remain independent. They did not ask for military bases but only for a political office at Beirut. Then he defended the right of the Palestinians to remain independent, emphasizing that the PLO vehemently rejected Arab sponsorship. No one Arab state should have the right to impose its views on the Palestinians and the PLO. The Palestinians, he added, never renounced their right to launch attacks against Israel from any Arab territory. This is a right for which Palestinians went to prison.[75]

The Jordanian Foreign Minister, Hazem Nusseibah, expressed the common Arab view of the Palestinian refugees as wards of the Arab nation and of the United Nations. The most important issue here was the perimeters of the Palestinian presence in Lebanon. He said the Arabs were marching to the brink while Israel watched from the sidelines. He also reminded Syria that Jordan had fought in 1967 because of rumors of Israeli troop concentrations along its borders. Because of that war, some of the same Palestinians for whom the Syrian delegate had shown enmity and hatred today suffered under an Israeli military occupation.[76]

Tareq ʿAziz, representing Iraq, insisted that the Arab League's responsibility to the Palestinians superseded the issue of Lebanon's absence from the meeting. What the PLO was proposing—namely, protection for the camps—did not touch on Lebanon's sovereignty. The Iraqi delegation, he added, condemned the shelling of the camps in the strongest of terms. Iraq did not sanction the killing of Palestinians either by Amal or the Israelis. The Palestinians did not represent a threat to Lebanon's sovereignty, either by their sheer numbers or in terms of the military situation. If a Palestinian carried arms to defend himself or his brother or his spouse, this did not constitute a threat to Lebanon's sovereignty. ʿAziz added that the Palestinians in Lebanon were the wards of the entire Arab nation, and the PLO was their representative.[77]

The Arab League session then adopted several resolutions mostly favorable to the Palestinian side. One of these authorized the Secretary-General of the League, Al-Shadli al-Qleibi, to mediate the dispute by arranging for an immediate cease-fire agreement and then reporting his findings to the League. The Council of the Arab League also voted to request the Lebanese authorities' cooperation with the Palestinians in order to ensure their protection and the safety of Lebanon. The resolutions also called for the lifting of Amal's siege around the camps and the release of hostages and prisoners, as well as facilitating the movement of the International Committee of the Red Cross. On the political level, the Council called for the reopening of the PLO's Beirut office and compliance with all previous resolutions of the Arab League pertaining to the Palestinian presence in Lebanon. The council also called on Lebanon to respect all the resolutions of Arab summits pertaining to the PLO.[78]

A profound change transformed the Palestinian view of the Ba'th regime in Syria as a result of the war of the camps. Prior to the war, the response to Syria's encouragement of the PLO's rebellion had been muted, often couched in brotherly terms. After the onslaught on the camps, the Syrian regime was perceived more harshly. During a meeting of the Palestinian Central Committee at Tunis on May 28, 1985, the language with which the PLO addressed Syria in its various resolutions changed. The Syrian regime was described as sectarian in nature because of its alliance with the Shi'ites of southern Lebanon. The language reflected the Palestinian realization that Syrian relations would never be restored to their previous levels. The change apparently came on the heels of news of Syria's transfer of 120,000 Syrians belonging to the 'Alawite sect to Tripoli and its outskirts. There were also rumors that an agreement had been reached to elect four to six 'Alawite deputies to the Lebanese parliament in the next elections.[79]

From 1982 until 1986, the PLO attempted to mend its fences with the Jordanian regime. This was Arafat's way of balancing Syria with another Arab alliance. Contacts and extensive PLO-Jordanian discussions, however, opened Arafat to the charge of going along with the Reagan plan, the latest of the American peace initiatives. Arafat resorted to extensive denials, arguing that the Reagan plan was never discussed and that he was merely working to secure a role for the PLO in the occupied territories. Hussein's desire to obtain the participation of the PLO in this plan and the proposed negotiations explain his readiness to host the seventeenth PNC meeting at Amman.[80] By February 1985, a working paper was drawn up in which Jordan and the PLO affirmed previous PNC and summit resolutions, particularly those of the Rabat and Fez summits. The understanding also declared the final rejection of the autonomy plan of the Camp David agreements, the Reagan plan, and Security Council Resolution 242. Both sides expressed support for a confederal union between the two "sovereign" states.[81]

Conclusion

It should always be borne in mind that the longest Palestinian-Arab confrontation was aimed not against Jordan but against Syria. With the PLO's flight from Jordan in 1970, no other Arab state stood to be affected by the PLO's decision to relocate to Lebanon more than Syria. The PLO entered Lebanon because of the maneuvering room provided by its intricate and segmented internal political picture. That alone afforded the Palestinians another territorial base from which to carry out the armed struggle against Israel. The presence of vast numbers of stateless Palestinian refugees, with no hope of ever assimilating within an Arab system, created boundless opportunities for the PLO. Lebanon also became a Palestinian autonomous zone, a nonterritorial state in which the PLO's institutions flourished and were stabilized. And when the host country disintegrated under the combined pressure of its ossified constitutional arrangement and the rising social expectations of its most unrepresented communities, the PLO was drawn into a civil war. The PLO's military presence became an asset to some and a source of danger to others, until the Palestinians themselves became part of the domestic problem. Perhaps this is the only explanation for the PLO's repeated victimization at the hands of successive local and foreign powers.

Lebanon, in Shafiq al-Hout's eloquent phrase, was "an unfenced garden." Arafat's entrenchment in Lebanon turned out to be a catastrophe for it brought out the worst in the militarized political culture of the PLO. Imagine for a moment the reaction of ordinary Lebanese when they heard of Arafat's boast, years later, that he was capable of running Gaza and Jericho just as he ran Lebanon.[82] Imagine the resentment of the Lebanese when the attention of the international media focused on the Palestinian victims and not on their own suffering. Imagine the Lebanese distress at finding the PLO returning to Lebanon, again and again, in order to reestablish themselves in the camps despite the cancellation of the 1969 Cairo agreement on May 21, 1987. This action, taken by a group of Phalangist and Shi'ite parliamentary deputies, enraged the PLO, which contended that this was a one-sided abrogation.[83] The PLO even portrayed its departure from Lebanon as a victory, claiming, in a 1986 statement by Khalil al-Wazir, that the Palestinian presence in Lebanon was never disrupted throughout the four years following the Israeli invasion. Typically, al-Wazir never distinguished between the refugees and the PLO. There were still half a million Palestinians in Lebanon's camps, he stated, and the PLO was under an obligation to secure for them peace and a decent life. He added that the Lebanese allies often said that the PLO played a crucial role in maintaining a balance among the various factions. Several Lebanese groups, he said, had asked the PLO to reprise its previous role, and the Palestinians were considering that suggestion.[84] This was a meaningful statement that only George Habash would have appreciated. Unexpectedly, Fateh was "forced" by the weakness of Lebanon to fight a progressive pan-Arab war before it fought the Israeli enemy. The road to Jerusalem appeared indeed to go first through Beirut.

The irony of the Lebanese imbroglio was that the PLO seemed oblivious to the true nature of its limitations and opportunities in that peripheral conflict. Armed with a powerful and internationally recognized cause, Arafat forged ahead always relying on his Arab and international friends for the rescue. He was also a victim of his own revolutionary mythology, which taught that justice would inevitably triumph over evil. At this stage of his career, Arafat was one of the finest political actors in the Arab world, and he knew how to parlay the PLO's weaknesses into strength. He did this through several means, one of which entailed readiness to switch sides regardless of the ideological compatibility of his new allies. Even old enemies like the Jordanian regime, the Phalangists, and post–Camp David Egypt were put to use in order to counterbalance the Syrians. Then there was his superb ability to force the Arab states to acknowledge their responsibility to the Palestinians while denying these same states a decision-making role. Rather than the PLO being annexed to the foreign policy of one state or another, he was able to annex the foreign policy of states to the Palestinian cause. This proved to be easy at times, given the mistrust and conflicting interests prevailing in different Arab regimes. He also managed to mask his policy blunders behind the suffering population of the camps. Any attack on his leadership style, his unrealistic tactics, or his undemocratic methods was pronounced to be an attack on the Palestinians themselves. But in the end, his disregard for the most basic democratic rules and principles of accountability cost him the unity of his movement. His autocratic leadership style (such as rewarding loyal but discredited military leaders with high office while ignoring highly regarded officers like the Sandhurst-trained Abu Musa) finally opened a wedge for the Syrians within his ranks.

Syria, as has often been pointed out, regarded the disintegration of Lebanon with great apprehension. Although ideologically predisposed to the Palestinian cause, Ba'thist Syria regarded it as an extension of the pan-Arab question. The PLO, tragically, was asserting its independent will at a time when Syria felt extremely vulnerable in neighboring Lebanon. Syria, furthermore, has always feared the consequences of independent guerrilla activity, especially against Israel. Once Syria intervened in Lebanon in 1976, Syria's boundaries, in a sense, moved westward. Therefore the PLO was considered to be operating from territory under Syria's quasi-jurisdiction. This explains why the PLO's deliberate lack of cooperation when negotiating with Philip Habib disturbed the Syrians tremendously.

It was revealed in an editorial in *Filastin al-Thawrah* (the PLO's official voice) that Assad considered Arafat's February 1982 attempt to secure medium-range Soviet missiles from the Libyans to be the gesture of a madman. If Arafat was allowed to acquire twelve such missiles, Assad said, the PLO leader would fire them immediately and expose everyone to Israeli retaliation. The PLO, for its part, considered it a shameful irony that the Israelis came as close as sixty kilometers to the outlying areas around Damascus without inducing Assad to confront them militarily. History will record, the PLO used to repeat, that the Israelis held Beirut under siege while Assad ruled Damascus.[85] Indeed, the PLO managed to sully the reputation of Syria throughout the Arab world. By the time of the convening of the regional Ba'th Party's seventeenth annual meeting in 1985, they were reviled throughout the area.[86] Syrians, as they were fond of emphasizing, were up against master propagandists. They also lamented the fact that they were never given credit for forcing the government of Amin Gemayel to abrogate the Lebanese-Israeli peace agreement. Assad's skill in putting together a Lebanese national coalition to join in the campaign of pressure against Gemayel was never recognized. But the PLO should have recognized Assad's steely determination to place the interests of Syria above everything else in any Arab struggle, particularly when a conflict was so close to his boundaries. Observing Assad's tactics in Lebanon and his readiness to switch allies with the same speed with which Arafat changed sides should have told the PLO that the Syrians were unwilling to abandon the Lebanese arena. Assad, for instance, said to a French interviewer in 1978, "We [the Syrians] have a national responsibility, and anything that is Arab concerns us. We are distinguished by an internationalized national, interventionist tendency. Thus, no Arab union can be imagined without Syria. No war can be imagined without us. Had we had common borders with Egypt, our army would have entered that country after Sadat's visit to Jerusalem. Yes, we are the heart, we are in the heart of the Arab world. Syria is the core of the problem and the key to the peace settlement in the Middle East."[87]

This frankly interventionist approach, however, did not mean a reckless willingness to fight on several fronts at once. What this approach meant was that anything short of war could be employed to further Syria's objectives. This interventionist approach was also employed against the PLO when Syria attempted to infiltrate the ranks of the organization and support the most serious rebellion in the history of the Palestinian struggle. Although the PLO claimed all along that Syria's intent was to create an organization to rival the PLO, this remains a matter of debate. Being the realists that they were, the Syrians appeared to recognize the difficulty in achieving this end, particularly when all of their Palestinian allies joined the ranks of Fateh in the war of the camps against Amal. The Syrians genuinely believed that Arafat was inimical to their own and the Palestinians' interests. *Al-Thawrah*, the Ba'th official organ at Damascus, claimed in 1984 that Arafat's removal was an urgent national task since he alone was responsible for all of Fateh's and the PLO's crises. *Al-Thawrah* also blamed Arafat for a variety of political, financial, and organizational deviations. Arafat, the paper added, was also responsible for the 1970 Jordanian civil war, the PLO's exit from that country, and the paralysis of the PLO's institutions.[88]

Syria's failure to rein in the Palestinians can be attributed to two main factors. The first of these was the reluctance of some of the pro-Syrian Palestinian leadership to make a total break with the PLO. This was particularly true of Khaled al-Fahoum's unwillingness to convene a rival PNC during the controversial seventeenth PNC at Amman. Abu Musa's reluctance to join Amal against the Palestinian camp population during the war of the camps was another example. Finally, there was always the resistance of the independent opposition factions in the PLO, such as the PFLP and the PDFLP, to making a complete break with Fateh. The Democratic Front, despite years of abuse under Arafat's leadership, never entertained the thought of moving over to the Syrian side and satisfied itself with demanding internal reforms. Thus, Assad was left with the pro-Syrian factions such as the PLO General Command and Sa'iqa, who, because of their known close ties to Syrian intelligence services and the military, lacked any credibility in the Palestinian community.

The second Syrian failure was their inability to gauge the emotional depth of the refugee issue and the tremendous capacity of the Palestine question to stir people's hearts everywhere. One of the achievements of the PLO, like it or not, was its ability to transform the Palestine issue into a metaphor for the oppression and injustice that befell Third World people in the twentieth century. Arafat knew the greatness of the cause he represented, and was able to arouse feelings of guilt and shame in the Arab world with the twist of a phrase. Assad and the Ba'th failed completely to understand that warring with the Palestinian camps at Beirut, Sidon, and Tripoli placed them in the same category as Sharon's Israeli forces.

The third Syrian failure was to instigate elements within the occupied Palestinian population against Fateh. One of the basic rules of the liberationist struggle of an occupied people is that success depends largely on the ability to maintain control over the exiled and occupied populations. Arafat continued to flatter, co-opt, and seek the support of Palestinian personalities from the West Bank and Gaza, recognizing all along that the right to represent them gave him Arab and international legitimacy.

Finally, it should be evident from this study that both Fateh and the Syrians shared one significant failure, namely, to heed the lessons of the Jordanian civil war. Although he was intimately involved in that war while still Syria's Defense Minister, Assad failed to recall the depth of Arab revulsion at the notion of Arab states warring against the PLO and its defenseless refugees. Arafat, for his part, does not appear to have attempted a dispassionate analysis of the Palestinian loss in Jordan. And, as his Palestinian critics would later claim, neither he nor his advisors ever attempted to understand the tragic loss of his Lebanese base. Instead, Fateh and the rest of the PLO, in a characteristic fit of revolutionary hyperbole, foretold destruction and disaster for erring Arab regimes. But then, neither Jordan, nor Egypt, nor Lebanon, nor Kuwait were seriously destabilized as a result of their tussles with the PLO. Therefore, in order to gain an understanding of the differences between Assad's realpolitik and the PLO's revolutionary tactics, it is necessary to focus on ideology, the most important facet of political life in the Arab world today.

6

The Clash of Nationalisms

There is no question but that the Syrian-Palestinian conflict, which began with the rise of the Palestinian armed struggle and saw its bloodiest moments during the mid 1980s over Lebanon, was ideological in its basis. No understanding of the passionate intensity of this dispute can be explained merely by reference to policy. Furthermore, the roots of the dispute go back to the beginnings of the modern Arab state system, when Syrian and Palestinian identities were no more than local variations on the larger Arab theme. Given these considerations, it should be obvious that both the pan-Arab and the Palestinian national movements emerged from local historical factors rather than from European ideologies. As Philip Hitti observed regarding the indebtedness of the Ba'th ideology to Western systems of thought, the representatives of the Ba'th always emphasized their own Arab and Islamic history.[1]

But it is also true, Ba'thists notwithstanding, that all the broad Arab ideologies of the twentieth century were largely a response to the crisis of colonization and the loss of independence. So was Palestinian nationalism, which developed as a reaction to the crises of colonialism, imperialism, and Zionism that culminated in the total loss of the homeland. Rather than drawing its inspiration from Arab history, Palestinian nationalism developed in reference to the Algerian and Vietnamese revolutions as other examples of Third World struggle. Then there was the vision of the Arab League and its perspective on relations between Arab states and how to substitute cooperation and coordination for the imperative of unification.

When focusing on nationalisms, one should keep in mind that some occupied a transitional position among major movements. It would not be too far-fetched to see that the thought of Ahmad Shuqeiri was a transitional phase in the developing ideology of the PLO. Similarly, no one can deny the ideological significance of the Arab nationalist movement, which bridged the thinking of the pan-Arabists and that of Palestinian nationalists until it self-destructed under the impact of the June 1967 War. Both of these movements are a reminder that no thought system ever developed in a vacuum and that most ideologies have strong historical roots and antecedents.

But whether one is looking at the Baʻth, the Syrian Social Nationalist Party, or Palestinian nationalism, the main difference between them concerned the definition of the ideal political society. This definition, in the main, touched not only upon geography but also on the economic and religious characteristics of the state. These differences are apparent in the case of the socialist-oriented Baʻth and the nationalist-oriented Arab Nationalist Movement. The same could be seen when contrasting the secularist orientation of the Syrian Social National Party (SSNP) and the Baʻth emphasis on the interconnectedness of Arabism and Islam. The major difference between all these movements, however, will always be in their approach to the Palestine question.

Not unlike the African colonial experience, World War I produced the kind of arbitrary and gerrymandered state boundaries in the Arab territories that only a nineteenth-century imperial mind was capable of conceiving. The SSNP was the first ideological attempt to counter the new system of state nationalism. But the breakup of the Syrian province of the Ottoman empire also saw a practical challenge to the fragmentation in the form of dynastic unification projects. These lost credibility with the Syrian and Iraqi political classes following the death of Kings Faisal and Ghazi of Iraq, who epitomized the dynastic pan-Arab idea. The assumption by King ʻAbdullah of Jordan and the Iraqi regent ʻAbd al-Ilah of leadership roles in these unification schemes rehabilitated the forces of regional nationalism in the 1940s. Once the dynastic brand of pan-Arabism was identified with the British policies of these two representative leaders, state or regional nationalism was identified with independence and acquired a certain degree of legitimacy. But regional nationalism, according to some experts, never acquired theoretical acceptance.[2] In the hands of defenders such as Shukri al-Quwatli, for instance, regional nationalism was a temporary shield against schemes hatched in Amman. In the hands of Adib al-Shishakli, it was a weapon in the struggle against British oil interests in Iraq.

The Syrian Social National Party

The first movement to propose the boundaries and characteristics of the ideal state in the heart of the former Syrian province was the Syrian Social National Party. Officially founded in 1932, only to be disbanded and reorganized in 1935, it proposed the novel idea that the issue of Syrian nationalism was independent of any other contemporary national question. The movement argued that what accounted for the cohesiveness of the Syrian people was the fact that the Syrian homeland enjoyed distinct geographic boundaries. This movement was the first in the region to appeal to the new social sciences, which seemed to strengthen its claims. In his book *Nushu' al-Umam* (The Rise of Nations), the founder of the SSNP, Anton Sa'adeh, went beyond the usual rhetoric of the politicians by appealing to an educated generation with ideas that seemed scientifically credible. Departing from the earlier focus on language as a unifying factor, Sa'adeh gave priority to geography in the formation of nations. The emphasis on geographic unity was drawn from the German geopolitical school, which flourished from the end of the nineteenth century to the 1930s. Sa'adeh was so taken with this idea that he considered the island of Cyprus to be related to the geographic environment of Syria and that the two should be politically integrated, irrespective of the differences of language and history separating the Arab and Cypriot peoples.[3]

In one of his fascinating and imaginative articles, Sa'adeh wades through the realms of literature and archaeology in order to prove his point. A collection of these articles, written while the founder was in forced exile in Argentina between 1938 and 1947, expresses Sa'adeh's view of the uniqueness and richness of ancient Syrian literature. These articles, moreover, were among the first to allude to the significance of Syrian myths and their relevance to the history of this nation. It pained him that the pan-Arabists and Islamists tended to ignore all that had been written before about ancient Arab history and Islam. Sa'adeh analyzes a poem by the Lebanese poet Sa'id 'Aqel (whom he refers to as Syrian) titled "Qadmous," in a way that showcases Syria's rich religious heritage. Qadmous, reminds Sa'adeh, was the ancient Syrian god who taught the Greeks the alphabet and the art of writing. This god was also the subject of several heroic legendary accounts. But 'Aqel did not treat the subject well, Sa'adeh argues, having chosen to present the legend of Qadmous in a local context and not in a universal framework.

In another article, Sa'adeh complains that the poet Shafiq Ma'louf had failed to present properly ancient Syrian legends and their relevance to modern Syrian life. Syrians and the whole world community had discovered, since the excavations at Ras Shamra, near Latakia, the greatness of the Syrian imagination and the Syrian approach to life and its complex issues. We have since discovered, added Sa'adeh, that the greatest Greek legends and the important Hebraic myths recorded in the Bible were Syrian in origin. Long before Homer wrote his *Iliad*, Phoenician authors (who were also Canaanites, added Sa'adeh) wrote at Uggarite several adventurous odysseys of a mythical hero named Tafen (or Tafoun).[4]

Newly discovered sites at Ras Shamra, wrote Sa'adeh, described 50 gods and 25 goddesses who were involved in the adventures of Tafen. The father of all the gods was sometimes called El or Al and sometimes Maled or Moloukh, meaning the King of the Year, and his greatest antagonist was Ba'al, who had been born with an authoritarian nature and a strong desire for absolutist rulership. The story of the struggle between the King of the Year, the Just Old Man, and Ba'al was the exciting struggle of old age versus youth, which Ba'al wins despite the sanctity of old age.

Other stories were recorded on the cuneiform tablets of Ras Shamra, such as the struggle of the god representing the fertility of the earth against the god of the wind and rain. There were many gods in these stories, explained Sa'adeh, such as the god of wisdom, who preaches patience to his devotees and the need to accept fate. There was also Adon, or Adonis of the classic Phoenician pantheon of gods, who inspired people with enthusiasm for beauty and love. Sa'adeh then goes to great lengths to explain how the same Syrian stories and gods appear in the Old Testament with slightly altered names. This borrowing, he wrote, was similar to the Gilgamesh epic, which ended up in the story of the great flood and which was discovered in the library of the great Assyrian ruler, Athur Banipal, and subsequently reproduced in its entirety in the Old Testament. Sa'adeh also reminded his readers that many of these Syrian myths appear later in ancient Greek history. He reflected on the themes they dramatize, such as old age, youth, fatherhood, prophethood, love, hatred, wisdom, courage, justice, and ambition.[5]

Sa'adeh thus presented his readers with a picture of a full and complete ancient society that placed Syria at the center of the universe. The ancient civilization that he portrayed, based on the discoveries of Ras Shamra and other Syrian sites, was the mother of all civilizations, including that of the ancient Hebrews and the ancient Greeks. To Sa'adeh, then, Syria was the center of this Syrian world, not Palestine or Cyprus or Iraq. When he gave the Palestine question some thought, it was in the manner of a parent acknowledging responsibility for a problem child. Palestine was Syria's ward.

Sa'adeh's insight into the hopelessness of the Arab approach to the Palestine question, however, showed great understanding of the limits of patronization. These insights were explained by the party's ideologues in the 1980s with references to real-life incidents from that period. There were always two approaches to the Palestine question, he is said to have preached, that of the generalists and that of the isolationists. This meant that once Egypt adopted a position on the question of Palestine, Syria adopted another one, and so did Morocco, Lebanon, Jordan, and Iraq. The problem was generalized, and ultimate responsibility lay with all of these states. There were also the isolationists, who considered the Palestine issue the responsibility of the Palestinians themselves. Neither of these approaches was accurate, since both denied the Palestinians recourse to the power of the entire Syrian nation. For example, the party ideologues offered President Sadat's monopoly of the Palestine question as the worst example of the generalists' approach. But the Arab world was not justified in condemning the Camp David agreements, since every Arab state was expected to fashion its own policy. Similarly, if Damascus issued an opinion on Palestine, proponents of the isolationist school resorted to the weapon of "the independent Palestine will."

Sa'adeh, according to his followers, adopted a completely different approach. In a letter to his devotees dated November 2, 1947, he maintained that the Syrian nation alone enjoyed the natural legal right to determine the future of Palestine. This assertion eliminated Britain's right, as well as that of the Soviets and the Americans, to have the final say over Palestine. The work of the Arab League itself must also respect the principle of Syrian monopoly over this decision. The Arab League of States did not have the right to cancel the sovereignty of the Syrian people over their homeland. The first principle of this party's constitution read, "Syria is for the Syrians, and these are a complete nation"; the second principle stated, "The Syrian question is an independent national question, totally separate from any other issue."[6]

The question of Palestine belongs to the Syrian nation, argued Sa'adeh, just as the question of the Nile Delta belongs to Egypt and Casablanca belongs to the Maghreb. As long as all of Syria (or the Syrian Fertile Crescent) remains a part of the Arab world, and since the Syrian nation is an Arab nation, then it is the duty of all the Arab states to assist the Syrian nation in its endeavor to retrieve Palestine. This would lead to an Arab front, responsible for defending the entire Arab world against the forces of colonialism and occupation. As long as the Arab states did not sidestep the principle of the sovereignty of the Syrian nation over its own soil, wrote Sa'adeh, the Arab states were obligated to struggle for the liberation of Palestine.[7]

Sa'adeh's distinction as to when the Palestine question became the responsibility of all the Arab states and when it was the sole responsibility of the Syrian people provided room for critiquing the pan-Arabists. Writing in 1938 under the title of "Nationalist Racialist Philosophy," he commented on an article by the Syrian ideologue Zaki al-Arsuzi, then the president of the 'Usbat al-'Amal al Qawmi (League of National Action). This party, which still clung to Alexandretta, according to Sa'adeh, still adhered to the notion of the "Arab-Jewish genius." Arsuzi advocated the dangerous but amusing notion that Arabs and Jews should achieve a common understanding throughout the world in order to restore past Arab glories and resurrect the Semitic genius, which is an Arab-Jewish genius. All that the Jews needed to do, wrote Arsuzi, was abandon the notion of creating a national Zionist homeland in Palestine. Instead, they should ally themselves with the Arabs and demand that Britain grant Palestine its independence within a larger Arab alliance. This way, the Arabs would befriend the Jews and grant them equality so that they might cease to be treated like a minority and return to their original status as a people descended from Arab roots.

Sa'adeh, who was influenced by the German theories of the 1930s, sarcastically wondered whether Arsuzi's "unique" ideas, which had not crossed any Arab mind, were learned at the Sorbonne or whether they were the product of the genius of the League of National Action. Arsuzi could not bring himself to realize that Syrian and Jewish interests in Palestine were irreconcilable. Being of one Semitic origin, however, did not justify joining the two people together as one nationality, in Sa'adeh's mind. He also argued that Arsuzi was mistaken in his belief that granting the Jews full equality would solve the Palestine problem. Would Arsuzi then, asked Sa'adeh, open the door for the immigration of fifteen million Jews on the grounds that they were "Arabs"? Apparently, those advocating Arab nationalism, concluded Sa'adeh, were pursuing dangerous objectives.[8] Clearly, Sa'adeh rejected unification projects based on common descent and manifested by the use of one language.

Sa'adeh was also critical of Islamic projects to save Palestine, commenting wryly on an Islamic conference convened in Egypt to proclaim solidarity with Palestine. Why did Egypt suddenly change its stand on the Palestine question after having sent an official representative (Ahmad Lutfi al-Sayyid, president of the University of King Fu'ad) to participate in the opening ceremonies of the Hebrew University at Jerusalem? Did Egypt's statesmen and Egyptian public opinion suddenly discover the danger of unrestricted Zionist immigration to Palestine? The uncritical Syrian mind, according to Sa'adeh, did not express any surprise, but it should be realized that this sudden and serious attention to the question of southern

Syria was merely the result of the continuing struggle between the king and the Wafd Party. Egyptian interest was directed to this issue simply in order to remove the Wafd cabinet from power and strengthen the monarchy and its desire for the caliphate.[9]

In practical terms, however, the SSNP was involved in Palestinian events only minimally. Part of this limited presence was due to the fact that the party never seized power in Syria, Lebanon, or Palestine. When Saʿadeh was allowed to return to Syria in 1947, after a nine-year exile in Latin America, he was greeted by large throngs, including representatives of the party's branches at Jerusalem and Haifa.[10] According to the publications of the SSNP, the party's effort on behalf of southern Syria dated back to 1933, when Saʿadeh was invited to speak at the inauguration of the Palestinian students' house at the American University of Beirut. It was there that he first warned of the Jewish threat to southern Syria and called for a concrete campaign by the SSNP in Palestine. He also offered to cooperate with the mufti of Jerusalem in standing up to the Jewish menace, but the mufti's two centers of power, the Supreme Muslim Council and the Arab Higher Committee, rejected this offer. The SSNP was thus deprived of the opportunity to participate in planning for the 1936 Arab revolt in Palestine. The party, however, did participate in this revolt with a small contingent. Among its casualties was the famed commander Saʿid al-ʿAss.

In 1937 Saʿadeh penned a lengthy memorandum to the League of Nations objecting to the report of the Peel Commission on Palestine. He protested in the strongest of terms not only Peel's idea of the partition of Palestine but the detachment of southern Syria from the rest of the Syrian nation. In 1947 the party would have carried out the largest demonstration at Beirut on the anniversary of the Balfour Declaration were it not for the threats of the Lebanese police. But when the situation on the war front in Palestine began to deteriorate, the central office of the party authorized Adib Qaddourah, the military training chief, to coordinate with the Palestine Arab Higher Committee office at Beirut in order to send an SSNP contingent. The Palestine office turned this offer down, claiming that the Palestine effort did not consist of parties and neither did the Palestinian leadership deal with parties. But the SSNP did send a volunteer force, numbering in the hundreds, that played a large role in the defense of Safad.

The party suffered many casualties in the Palestine War, particularly in the Jerusalem, Haifa, and Acre areas. There was also a serious proposal to outfit a large company of SSNP volunteers if the Syrian army in Jerusalem was willing to provide weapons, but the deal fell through, apparently because of reluctance to arm the volunteers. When the Palestine War ended, the SSNP's branches in various Syrian and Lebanese cities provided a great deal of humanitarian assistance to the flood of Palestinian refugees entering Syria at the time. One of the party's most prominent Palestinian members, Comrade Fu'ad Nassar, and his mother, Sathej Nassar, volunteered in this war.[11]

Sa'adeh, his devotees always emphasized, never forgot Palestine, but he also never forgot Lebanon, Syria, Jordan, and Iraq, for all were part of the Syrian homeland. Palestine, therefore, was not the main focus of the SSNP but merely one issue of concern.[12] The party remained basically Syrian in outlook, particularly in its emphasis on the ancient religions of Syria. The party's greatest advantage was that it inherited a radicalized and disillusioned elite searching for the ideal state model with which to mobilize the populace. But the SSNP's main weakness was that it was constantly swimming against the current of pan-Arabism. Although the SSNP insisted that its vision of the ideal unity project of natural Syria was merely a step toward the ultimate unity of the Arab world, its vision did not prevail against the ideal of pan-Arabism.[13]

The Ba'th Party

The Ba'th was the second party to touch the hearts and minds of Syrians, as well as reach out to a wider Arab constituency. Although not the first to build its program around an ideal of pan-Arabism based on a shared history and a common language, the Ba'th genuinely transcended the boundaries of Greater Syria. Greatly indebted to Arsuzi's League of National Action, founded in 1933, the Ba'th was not limited to issues affecting only Syria and Lebanon. Officially organized as a national party in 1947, the Ba'th considered various ideas, such as the concept of regional nationalism represented at the time by the Nationalist Party. In the late 1940s and in the 1950s, the Ba'th was in a constant ideological confrontation with the Communist Party and the SSNP because of their de-emphasis of the idea of Arab unity. The party also challenged the Muslim Brotherhood's concept of a pan-Islamic ideal. In the 1940s, and in defense of pan-Arabism, the Ba'th declared that the party was committed to unity and constitutionalism but not necessarily to republicanism. The party, therefore, asserted the precedence of the national over the regional idea and favored Syria's "advancement" over Jordan's and Iraq's monarchic "backwardness."[14]

The Ba'th Party was opposed not only by the pragmatic current of regional nationalism, which defended the colonial boundaries of the First

World War settlement, but also by the gradualist approach to unity represented by the Arab League of States. Lacking a clear enunciation of the idea of Arab unity, the League's charter instead stipulated respect for the boundaries of its member states while promoting the idea of pragmatic cooperation in the economic, cultural, and educational spheres. The Ba'th, on the other hand, saw the League as a British-inspired design to contain, not promote, Arab unity. Furthermore, the Arab League represented the views of the Arab regimes while the Ba'th represented the Arab masses. The League, nevertheless, was tacitly tolerated until the unity with Egypt as an arena for the anti-Hashimite struggle that consumed Syria in the 1940s and 1950s.[15]

For the Palestinians, the Ba'th represented the greatest obstacle to their desire for self-direction. However, the Ba'th was also greatly affected by the loss of the Palestinian homeland. While it was still a revolutionary mass party, the Ba'th often proposed radical solutions to the Palestine question. In a May 7, 1947, editorial in *Al-Ba'th*, party leader Salah al-Din al-Bitar proposed that Arabs should not hesitate to use economic pressure against the West. Arab oil should not be sold to Western states until they were persuaded to change their Palestine policies. The Ba'th, which believed in the possibility of total unity among the Arab states, did not accept the idea of regional state control over the natural resources of any corner of the Arab world. Bitar also suggested a few days later that Syria should take itself out of the UN as a gesture of protest against the pro-Zionist policies of the world organization.[16]

Neither of these two ideas was novel. Both had been proposed by other groups to express their anger at the partitioning of Palestine and the UN abandonment of its Arab population. The Ba'th also saw in the loss of Arab Palestine the greatest incentive to the achievement of Arab unity. Palestine was the subject of a significant historical debate in the Syrian parliament during the March 28, 1945, session, which revolved around the rationale behind the Greater Syria plan and the relevance of this issue to Syria's proposed membership in the Arab League of States. According to one viewpoint, Palestine was a great motivator for unifying the Syrian lands and this unity carried within it an obligation to defend Palestine. Rejecting the Greater Syria plan, argued the same group, amounted to an abandonment of Palestine. Another viewpoint, which saw the Palestine question as a barrier to Syrian unity, argued that the realization of unity would open up the possibility of a Zionist takeover of all of natural Syria. Seen from this perspective, the Palestine issue was a source of great danger to Syria and must not be included in Greater Syria.

One advocate for the first viewpoint, Hilmi al-Atassi, the representative of Homs, charged that the Syrian government was using Palestine in order to defend other Arab lands, whereas the best means of standing up to the Zionists was to unify all of Syria. Akram Hourani, then a parliamentary deputy, supported Atassi's argument. When the charter of the Arab League of States came up for ratification, Hourani and another deputy offered a signed brief stating that the Syrian parliament reserved for itself the right to create a Greater Syrian homeland. Parliament did not recognize the British mandate system over Palestine, it read, since Palestine was considered a part of southern Syria. The counter viewpoint represented by the government was more subdued. A declaration by Prime Minister Faris al-Khouri merely stressed that the current situation in Palestine constituted an obstacle to the creation of Greater Syria. The premier implied that to unite with Palestine would expose the Syrian republic to a Zionist assault. But the government also held on to the vague notion, not yet officially adopted, that the Palestine issue constituted the greatest incentive to the creation of a united Arab state dedicated to repelling the Zionist threat. Thus, the rise of a hostile and foreign state in Palestine, in the midst of the Arab homeland, strengthened faith in the transitional nature of the Syrian republic. Total Arab unity was seen as the necessary second stage in this process of independence in order to face the postcolonial crisis of Zionism and Western imperialism.[17]

As was the case for the SSNP, the Ba'th saw in the first Palestine War an opportunity to increase its ranks and gain military experience for its members. The Ba'th also firmly believed in the Arab credentials of the Palestinian struggle. The party was involved in collecting funds, registering volunteers, and sending some of its most prominent members, such as Salah al-Din al-Bitar, Michel 'Aflaq, and Wahib al-Ghanim, to the Palestine front. When the Arabs lost the war, the Ba'th went on the offensive, pointing a finger at the regimes and their failure and at the consequences of relying on the UN. By the early 1950s, the Ba'th had achieved prominence as a political force in Syria, as well as in Jordan and Iraq. Branches of the party sprouted in most Arab countries. An ideological transformation was also noticeable by 1949, when the party adopted a strong position against unification with Arab monarchical regimes, defended Syria's republican tradition, and challenged advocates of greater Syrian unity such as the Hashimite regimes and the SSNP. After its merger with Akram Hourani's Arab Socialist Party, the Ba'th's role in Syrian politics was strengthened by Hourani's following in Hama.[18]

When the Ba'th gave up hope for achieving Arab unity within the framework of the Arab League summit meetings, the party began to advocate two alternate approaches to unification. The summits were found lacking because of their spirit of reconciliation, their conservative orientation, and regime-domination. The Ba'th mistrusted the domination of any regime, even that of Nasser. Two alternative strategies were developed and debated before and after the June 1967 War, emphasizing the people's struggle versus the formal, state-level efforts. The first of these ideas raised the slogan of the people's war of liberation and was probably influenced by the views of the second PLO, particularly the rise of Fateh and the concept of the armed struggle.

It should be remembered that Fateh generated a great deal of enthusiasm on all popular levels when it first appeared in Syria. The Ba'th regime, in power since 1963, favored a new Palestinian operative methodology and began to debate the new concept of liberation during the eighth annual congress of the national party. In the final report of the congress, the Ba'th defined commitment to Palestine as a commitment to its liberation, thereby distancing itself completely from the view of the Arab League and the various Arab regimes that called only for application of the UN partition resolution. The Ba'th report continued by asserting that the first and most essential instrument for liberating Palestine was the Palestinian people themselves, who should be organized and unfettered from their chains in order to do so. The report thus adopted Fateh's operative philosophy, which called for granting the Palestinians freedom of action within any Arab territory.

The Arab summits' approach to liberation was viewed as a continuation of the Arab League's traditional orientation and not a proper revolutionary method. With the Arab defeat of 1967, the anti-summit policy of the Ba'th became entrenched, as was clear from the ninth emergency congress in 1967 and the tenth congress in 1968. As has already been mentioned, the ninth congress was the first to debate the idea of a people's liberation struggle. Positions taken by these two congresses explain why the Syrian Ba'thist government declined to be represented on the presidential level at the Khartoum summit meeting of the Arab League and the Rabat summit meeting of September 1969.

The second alternative to the traditional summit meeting of heads of states, and the natural corollary to the people's war of liberation, was said to be the convening of a popular meeting for all the progressive Arab groups and regimes. This meant a meeting in other countries and within frameworks other than the Ba'th. This second alternative was described in the ninth emergency meeting of the national Ba'th Party, which finally acknowledged the revolutionary and progressive nature of the Egyptian regime. The ninth congress also called for a popular meeting of all progressive parties, movements, popular organizations, and professional associations in the Arab world, in order to work for the armed struggle on the level of the larger homeland. The fact that this meeting was never convened did not prevent successive party congresses from repeating this call.[19]

Within the realm of practical politics, opposition by the Ba'th to Palestinian nationalism was more emphatic than befits the ideals of the Ba'th Party. The main reason for this was that the so-called progressive Arab regimes expressed their interest in the Palestinian organizations of armed struggle by attempting to co-opt them. This approach contrasted with the policies of the traditional regimes toward the Palestinians, which sought to assimilate the refugees in their societies by providing them with increased work opportunities and with other economic and social benefits designed to discourage them from joining the new revolutionary organizations. Some progressive regimes, on the other hand, desired to contain and circumvent Palestinian activism by patronizing a Palestinian national and representative organization.

The first Arab progressive regime to establish this pattern was the Nasserite government, which created an official popular organization for the Palestinian people in the Gaza Strip and permitted the election of the first Palestinian legislative council. Thus, a quasi-government for the Palestinians emerged in Gaza in 1958, including a constitution and an executive council. Nasser followed this by pressuring the Arab League to sponsor a Palestinian framework so that the world would hear the voice of the Palestinians through their own representatives. By 1959 the political committee of the League issued a recommendation for the creation of a Palestinian army in the Arab states. Nasser's project faced some opposition from the backers of the Government of All Palestine, which by that time existed in name only. All of this changed with the 1964 Arab summit meeting, the first of the summits, in which Ahmad Shuqeiri was chosen to represent the Palestinians as the head of an Egyptian-and-League-sponsored organization. This represented the epitome of Arab co-optation and containment.[20]

The Arab Ba'th Party responded to these developments by issuing on May 20, 1964, a statement titled "The Proposed Palestinian Framework" (Mashrou' al-Kiyan al-Filistini), which explained the party's nationalist perspective on the Palestine issue and the ideal manner of creating a Palestinian framework, on the principles it should represent, and on the makeup of its institutions. The statement emphasized that the new framework recently approved by Arab kings and presidents was neither new nor accidental. The idea of creating such a Palestinian framework was born at the time of the *nakba* (the Arabic term for disaster, or the loss of Palestine) and was nurtured by the revolutionary experience of Algeria. The idea then forced itself on the Arab governments until it emerged as a collective decision. But the Ba'th insisted that for any such framework to become a real entity leading to the formation of a state, the three conditions of real statehood must first be met: land, people, and sovereignty.[21]

Expressing further skepticism about Shuqeiri's PLO, the National Command Council of the Ba'th Party issued an additional declaration on May 15, 1965, in which it discussed its fears that the new organization could come to embody all the contradictions of the Arab summit meetings. Michel 'Aflaq added in a meeting on June 21, 1964, that the party's own proposal for a Palestinian framework was not merely a tactical maneuver but represented its assessment of the best means of preparing the Palestinians for the liberation battle. He denied that the party's emphasis on the issue of Palestinian sovereignty over their own land was intended to embarrass the governments of Egypt and Jordan. The party recognized the complexity of realizing this condition but also insisted that it be met before Shuqeiri's project could be taken seriously. Revolutionary honesty demanded that the Ba'th provide this critique of "Shuqeiri's project," as 'Aflaq referred to it, in order to demonstrate that this framework was no more than the outcome of a compromise between different Arab governments. 'Aflaq insisted that the only way to realize the project of a Palestinian framework was to establish the Ba'th revolution in Syria and other countries.[22]

'Aflaq's commitment to the Palestine cause led to the creation of a special section within the Ba'th for its Palestinian members in order for them to carry out the task of Palestinian liberation. All parties, with the exception of the Nasserite and the Communist parties, followed this pattern. But all Palestinian activity within the ranks of the Ba'th Party was under the control of the Ba'th leadership. This design was intended to prevent any deviation by an organization like the PLO, which, posing as the representative of all Palestinians, had the potential to attract fellow Palestinians irrespective of their political affiliation. Therefore, a special section within the Ba'th came into being and was known as the Branch of Palestinian Action, which specialized in mobilizing the Palestinian masses.

Lutfi al-Khouli, a veteran Egyptian progressive journalist, reported that Nasser had received a suggestion to organize a Palestinian project exactly along Ba'thist lines. This information came from Amin Howaidi, the former Egyptian Minister of Defense and intelligence chief, who claimed that he was asked to set up a meeting between Nasser and the the late Dr. 'Issam Sartawi in late 1963. Sartawi apparently proposed to Nasser the creation of a Nasser-supported Palestine liberation front that would pursue the armed struggle under Nasser's direct control. Nasser professed willingness to support any Palestinian initiative to liberate their land as long as the effort avoided becoming entangled in inter-Arab disputes. Nasser added that he had actually considered for some time inviting Palestinians to create their own organization. His final advice to Sartawi was to avoid splintering into competing groups. But it should be noted that, in the case of the Ba'th, the party feared the rise of independent Palestinian organizations so much that it labeled all of its Palestinian followers who quit the party as "separatists." The Ba'th also made a serious attempt to infiltrate Fateh by planting several Ba'thist cadres within its ranks, but this plan failed.[23]

The Arab Nationalist Movement

Perhaps the richest experience of a group bridging Arab and Palestinian nationalism was that of the Arab Nationalist Movement (Harakat al-Qawmiyeen al-'Arab). Until recently, this movement received scant scholarly attention because of its frequent ideological transformations. Several of its founding leaders eventually left the movement and denied any links to it, only to form other, more narrow and ideologically defined fronts and parties. Two factors contributed to the emergence of the Arab Nationalist Movement: the ideological ferment among the student circles at the American University of Beirut (AUB) during the late 1940s and early 1950s, and the loss of Arab Palestine as a result of the failure of the Arab armies in the first Palestine War. The movement was responsible for accelerated attacks on the traditional regimes, and it gained political mileage during the period of despair and disgust following the events of 1948. The ANM was also among the first in the Arab world to rationalize the use of violence as the language of political revolutionary rejectionists. No other movement, not even the Ba'th, reached all corners of the Arab world as did the ANM. At one time its activities contributed to regime disturbances in Yemen, Jordan, and Iraq. The movement's importance, in a sense, was its role as the fountainhead of most contemporary Arab nationalist and Palestinian movements. It focused on all Arab national questions and envisaged a struggle in two stages: the first to overcome the forces of imperialism and Zionism in order to create a unified Arab state, and the second to achieve democratic Arab socialism. Though heavily Palestinian, the ANM was joined by Arab activists from a variety of countries.[24]

The earliest manifestation of the ANM was a shadowy group known as Kata'ib al-Fida' al-'Arabi, which appeared as a direct response to *al-Nakba*. What distinguished al-Kata'ib was its open reliance on violence. Al-Kata'ib first came to the attention of Syrian authorities with its failed attempt on the life of Adib al-Shishakly in 1950, when he was the deputy chief of the Syrian armed forces. Most of those involved in the plot were young men in their twenties who had experienced the first Palestine War through participation in the Salvation Army. Apparently, when the war ended, several political groups began to surface in order to respond to the defeat, among them a Beirut-based group headed by George Habash and Hani al-Hindi, a Syrian-based group led by Jihad Dhahi, and a group of Egyptian political exiles led by Hussein Tawfiq. The three groups met in Beirut in March 1949 and created al-Kata'ib, an organization dedicated to punishing those responsible for the Arab defeat. A debate ensued among the various groups concerning the role of violence in the national struggle and the possible targets of that struggle. According to most accounts, the Beirut group led by Habash was reluctant to sanction an all-out campaign of violence and emphasized the role of political education and mass participation in the organization's activities. The Egyptian group, on the other hand, opted for the sole use of violence and was eventually persuaded by some Syrian activists to target not only Shishakly but also Akram Hourani for assassination.[25]

The elite nature of this early nucleus of the ANM and the inter-Arab character of its leaders should be noted. This was truly an intelligentsia dedicated to revolutionary politics. Hindi was a Syrian whose father was Lt. Col. Mahmoud al-Hindi, who, as one of King Faisal's Syrian officers, followed the monarch to Baghdad. Hani was born in Iraq in 1927, where he was greatly influenced by his father's involvement in the secret organization of Younis al-Sab'awi and the defense of Baghdad in 1941 against British efforts to retake the city. After being discharged from the Iraqi armed forces, the senior al-Hindi returned to Syria, where his son received an elite education. Hani studied at private schools in Lebanon and the American College of Aleppo, where he met Dhahi, and eventually at AUB, where he concentrated on political science. Dhahi, on the other hand, was a law student at Syrian University, and hailed from a Greek Orthodox family from near Homs. According to recent studies, his baptismal name was 'Abd al-Masih, but he changed it to Jihad when he converted to Islam in 1945. His conversion was more out of patriotic considerations than anything else since he was inspired by Michel 'Aflaq's presentation of the life of the Prophet Muhammad as a truly Arab experience. When Dhahi met al-Hindi at the Aleppo American College, the two became the center of a group of students imitating the nationalist pro-German unity students of the nineteenth-century, mixing romance and patriotism and revolutionary action. Dhahi, for instance, was involved in an assassination attempt against a French officer in 1945, and was greatly influenced by the writings of Nietzsche.

George Habash, perhaps the most influential Arab nationalist and revolutionary figure of the twentieth century, was the son of a prosperous Palestinian merchant from the town of Lyddah. At the time of the founding of al-Kata'ib, Habash had already concluded his medical studies at AUB. The Egyptian group was equally revolutionary and elitist in background, but was distinguished from the others by its actual experience of revolutionary activity. With the exception of Hussein Tawfiq, all members of this Syrian-based group of exiles had belonged at one time to Misr al-Fatah, a neo-Nazi party. Misr al-Fatah first surfaced in Egypt following the signing of the Anglo-Egyptian Treaty of 1938, as a protest against the policies of the dominant Wafd Party. Three members of the "Green Shirts," Misr al-Fatah's militarized youth organization, were imprisoned for throwing hand grenades against the British Officers' Club of Alexandria. The three fled to Syria, where they joined the Salvation Army to fight in Palestine. Their leader was Hussein Tawfiq, the son of Egyptian deputy minister of defense Tawfiq Ahmad Pasha, who fled to Syria after being implicated in the assassination of the Wafdist Minister of Finance, Amin 'Othman, in 1946. The Egyptians who carried out the attempt on Shishaskli's life were interested in action and contemptuous of attending lectures like the rest of the members. Through the help of some Syrian intelligence groups, the Egyptians were able to organize underground cells in order to "behead the traitors" who had lost Palestine. They succeeded in recruiting Iraqis, as well as Palestinians and Syrians, to their organization.[26]

Habash was to admit later on that although he was not opposed to punishing the traitors, he was mystified by the targeting of Shishakli. Habash had already participated in grenade attacks on some embassies and had plotted the assassination of both John B. Glubb Pasha, chief of Jordan's Arab Legion, and Iraqi premier Nouri al-Sa'id.[27] Shishakly was apparently targeted more by Syrian intelligence than by the angry Egyptian exiles.

The ANM was also greatly influenced by the nationalist atmosphere at AUB and the early student activism within an organization known as al-'Urwah al-Wuthqa. Founded as a cultural club, al-'Urwah catered to the needs of students from various Arab countries. It became famous as a laboratory for the principles of Arab nationalism through the work of its advisor, Professor Qustantin Zureiq, who acquired a reputation as one of the leading ideologues of Arab nationalism with his pioneering work *Al-Wa'ii al-Qawmi* (National Consciousness), published in 1939. The university became the center of intellectual ferment through the gathering of the best minds on its campus and the relative intellectual freedom enjoyed by Beirut.

It has been said that at first Zureiq hand-picked the members of his club. He believed in the role of the elite in modern societies and viewed himself as a guide and a nurturer of a new Arab nationalist generation. He had been an activist of sorts in the 1920s, when he organized Jama'at al-Qawmiyeen al-'Arab, which in turn inspired such groups as Hizb Filastin al-'Arabi and 'Usbat al-'Amal al-Qawmi. Zureiq regarded al-'Urwah as a new nationalist effort for the post–Second World War period. Following the first Palestine War, he had openly called for the creation of an Arab nationalist party and encouraged debates between his followers and members of other parties. Zureiq was particularly interested in seeing his students debate the ideas of Sati' al-Husri and Michel 'Aflaq.[28]

During the early 1940s, Zureiq's nationalist group was greatly influenced by German theories of nationalism, believing that every nation has specific characteristics. The Arab nation was said to have a special mission in the world, a Zureiq idea that influenced 'Aflaq. Since the Arabs were segmented and denied the life of a normal nation, Zureiq felt the need to study the European experience of unification, particularly that of Germany and Italy, by looking at the careers of Bismarck, Garibaldi, and Mazzini. His group also studied the thoughts of Fichte, Spengler, and Bergson and was highly interested in the comparative study of nationalism. At AUB, Zureiq's lectures on nationalism paralleled those of another Arab nationalist, Nabih Amin Faris.

It is reported that Habash, who was the president of al-'Urwah, discussed the founding of a secret revolutionary society with Zureiq, but was discouraged by the latter, who appeared to his followers to be more of a reformist than a revolutionary. But Zureiq's rejection of an underground organization along the lines of nineteenth-century German student groups could not stop the revolutionary trend from moving in the direction of a secret society after the Palestine War. Zureiq himself felt deeply the agony and humiliation of the 1948 defeat when he published his famous work *Ma'na al-Nakba* (The Meaning of the Disaster) and coined the term *nakba* for succeeding Arab generations. In this seminal work, Zureiq predicted that the battle against Zionism would be a long one and that the key to its success was to change the political picture of the Arab world and produce a complete radical transformation in the way people thought, worked, and lived. His book was a call to modernize the Arab world. But when the lectures of al-'Urwah al-Wuthqa turned to discussions about the armed struggle, the university protested.[29]

After Zureiq's rejection of the violent ideas of some of his student followers, these same students failed to infiltrate the traditional political parties, such as al-Ba'th. Habash's first reaction to al-Ba'th was that it approximated a cultural and political club more than a genuine party because of its different wings and currents. Habash protested the Ba'th's lack of interest in becoming an iron-fisted socialist organization. He suggested to 'Aflaq that Kata'ib al-Fida' become the military wing of the Ba'th Party, but 'Aflaq refused to work with the guerrilla organization and would only agree to work with its individual members. Therefore, some of the Kata'ib members joined the Ba'th while others drifted away to found a new organization known as the Arab Nationalist Movement.[30] Habash also felt that the Ba'th did not give priority to the question of Arab unity, was predisposed to parliamentarism, engaged in hero worship (such as 'Aflaq), and saw the Ba'th Party as an end in itself. The disbanded al-Kata'ib members also tried to dialogue with the SSNP but rejected its ideology as a dangerous distraction from the idea of total Arab unity. Dialogues with the communists also faltered because of the latter's acceptance of the UN partition resolution on Palestine.[31]

It is important at this point to trace the origins of the ideas of armed struggle and revolutionary violence since they came to dominate the ideology of the ANM and, later, that of all the Palestinian guerrilla organizations. It should also be reiterated here that Qustantin Zureiq's relationship to the Kata'ib was no more than that of a guide rather than a formal organizational one. Habash and his associates continued to look to his ideas on Arab nationalism as the foundation for their own ideology, and they made his two books, *Al-Wa'ii al-Qawmi* and *Ma'na al-Nakba,* as well as Sati' al-Husri's works, required reading for all new recruits. Thus, as one writer put it, Zureiq was never to this organization what Sa'adeh was to the SSNP and 'Aflaq to the Ba'th. Zureiq's role could only be compared to Arsuzi's in the Ba'th. The ideas about violence should be attributed to the Lebanese Druze activist 'Ali Nasser al-Din, who was invited to lecture at al-ʿUrwah al-Wuthqa in April 1951 and delivered his famous lecture titled "Revenge, or Erasing Shame" (Al-thaʾr aw mahwi al-ʿaar). By the time Habash's secret group issued its second leaflet at the end of 1952, it had already adopted the slogan "Unity, Liberation, Revenge." Nasser al-Din was invited to Amman in 1954 to be present at the birth of the ANM, which translated his ideas from theory to action.

Nasser al-Din enjoyed a background typical of that of the early generation of pan-Arabists. He was born in 1892 and shared the dream of the Arab revolt of 1916 with those of his Arab generation. He rallied to King Faisal's side, first in Syria and then in Iraq, and used to refer to him as "the great Faisal." After Iraq achieved its independence and was admitted to the League of Nations in 1932, Nasser al-Din and others of his generation saw Iraq as the regional base for the realization of Arab unity. Iraq was considered capable of performing the role of Prussia in the German unification. This led to the founding of the League of National Action in 1933, in which Nasser al-Din participated. He founded the Lebanese branch of Arsuzi's organization in 1936, and continued to guide its affairs during the early years of Lebanon's independence until the early 1950s. He also served a long prison sentence when French authorities accused him of Nazism, as they did to all the pan-Arabists.[32]

Nasser al-Din impressed upon the nationalists the need to organize as an ideological society in the form of a cell or as a kind of fraternal order. This was to be a society of believers, keeping watch over the nationalist ideal. Members of the cell should maintain high standards of behavior and be dedicated to the nationalist struggle, denying themselves all diversions, even watching a movie. This puritanical behavior was, in the eyes of the movement, what distinguished them from the Baʿth. The society should also boycott foreign goods, and stage a popular campaign on behalf of this idea as a demonstration of its antipathy toward Westerners.

In his famous "Revenge, or Erasing Shame" speech, Nasser al-Din said that he had resolved following *al-Nakba* never to lecture, write, or attend a meeting unless it concerned a serious discussion of how to erase shame. This shame had been attached to the Arabs by other Arabs even before the British, Americans, and Zionists had imposed it on them, and he believed that erasing it must come before any reform or any progress to which Arabs aspired. And what could erase this shame, he asked. Was it an amended constitution in some corner of the Arab world, an increased share in the oil windfall somewhere, an amended or canceled treaty, or profitable new commercial or cultural pacts with foreign countries? Would the Arabs' shame be erased through the construction of another royal palace, another port, another university, or through a lavish banquet demonstrating the Arab tradition of hospitality? Would it be erased by delivering another bombastic speech? Would it be erased by the creation of a new state (a reference to Libya) without the participation of its courageous sons? None of these erases the shame, he concluded. Even if all the Arabs united in a single state or succeeded in convincing General Franco of Spain to restore to them al-Andalus (Andalusia), this would not erase the shame.[33] He concluded, "Only one thing would erase our shame, nothing would do that except for revenge. . . . Even if the UN through a heavenly miracle decided to apply its laws concerning the right of people to liberty, independence, and dignity, . . . do you think that our shame would be erased? No, because a shame of this kind . . . will not be erased . . . except by those who endured it."[34]

Nasser al-Din asserted that there was only one law that justified, and even sanctioned, revenge. This was a "law unwritten on paper, but etched on skulls and on the bones of the chest. It is the law of national honor . . . which is a fact of human honor."[35] Among his recommendations was the creation of a national draft in all the Arab countries and the conscription of the sons of the refugees into these armies. Each state should support and sustain refugee families within its borders. He also advocated that all Arabs—youths and children, men and women—should be indoctrinated so that they would never forget Palestine, just as the French had taught their children never to forget Alsace-Lorraine. And even if the United Nations was able to facilitate the return of some or all of the refugees to Palestine, this would not be the same as if the Arabs had regained Palestine, or had erased the shame. On the contrary, the UN action would mean only that the Arabs had acquiesced in the rape of Palestine, which would only increase their shame. Nasser al-Din stressed that only when the Arabs themselves restored Palestine would shame be erased through revenge.[36]

The Arab Nationalist Movement went through three distinct intellectual phases before splintering into separate groups. During the first of these, which began in 1951, the movement was dominated by the ideas of pure or idealistic nationalism. The second phase, during which the movement spread throughout the Arab world, nationalism was defined along Nasserite lines as socialist nationalism, or Arab socialism. In the third phase, which was preoccupied with internal struggles and factionalism, the movement finally adopted Marxism-Leninism. During the first phase, the movement was influenced by the ideas and writings of Zureiq, al-Husri, and Nasser al-Din whose most influential book was *Qhadhiyat al-'Arab* (The Arab Question). In its second phase, the movement adopted

Nasserite thought exemplified by Nasser's works, beginning with *Egypt's Liberation,* and accepted most but not all of his ideas. The third phase, its most divisive, was dominated by disputes over different forms of socialism and reasons for the 1967 Arab defeat. The movement was influenced by ideas of the new left and revolutionary violence as embodied in the new African, Asian, and Latin American revolutions.[37]

When the movement turned from planning to the building stage, it accomplished three steps. The movement succeeded in dominating al-'Urwah al-Wuthqa Club in Lebanon, organized through the effort of Ahmad al-Khatib. The latter was also credited with establishing the prestigious al-Nadi al-Thaqafi al-Qawmi (the National Cultural Club) in Kuwait. At the same time, George Habash and Wadi' Haddad set up medical practice in Amman. By offering free medical services, the two were able to mobilize the residents of the camps and organize the Committee to Resist Peace with Israel, as well as publish their bulletin, *Al-Tha'r* (Revenge). Small cells were then organized from among the refugees and infiltrated into the occupied territories to carry out attacks against the enemy, only to be frustrated by the military response of Glubb Pasha and the Jordanian army.

Two other Arab nationalist groups emerged in Jordan at the same time. One was led by Dr. Salah 'Anabtawi and other Zureiq students; it was organized in the Jordanian-ruled West Bank for the purpose of resisting the Jordan water scheme of Eric Johnston. The other was led by Hamad al-Farhan, an East Jordanian graduate of AUB and London University. It operated in the East Bank and was determined to end the Anglo-Jordanian agreement that defined Jordan's independence. Other scions of bourgeois families who participated in Habash's and Farhan's groups included 'Ali Mango and Nizar Jardaneh. Eventually, the two groups merged in 1953 as the Amman branch of the ANM, while 'Anabtawi's group became located in Gaza. The group's publication, *Al-Ra'ii,* began to publish severe attacks against the Baghdad Pact and Britain's domination of Jordan and called repeatedly for the expulsion of Glubb from Jordan and the cancellation of the treaty with Britain. *Al-Ra'ii* was muzzled by the authorities in 1955 but managed to appear at Damascus. By 1954 Habash called for a secret organizational meeting at Amman, which was also attended by Al-Hakam Darwaza (Palestinian), Mustafa Baydhoun (Lebanese), Thabet al-Mahayni (Syrian), Muhammad Zayyat (Lebanese), and 'Umar Fadhel (a Moroccan living in the Cameroons).[38]

The most important item on the agenda was the proposed Iraqi-Syrian union declared in 1954 by Fadhel al-Jamali, the Iraqi Prime Minister, in anticipation of Shishakli's imminent fall from power. This was one of the most serious Iraqi unity projects offered for discussion at the Arab League. The proposal entailed a federal union to be achieved in stages, beginning with Iraq, Syria, Jordan, and a unified army financed by Iraq's petroleum assets. The union was strenuously opposed by the Riyadh-Cairo axis as another Fertile Crescent scheme to fortify British influence in the Arab world. 'Ali Nasser al-Din urged that the movement come out in support of the project as the necessary cornerstone of any unified Arab state. He was able to persuade the meeting that this union, even if it was "a union of crowns," should be supported despite its political orientation. Thus, *Al-Ra'ii*, the movement's publication, published several articles in April and May calling for support for this project. The conference also tacitly approved the slogan of "Freedom, Unity, and Revenge," thereby distinguishing itself from the Ba'th by giving precedence to the liberation of Palestine and upholding the principle of the armed struggle. In addition, the conference adopted a plan to establish branches for the movement throughout the Arab world. Thus, the members dispersed to various Arab countries to establish new affiliates, the most important being the Kuwaiti section established by AUB graduate Ahmad al-Khatib, which was to have a great impact on the Arab Gulf countries and on the Arabian Peninsula.[39]

Among the most crucial activities of the movement was the creation in 1952 of the Committee to Resist Peace with Israel, which specialized in the mobilization of the refugee camps. The committee was also able to reach students through this effort and to recruit them as organizers in the camps. Among these were Abu-Maher al-Yamani, who later became a member of the political office of the PFLP, and Abu-'Adnan Qays, future member of the political office of the PDFLP. The committee called for drafting the refugees and the Arabs of Palestine, at first avoiding the term "the Palestinian People" because of its regionalist implications. It was suggested that the refugees be placed in special camps or colonies along Israel's borders, and the committee called upon them to elect their own representatives and create their own committees. By 1956 a special refugees conference was held with representatives from the various camps, and it called for condemnation of the Johnston Jordan River plan, the removal of travel restrictions for the refugees, and the tightening of the Arab boycott against Israel. The conference also called on the refugees to boycott UNRWA (UN Relief and Works Agency, created in 1948 to aid the refugees) and decline its services, except for humanitarian aid.[40]

During its first phase, the movement avoided being designated as a political party until the breakup of the UAR in 1961. The movement condemned the entire experience of party life in the Arab East, which explains why they preferred the term "movement" or "organization" to "party" until as late as 1958. One explanation for this stand was that the ANM developed in the general context of Nasserite ideology, which de-emphasized parties. Thus, it was not surprising that some of the movement's leaders recommended seriously in 1958 that the "movement" should be disbanded since its objectives had been achieved through Nasserism and the UAR. This negativism toward parties was also due to the movement's concept of the nation as a single cohesive body. The movement viewed itself as a group with a mission or a national iron guard (or the military shield of the nation), while the parties were seen as traditional groups dedicated to professional politics. Although the movement later became involved in parliamentary politics (in Jordan in 1956, in Lebanon in 1960, and in Kuwait in 1962), it continued to excuse this deviation as simply participation in outward or superficial institutions.[41]

The ANM and Nasser

The most revealing example of the movement's antipathy to party politics was its relationship to Nasserism. In order to understand how the ideology of the movement shifted from a fixation on Iraq to an obsession with Egypt, it is necessary to assess the political weight and numerical strength of the movement in the 1950s. As Nasserism reached the apex of pan-Arabist politics following the Suez War and the creation of the UAR, the ANM appeared weak and marginalized. It operated only in Jordan and Kuwait. It is estimated that the membership of the Syrian branch until 1960 was anywhere from 15 to 50; apparently the branch was almost disbanded. At the time of the revolution of July 1958, the Iraqi branch of the movement numbered around 20 to 27. In Lebanon the ANM was an extension of Palestinian political life. In Egypt the movement was composed entirely of a limited student group called Al-Qawmiyoun (The Nationalists). It was made up of students expelled from AUB in 1954 and 1955, who later superimposed themselves on the Union of Kuwaiti Scholarship Students. The secrecy and limited membership of the movement forced some to advocate the recruitment of workers, peasants, and soldiers in order to escape the limitations of a student organization.[42]

Following the defeat of the tripartite Suez attack on Egypt, the movement held a meeting at Beirut on December 25, 1956, to organize a national leadership to guide Arab nationalist youths. It was then that the movement adopted the slogan "the unity of Egypt, Syria, and Jordan," thereby discarding its historic slogan upholding "the unity of Iraq, Syria, and Jordan." By that time, the infatuation of the movement with the Iraqi region (*iqleem*) as a base for the realization of Arab unity had faded. But the centrality of Iraq to this vision lingered on, which explains why Habash insisted on maintaining the movement's organizational independence from Nasserism, to which he referred as "the official leadership of the Arab revolution."

The obsession of the movement with Iraq as the Prussia of the Arabs can be traced to the 1930s and 1940s, when all the nationalist circles of the Arab intelligentsia adopted this idea, ranging from the League of National Action to al-Ba'th. Not only did these two parties in their early phase display the flag of the Great Arab Revolt of 1916, but the Ba'th itself first appeared in 1941 under the name of Harakat Nassret al-Iraq (the Movement to Champion Iraq). King Faisal I of Iraq was referred to by the Ba'th and the movement as the Bismarck of the Arabs. Also, Kata'ib al-Fida' al-'Arabi was said to have plotted the assassination of Hourani because of his determined opposition to plans for the union of Syria and Iraq.[43]

By Habash's own estimation, the movement remained a vanguard of Arab nationalism rather than a genuine political organization until the Egyptian-Syrian union of 1958. During its second phase, however, the movement changed into a populous political organization with a strategy that was compatible with that of Nasser. Apparently, what helped in the popular mobilization throughout the Arab world was the fact that most Arabs were Nasserite in orientation. But since Nasser had no political party outside of Egypt, the movement founded a nucleus in Southern Yemen, having participated in the revolution that led to the creation of this republic. Soon after, another small group was founded in Northern Yemen; then branches of the movement sprouted in Libya, the Sudan, and in Bahrain. In Syria, the movement benefited from its warm relationship with the UAR and 'Abd al-Hamid al-Sarraj, the security chief of the Northern Province. But because of its close ties to the government of the UAR in Syria, the movement, according to Habash, became aware of some pitfalls in the Nasserite experiment. The movement refrained from public criticism of Nasser in order to offset the separatist current.

After 1961 the movement continued to agitate for the reunification of the two UAR provinces. This stand, naturally, disrupted relations with the Ba'th and the Syrian Communist Party. Indeed, the movement was able to maintain direct channels to Nasser after the separation because of its proven loyalty. Before that, the movement's contacts were with Sarraj and Vice-President 'Abd al-Hakim 'Amir; but after the separation representatives of the movement, such as Muhsin Ibrahim and others, were able to meet Nasser personally and level serious charges against the experience of unification. When the tripartite unity talks between 'Aref's Iraq, Syria, and Egypt began in 1965, Hani al-Hindi participated as a member of the Syrian delegation. Habash was in hiding until early 1964 because of his alleged involvement in the Jasem 'Alwan coup attempt to restore the unity of Syria and Egypt.[44]

Despite the close identification of the movement with Nasserism, the ANM never seriously considered infiltrating the military as the Ba'th had. Habash had contended all along that he was not interested in backing one more failed coup attempt in Syria. Indeed, the movement hesitated to support the July 23, 1952, coup in Egypt until it was proven that it was a revolution and not merely a coup. Habash conceded, however, that after a while the movement recognized that its neglect of the military institution was a mistake. Habash always believed that change could only come about through the use of force, but he also held the view that total reliance on the military institution would inevitably change the nature of the movement during its formative stage. The movement's disassociation from the military thus forced it to be more dependent on the Nasserite regime. But the close relationship with Egypt, which always supplied training facilities for the ANM fighters, was ruptured after the Arab defeat of 1967. The movement did achieve some presence later on in the Iraqi army, and Nayef Hawatmah used to contend that only in Iraq after 1959 did the movement succeed in combining party, popular, and military activity.[45]

Habash, who began in 1964 to meet personally with Nasser every three or four months, had ample opportunity to assess Nasser's views on the Palestine struggle. Nasser was eager to help the ANM in its role as a supporter of the liberation struggles in the southern Arabian Peninsula, but he cautioned that since the United States was always behind Israel, any confrontation with the Zionists would need careful preparation. During Habash's first meeting with Nasser after the 1967 defeat, Habash lectured Nasser on the significance of supporting the Palestinian armed struggle and a people's war of liberation. But despite Nasser's cautious stand on this issue, Habash began to notice a wave of questioning and skepticism in the refugee camps following the breakup of the UAR. Palestinians were disillusioned with the practical outcome of pan-Arabism and were searching for the appropriate Palestinian organization to express their uncertainty and fear. Habash also could not fail to notice that between 1961 and 1962, around 36 Palestinian organizations came to the forefront, not including the PFLP and Fateh. Political groups who were fixated on Arab nationalism received a powerful jolt. The challenge to the ANM was whether to continue addressing the Palestinian question through the Arab nationalist struggle or to revise the strategy of the movement by creating a special niche for this issue within its wider program. Since the Palestinian armed struggle was not yet an option, Habash dealt with this issue organizationally. Thus, Palestinian members of the movement in the Lebanese, Kuwaiti, and Syrian branches were grouped in a new sector in order to begin laying the intellectual groundwork for future military activity. By 1964 some units of the movement began to mount guerrilla attacks in the Galilee and suffered their first casualty, an Egyptian-trained fighter referred to as "the martyr Khaled."[46]

Palestinian activity within the movement widened considerably after the Arab defeat of 1967, and a special command, including the five guerrilla sections operating in the Palestinian arena, began to coordinate strategy. These four were Fateh, the Syrian-trained Sa'iqa, Jibril's Front for the Liberation of Palestine, and the Youths of Revenge (Shabab al-Tha'r), which was an arm of the movement. Fateh attempted to lead this new formation, while Dr. Wadi' Haddad, another AUB intellectual, led the negotiations on behalf of the movement. The ANM succeeded in unifying Jibril's group, the Youths of Revenge, and another military unit of their own, the Heroes of Return (Abtal al-'Awdah), which became the PFLP on December 10, 1967. Within a short period of time, however, Ahmad Jibril and some independents pulled out because of organizational differences and because the Jordanian independents resented Habash's determined opposition to the Jordanian regime. The PDFLP, however, split from the PFLP in 1969 for purely ideological reasons. Nayef Hawatmah argued that the PFLP should not join hands with the PLO, which was a bourgeois organization led by a traditional and rightist leadership. Habash complained later that this group was to the left of Mao Zedong by a hundred meters and always indulged itself by mounting written attacks against the Soviet Union. Another group to emerge from the ANM in 1969 was the Organization of Lebanese Socialists, led by Muhsin Ibrahim and Muhammad Kishli.[47]

The metamorphosis of the ANM came as a result of the last break with Nasser. The confrontation with Nasser began as a serious dispute over the ANM's operations in South Yemen and attempts by Egyptian intelligence services to recruit Yemenis to pan-Nasserism. This led to a total withdrawal of the movement from the Nasserite front in Yemen following the disintegration of the UAR. The dispute with Egypt simmered until the final denouement of 1967, which confirmed the earlier and growing disillusionment of the ANM. In examining the causes of Nasserite failure, first in Syria and later in the 1967 War, the ANM turned to class analysis and began moving in a Leninist-Marxist direction. Some ANM members were beginning to describe Nasserism as a movement of the petite bourgeoisie and as such not capable of carrying out an extended struggle. The ANM began to argue the necessity of shifting the leadership of the movement to the laboring class, who were more capable of sustaining a prolonged struggle. By the end of 1969, the movement renamed itself the Arab Socialist Labor Party (Hizb al-'Amal al'Ishtiraki al-'Arabi) under Habash's leadership. The party disintegrated shortly thereafter as a result of disputes between members of its Jordanian and Palestinian "wings." But since all currents within the movement professed Marxism, it is difficult to explain the causes of the final split, except in terms of strategic differences over the timetable of the Arab and Palestinian struggle.[48]

Shuqeiri's Balancing Act

Nasser's involvement with Palestinian activists transcended his backing of the ANM. It is a tribute to Nasser's flexibility that he supported an official Palestinian movement under Shuqeiri's leadership while at the same time supporting the ANM and its Palestinian agenda. It is clear that Shuqeiri was chosen in order to co-opt the Palestinian popular current, but at the same time Shuqeiri's own ideological position was solely responsible for attracting numerous Palestinian organizations to his side. Groups such as the General Union of Palestinian Students and the General Union of Palestinian Women joined the PLO in 1965. The Union of Palestinian Writers followed in 1966. Shuqeiri also moved quickly to organize Palestinian military units and stationed them in Syria, Iraq, and Gaza, to be collectively known as the Palestine Liberation Army.[49]

Shuqeiri, however, was also aware of the rising tide of popular Palestinian organizations and the call for the armed struggle. He asked the ANM to organize a guerrilla arm of the regular Palestine Liberation Army, which came into being as a group called Abtal al-'Awdah, the Heroes of Return.[50] But Shuqeiri was generally mistrustful of guerrilla organizations. He attacked Fateh as an organization that could only serve the enemies of Palestinian liberation.[51] Shuqeiri's suspicion of organizations devoted exclusively to Palestinian liberation was understandable, however, in view of his overarching ideology. If Habash and the ANM represented the powerful current of pan-Arabism, Shuqeiri occupied a position midway between pan-Arabism and Palestinian nationalism. A transitional figure, he struggled much of his life to reconcile his commitment to Palestine with his devotion to the Arab idea. For a while he succeeded admirably in satisfying both commitments and sounded at times as though he partook of the ideology of the ANM.

Shuqeiri differed from the ANM in that he made Palestine the raison d'être of the unified Arab state. Palestine tests the devotion of the nationalists to their cause, he wrote, as Zionist ideology was able to challenge Arab objectives and desires. After all, Zionism appeared as one last link in the chain of Western aggression against the Arab world. As a result of these acts of aggression, Shuqeiri wrote, each liberation struggle was forced to focus on a single state at a time, thereby remaining a prisoner of narrow regional goals. Shuqeiri, writing in 1967, was even ready to acknowledge the detrimental impact of the Arab League of States on the goal of Arab unity, since the charter of the League mandated respect for the boundaries of member states. Shuqeiri once wrote a proposal for the creation of the unified Arab state and stipulated optimal conditions for its survival. Among these was that no single region in this unified state should have the right to secede without holding a plebiscite on the issue. The unified Arab state should enjoy one foreign policy, including a single representation in international organizations. He called for the creation of a unified military command as well as the unified production of military armaments. Regional governments within the unified state should be limited to local issues and should not enjoy the privileges of the unified central government. Until such time as the unified state was realized, all the regional members of this state should participate in a council of heads of state and in a unified military command under a single leadership.[52]

Since he was writing after the defeat of 1967 and after his own resignation from the PLO, Shuqeiri felt free to assess the lessons of a regime-sponsored PLO. In his view, the experience of the Arab summit meetings showed that the League of Arab States pursued the goals of Arab unity according to the lowest common denominator. Israel was made up of people of diverse origins who all enjoyed a single government, while the Arabs were a single nation with thirteen governments (the number of Arab states at the time). Shuqeiri also noted that all the Arab states had been given their current boundaries by the colonizing powers and were assigned names that were really the geographic names of regions or provinces, such as Syria, Iraq, Tunisia, and Palestine. Ironically, he added, every Arab head of state described these boundaries as an artificial creation, but each nevertheless had established border checkpoints to examine travel documents and collect customs duties. Then he addressed the PLO's relationship to the issue of unity. No Arab people, he wrote, had more of a right and sacred duty to call for unity than the Palestinians. No Arab people were more committed to a unified Arab state than the Palestinians, who had called for unity since 1919.[53]

The period from 1964 until 1967 witnessed what can best be described as a dualism of responsibility in the Palestinian arena, with Shuqeiri's PLO enjoying political legitimacy while the guerrilla organizations such as Fateh enjoyed considerable popular support. While all the other Palestinian organizations in the field were highly critical of Shuqeiri and his work, Fateh was just mildly negative. All the guerrilla organizations, however, demanded inclusion in the PLO's decision-making apparatus and a say in how Shuqeiri interacted with Arab and foreign governments. The defeat of 1967 left the PLO weakened and leaderless, which opened up room for the guerrilla organizations to make a serious bid for general popular support. Following the battle of Karamah, Fateh in particular began to develop an Arab policy on two levels. One was on the popular level, and it involved strengthening its ties to the Arab populace. The other entailed building bridges to the progressive Arab regimes and using these relationships to pressure the rich states, such as Saudi Arabia, and the states with strategic depth, such as Jordan and Lebanon. As to the progressive regimes, Fateh, and later the PLO, enjoyed Nasser's unhesitating support until his death in 1970. Fateh's relationship with Syria, the other ranking progressive regime in the Arab world, oscillated between peaceful co-existence and fierce competition and struggle. Much of the problem of living and operating in Syria issued from the struggle within the Ba'th and its attempt to seize power and co-opt the Palestinians. Fateh also suffered from Syria's historical determination to maintain nationalist involvement in the Palestinian struggle. As soon as Fateh at the head of the new PLO succeeded the first PLO, its long-range strategic goal became achieving the total liberation of Palestinian soil and the establishment of a democratic state free of racial or religious prejudice. All existing political parties supported this objective except for the Arab Communists, including the Palestinian Communists, who at the time were members of the Jordanian party. The emergence of the Fateh-led PLO induced the Palestinian Communists to form their own independent party.[54]

One of the major ideological tensions within the PLO developed out of the strategy of stages that was adopted by the PNC at its twelfth session, at Cairo in June 1974. This strategy was ostensibly adopted as a result of the October 1973 War and called for "the establishment of the people's independent and national fighting authority [later referred to as the "independent Palestinian state"] on any part of liberated Palestinian territory." The resolution added that "any liberation step achieved will be one link in a series of steps to pursue the realization of the strategy of the liberation organization for the establishment of the democratic Palestinian state stipulated in the resolutions of the previous national councils."[55] The strategy of stages was also called the Ten Point Program, and it elicited serious opposition from the Iraqi Baʻth Party, which viewed it as a conspiracy to liquidate the Palestinian national program. This resolution caused the first major split in the organization and the withdrawal of several of its constituent groups.[56]

Beginning in 1974, major shifts away from pure ideology in the direction of pragmatism were to characterize the policy of the PLO. For instance, after vehemently condemning and opposing the Camp David agreements, the center groups within the PLO headed by Fateh opened up a dialogue with Egypt in June 1982. This move was justified on the grounds that President Mubarak had renewed recognition of the PLO as the sole legitimate representative of the Palestinian people after President Sadat had dropped this policy following the signing of the agreements. Mubarak's policy of supporting the PLO while refraining from applying any pressure on the organization was a sharp contrast to Sadat's attempt to bring the PLO in line with the Camp David agreements. The PLO, for instance, rejected Sadat's argument in favor of setting up a Palestinian state in exile and adopting a diplomatic rather than a military solution.[57]

First raised in 1981, the issue of a Palestinian government in exile was also viewed by the PLO as an Arab attempt to control and confine the Palestinian struggle. The PLO was most apprehensive about the implications of this scheme, since it would entail determining the role of the occupied territories and who would be the leading exile community. But the idea was not without its supporters, particularly when voices favoring this strategy rose from within the occupied territories following the intifada. At one point in the late 1980s, the PDFLP and Hani al-Hassan (one of the three Hassan brothers within Fateh) favored this idea. But three of the most powerful figures of the PLO, Khaled al-Hassan, Khalil al-Wazir, and Salah Khalaf, led the opposing camp, which argued that this government would deflect attention from the intifada.[58]

The Palestinian State Deferred

The 1987 intifada placed in bold relief the PLO's determination to fashion the Palestinian destiny independently of the wishes of Arab states. The most immediate impact of the intifada on the PLO leadership in Tunisia was that it provided an alternative for the loss of Lebanon. Qaddumi claimed that the West Bank and Gaza uprising meant that the Lebanese theater had become obsolete. He did not, however, elaborate on the original intent of carrying out the armed struggle from Lebanon. From the PLO's vantage point, the future of the Palestinians could now be determined solely in reference to the armed struggle in the occupied territories. Lebanon was by now a Syrian protectorate, and the PLO became increasingly anxious to put that phase of the Palestinian-Syrian confrontation behind it. The intifada also freed the PLO from Jordanian suzerainty since the Jordanian monarch quickly disengaged himself from the West Bank. More importantly, the intifada paved the way for opening up contacts with the United States. This was the PLO's second significant opportunity, after adopting the strategy of stages, to join the international community via the declaration of a Palestinian state and the abandonment of the armed struggle.[59]

The declaration of a Palestinian state posed several advantages over the option of a government in exile. The declaration of a state was issued minus the delineation of borders. Such a state could then become the initial topic of an international peace conference, and not a bargaining point between the parties. Arafat's declaration of statehood thus rested on an important international document, namely, UN Resolution 181 of 1947, authorizing the partition of Palestine. Completely oblivious to the legalities of the issue, the PLO overlooked the unequivocal rejection of this resolution in the covenant. When the declaration was approved by the top leadership in October 1988 prior to its announcement, a small faction of the Palestine National Salvation Front, the Syrian-backed opposition group, approved the declaration. The rest of the opposition absented themselves, as they had done since the eighteenth annual meeting of the PNC. The PLO had also assured itself a role in any future Middle East peace negotiations.

The declaration of statehood forestalled the emergence of any Western- or Israeli-backed Palestinian government from the territories, a genuine fear of the PLO given the constitutional vacuum created by Jordan's disengagement from the West Bank. But the greatest motivating fear was of a government in exile that would quickly replace the authority of the PLO's executive committee. Thus, the PNC approved a provisional (or temporary) government in exile to be set up by the executive committee at a later date. But the PLO had to fight a more strenuous battle against its constituent factions before gaining acceptance of Resolution 242. When the declaration of independence was presented to the nineteenth session of the PNC, which met in November 1988 at Algiers, the resolution did not invoke the authority of the covenant. Arafat's subsequent remarks at a special UN General Assembly meeting held at Geneva, Switzerland, in December, in which he complied with U.S. demands to renounce terrorism and accept Security Council Resolutions 242 and 338, were also denounced by the opposition as contravening articles in the covenant. Once the PLO controlled the intifada, Arafat's stature both internationally and in the Arab world grew. Syria became increasingly isolated through a combination of factors, including the resumption of Soviet diplomatic relations with Egypt and Israel, and the defeat of its ally Iran.[60]

The departure from the covenant and steady incline toward pragmatism continued throughout 1989. Among Arafat's shocking statements during that year was an expression of willingness to go to Jerusalem, à la Sadat, if this would improve the chances for peace. The statement was made in an interview in an Italian paper and was later severely criticized for its departure from the PNC consensus. Habash responded that Arafat's concessions were unnecessary since the intifada was growing and Israel was losing international support.[61] And when Arafat, in a moment of extreme pragmatism, announced that the covenant was, in his words, "caduc" (obsolete), Habash responded with bitterness: "Brother Yasir Arafat can establish a new organization if he wants," he said on Radio Monte Carlo on May 3, 1989. "But," he continued, "the PLO, as understood by our Palestinian people and by our masses, is the Charter."[62]

The PLO, however, backed away at the last minute from declaring itself a provisional government because of Western European advice indicating that this step would complicate the PLO's march toward international recognition. The most sizeable opposition group, the PFLP, did not appear to mind, fearing that it might be removed from the new government. But the PDFLP approved the provisional government proposal, believing that its approval and participation would force the PLO to take legal steps and seek ratification by the national leaders of the intifada. This would ensure a stronger role for the PDFLP in constituting the new government because of its influence with the West Bank leadership of the intifada.[63]

The PLO's bypassing of the Palestinian consensus also signified its abandonment of the Arab consensus, with disastrous consequences for both the Palestinians and the Arab states. The PLO's determination to pursue its own course dated back to the earliest days of Fateh's takeover of the PLO's institutions. Arab critics of the PLO, for instance, have always charged that although the Palestinian revolution enjoyed its own particularist characteristics, the Palestine question should never have been considered the sole responsibility of the Palestinians. While recognizing that the emergence of an independent Palestinian national movement in the 1960s was a great political achievement of the Palestinian people, this did not mean that Israel's aggression was confined to the Palestinians. Arab nationalists have always recognized that Israel posed a serious threat to the entire Arab world. Indeed, when some Arab regimes encouraged this Palestinian particularism, the result was a strengthening of Arab regionalism in general. Arab observers and critics, therefore, always insisted that the relationship of the Palestinian liberation movement to the Arab regimes was one of simultaneous affinity and independence.

The undeniable affinity of this struggle to the larger Arab nationalist movement was actually stronger than was the case in comparable liberation struggles. Thus, whereas the Algerian struggle was primarily the responsibility of the Algerian people and was assisted by a secondary Arab campaign of support, the Arab dimension was an essential aspect of the Palestinian struggle right from the start. The PLO's determination to be admitted as a full-fledged member to the League of Arab States in 1974 was perhaps the gravest consequence of this trend, since it plunged the weak and stateless Palestinians into all aspects of inter-Arab questions. Recognition of the PLO's legitimacy, according to this view, should not have come through the Arab League but should have been granted as a parallel policy. Thus, while the Algerian struggle managed to penetrate the Arab arena, the Palestinian question suffered from Arab penetration that could only be described as "intervention" or "sponsorship."[64]

The greatest criticism leveled at Fateh and the PLO has always been in regard to its relationship with Syria. Syria extended support to the Palestinian guerrillas as early as 1963, offering more than any other modern Arab regime. Syrian territory was willingly opened for the PLO's bases as early as 1965. Syria continued to support the guerrillas after the 1967 War. But then the PLO's own mistakes forced a crisis with the Syrian regime, one of the most progressive in the Arab region. For instance, the PLO had studied the revolutionary experiences of Vietnam and Cuba but did not bother to examine Arab revolutionary movements, particularly that of Algeria. The PLO never grasped the nature of the relationship between revolutionary bases of support in neighboring countries and the war of liberation. Therefore, grave mistakes were made in Lebanon, where the PLO fought its battles for over twenty years, believing it had a right to be on Lebanese soil since Lebanon was Arab territory. The PLO also entertained the delusionary idea that it could fight in someone else's territory without getting involved in that country's politics. The PLO seriously believed that it continued to enjoy an independent political will even while it fought its battles on a territory other than its own.[65]

In tracing the cause of Fateh's inability to manage the Arab dimension of the Palestine question, a ranking member of the PFLP's political bureau, Maher al-Taher, blamed the guerrillas' reaction to the 1967 Arab defeat. While the Arab nationalists turned to examining reasons for the defeat, Fateh shifted its emphasis to the Palestinian regional struggle. It should be remembered that at first Egypt and Syria supported the Palestinianization of the struggle. Some of these changes were reflected in the amendments to the covenant, beginning with a change in its title from "The National Covenant" (al-Mithaq al-Qawmi) to "The Regional Charter" (al-Mithaq al-Watani). Fateh pushed for the strengthening of the Palestinian national identity, although it did yield to pressure by various Arab nationalist constituent groups to maintain the article specifying that the goals of Arab unity and the liberation of Palestine were complementary. The amended charter nevertheless emphasized in Article 2 that the Palestinian people enjoyed the exclusive right to liberate and retrieve their homeland as well as to reject all forms of intervention, sponsorship, and co-optation. In accordance with this emphasis, Article 24, which proclaimed that the PLO did not claim any sovereignty over the Jordanian-ruled West Bank and the Egyptian-administered Gaza strip, was deleted.

The Camp David negotiations, in which Egypt pursued a unilateral track to peace, further strengthened the independent Palestinian rather than the Palestinian-Arab trend within the PLO. This gave rise to Palestinian solutions, such as the policy of stages in 1974, which endorsed the strategy of negotiating with the enemy and defining a goal short of the liberation of all of Palestine. The key change in this new resolution, which was adopted by the twelfth session of the PNC, was in substituting the phrase "the liberation of the Palestinian lands and the establishment of a national authority on any part of the liberated Palestinian territory" for that of "the liberation of Palestine."[66]

Following the approval of this new political program, the seventh Arab summit meeting, at Rabat in October 1974, adopted the resolution that recognized the PLO as the sole and legitimate representative of the Palestinian people. By undertaking this step, the Arab states committed themselves not to interfere in internal Palestinian affairs. This step was quickly confirmed by the UN bestowal of observer status on the PLO. Both of these measures enabled the PLO to stake out a claim for itself in any peace conference or international negotiations concerning Israel, the Arabs, and the Palestinians. The PLO's exit from Lebanon after the 1982 Israeli invasion coincided with a severe crisis within its leadership ranks that threatened the future of the organization. Its arrival at Oslo to initiate direct talks with Israel in 1993 was, therefore, the culmination of a particular political outlook that exaggerated the regional particularism of the Palestine question and produced a serious separation between regionalist thought and the Arab question. But blame cannot be confined to the Palestinians. The Arab states that favored regionalism and abandoned Arab nationalism succeeded in encouraging the same attitude on the part of the Palestinian front in order to absolve themselves of any responsibility toward the Palestinians.[67]

Palestinian revisionism was particularly visible after the Lebanese debacle. Representatives of this school used the Lebanese experience as an occasion for reassessing the past missteps of Fateh and the PLO. Represented by independents who worked with the PLO, such as Shafiq al-Hout, the new revisionism harped on the abandonment of the Arab cause. Admitting that the Arab and Palestinian leadership had both failed to develop a coherent strategic plan on the same level as that of the enemy, before and after the Palestine War of 1948, this revisionism argued that the new Palestinian thinking represented by Fateh did not justify the mistakes of the later PLO. The separation of Egypt and Syria in 1961 was recognized as one of the major developments that had led to the regionalization of the Palestinian struggle and the rise of slogans proclaiming that "Palestine can only be liberated by Palestinians." Thus, regionalist thought argued that reviving the Palestinian national identity and creating a political framework for the Palestinians were necessary for the resumption of the struggle. But Arab nationalists within the Palestinian community continued to believe that the new Palestinian framework of the 1960s should remain within the Arab fold and transform itself into the vanguard of the progressive Arab nationalist movement. A third Palestinian trend, represented by the PDFLP, emphasized a Marxist-Leninist line and insisted on the class struggle as a way of organizing the national struggle.[68]

According to Shafiq al-Hout's revisionist interpretation, regional Palestinian modifications of the covenant had produced great confusion. There was a lot of uncertainty as to which aspects of the Palestine question were to be considered nationalist and which were regionalist in nature. Stressing the independence of the Palestinian political will, for instance, contradicted Shuqeiri's last stand at the Khartoum summit, when he insisted that no single Arab regime could determine the fate of the Palestinians without reference first to the decision of an Arab summit meeting. The revisionist view also regarded the Jordanian-Palestinian clash in 1970 as the natural outcome of this ideological confusion, leading eventually to a series of Palestinian confrontations with the surrounding Arab states. The culmination of this ideological uncertainty was Lebanon, where the Palestine national movement wasted a decade of its life in inter-Arab entanglements rather than in confrontations with the real enemy. Astonishingly, the PLO raised the slogan of nonintervention in the affairs of Arab states while retaining the final decision on peace and war in some states.

The revisionists expressed dismay over the PLO's refusal to examine its strategy of utilizing other territories from which to stage attacks against Israel. The discussion of the sixteenth PNC in February 1983, and the secessions that developed over the issue of the PLO's withdrawal from Lebanon, were indications of considerable internal turmoil. But the PLO persisted in its blindness toward the issue of relations with Arab states and attempted a second return to Lebanon, only to find itself mired in inter-Palestinian and Syrian-Palestinian fighting. The organization's second ejection from Lebanon encouraged new directions seeking peaceful solutions on the Sadat model. Thus, the fact that the PLO became the first member of the League of Arab States to lift the post–Camp David embargo against Egypt was an important indication of the abandonment of the armed struggle. The absence of a firm ideology of any kind permitted the various factions of the PLO to coexist over a period of thirty years, not as a single and unified organization but as a confederation. There was never any real Palestinian national unity. Thus, factional identity was always considered above national identity, which in the end drove many qualified people from participating directly in the national movement.[69]

Another explanation for the PLO's uncontrollable drift toward a separate rather than comprehensive Arab solution located the problem in the competition of the superpowers rather than in the PLO's disregard for the surrounding Arab states. According to this view, the Soviets were responsible for strengthening the PLO's separatist foreign policy for purely Soviet considerations. It should be recalled that the Soviets had always focused on Egypt as their entry point to the Arab world. The Soviets' affinity for Egypt was historical, having to do with the fact that they first established themselves in the Middle East via Egypt, and that they left that region in the 1970s also via Egypt. Thus, the Soviets were anxiously awaiting Egypt's readmission to the Arab world following the signing of the Camp David agreements. The Soviet attitude toward the Iran-Iraq War was also consistently on the side of mediation. Soviet strategy in the Middle East, hence, always rested on diplomacy and was never intended to produce a military confrontation with the United States. Soviet strategy, moreover, was strongly committed to a peaceful solution to the Arab-Israeli conflict and considered the notion of a Middle East peace conference to be the cornerstone of its diplomacy. But an international conference depended on PLO participation; hence the Soviet determination to push the Palestinians, as well as the Western powers, to provide seats at the peace table for the two parties. The Soviets, in addition, always backed Arafat's leadership and pressured the Syrians against creating a serious rival leadership. Fearful of betting on a new horse, the Soviets backed the tried-and-true Fateh leadership of the PLO.[70]

Conclusion

It is clear from the above discussion that Palestinian nationalism was nurtured in an environment of intense ideological debate concerning the fate of the Arabs in general. It should also be apparent that Palestinian nationalism as such was distinguished from the Palestinian identity, which developed over a long period of time in reaction to powerful external and internal forces. The Palestinian identity, for instance, was not a manifestation of a specific national or political program but continued to express itself within various ideologies and sub-ideologies. Indeed, what is regarded today as Palestinian nationalism is traceable to the mid 1960s, when great forces converged to exaggerate Arab failures and the national paralysis of will. This new outlook on the fate of the Palestinians, moreover, underwent fundamental changes during the 1960s, 1970s, and 1980s.

It is also evident that the steady detachment of Palestine from the Arab body politic, and particularly from Syria, occupied the attention of practically all ideological schools of the Fertile Crescent. Fueled by a devastating sense of powerlessness over the permanent alienation of this vital Arab territory, Arab ideologues continued to ponder the eternal question of how Palestine could be restored to the Arabs. Long after the consolidation of the post–World War I territorial settlement in the Middle East, Arab writers and thinkers were searching for common ideological grounds in order to organize as a whole and restore Palestine's relationship to this unified Arab state. The debate concerning Palestine was the centerpiece of this search. Thus, no single Arab political party or ideological movement neglected to address the Palestine question, even after certain Palestinian groups sought pragmatism and separation.

One of the main characteristics of Palestinian nationalism is that it has shunned formal ideology. This was true especially of Fateh, which came to control and define much of the Palestinian movement of the post-1967 era. But, as in all national movements, groups much smaller than Fateh exercised an enormous influence on Palestinian thinking irrespective of their numbers. Thus, the Arab Nationalist Movement, which preceded the rise of Fateh by a decade and a half, struggled to define the most urgent question confronting Arabs and Palestinians following *al-Nakba*, namely, the universalist and particularist aspects of the Palestine question. Unlike the SSNP, which grappled with the same issue during the 1930s and 1940s, the ANM intellectualized the issue of violence and applied it to the Palestinian cause while at the same time allowing itself to ride the crest of the Nasserite Arab ideology. But even the ANM, which fomented an Arab nationalist unrest in several parts of the Arab world, could not resist the tide of Palestinanism after 1967. Realizing that Palestinian refugees and the Palestinian populace were the leavening of Arab nationalism wherever they existed, the ANM leadership could not ignore their voices. Before splintering into the PFLP and other factions, the ANM subsumed the Palestine question in the Arab nationalist question. After 1967, however, the ANM allowed Arab nationalism to be subsumed in the Palestinian question. When the PFLP became officially part of the Palestine national movement in the 1960s, it joined the ranks of the opposition. Habash's faction remained the voice of Arab nationalism, constantly reminding the Fateh-led PLO of the natural place of the Palestinian national movement at the center of the Arab nationalist current and the heart of the progressive Arab states.

The Palestinian nationalism of the 1960s metamorphosed from a regime-dependent and transitional framework created by a Nasser-dominated Arab League into a fully independent movement that often defied its regime antagonists with confidence. Fateh led its greatest ideological battle with the Ba'th Party, which, unlike the ANM, presided over two governments in Syria and Iraq. The Ba'th was leery of subnational movements that deemphasized the Arab nationalist ideology in the campaign to liberate Palestine. But because the Ba'th was the major party in specific progressive regimes, it developed a specific outlook on the nature of the Palestinian struggle. The Ba'th embraced the ideology of the armed struggle but clearly specified its spheres of action. And because the Ba'th was an overall social and political movement advocating not only Arab unity but socialist economics and republicanism as well, it perceived Palestinian nationalism not as a competitor but as an aberration of the larger, pan-Arab nationalism.

At first, the Fateh-led PLO rode the tide of Palestinian discontent with confidence. Much of its initial popular success was due to the ideological vacuum resulting from the breakup of the UAR. Although most commentators, including supporters of the PLO, emphasized the general Arab disillusionment following the 1967 Arab defeat, a greater disillusionment resulted from the demise of Nasserism in Syria. This, coupled with the disintegration of the first PLO and Shuqeiri's departure from the center stage of Palestinian politics, encouraged the more radical and more regionalized brand of Fateh Palestinianism to emerge. When a series of violent confrontations with the Jordanian, Lebanese, and Syrian regimes became the norm, the Palestinian guerrilla groups, including the PFLP, intensified their emphasis on the Palestinian identity. Palestinian separateness and distinctness began to replace faith in a larger Arab entity. What is also significant is the degree to which the conservative and pro–status quo Arab regimes supported the latter PLO, once it became clear that the organization's main objective was gaining acceptance as a member of the Arab League.

The PLO under Fateh's leadership began its perceptible abandonment of the strategy of armed struggle in Lebanon when it became clear that survival in that Arab theater had its own state imperatives. It was in Lebanon that the PLO became a nonterritorial state before its time and sank deeper and deeper into inter-Lebanese and inter-Arab politics. Arafat demonstrated as a result of his Lebanese involvement that he could survive in the fractured Arab state environment by playing off one state against the other and by using his Arab League membership to become a genuine state actor. Membership in the League was, therefore, used to extricate him from Lebanon and bring added pressure against his Lebanese foes, as well as against Syria. Membership in the League was also suitable as an alliance-building forum. Arafat's success in gaining acceptance for post–Camp David Egypt was a demonstration of his ability to play state maker even before he actually controlled a state.

The PLO's deviations from its ideological roots, modest as they may have been, are best seen in the steady separation of the PNC resolutions from the covenant. Arafat, the master manipulator of an extremely factionalized guerrilla organization that had absorbed over the years all manner of professional organizations and political groups, was able to neutralize the maximalist and revolutionary articles of the covenant in the interest of gaining international acceptance. This action not only divided the PLO ranks further, it also alienated ideological parties and groups committed to the pan-Arabist ideal. Two changes in particular altered the covenant drastically and permanently changed the entire course of Palestinian liberation. The first was the adoption of the strategy of liberating Palestine in stages, which canceled the intent of the PLO to liberate all of Palestine and restore total Palestinian political rights. The second was the declaration of a Palestinian state in 1988 based on UN Resolution 181, which created a state for Jews in Palestine, despite the firm rejection of that resolution by the covenant authors. It was no surprise to Arab and Palestinian observers, therefore, that the chairman declared the covenant "caduc" before the international media in the late 1980s in order to signify his seriousness regarding the abandonment of terrorism and willingness to recognize Israel. That he was able to declare the covenant in effect null and void, when the covenant articles themselves could not be amended except by the absolute consensus of the PNC, is proof of the paralysis of the PLO and the death of its institutions.

Arab ideologues, on the other hand, were aware from the beginning of the deviation of the covenant authors from the Arab consensus on major issues such as the goal of Arab unity. It was noted, for instance, that while Shuqeiri, author of the first covenant, went to extremes in order to allay Arab fears about the separatist intent of the new Palestinian framework, those who amended the covenant when Fateh came aboard did not. First, there was the name change, from the National (*qawmi*) Covenant to the Regional (*watani*) Covenant. Then there was the article describing the Palestinian state of the future as a secular democratic state in which Christians, Muslims, and Jews could live in equality and peace. Totally in opposition to the prevailing ideal of Arab unity, this stipulation alienated many Arab supporters. This was particularly true of the Ba'th Party and Ba'th government in Syria, which noted Arafat's reference to this concept in his UN speech in a bid to gain international acceptability.

In addition, commitment to the principle of the armed struggle was steadily weakened through a policy of premature diplomacy before the achievement of the major goals of that struggle. Arafat quickly adopted an extreme incremental policy that led to confusion, loss of Arab allies, and the destruction of the fragile unity of the PLO. Officially, the PLO was said to have been inspired by the Chinese, Vietnamese, and Cuban revolutions, but none of the lessons of these revolutions were applied. More importantly, the lessons of the Algerian revolution, the most celebrated war of liberation in recent Arab history, were totally ignored. Although the newly independent Algeria was Fateh's greatest supporter, the latter never seriously examined how that war against a sizeable community of determined settlers and a powerful colonial power had been won. Fateh never paid attention to the Algerian FLN's management of its relations with its neighboring Arab states, nor to how it achieved revolutionary consensus before the enemy's onslaught. The PLO's willingness to deviate from principles of the armed struggle on which it based its revolutionary legitimacy also stunned the progressive Arab camp. Many of the PLO's early supporters fell by the wayside as the movement shifted toward the pro-Western Arab states in an open bid for Western recognition and support.

Critics of Fateh's leadership of the PLO, however, rarely broach the subject of its survivability. Arafat's ability to withstand attacks by a host of external and internal foes was never fully explained. His remarkable success in maintaining his freedom from any Arab government created the illusion of genuine independence. But the PLO never managed to be its own master and continued to lurch to the right. Perhaps Arafat's greatest asset remained the unshakable support of the occupied segment of the Arab population. Although much of their steadfastness was due to the harshness of Israeli rule, it was also a natural reaction to the Arab onslaught against other segments of the Palestinian community. Similarly, the development of a powerful Palestinian political identity and a distinct ideology was the result of years of suppression inside and outside the occupied Palestinian areas. Somehow, Fateh's leadership failed or declined to direct this newly emerging Palestinian nationalism into the mainstream of Arab nationalism. The only possible result was to create Shuqeiri's nightmare, namely, another regional Arab nationalism and a separate set of national interests. Seen in this light, it is not surprising that the Fateh-led PLO ended up reliving the Camp David experience by pursuing a separate and unchecked drive toward peace.

7

Peace or Pax Americana?

Syria's disappointment at the PLO's decision to seek a unilateral peace settlement with Israel was based on pragmatic considerations as well as deeply felt emotional ones. As late as September 1987, Syrians were reminded in official pronouncements of the unbreakable link joining them to Palestine. In his inaugural speech before the Tenth Session of the Mediterranean Games at Latakia, President Assad intermixed inspirational messages to Syrian youth with the regime's Arab nationalist claims. This Mediterranean Sea which links Syria to the rest of humanity has known ancient cultures and civilizations and carried the first alphabet to the rest of the world, he said. Thus Syria hoped that its youth would always bear a humanistic message to the world, a message based on love and peace. For in this Syrian land, he added, lived all the prophets. Jesus, peace be upon him, lived in Syria and spoke the Syrian language, since there was no Palestine, Jordan, or Lebanon in Greater Syria. To this land also came the prophet Muhammad as the business agent of Khadijah. Muhammad met here the monk Buhaira, and from Damascus Muslim armies issued forth to al-Andalus and China. He then concluded that since this land was the land of prophecy, civilization, and the alphabets, it should always remain the land of peace.[1] After Arafat signed the Oslo peace accords, however, the Syrians were full of bitterness, refusing to concede the right of one Arab entity to conclude a peace agreement on its own. Palestine had never been simply another state, another land, wrote a Syrian military historian, until the PLO and Yasir Arafat began to endanger the Palestinian cause as a follow-up to his regrettable slogan speaking of "the independent Palestinian will."[2]

The Radical Arab Camp Weakens

The road to Oslo was thus the break in the fragile link that still tied the Palestinians to Arab decision making. It was also a by-product of the immense weakening of the PLO. Similarly, Syrians were aware that the peace process forced upon them by the Bush administration was a consequence of their general weakened state. But Syrians were adamant about rejecting partial solutions and pursuing what was, in their view, an attempt to achieve a total Arab peace. Part of this hardened position was the result of Egypt's defection after the Camp David agreements. Unlike Egypt, Syria's central position in the Arab region and its geographic exposure to Israel's front lines had taught the necessity of Arab coordination and strategic cooperation. After all, it was Egypt's premature acceptance of a cease-fire during the October 1973 War that exposed the Syrian northern front to intense Israeli pressure. Syria's trial by fire in Lebanon during the late 1970s and the 1980s further demonstrated Syria's geographic vulnerability to Israeli attacks on any Arab territory. Furthermore, the decade of the 1980s was Syria's isolationist decade, in which its support for the Iranians during the Iran-Iraq War was a cause of serious alienation from other Arab states, particularly those in the Gulf region.[3]

Syria's capacity to survive its inevitable confrontations with Israel depended largely on its ability to achieve a certain strategic depth vis-à-vis the Israeli state. Assad's strategic instinct led him to believe that only Iraq, with its vast resources and insularity from Israeli land attacks, could provide that depth. But much to his disappointment, Syria's Ba'thist ideological disputes with Iraq were compounded by Iraq's military confrontations with its eastern neighbors. Syria was also infuriated to learn that George Brown, the former British Prime Minister, had secretly advised Saddam Hussein against concluding a union agreement with Syria, since this unification would inevitably lead to an Iraqi-Israeli confrontation. This unity, if it ever materialized, advised Brown, would also embroil Iraq in the Lebanese quagmire.[4]

Perhaps the greatest blow that Syria suffered on the eve of the Gulf War was the collapse of the Soviet Union, its greatest ally and chief source of weapons and economic assistance. Signs of waning Soviet support apparently developed gradually, and Syrians were initially unable to assess the cumulative effect of the loss. The first to receive an indication of the Soviet's loss of interest in the Middle East was actually Arafat. Meeting Mikhail Gorbachev in 1987, Arafat complained that the Americans always allowed themselves full license in that part of the world. Gorbachev responded that although both the Soviets and the Americans had experienced many competitions and confrontations in the Middle East in the past, that phase of their relationship was over. During that same year, Assad received an even greater revelation. While he was detailing his theory about the need to achieve "strategic parity" between the Arabs and

Israel as the only means of achieving a balanced peace in the Middle East, Gorbachev offered the counter thesis of "interests parity." This was the first time Assad had received a full acknowledgment of the changed Soviet posture. On another occasion, in 1988, Assad heard a variation on the same theme while on another visit to Moscow. Gorbachev indicated clearly that the Soviet Union would be preoccupied for many years to come with reordering its house internally. The Soviet Union, he added, would now be less inclined to play a role in regional conflicts.[5]

The convergence of three other events during the late 1980s demonstrated not only the weakening position of the radical Arab camp but also the fracturing of the Arab bloc in its American and Israeli posture. First was the Iran-Iraq War, one of the longest in recent Arab history. The war initially created a false sense of security and optimism among Palestinians, who came to believe that the recently acquired field experience of the Iraqi forces would eventually be used against Israel. This estimation, which may have contributed to the PLO's determination to side with Iraq during the initial phase of the Gulf crisis, overlooked Iraq's immense political and economic difficulties following the war. Then, there was the matter of growing Iraqi military dependence on the Egyptian military and the participation of Egypt in the newly formed Arab Cooperation Council. Egypt was thus afforded an opportunity to be readmitted to the Arab League of States and be rehabilitated in the Arab world, almost ten years after its expulsion from the League as a result of signing the Camp David agreements.

Although the return of Egypt to the fold may have been inevitable, the Iran-Iraq War certainly speeded the process. But the readmission of Egypt to the League was also a cause for friction between supporters and opponents of this move. During the 1989 Casablanca Arab summit, Syria dropped its opposition to Egypt's return expressed a year earlier during the 1988 Algiers summit. Qaddhafi was infuriated by this move, but Assad was now friendly to Egypt, perhaps in realization of the loss of his Soviet base of support. Among the most angered by Egypt's return to the Arab fold and the unfreezing of its membership in the League was Saddam Hussein, who lost much of his interest in the Arab Cooperation Council upon his return from Casablanca. Hussein expressed the view before a member of Iraq's summit delegation that Egyptians used Iraq in their drive to regain admission to the Arab world.[6] Arab alignments were shifting again, with Syria trying to break away from its isolation and the PLO looking to Egypt as a means of escape from Syrian domination.

The PLO created the greatest division in Arab ranks by undertaking a series of concessions beginning in November 1988. During the PNC Algiers meeting of that year, the PLO rammed through its acceptance of UN Security Council Resolution 242, as a signal to the United States that the Palestinians were ready for a peaceful settlement. This painful concession, which sabotaged the covenant and reversed the PLO's long-standing rejection of measures that failed to guarantee Palestinian political rights, created serious divisions within the Palestinian movement and between member Arab states. Arafat, who for years had said that he would rather see his right hand severed than sign Resolution 242, offered two justifications for this radical turnabout. First, he claimed that this pragmatic move was necessitated by the intifada, which called for serious political initiatives in order to persuade other Arab states that the Israelis and not the Palestinians were the main obstacle to peace. The Israelis, he added, would not be satisfied with anything less than all of Palestine. Therefore, these Palestinian concessions were offered to the Arabs and not the Israelis. Much of the Arab world, friend or foe, understood, however, that even before the Gulf War, Arafat was reacting to the loss of his Soviet allies and seeking to forge a new, but difficult, American alliance. The fact that the United States did not recognize the significance of this offer, and was not satisfied even when the PLO renounced terrorism, merely fueled Arafat's determination to execute more and more concessions.[7]

Syria, naturally, was the first to grasp the importance of this move. A new American peace initiative was unfolding, and a weakened Syria began to feel the pressure. Syria had implicitly accepted Resolution 242 and its principle of land for peace when it accepted Resolution 338 following the October 1973 War. But this acceptance was a prelude to the signing of the Syrian-Israeli disengagement agreement. Syria, according to Assad in his March 2, 1992, speech before the People's Assembly, had not changed its basic position on the issue of land for peace by accepting this resolution. Syria's position remained based on the exchange of all of occupied Golan territory in return for peace.[8] The PLO's acceptance of this resolution was viewed by the Syrians as something more problematic and a marked tilt in the direction of the United States.

The U.S. Peace Strategy

The United States, however, was ahead of the Palestinians, Syrians, and other Arabs in strategizing the way to a peace settlement in the Middle East. As soon as James Baker took over the post of Secretary of State under the presidency of George Bush, he expressed apprehension over the ability of the Middle East region to use up a lot of the time of U.S. foreign policy officials without yielding any results. Middle East experts in the State Department, nevertheless, were predicting a resolution of the deadlock between the Arab demand for an international peace conference under UN auspices and the Israelis' rejection of this formula. By early 1989, the chief of Baker's policy planning staff, Dennis Ross, had prepared a memorandum for the National Security Council in which he explained that a new picture was emerging in the occupied West Bank and Gaza as a result of the intifada. Other influential members of the policy planning staff (such as Bill Burns, Dan Kurtzer, Aaron Miller, and John Kelly, who served as Assistant Secretary for Near Eastern Affairs) agreed with Ross. They all believed that the intifada had provoked much Israeli military repression and as such was an embarrassment to the government of Yitzhak Shamir and the cause of an increasingly divisive debate within Israel's political circles. Yitzhak Rabin's position, when he was a Defense Minister in the Shamir coalition cabinet, was that the intifada could only be overcome by political, not military means.[9]

The American policy group also speculated that the intifada had created schisms of a different kind within the Palestinian camp. Since the intifada was a grassroots uprising, it had already given life to a different set of goals than those of the Tunis-based PLO leadership, and the possibility of the grassroots breaking ranks with that leadership was tantalizingly at hand. There was even a slim chance, the Americans felt, that the uprising's leadership might enter the peace process on their own. This might open doors for direct negotiations between the new Palestinian leaders and the Israelis, who adamantly refused to deal directly with the official PLO leadership. When the Israelis were prodded about their peace plans, Prime Minister Shamir proposed that elections be held in the occupied territories to select a non-PLO-affiliated negotiating team. The possibility of this happening or of its being accepted by Palestinians of various factional persuasions was very slim, however. The PLO's patron protector at the time, Egypt, had already spoken on behalf of Tunis, insisting that the PLO must be included in the negotiations. During this Israeli-U.S. impasse, the Bush administration found another way of pressuring the Israelis, namely, to speak publicly against the Israeli settlements as an obstacle to peace. Baker began to call on Israel in his public statements to abandon the dream of Greater Israel in the interest of achieving a meaningful peace with its Arab neighbors. Baker called this tactic "finessing the irritant of settlements."[10]

But the time was not yet ripe to launch a major Middle East peace initiative. This notion of "ripeness" or timing had already been broached by Dennis Ross, who, in an important internal pamphlet titled "Building for Peace," had advocated that the Bush administration delay the attempt at an international peace process until the situation was more amenable to reaching a settlement. Ross also favored the incremental rather than the comprehensive approach. Another Middle East expert who advised the State Department and the National Security Council, Richard Haass, advocated a patient policy that awaited the "ripeness" of the parties, or their readiness to negotiate. William Quandt concluded that the incremental approach appealed immensely to the Israelis, who looked forward to a reciprocal process in which not all concessions would come from their side. Even though this formula was unfavorable to the Palestinians, they tried to live with it by bargaining for some modifications. Thus, by the summer of 1989, U.S.-PLO secret talks netted small gains as the PLO, even before the Gulf crisis, was trying hard to secure a seat at the peace table. The PLO suggested that it could accept its exclusion from the talks if it could control the process by which the Palestinian team was chosen, and if one delegate were chosen from the Palestinian diaspora. The PLO also protested the exclusion of any delegate from East Jerusalem. That is where the Bush administration's initiatives rested until the Gulf crisis changed the Arab balance of power perceptibly and overturned all Palestinian gains made during the intifada.[11]

When the dust of the Gulf War settled, the Palestinians were among the greatest losers. The Syrians did not fare badly at all and were able to demonstrate their remarkable bargaining skills before Secretary of State Baker. In a fit of Orientalist amnesia, Baker called President Assad a "vintage horse trader" when the latter attempted to extract additional concessions as the price of his participation in the Gulf War.[12] Yet during the initial months of his appointment as Secretary of State, Baker clearly expressed a preference for seizing the moment when his opponent was at his weakest. He remarked to Michael Kramer, in an interview in *Time* titled "Playing for the Edge" and published on February 13, 1989, that it was not the U.S. intention to pressure the Israelis but that both sides, Israelis and Palestinians, "have got to find a way to give something."[13] Baker proved willing to bargain with Assad, whose support the United States needed during the war; but for the prostrate Palestinians who had backed the wrong side there would be no mercy.

When the Syrians resisted pressure to fight on the front lines in the Gulf, fearing that their Soviet military equipment, which was like that of the Iraqis, might make them the target of American firepower, Baker found a solution. He arranged for the Syrians to avoid entering Iraq and to serve instead as the back-up units behind the Egyptians when the latter entered Kuwait.[14] The Syrians were thus afforded a big leaf with which to cover themselves, and they proceeded to declare that their participation in the international coalition was only a response to a sisterly Arab state in distress, namely, Saudi Arabia. Thus, Syrian troops moved to Saudi Arabia at the request of King Fahd, who had been encouraged by Baker and his military team to issue the call.[15] Syria was also able to claim that the willingness of Syrian and Egyptian troops to liberate Iraqi-occupied Kuwait was undertaken in the interest of insulating Arab Gulf soil from occupation by foreign troops.[16]

For the Palestinians, however, Baker offered no fig leaf. When the time came to pressure them into joining the international peace talks at Madrid, they acceded to the Israeli demand that they participate as part of the Jordanian delegation and that there be no representation from the Palestinian diaspora. When Arafat finally assembled a seemingly autonomous Palestinian team, it had to be composed of unknown figures with no previous ties to the PLO and no history of struggle against the occupying forces. Indeed, the negotiating team was just that, with the exception of Haidar 'Abd al-Shafi, a highly respected figure from the Gaza area. One member of the team, Hanan 'Ashrawi, a comparative unknown, was anointed by the American media as the voice of the new Palestine, to the chagrin of most Palestinians, who had no sympathy for such political opportunism. Baker was consistently harsh in his dealings with this team, reminding them that Arafat's visible support for Saddam Hussein during the war had eliminated a great deal of international sympathy for the Palestinians in general.[17] Baker was also brutally blunt with them, saying, "I have sat with leaders of eight Arab states, and all said they will not support your leadership. You are moderate people of good sense. You have to realize that we're not going to renew a dialogue with the PLO in the face of Arafat's embrace of Saddam Hussein."[18]

Baker's greatest blind spot was that he was unable to see the similarities in the American and Israeli positions on the desired peace, and the impact of this posture on the Arabs. The Syrians, for instance, resisted the idea of attending an international peace conference on what appeared to them to be Israel's terms. But Baker even went as far as to request their commitment to the "process" and to attend the regional conference (which he refused to label as international until much later), and at the same time to avoid criticizing those Palestinians ready to dialogue with the Israelis.[19]

Baker was not above pressuring Syria to pressure the Palestinians on the matter of joining the Jordanian delegation. He wanted Assad to signal the PLO at Tunis that if they refused, Syria and Jordan would proceed to the negotiating table without them. Baker, of course, pretended to be unaware of the absence of communications between Arafat and Assad. Baker also used his knowledge of the fractured Arab front to place additional pressure on the Palestinian negotiating team. When Arafat's hesitation prevented it from moving to join the Jordanian team, Baker delivered a blunt message. He told 'Ashrawi, who began her role on the team as Faisal Husseini's translator but rose to be its chief spokesperson, that if the Palestinians remained outside the peace process, they would be ignored. He also saw through 'Ashrawi's bluff when she attempted to persuade him that the rest of the Arab states would not consider participating in the proposed conference unless the Palestinians were there.[20] Baker's strategy was based on the tactics of divide and conquer. He was to return again to the metaphor of the Oriental horse trader. With great cultural insensitivity, he protested loudly when the Palestinian negotiating team at Jerusalem attempted a last-minute holding action, demanding that a Jerusalemite be part of the team. Baker blurted out in anger, "How many times have we done this? I am sick and tired of this. With you people, the *souk* [market] never closes."[21] One wonders how Assad might have responded to this remark.

Part of the success of the American diplomats in bringing about an Arab-Israeli peace settlement of sorts was due to the successive U.S. attempts to break down Arab defenses. This was achieved largely by refining the art of negotiation and forcing the Arabs to learn what the Americans meant by negotiations. To the Americans, negotiations were not about the recovery of internationally recognized rights but rather an entirely new game, the rules of which were first developed by Secretary of State Henry Kissinger. According to Amos Perlmutter, an American expert on Middle Eastern affairs, Kissinger recognized the Arab love for words early on and began to drill them in the meaning of his latest terminology. Kissinger played the role of drill master very subtly, without arousing the sensitivities of his audiences. He would begin by repeating such terms as "peace process," which, according to him, meant changing the peace from the end product of war to a process, beginning with sitting around a table and allowing the dynamics of negotiations to take their own course. He used terms like "momentum," meaning that the peace process was constantly in need of refueling in order to prevent it from floundering. Since it was the Arabs who were interested in a settlement to facilitate the return of their lands, they were obligated to supply the fuel. Kissinger's most intriguing concept was "confidence-building measures," which he explained as the need to sustain the momentum of the negotiations by undertaking measures designed to build the confidence of the other party. Clearly, Kissinger felt that Israel was badly in need of these measures since it would be required to give up something tangible (land) in exchange for something intangible (peace) that would be granted by Arabs. The whole idea was to proceed step by step.[22]

This background may explain the readiness of many Arab parties to accept the American invitation to the negotiating table following the Gulf War. The Palestinians, said Arafat, could not absent themselves from a conference attended by all the Arab parties. According to Arafat, the Palestinians' mere presence at such a conference would be a confirmation of their rights and the role they must play. They should never refuse but should leave to Israel the choice of doing so if it wished.[23]

When Baker intensified his efforts to get the parties to the peace table in 1991, Syria and Egypt eventually yielded and issued a call for the convening of an "international" conference on the Arab-Israeli conflict. Prime Minister Shamir, however, made it clear that he would only join a "regional" conference convened not by the UN but by the United States and the Soviets. Baker then proceeded to induce the Israelis to join this project by making attendance at the conference a purely voluntary decision. Assad insisted on the UN formula, arguing that if the Gulf War was waged under the auspices of the UN, why not this peace conference? Israel was finally brought into the negotiations after its demand for a non-PLO Palestinian delegation, which would include no one from Jerusalem or from outside the West Bank, was met. According to Quandt, Baker accepted the Palestinian stipulations in 1990, but when the PLO backed the losing side in the Gulf War, he moved to extract his price by yielding to the Israeli position. The United States also yielded to Israel's demand for the repeal of the UN resolution equating Zionism with racism by calling publicly for such action. Once the Madrid talks started, knowledge of ongoing Syrian-Israeli negotiations frightened the Palestinians into believing that a separate Syrian-Israeli peace agreement was in the works. Lack of communication and trust between these two crucial players accelerated the pace of Palestinian concessions.[24]

Palestinians Oppose Oslo

The last holdouts among the Palestinian diaspora community, particularly those in Syria, could not help but notice the stark contrast between the

PLO's negotiating posture and those of other successful revolutionary movements like the Vietnamese Liberation Front. One reason why the Vietnamese quickly came to mind was the alleged affinity between the Palestinian and Vietnamese revolutions. The Vietnamese, Chinese, and Cuban revolutions served as inspirational models for Fateh in the mid 1960s. The Vietnamese experience was also a topic of hot debate among PLO supporters, who claimed that Ho Chi Minh, Lenin, and Mao Zedong all made substantial tactical concessions to the enemy early in their struggle in order to avoid total annihilation. There were those who pointed to the toughness of these negotiators around the peace table. However, Fateh supporters insisted that the PLO's concessions at Madrid were in the category of "the Arab peace attack" or strategy.[25]

Critics of Fateh insisted that the Vietnamese "bamboo diplomacy" and its lethal effect on the Americans could best be appreciated by reading Richard Nixon's and Henry Kissinger's memoirs, both of which were duly translated into Arabic. The PLO detractors insisted that the strategy of negotiations was not the only strategy used in the Vietnamese experience. The strategy of negotiations was related to the diplomatic struggle, which in turn was a by-product of the political struggle. All these, however, were perceived as emanating from revolutionary violence, or from a specific military strategy. The Vietnamese negotiating strategy was not influenced by the Harvard University studies on negotiations authored by Roger Fischer and William Uri, but neither were they spontaneous initiatives. The Vietnamese based their negotiating strategy on three principles: (1) a clear analysis of the political, economic, and military condition of the opposing side; (2) a clear analysis of the American Democratic Party and of the interrelationships among the White House, the Pentagon, and the State Department; and (3) an objective evaluation of the Vietnamese front itself and of its regional and international alliances. But the greatest victory of the Vietnamese, according to this view, was achieved three months before the actual negotiations took place, when President Johnson was forced to stop the aerial bombardment of North Vietnam as the price of Vietnamese willingness to negotiate. The mixture of toughness and flexibility displayed by the Vietnamese negotiators came to be called "bamboo diplomacy." What shocked the PLO's critics was the willingness of Arafat to enter into negotiations without compelling the enemy to promise the return of occupied Arab lands, even if only rhetorically, or to demand the application of international resolutions, even if only symbolically. Without any victory on the ground, and given the recent Arab defeat during the Gulf War, the PLO could not hope to achieve serious results from the peace conference.[26]

The PLO's internal critics were equally censorious in their comments on the Madrid peace conference. The leaders of various factions and military organizations within the PLO were shocked to learn that decisions concerning the peace at Madrid had been made by just a few individuals since Baker's trips to the region began in March 1991. This was considered not only inimical to Palestinian interests but to the Arab-Arab regional balance. Right from the start, Arafat presented Fateh's Tunis leadership with a fait accompli, claiming that all the concessions he was making were at the request of Egypt. He reiterated his desire to persuade the Egyptians of his flexible position and his willingness to reciprocate. Talks with the United States through the Egyptians apparently extended from 1988 until 1990 and the Gulf crisis. Hoping to reestablish its regional position in the Arab world with help from the United States, and pushed by a wide circle of pro-Israel states ranging from Romania to the Scandinavian countries, Egypt became the intermediary for all the PLO's contacts. The states mentioned above, moreover, shared more with Israel through the network of West European socialist parties and Israel's Labor Party than they did with the PLO's executive committee. Thus, throughout the 1988–90 period, U.S.-Israeli proposals to the PLO always arrived via Cairo accompanied by the Egyptians' suggestions and advice. Arafat gratefully agreed to play by Egypt's rules, forgetting that the latter was entrenching itself at the core of one of the Middle East's most serious issues.[27]

Fateh's executive committee knew, however, that what was being proposed was a unilateral peace not unlike the Camp David agreements. No Arab dimension to these talks, no Syrian, Lebanese, or Jordanian links, were ever discussed. It became apparent during that phase of the secret negotiations that what was being proposed was the decoupling of the Palestine issue from the Arab states as in the Camp David agreements. When Baker launched his contacts with the Palestinians chosen from Jerusalem and Ramallah, the PLO was inundated with rumors of the impending signing of Syrian, Jordanian, and Lebanese agreements with Baker. This frightened those sitting on the sidelines, who were told that all the Arabs were on their way to the peace conference except for the Palestinians. Faisal Husseini, a leading member of the Palestinian negotiating team, even repeated Baker's words to the PLO's inner circle at Tunis. Baker had emphasized to the Palestinians that they might be able to sabotage the settlement, or the American solution, but this would hurt them because they were already hurting. The PLO opposition forces, however, continued to resist this game of bluff, suggesting instead a move to slow down the rush to the conference.[28]

Once it was announced in Tunis that Faisal Husseini had informed Baker of the Palestinians' willingness to join the Jordanians as one delegation, in the formula preferred by Israel and the United States, discussions commenced concerning ways to limit the damage. To the opposition, the shock was not solely at the choice of the delegation but also concerned the unconditional Palestinian surrender to the U.S. and Israeli demands. The PLO's agreement to postpone meaningful discussions of the Jerusalem question, notwithstanding its inability to extract an Israeli commitment to halt the expansion of the settlements or to engage in any meaningful talks regarding sovereignty on the land, spelled utter disaster. Thus, Farouq Qaddumi, the PLO's foreign affairs expert, after consulting Arafat, recommended dispatching a delegation to meet President Assad in October 1991 and then proceeding to visit President Mubarak. The delegation was to include Qadummi and Arafat along with others, but some of the opposition leaders declined to join. For instance, Hawatmah of the PDFLP decided to go public with his rejection of Arafat's concessions and castigated him for not informing the executive committee of his approval of the American-Israeli stipulations regarding the composition of the delegation. The idea of an Arab tour fizzled, and criticism of the PLO mounted, particularly by Algeria. The PLO's old ally had expected, following the declaration of the Palestinian state, that a provisional Palestinian government would be formed according to the resolutions of the 1988 PNC in Algiers. It was this government that many expected to spearhead the negotiations. Arafat did meet the vice president of Syria, 'Abd al-Halim Khaddam, during Libya's celebrations of the completion of its Green River Project in September 1991. But the two were among several officials invited for the occasion, and no meaningful talks ever took place.[29]

The Madrid formula for peace thus was based on the principle of multiple tracks, a demand made by the Israelis as early as the 1948 armistice agreements. Israel was once more able to resist Arab demands to negotiate as one bloc, which left the Palestinians completely on their own. Direct pressure on members of the Palestinian delegation was applied by some Palestinian opposition members but failed to produce any results. The opposition, as well as several diaspora leaders, looked to Haidar 'Abd al-Shafi, the head of the delegation, to change the direction of the talks. 'Abd al-Shafi and his team, however, were unresponsive. He continued to avoid arousing the sensitivities of the Israelis, particularly during his grand and dignified speech at Madrid, in which he avoided any mention of the need to link the other Arab tracks to the Palestinian track. As pressure mounted on the negotiating team to force the suspension of the negotiations until the building of Israeli settlements ceased, the delegation also became frozen for fear of being seen as an alternative to the PLO. Indeed, Arafat often accused them of plotting against his leadership, hinting at the possibility of treason whenever they expressed disagreement with his instructions. Arafat's edicts continued to be channeled through his trusted aid, Nabeel Sha'ath, who stayed close to the delegation at Washington, and through Sa'ib 'Ireqat, who served on the delegation. The entire negotiations focused on the issue of Palestinian self-rule. When 'Abd al-Shafi suggested to Tunis, during the fourth of the eleven rounds, suspending the negotiations until the Israelis agreed to stop building settlements, he was completely ignored. By that time, additional secret channels were opened with the Israelis that made the entire delegation's mission an exercise in futility. The secret talks at Oslo were apparently launched in December 1992.[30]

The secret road to Oslo was also paved with bluffing and deception. When Shimon Peres arrived at Oslo in August 1993, Tirgi Larsen, head of the Norwegian Research Institute (FAFO, or Fagbevegelsens Senter for Forskning), called Arafat by telephone to prod him to finalize the talks and sign the declaration of peace. He said that Foreign Minister Johan Jorgen Holst and Israeli Foreign Minister Peres were with him and that the talks should be concluded that evening since Israel was about to sign a peace with the Syrians. Since Israel preferred to move along these two tracks quickly and simultaneously, it would sign with the Syrians if the PLO hesitated.[31] As for the official Washington delegation, no one bothered to inform them of the contents of the draft agreement on Palestinian self-rule at Gaza and Jericho until the Washington-based representative of the Israeli paper *Yediot Ahronot* translated the document for them from Hebrew.[32]

Syria, unlike the PLO, resisted separate deals. According to Shlomo Gazit, a senior researcher at the Jaffee Institute in Tel Aviv, Israel was more anxious to secure a deal with Syria than to achieve a breakthrough with the PLO. But Syria insisted on employing a new term, "the comprehensive peace," and Assad resisted opening up parallel secret talks with Israel, asserting his preference for the talks conducted by his official negotiating team at Madrid.[33] When news of the Oslo agreement was leaked out, Syria expressed great dissatisfaction with this separate agreement but made no threats to sabotage it.[34] When Assad met with Arafat at Damascus on September 5, 1993, during the latter's whirlwind tour of the Arab countries, he refused to grant Arafat's request for an open endorsement of the agreement. Even though Egypt and Jordan extended their support, Assad declared that Arafat was proceeding "at his own risk."[35]

Although the United States and Israel continued to pressure Syria for an agreement similar to that reached with the PLO, the United States in particular began to advocate slowing the talks down and exercising caution in granting Syria all of its demands. The theory in Washington was that the Israeli public's lack of preparedness to give up concessions and territory at Gaza and the Golan simultaneously must be taken seriously. Clearly, Syria viewed the timing of the Oslo accords as inimical to its own interests. Once the PLO signed, there was heightened pressure on Syria to modify its demands. Thomas Friedman of the *New York Times* stated bluntly that the United States had been exploiting Assad's and Arafat's mutual suspicions in order to bring pressure on Arafat to sign an agreement. This was certainly the explanation for Secretary of State Warren Christopher's frequent trips to Syria, which were intended to create the impression that a deal between Syria and Israel was imminent.[36]

Syria's reluctance to sign a permanent peace treaty with Israel arose in part from its apprehensions regarding the Israeli-Palestinian negotiations. Syria was unwilling to sign a separate and independent peace, irrespective of the outcome of Israel's negotiations with the other Arab parties to the conflict. The Syrians admitted that their reluctance to sign quickly was also a function of Israel's unwillingness to meet Syria's demands in the Golan area. Prime Minister Rabin was willing to offer a partial Israeli withdrawal from a small part of the Golan, in what he termed Golan II (he considered the 1974 disengagement agreement to be Golan I), in exchange for a Syrian commitment to peace and a reduction in the number of its troops in the area. But Syria rejected this offer categorically, claiming that it was motivated by its long-standing rejection of the principle of a separate peace. Such a peace agreement, according to the Syrians, would never ensure Syria's security in the region and would only pave the way for Israeli hegemony over Syria and the entire region. Syria continued to reiterate its full set of demands to the American intermediaries, indicating that it would never settle for anything less than the return of the entire Golan, Israel's withdrawal from southern Lebanon, and recognition of the national rights of the Palestinians.

Syria continued to emphasize its perception of peace in the region as being an interconnected phenomenon. Syria's central location at the heart of the Arab world meant that a less than satisfactory peace between Israel and its neighbors would pose grave dangers to Syria. Syrian-Lebanese-

Jordanian security was strategically interdependent since the three, together with the PLO, constituted the area's confrontational states. Thus, even though Syria failed in its attempt to force coordination among the various Arab negotiating teams, it was not ready to yield further on this point by undertaking a separate and unfavorable peace agreement on its own. Syria never abandoned its maximalist position as a compensatory measure to large-scale Arab concessions. Syria considered the Palestinian-Israeli accords to be tantamount to a Palestinian act of suicide since so much had been given away.[37]

Syria's willingness to accept the U.S. peace initiative was clearly a pragmatic step in recognition of the realities of the so-called new world order. But Syria maintained a high threshold for its demands because the basis of its participation in the peace negotiations had been established in UN Resolution 338, which also encompassed Resolution 242. President Assad's insistence on viewing the peace conference as "international" challenged the U.S. secretary of state, who preferred the term "regional." From the beginning, then, Syria insisted on a full application of the principle of land for peace. Assad made it clear that unlike the Syrian-Israeli disengagement agreement of 1974, which was merely a step toward "a just and permanent peace," what was being negotiated in 1991 was a full peace agreement. For that to happen, full withdrawal from Syrian lands was needed and not merely partial Israeli withdrawal.[38]

Peace, according to Assad, was a question of rights and obligations, and not merely a question of striking a deal. More importantly, Assad in his public statements rejected the notion of interim agreements and the eventuality of surrendering national claims for land in exchange for a permanent peace. Perhaps alluding to Arafat's negotiating posture, Assad insisted that no Syrian would ever surrender a foot of land. Anyone who did so, Assad emphasized, was a traitor to his people; therefore interim arrangements and moderate solutions were not acceptable. Furthermore, Israelis now understood that geography alone would not ensure their security. Only a permanent peace would. Thus, the Israelis knew that a strategic depth of twenty kilometers would not provide total security since the range of Syrian guns had vastly improved following the June 1967 War.[39]

Conclusion

Arab public opinion in general was aware of Washington's determination to force a peace settlement on the region after the Gulf War. Moreover, there was a perception that Washington would pursue its goal with unusual ruthlessness, based on its calculations of who the winners and losers of that war were. Those who emerged weakened in the 1990s had been generally cut off their moorings earlier as a result of the collapse of the Soviet Union. For several of these political actors, particularly Syria and the PLO, the Gulf War merely accentuated their fading influence and power. None of this escaped notice in Washington, which was determined to force the kind of settlement on the concerned parties that would neutralize them permanently. As exercised by U.S. Secretary of State James Baker, the new diplomatic approach was based on a mix of realpolitik and pure racism. Psychological pressure, the art of the bluff, and intimidating tactics were put to heavy use.

The greatest victims of these tactics turned out to be the Palestinians, who, because of their deep divisions and their undemocratic leadership, succumbed easily to them. The PLO leadership, represented mostly by Arafat, was too accustomed to separate deals and secret arrangements to bring its negotiations out in the open. By the post–Gulf War period, decision making within the PLO had been monopolized by the chairman of the executive committee. Arafat was experiencing unprecedented unity at the top because of the recent demise of his two top co-leaders, Salah Khalaf and Khalil al-Wazir. By contrast, Syria was enjoying a long stretch of stability under autocratic leadership, including an absence of challenges to Assad's monopoly over foreign policy. Unlike previous rulers, Assad was unusually well suited to making vital decisions regarding defense and foreign policy issues, given his long experience in those two areas. His history, moreover, was uncompromising and strongly predisposed to comprehensive, rather than incremental, solutions.

When the U.S. negotiating tactics became known, the Palestinian opposition was against the idea of giving up Arab land for peace. Their understanding was that peace negotiations should be based on an exchange of Israeli-occupied land for peace. Not so the PLO's leadership, which was desperate for recognition and an opportunity to cement its claims to permanent leadership of the Palestinians. But since the Palestinians were not actually in possession of any land, what they were expected to give up was their right to land. The Syrians, for their part, had become familiar with the tactics of another U.S. Secretary of State, namely, Henry Kissinger, before Baker confronted them with the realities of the new world order. But even that experience did not insulate Syria against the U.S. manipulation of Arab divisions and lack of communications. No one, for instance, could have circumvented Washington's subtle pressure on the Palestinians created by frequent contacts with Damascus.

For the Israelis, the main incentive for seeking a peaceful solution was to neutralize Syria. Indeed, a peace settlement with the Palestinians was the least desired objective since it would also mean giving up occupied land. But if an agreement was reached with Syria first, the Israelis assumed that the domino theory would come into play. Not only the Palestinians but other Arab states, including Lebanon, would soon cave in. Thus, Syria was the key to Israel's regional hegemonic plans. But Syria did not cave in because it viewed its strategic posture precisely in the same hegemonic terms. Syria saw itself as the leader of the confrontation states, which were destined by the forces of history and geography to propel the sagging middle ground (the Levant region) of the Arab area.

8

The Search for a Unified Strategy

In a 1978 conversation with a French reporter, Assad attempted to justify Syria's deep involvement in Lebanon's affairs by reference to his country's special characteristics, especially its geography:

> Syria is different from any other Arab country.... We have a national responsibility and all that is Arab is our responsibility. We are distinguished by our nationalist interventionist tendencies. Therefore, no Arab unity project can be imagined without Syria. The same goes for war. Had we had common borders with Egypt, our armed forces would have entered following Sadat's visit to Jerusalem. Certainly, we are the heart, and we are in the heart of the Arab world. Syria is the crux of the question and the key to the Middle East solution.[1]

No other Syrian president has voiced similar views with the same conviction. Yet Assad was expressing a familiar national sentiment, albeit one backed by the rhetoric of a military strategist. His comments, moreover, suggest that Syria's role in the region has always been that of a dominant, interventionist state, which obviously has not always been the case. Perhaps the only theme that emerges from Assad's remarks concerns Syria's capacity to assume a central role when led by a determined and geopolitically conscious ruler. It is the ruler who, seizing the moment, can expand or contract Syria's influence in the region. It is only the ruler who has the potential to translate Syria's geography into a policy of natural intervention and strategic restructuring.

Syria's long and tortuous relationship to Arab Palestine was also an extension of the former's definition of what could be considered its natural and unnatural boundaries. Syria's history during much of this century can only be described as a continuous quest for geographic coherence and strategic security. The experience of colonial dismemberment and territorial rezoning taught the Syrians the hard lesson of what happens when a country's natural defenses are deliberately weakened. The loss of parts of the Syrian north, the granting of independence to Lebanon, and then the implantation of a foreign and expansionist power in the Syrian south all spelled disaster to the Syrian generation of the post–World War I settlement. The early nationalist leaders attempted self-consciously to reconcile their truncated and externally imposed geographic identity with the schemes of Arab unity hatched first by the Hashimite royalist camp and later by the Ba'th revolutionary camp. These new realities, however, invariably dictated caution toward the more grandiose unity plans, which were led by stronger regional powers. The Syria of Quwatli, Shishekli, and Hourani was unwilling to sacrifice its independence on the altar of Hashimite nostalgia for the bygone Arab Kingdom of Syria or the futuristic dream of a Nasserite pan-Arab and revolutionary state.

Ironically, many of the conflicts with the Iraqi-Jordanian or Egyptian axis were the result of the Palestine issue as it developed in the wake of the 1948 Palestine War. This issue was added to all the other pitfalls on the road to unity. The Palestine question threatened Syria with the loss of independence if the Jordanian royalist regime succeeded in inserting its troops in Palestine by virtue of an Arab League mandate. The Syrian government at the time saw any territorial gain on the part of the Jordanians as the first step in realizing the dream of Greater Syria in the south. The experiment in revolutionary unity under Nasser posed a different threat, as the Egyptians dominated the Syrian province to the extent that Israeli threats to Syria's waters were sacrificed in the interest of Egyptian economic and military stability.

But the threat was invariably centered in the south. Without minimizing the other dangers to Syria's survival, clearly what threatened to destabilize Syria the most was the loss of Arab sovereignty in Palestine and the resultant dangers in the form of refugee, water, and security issues. This explains Syria's preoccupation with managing the Palestinian problem, first by the diplomatic co-optation and representation of the Palestinian leadership, and later by various attempts to nurture a Syrian-dependent Palestinian leadership. The clash of Syrians and Palestinians, therefore, was inevitable by virtue of their shared claim to what constituted the legitimate staging ground and center of gravity against Israel.

The Palestinian maelstrom burst on an Arab region barely free of its colonial crisis. Of all of the Arab states surrounding Israel, Syria was the least secure, combining a fragile republican form of government with a strong and fractious military institution. The Palestinians, it turned out, could not be contained after 1948. Physically dispersed throughout the former Syrian region, they became involved with most ideological movements of the day. They too saw the lands of the former Syrian provinces as their theater of operations. They were determined to confront the usurpers of their land either by radicalizing and leading pan-Arab movements or directly through their own organizations and guerrilla formations. The pull and push factors exercised by the pan-Arab ideologies on the Palestinians illustrated their basic dilemma: were they part of the Arab nation, or was their survival dependent on their own independence?

Nothing illustrates this dilemma better than the ideological odyssey of George Habash, whose revolutionary career spanned the entire gamut of national and regional political beliefs of the post-1948 years. Habash also grappled, both intellectually and politically, with the issue of Arab sponsorship. At first devising a nihilistic philosophy of his own, he then surrendered to Nasser while the latter was practicing the strongest forms of Palestinian co-optation with Shuqeiri's PLO. Habash then devised a Palestinian ideology combining elements from his previous credo. The restless revolutionary spent the rest of his years in a futile attempt to reconcile the Palestinian revolution to the principles of the Arab Nationalist Movement. Significantly, his flirtation with the Syrian Ba'th came to an ignoble end as he discovered it lacked a serious interest in the Palestine issue as well as any real emotional commitment to it. Habash, as well as others of his Palestinian generation, saw no contradiction between commitment to the Yemeni revolution and the anti-Hashimite struggle in Jordan, and his allegiance to the Palestine cause. His tragedy was his inability to stem the tide of Palestinian pragmatism as he watched the Fateh current steadily veering to the right.

Fateh itself grappled with the issue of Arab sponsorship and co-optation. But its dilemma turned out to be twofold: how to graft the principles of foreign struggles, such as the Chinese and Vietnamese revolutions, on a tide of Palestinian discontent while remaining in control of that tide. Fateh, lacking the checkered history of Habash, was truly the child of the June 1967 War, and seemed to have been scarred by the ensuing Palestinian marginalization in inter-Arab circles. Determined not to suffer a fate similar to that of Shuqeiri, Fateh adopted the unrealistic policy of total independence from any Arab regime. But in the course of its violent confrontation with the Jordanian regime, it did not reject the friendship and mediation efforts of Nasser. The Jordanian confrontation confirmed Fateh's faith, when not yet assured of its leadership of the PLO, in its tremendous moral credibility in popular Arab circles. This conviction, in turn, encouraged the view that Arab regimes could not risk the wrath of their own people in any future struggle against the PLO.

The revolutionary mystique of the PLO, which was largely Fateh's at that point, was born out of the battle of Karamah. Fateh took on its subsequent struggles as though they were all a future Karamah. The mystique of the outnumbered Palestinian guerrilla fighters carried Fateh through the years of glory in Lebanon, when official Arab resistance to Fateh's revolutionary plans was plotted away from public view. The Israeli invasion of Lebanon in 1982 also augmented this perception by providing overwhelming force against the Palestinians. The victimization of the Palestinians, through massacres and mass expulsions, which stunned not only Arab but also international public opinion, provided another escape from self-assessment and reevaluation of strategies and goals. The Lebanese fiasco, though genuinely the result of failed policies, reinforced the Karamah mythology.

Syria's bid for control over Lebanon inevitably clashed with Fateh's near-successful attempt to dominate the Lebanese progressive camp. The Israeli invasion and the subsequent American failed foray into the Lebanese quagmire raised the stakes for Syria. The pan-Arabist quest was temporarily subsumed under Syria's quest for strategic security. Because the stakes were so high for both Syria and Fateh, their military and verbal clashes were unrivaled. Both were fighting for survival as two threatened entities caught in the grip of Israeli militarism and Lebanese factionalism. It was during this juncture that the Syrians launched their strongest campaign to separate Fateh from the rest of the Palestinian national movement. This was the first time that the PLO had to face massive defections and the potential rise of an alternate leadership. Fateh resisted, however, and neither allowed itself to be absorbed by Syria nor to be exterminated by the combined force of Syrian and dissident Palestinian troops. Fateh's leadership, under Arafat's personal direction, made a last symbolic stand at Tripoli. Fateh's ejection from the Syrian heartland was neither heroic nor totally ignoble. The PLO made a stand, suffered additional refugee casualties, and exited under the protection of foreign ships.

Its departure from Lebanon, however, did not eliminate all of the PLO's options. The confrontation with Syria merely emboldened Arafat to seek new allies. He also embraced the Machiavellian game of abandoning morals for the stratagems of war and survival, which eventually drove him to post–Camp David Egypt.

It was Egypt that bought time and provided sponsorship for the PLO. With the independent Palestinian opposition angered and despondent, Fateh led the PLO to a simple deal with Egypt's Mubarak. The deal entailed legitimation by the Arab world's most injured victims in exchange for Egyptian friendship and support. The PLO, using its status as the moral gatekeeper of the Arab world, opened the door for Egypt's admission to the Islamic Conference, and later to that of the Arab League of States. Syria's rejection of Egypt remained frozen until the Iran-Iraq War demonstrated Egypt's indispensability to any major war effort in the region. Thus, despite all of Fateh's rhetoric about the independent Palestinian decision, reality dictated a pragmatic course of manipulating one Arab state against the other. The mufti of Jerusalem had used this tactic when the centers of power within the Arab League of States threatened to swallow his cause. But his success in manipulating the Saudi-Hashimite dispute was limited by his own constrained military situation and the squabbles of his lieutenants at home.

Arafat was able to raise the art of using one Arab state against the other to new heights, largely because of two factors: the murky Palestinian nationalist ideology, which left undefined its own relationship to the wider Arab ideology; and the steadfast support of Palestinians living in the Israeli-occupied areas. Palestinian nationalism, which was often confused with the Palestinian identity, became a necessary development in the struggle against Zionism. The Palestinian national identity, a much older phenomenon, had always had a definite role within the Arab ideology. Shuqeiri struggled with these three issues as he formed his first PLO and tried valiantly to silence his critics in the pan-Arabist camp. This was the significance of the first PLO covenant, which addressed the relationship of the Palestine of the future to the rest of the Arab world. A careful reading of the second PLO covenant, amended after Fateh assumed the leadership of the rest of the guerrilla organizations, reveals a strong and conscious effort to assert the primacy of the particularist Palestinian ideology over the pan-Arab tide. The very notion of the secular democratic state in the second covenant presumes a certain specificity and exceptionalism distinguishing future Palestinian revolutionary society from Arab society.

There was always an urgent need, of course, to establish the Palestinian credentials as a national community in order to assert Palestinian rights in the face of Zionist claims to nationhood and communal integration. As the Zionist insistence on their exclusive national rights heightened, so did the Palestinian effort to emphasize their historical rootedness in the land and their cohesiveness as a national community. Clearly what needed to be emphasized was that the Palestinian case fit Max Weber's definition of a communal relationship based on "emotional, affectual, and traditional" ties.[2] But in the project of affirming the Palestinian transformation from a linguistic to a political nation and asserting their cohesiveness as a community (particularly in comparison with the weak Jewish communal ties), one should not overlook the fact that the Palestinians were always part of the larger Arab group.

This definition, moreover, was not a matter of philosophical urgency as much as it was a practical necessity. This ideological failure produced the previously discussed Palestinian conflicts that took place against the Jordanians, the Lebanese, and then the Syrians. This argument is not intended to place the blame for these inter-Arab wars exclusively on the Palestinians, but it does assume the need to sort out all these long-range regional tactics and strategies before one leads the refugees into another diaspora outside the Syrian region altogether. Blame will always be placed on some of these states for putting their state interests above those of the victimized Palestinians. But the damage to the Palestinian side was greater, not the least of which was the ideological discord it produced, which prevented a genuine integration of the various PLO factions. Many of the factional differences within the PLO were always over relations with other Arab regimes, particularly Syria, as well as over the question of accountability and democracy.

The steadfastness of the West Bank and Gaza and their determination to grant their full support to the PLO in its various factions also permitted the exchange of one Arab base of operations for another. Lebanon substituted for the loss of Jordan. But following the tragic Palestinian experience in Lebanon, the PLO was in total disarray and retreat. When the PLO's expulsion from Tripoli appeared to spell the end of its political and military apparatus, the West Bank opened up as a new Palestinian front in the form of the intifada. Bearing the brunt of the Israeli occupation made the occupied population anxious to support the unity of the leadership abroad. Their need for the political and economic support of the PLO made the intifada's grassroot leadership accept the superimposed PLO leadership. Having lost several bases of operations and alienated more than one regime, the PLO became very conscious of the threats to its existence.

The intifada, therefore, was an unexpected boon to the PLO. It generated a great degree of international support and convinced the Israelis of the ungovernability of certain occupied territories such as Gaza. These factors encouraged the Palestinians in their belief that the Israelis were battle weary and that the time was right to strike a deal. Perhaps what encouraged the PLO even more to desert the path of revolution and to seek its reincarnation as the quasi-legitimate representative of the Palestinian people, now on the path of negotiations and peace, was its long-established, albeit informal, contacts with the Western powers. This parallel strategy, which dated back to the early 1970s, reinforced the transformation of the PLO from a guerrilla organization to a political committee in search of a territorial base. If the Palestinian opposition and the radical Arab states viewed this change as a turn to the right supported by the likes of post–Camp David Egypt and the Saudi regime, that was the result of the opposition's failure to notice that the PLO's priorities had changed.

By the time the U.S. opposition to dealing with the revolutionary PLO had softened, the Gulf War radically altered the Arab balance of power. Among the weakened groups were definitely the PLO, which emerged shorn of its Arab sources of financial support and minus its decimated radical Arab allies. In addition, what increased the catastrophic dimensions of the Gulf War not only for the PLO but also for the entire Arab region was that it followed on the heels of the demise of the Soviet Union. This was a reality well understood by U.S. Secretary of State James Baker, who proceeded to prod the PLO and all the Arab states to the peace table. Thus, the Gulf War led to a "new world order" that was disastrous to all the Arabs. The PLO, for its part, should have been the one to understand that negotiating out of weakness would only result in further weakness.

This was the lesson of the Vietnamese experience, a much-touted example of revolutionary success. The Vietnamese demonstrated and wrote about the necessity of achieving victory on the ground before proceeding to negotiations. They also demonstrated that there was a time for war and a time for diplomacy and that the role of a mature leadership was to distinguish between the two. The question of timing, tactics, and a peace strategy was apparently raised in some PLO circles. The Palestinian leadership, however, proceeded to the bargaining table, and eventually to a secret set of negotiations, as though its very life depended on it. Worse yet, the PLO acted in isolation from all the other Arab states. Even its coordination with Jordan, prior to proceeding to Madrid as a single delegation, was done through the United States. The PLO's decision to proceed to the Oslo talks was reached in full secrecy, with the possible exception of some cooperation from the Egyptian secret service. Astoundingly, the decision to work out a deal by which Israel would be legitimized by its foremost adversary was not viewed as something that would affect all of Israel's Arab neighbors. The result was further weakening at the hands of the Israeli negotiators, who erased most of the PLO's international gains. In a stunning volte-face, the PLO executed a second Camp David deal, leaving the rest of its Arab allies behind. Syria, by virtue of its central position, felt the threat of isolation again and feared the loss of Israel's incentive to negotiate the return of the Golan.

As for the Palestinian remnants in Lebanon, they were doomed to await an uncertain fate until such time as the question of refugees was slated for discussions between the Israelis and the Palestine Authority. Of all the Palestinians in the diaspora, those in Lebanon bore the deepest scars of the PLO-Arab wars. Furthermore, Lebanon's own unsettled situation perpetuated the mistrust of the various Lebanese factions toward the Palestinians in their midst. In a 1998 *Christian Science Monitor* article, for instance, the Palestinians in Lebanon were described as safely encircled in their own refugee camps and absolutely neglected by their own exiled leadership. Feeling unduly burdened with the Palestinian question, the Lebanese finally enacted parliamentary legislation forbidding Palestinian naturalization in Lebanon. One reason for this is that the Palestinians constitute 13 percent of the total Lebanese population. Few professional jobs are open to them outside the camps, and the importation of building materials into the camps is also restricted. Condemned to cramped quarters and living on a meager UN dole supplied by UNRWA, the Palestinians do not figure in the plans of any official Lebanese group. Furthermore, they exist in a legal limbo, unprotected by local or international laws. Tragically, UNRWA has provided only physical assistance, since its 1948 mandate did not extend beyond humanitarian aid. The creation in 1951 of the UN High Commission for Refugees, which called for the protection and repatriation of international refugees, never extended its mandate retroactively to the Palestinians. The situation of the Lebanese Palestinians is further complicated by the lingering factionalism in the camps. Most of the remaining 17 to 18 Palestinian factions still retain their weapons and often fight violent battles against each other. As one might imagine, there is little love left for Arafat or Fateh, but the small battles over turf continue.[3]

The refugees in Lebanon, numbering around 370,000 and scattered in 12 camps, continue to bear the scars of the Lebanese civil war. Lebanese troops still surround some of the camps, particularly in the south, and it is estimated that 60 percent live below the poverty level. Although the war ended in 1989, a large number of schoolchildren, around 40 percent, are still out of school. The PLO leadership also severed all financial assistance to around 10,000 of the families of deceased fighters. UNRWA, claiming to be suffering a severe deficit, trimmed its health and education spending in 1997, provoking large-scale demonstrations and protests. The refugees often suspect UNRWA of collusion with official Lebanese plans to disperse the refugees to other parts of the Arab world. The Lebanese authorities also provoked deep-seated fears with their declared plans to raze the refugee camps as part of a blueprint for the reconstruction of peace-time Lebanon.[4]

The refugees in waiting were merely a fraction of the total Palestinian problem. At least they can be classified as something, which is not the case of other remnants of the Palestinian people, such as the Arab citizens of the state of Israel. For these, Oslo and its accomplishments must have seemed an irrelevant theater of the absurd. Other Palestinian communities, such as the Syrian Palestinians, who number around 360,000 or close to 2.5 percent of the total population, have been spared some hardships through the ability of their leadership to maintain open lines of communication to the regime. By virtue of their oppositional policies toward Fateh, these leaders have managed to assure a normal life to the refugees short of full citizenship and higher government employment.[5] Thus, if the Oslo accords turn out to be limited in application solely to the West Bank and Gaza, the status of the PLO will come into question. What kind of leadership can afford to decree a truncated definition of the homeland and its people and still claim to represent the Palestinian community at large?

Notes

1. The Struggle for Geographic Coherence: Reclaiming Southern Syria

1. Salem, *Al-hukm al-Misri*, 7.
2. Anton Saʿadeh, *Al-muhadharat*, 61–62.
3. Salem, *Al-hukm al-Misri*, 17–19.
4. Ibid., 20–22.
5. Ibid., 32, 71–82.
6. Ibid., 296–300.
7. Basily, *Souriya wa Lubnan*, 57–88, 287–302.
8. Ibid., 330–45.
9. Al-Solh, *Tarikh rajul*, 12–15, 24–25.
10. Ibid., 26–30.
11. Al-Yafee, *Jamal Pasha al-saffah*, 14–15, 57–58, 66–67, 115–18.
12. Al-Solh, *Tarikh rajul*, 30–31.
13. Al-Yafee, *Jamal Pasha al-saffah*, 64–65.
14. Khouri, *Awraq Faris al-Khouri*, 1: 111–20, 120n.4, 219–27, 250n.1; al-Solh, *Tarikh rajul*, 28–29.
15. Qasimiyeh, *ʿAbd al-Hadi*, 19–25.
16. Ibid., 13, 32–35.
17. Ibid., 37.
18. Ibid., 51–55, 57n.1.
19. Al-Kayyali, *Diraseh*, 36.
20. Qarqout, *Tatawur*, 6.
21. Al-Husri, *Muthakarat*, 1: 6–7.
22. Al-ʿAzm, *Muthakarat*, 1: 59.
23. Muhafathah, *Imaret*, 90–92.
24. Qarqout, *Tatawur*, 31–33, 105.
25. Mardam Bayk, *Awraq*, 48–49.
26. Abaza and Shishakli, *Al-Julan*, 40.
27. Ibid., 41–44.
28. Al-Samman, *Al-miyah*, 62.
29. Abaza and Shishakli, *Al-Julan*, 44–46.
30. Mardam Bayk, *Awraq*, 48–50.
31. Al-Kayyali, *Diraseh*, 64–66.
32. Ibid., 65–66.
33. Ibid., 66–68.
34. The Papers of Hizb al-Shaʿb, document 2, p. 8, the Syrian National Archives (hereafter referred to as SNA).
35. Qarqout, *Tatawur*, 103–4.

36. Qasimiyeh, 'Abd al-Hadi, 66, 66n.5.
37. Ibid., 66, 667.
38. Naddaf, *Nayef Hawatmah*, 184.
39. Zaitoun, *Min thawrat*, 15, 38.
40. Al-Sharif, *Al-Muslimoun*, 168.
41. Nuwayhedh al-Hout, *Al-Sheikh*, 32.
42. Zaitoun, *Min thawrat*, 47, 55.
43. Nuwayhedh al-Hout, *Al-Sheikh*, 25–29.
44. Ibid., 34–36.
45. Ibid., 39–52.
46. Ibid., 51–58.
47. Zaitoun, *Min thawrat*, 91–98.
48. Nuwayhedh al-Hout, *Al-Sheikh*, 53, 61–63.
49. Ibid., 49, 70–73.
50. Zaitoun, *Min thawrat*, 78.
51. Darwaza, *Hawl al-haraka*, 3: 119–21.
52. Nuwayhedh al-Hout, *Al-Sheikh*, 63.
53. Darwaza, *Hawl al-haraka*, 136.
54. Nuwayhedh al-Hout, *Al-Sheikh*, 66.
55. Al-Dassouqi, "Thawrat Rashid," 76–77.
56. Al-Sa'idi, *Fursan*, 139–41.
57. Al-Husri, *Muthakarat*, 1: 229–30.
58. Al-Dassouqi, "Thawrat Rashid," 77.
59. Nafi, "The Arabs," 9.
60. Al-Husri, *Muthakarat*, 2: 25.
61. Al-Dassouqi, "Thawrat Rashid," 78–81; Nafi, "The Arabs," 15–16.
62. Al-Sa'idi, *Fursan*, 262.
63. Al-Dassouqi, "Thawrat Rashid," 83–84.
64. Mardam Bayk, *Awraq*, 130–36.
65. Ramadhan, "Al-diplomasiyah," 67–70.
66. Talhami, *Palestine*, 32–33.
67. Weitzman, *The Crystallization*, 11–12.
68. Talhami, *Palestine*, 33–34.
69. Mardam Bayk, *Awraq*, 377.
70. Qasimiyeh, *'Abd al-Hadi*, 138n.3, 142–43.
71. Qasimiyeh, *Ahmad Shuqeiri*, 55–58.
72. Al-'Azm, *Muthakarat*, 1: 290–91.
73. Al-Husri, *Muthakarat*, 2: 153.

2. The Earthquake of the 1948 Palestine War

1. Silverfarb, *The Twilight*, 21.
2. Al-Kayyali, *Diraseh*, 275n.6.
3. Qasimiyeh, *Al-Barazi*, 31n.2.

4. Al-Kayyali, *Diraseh*, 240–42.
5. Mahfouth, *Taht rayet*, 25–29.
6. *The Papers of Fawzi al-Qawuqji* (hereafter FQ), SNA, 1925 Report, 1–2.
7. FQ, 1917 document, in Turkish and English, signed by Commander von Layser.
8. FQ, an article from *Al-Ayyam*, based on a story in the British *Daily Herald*, August 22, 1926.
9. FQ, file no. 153, Document 80.
10. FQ, file no. 153, Memorandum 711.
11. Ibid.
12. FQ, file no. 153, Communiqué no. 16, October 12, 1936.
13. FQ, file no. 153, Communiqué no. 17, October 20, 1936.
14. FQ, file no. 153, Document 89.
15. Al-Kayyali, *Diraseh*, 248–49.
16. Al-Husri, *Muthakarat*, 2: 157–58, 165–66, 179–82.
17. FQ, file no. 153, Document 113–15, pp. 26–29, 34.
18. Ibid., 34–40.
19. Ibid., 43–50.
20. Ibid., 80, 96, 105.
21. Ibid., 128–30, 136–37, 143, 148.
22. Ibid., 1.
23. Qasimiyeh, 'Abd al-Hadi, 146.
24. Qasimiyeh, *Al-Barazi*, 15–19, 54–57.
25. Ibid., 79–80, 116, 150–53.
26. Al-'Azm, *Muthakarat*, 1: 343, 384–85.
27. Al-Kayyali, *Diraseh*, 250.
28. Qasimiyeh, *Al-Barazi*, 3 1n.2.
29. Al-Kayyali, *Diraseh*, 250.
30. Ibid., 314–17.
31. Al-'Azm, *Muthakarat*, 1: 379–80.
32. Ibid., 381–82.
33. Qasimiyeh, *Al-Barazi*, 157–58.
34. Hamdan, *Akram Hourani*, 179.
35. Al-'Azm, *Muthakarat*, 2: 181–89.
36. Fansah, *Al-nakbat*, 94, 111.
37. Owen, *Akram Hourani*, 85–87.
38. Al-Mallouhi, *Akram Hourani*, 91–92.
39. Fansah, *Al-nakbat*, 113, 117–18, 143.
40. Owen, *Akram Hourani*, 87–90.
41. Fansah, *Al-nakbat*, 206–8.
42. Al-Kheir, *Akram al-Hourani*, 55–56.
43. Bazzi, *Souriya*, 245–47; Owen, *Akram Hourani*, 98.
44. Fansah, *Al-nakbat*, 220.

45. Al-Kayyali, *Diraseh*, 350–57.
46. Al-'Azm, *Muthakarat*, 2: 218.
47. Owen, *Akram Hourani*, 98–100.
48. Al-Kheir, *Akram al-Hourani*, 56–60.
49. Bazzi, *Souriya*, 252–61.
50. Owen, *Akram Hourani*, 153, 156–57.
51. The Papers of Hassan al-Hakim (hereafter HH), SNA, file no. 38, Document 13, May 23, 1956.
52. HH, file 38, Document 6.
53. Ibid.
54. Bazzi, *Souriya*, 270.
55. Al-Kheir, *Adib*, 125.
56. Bazzi, *Souriya*, 262, 267–68, 271.
57. Al-Kheir, *Adib*, 135.
58. Owen, *Akram*, 206–7.
59. Al-Kheir, *Adib*, 135.
60. Rokach, *Israel's Sacred Terrorism*, 19.
61. Ibid., 19–21.
62. Al-Kheir, *Adib*, 144–46.
63. Ibid., 141, 147–51.

3. The Political Co-Optation of the Palestinians

1. 'Ali Ridha, *Souriya*, 57.
2. Qasimiyeh, *Ahmad Shuqeiri*, 60–65.
3. Al-'Azm, *Muthakarat*, 2: 367–68, 373–78.
4. Ibid., 401.
5. Qasimiyeh, *Ahmad Shuqeiri*, 68.
6. Mattar, *Hakim*, 28–35, 39–43.
7. Lesch, "The Saudi," 40, 40n.31.
8. Bazzi, *Souriya*, 283.
9. Al-Madani, *'Adnan al-Malki*, 100–101, 122, 150.
10. 'Abd al-Mawlawi, *Al-inhiyar*, 26–31.
11. Ibid., 36–38, 51–52.
12. Haykal, *Li-Misr*, 121–23.
13. Haykal, *Waqa'i*, 36.
14. Ibid., 36–37, 59.
15. Hamdan, *Akram al-Hourani*, 249n.1.
16. Al-'Azm, *Muthakarat*, 3: 110.
17. 'Ali Ridha, *Souriya*, 178–80.
18. Bazzi, *Souriya*, 289.
19. Al'-Azm, *Muthakarat*, 3: 87–88, 92.
20. Embassy of Syrian Arab Republic, Washington D.C., "The Golan Heights: Fact and Fiction," n.d., 1–2.

21. Al-Samman, *Al-miyah*, 59–60.
22. Quoted in Embassy of Syrian Arab Republic, "The Golan Heights," 3–4.
23. Ibid., 5.
24. Drake, "The Golan Belongs to Syria."
25. Embassy of Syrian Republic, "The Golan Heights," 5.
26. Al-Samman, *Al-miyah*, 58–59, 60–61.
27. Kally, *Al-miyah*, 43–45.
28. Cowell, "Hurdle to Peace," 1, 6.
29. Baker, "Al manthour," 132–37.
30. Kally, *Al-miyah*, 43.
31. Cowell, "Hurdle to Peace," 6.
32. Kally, *Al-miyah*, 43.
33. Hamdan, *Akram al-Hourani*, 341–42, 341n.1.
34. Ibid., 342–43.
35. Ibid., 343–47.
36. Ibid., 346–50.
37. Kally, *Al-miyah*, 43–44.
38. Al-Hout, *Ishrouna*, 65–68.
39. Al-'Azm, *Muthakarat*, 4: 345.
40. Al-Hout, *Ishrouna*, 71.
41. Qasimiyeh, *Ahmad Shuqeiri*, 68–70.
42. Ibid., 70–71, 261–62.
43. Ibid., 72–74.
44. Ibid., 74–75.
45. See the first chapters of Rosemary Sayegh's book *Too Many Enemies*.
46. Al-Ghouri, "Rad," 10.
47. Ibid., 4, 19–20.
48. Al-Hout, *Ishrouna*, 86.
49. Mattar, *Hakim al-thawrah*, 60.
50. Ibid.
51. Ibid., 60–67, 88.
52. Ibid., 95–96.
53. Al-Hout, *Ishrouna*, 87.
54. 'Abd al Rahman and Darweesh, "Hiwar," 22–24.
55. Al-Hout, *Ishrouna*, 88.
56. Qasimiyeh, *Ahmad Shuqeiri*, 76.
57. Ibid., 76–77, 228, 286.
58. Ibid., 553.
59. Ibid., 571, 573.
60. Ibid., 552.
61. Ibid., 561.
62. Ibid., 79, 80–81, 566.
63. Ibid., 299–300.

64. Ibid., 91, 301–4.
65. Ibid., 82–85, 93.
66. Ibid., 85, 93.
67. Shafiq al-Hout, *Ishrouna*, 96–97.
68. Qasimiyeh, *Ahmad Shuqeiri*, 89, 91.
69. Shafiq al-Hout, *Ishrouna*, 109–10.
70. Ibid., 110–18.
71. Ibid., 118–53.
72. Ibid., 146–48.
73. Ibid., 154.
74. Qasimiyeh, *Ahmad Shuqeiri*, Appendix, Document 6, p. 581.
75. Shafiq al-Hout, *Ishrouna*, 98, 175.
76. Ibid., 125.

4. The Guerrilla Factor

1. Tlas, *Al-kifah*, 11, 96, 116.
2. Ibid., 121–26, 133–34.
3. Ibid., 198, 224.
4. Ibid., 219, 221, 221n.1, 225–26.
5. Bitterlin, *Hafiz*, 65–67.
6. Ibid., 778–83.
7. Ibid., 83–87.
8. Ibid., 91–94.
9. Ibid., 94–97.
10. Ibid., 101–6.
11. Ibid., 106–8.
12. Wallach, *Arafat*, 189–90.
13. Ibid., 191–94.
14. Ibid., 194–97.
15. 'Adel Ridha, *Qira'ah*, 149–50, 156.
16. Bitterlin, *Hafiz*, 112–16.
17. Ibid., 117–19.
18. Ibid., 119.
19. 'Adel Ridha, *Qira'ah*, 15, 157–60.
20. Bitterlin, *Hafiz*, 121–23.
21. 'Adel Ridha, *Qira'ah*, 171.
22. Bitterlin, *Hafiz*, 124.
23. 'Adel Ridha, *Qira'ah*, 336–37.
24. Bitterlin, *Hafiz*, 124.
25. 'Adel Ridha, *Qira'ah*, 339–41.
26. Seale, *Assad*, 157–58.
27. Naddaf, *Nayef Hawatmah*, 56–57, 57n.1.
28. Shafiq al-Hout, *Ishrouna*, 182–83.

29. Bitterlin, *Hafiz*, 124–25.
30. Mattar, *Hakim al-thawrah*, 89.
31. 'Abd al-Rahman and Darweesh, "Hiwar," 22, 25.
32. Haykal, *Al-salam*, 164.
33. Haykal, *Waqa'i*, 217.
34. Abu Iyad, "Fateh," 51.
35. Bitterlin, *Hafiz*, 126–27.
36. Shafiq al-Hout, *'Ishrouna*, 180–81.
37. Bitterlin, *Hafiz*, 127–30.
38. Ibid., 135–38.
39. Ibid., 138–45. See also Quandt, *Peace Process*, 111–12.
40. Naddaf, *Nayef Hawatmah*, 86–87, 87n.12.
41. Shafiq al-Hout, *'Ishrouna*, 184–85.
42. Interview with Sa'ad al-Sayel, "Taqyeem," 61.
43. 'Adhel Ridha, *Qira'ah*, 344.
44. Bitterlin, *Hafiz*, 156–57.
45. Ibid., 171–73.
46. Shafiq al-Hout, 186–87.
47. Bitterlin, *Hafiz*, 173.
48. Al-Assad, *Al-nass*, 11.
49. Hamma, *Al-murtafa'at*, 48.
50. Bitterlin, *Hafiz*, 183–86.
51. Ibid., 187–95, 198.
52. Tamir, *A Soldier*, 192–97.
53. Bitterlin, *Hafiz*, 198, 201–5.
54. Tamir, *A Soldier*, 8–9.
55. Bitterlin, *Hafiz*, 215–16.
56. Tamir, *A Soldier*, 204.
57. Bitterlin, *Hafiz*, 198–99. See also 'Adel Ridha, *Qira'ah*, 343.
58. Quandt, *Peace Process*, 226–27.
59. "Ghusn al-zaitoun," 121.
60. Bitterlin, *Hafiz*, 276.
61. Abu 'Ammar, "Bada'at," 32–33.
62. "Hiwar ma' Abu al-Luttof," 41.
63. Bitterlin, *Hafiz*, 276–77, 279–83.
64. "Al-dowrah al-rabi'ah," 71.
65. Ibid., 71–75.
66. Bitterlin, *Hafiz*, 257.

5. When Brothers Collide: The Confrontation over Lebanon

1. Dawisha, "The Motives," passim.
2. Cooley, "The Palestinians," 34–36.
3. Naddaf, *Nayef Hawatmah*, 117.

4. Snider et al., "Israel," 97.
5. Bitterlin, *Hafiz*, 232.
6. Cooley, "The Palestinians," 26, 37, 39, 45.
7. Ibid., 39.
8. Bitterlin, *Hafiz*, 243–44, 246–49, 246n.1.
9. Ibid., 252–55.
10. "Inter-Arab Relations," 147–50, 153.
11. "Palestine Issues," 183–85.
12. Ibid., 185–86, 190–92, 194–95.
13. Ibid., 196.
14. Bannerman, "Saudi Arabia," 113, 117–18, 122–23.
15. Ibid., 124–32.
16. Bitterlin, *Hafiz*, 241, 247, 292.
17. Ibid., 307.
18. Barakat, "The Social Context," 4.
19. Tamir, *A Soldier*, 113–14.
20. Ibid., 114.
21. Snider, "Inter-Arab," 196.
22. Cobban, *The Superpowers*, 20–21.
23. Tamir, *A Soldier*, 115–16.
24. Ibid., 116–18.
25. Ibid., 118–23.
26. Ibid., 123–27.
27. Haykal, *Salam*, 107, quoted in Naddaf, *Nayef Hawatmah*, 143n.5, 144n.1, 148–50.
28. Khalidi, "Behind the Fateh Rebellion," 10.
29. Naddaf, *Nayef Hawatmah*, 153, 157–61.
30. Bitterlin, *Hafiz*, 340–41.
31. Ibid., 343–45.
32. Naddaf, *Nayef Hawatmah*, 162.
33. 'Adel Ridha, *Qira'ah*, 345.
34. Naddaf, *Nayet Hawatmah*, 162–63.
35. "Palestinian Issues," *Middle East Contemporary Survey* 7: 276–79.
36. Ibid., 286, 297, 303.
37. Ibid., 303–10.
38. Ibid., 310–12.
39. Ibid., 312–13.
40. Bitterlin, *Hafiz*, 353.
41. Ibid., 347–49.
42. Cobban, *The Superpowers*, 50–58.
43. Naddaf, *Nayef Hawatmah*, 169n.22.
44. Cobban, *The Superpowers*, 46–48.
45. "The PLO," *Middle East Ccontemporary Survey* 8 (1983–84): 204–6.

46. Naddaf, *Nayef Hawatmah*, 169n.22.
47. Bitterlin, *Hafiz*, 352.
48. Naddaf, *Nayef Hawatmah*, 190.
49. Abu 'Ammar, "Al-tabadul," 9.
50. Abu 'Ammar, "Multazimouna," 6.
51. "Buyut faqirah," 10.
52. "Tahleel li-asbab al-khilaf," 4.
53. Ibid.
54. Ibid., 4–5.
55. Ibid., 5.
56. "The PLO," *Middle East Contemporary Survey* 8 (1983–84): 207.
57. "Al wafd," 6.
58. Ibrahim Shukri, interview, *Filastin al-Thawrah* no. 486, Dec. 3, 1983, 20.
59. Naddaf, *Nayef Hawatmah*, 171.
60. "The PLO," *Middle East Contemporary Survey* 8 (1983–84): 207–11, 221–22. See also ""Al-qimmah al-Islamiiyah al-rabi'ah," 11.
61. "Al-tanseeq," 5.
62. Ibid.
63. "The PLO," *Middle East Contemporary Survey* 9 (1984–85): 181–85.
64. Ibid., 185–87.
65. Ibid., 188–91.
66. Ibid., 194–216.
67. "The PLO," *Middle East Contemporary Survey* 9 (1984–85): 217–21.
68. Ibid., 221–22.
69. Sayegh, *Too Many Enemies*, 3–4, 6, 168, 184. See also "Kayfa," 10–11.
70. "'Al-hukumdar Khaddam yu'len al-harb," 8.
71. "The Palestinians," *Middle East Contemporary Survey* 10 (1986): 194–96.
72. Al-Hassan, editorial, "Min," 12.
73. "Qhadhiyat," 12.
74. "Mahdhar," 6–7.
75. Ibid., 9.
76. Ibid., 8.
77. Ibid., 7.
78. "Qhadhiyat," 13.
79. "Mudawalat," 20–21.
80. "Najah," 476–83.
81. "Rafdh," 6.
82. Naddaf, *Nayef Hawatmah*, 96n.8.
83. "The Palestinians and the PLO," *Middle East Contemporary Survey* 11 (1987): 230.
84. Abu Jihad, "Lam nakhruj," 4.
85. "Taqrir al-Ba'th," 4.
86. Sadowski, "Cadres," 3.

87. Bitterlin, *Hafiz*, 377.
88. Samaha, "Moscow," 10.

6. The Clash of Nationalisms

1. Hitti, "Foreword," in Abu-Jaber, *The Arab Ba'th*, vii.
2. Jabbour, *Al-fikr*, 54.
3. Ibid., 161–62.
4. Sa'adeh, *Al-sira'*, 46, 62.
5. Ibid., 62–65. See also Haddad and Mujais, *Ba'l Haddad*, passim.
6. Haj Isma'il, *Tarikh*, 111–14.
7. Ibid., 112–17.
8. Sa'adeh, *Fi al-mas'alah*, 73–76.
9. Ibid., 100–101.
10. Haj Isma'il, *Tarikh*, 138.
11. Sa'adeh, *Fi al-mas'alah*, 173–88.
12. Haj Isma'il, *Tarikh*, 148–49.
13. Jabbour, *Al-fikr*, 162–63.
14. Ibid., 164–67.
15. Ibid., 171.
16. Abu Jaber, *The Arab Ba'th Socialist Party*, 28–33.
17. Jabbour, *Al-fikr*, 181–83.
18. Abu-Jaber, *The Arab Ba'th Socialist Party*, 28–33.
19. Jabbour, *Al-fikr*, 227–29.
20. Al-Khouli, "Mulahathat," 144.
21. Ibid., 144–46.
22. Ibid., 146.
23. Ibid., 146–48.
24. Al-Tal, *Harakat*, 26–33.
25. Ibid., 28–30.
26. Barout, *Harakat*, 30–34.
27. Mattar, *Hakim al-thawrah*, 28–29.
28. Barout, *Harakat*, 34–35.
29. Ibid., 35–38.
30. Ibid., 47–48.
31. Al-Tal, *Harakat*, 31.
32. Barout, *Harakat*, 55–58.
33. Ibid., 58–59. 521–23.
34. Ibid., 523–24.
35. Ibid., 524–25.
36. Ibid., 525–28.
37, Al-Tal, *Harakat*, 51–54.
38. Barout, *Harakat*, 60–62.
39. Ibid., 62–64.

40. Ibid., 66–67.
41. Ibid., 75–76.
42. Ibid., 103–4.
43. Ibid., 104–6.
44. Mattar, *Hakim al-thawrah,* 56–57, 62, 65–67, 71, 87–89.
45. Ibid., 78, 85–86; Barout, *Harakat,* 266.
46. Mattar, *Hakim al-thawrah,* 92, 107, 114–17.
47. Ibid., 117–21. See also Barout, *Harakat,* 60.
48. Al-Tal, *Harakat,* 38–45.
49. Al-Khouli, "Mulahathat," 144–45.
50. Barout, *Harakat,* 311.
51. Al-Khouli, "Mulahathat," 148.
52. Shuqeiri, *Mashrou'* 9, 15–16, 27–30.
53. Ibid., 40–41.
54. Al-Khouli, "Mulahathat," 148–51.
55. Ibid., 154.
56. Ibid., 154, 156–57.
57. Ibid., 152–56.
58. "The PLO and the Intifada," *Middle East Contemporary Survey* 11 (1987): 232.
59. "The PLO-Palestine Issues," *Middle East Contemporary Survey* 12, (1988): 237–38.
60. Ibid., 244–48, 728.
61. "Palestinian Issues," *Middle East Contemporary Survey* 13 (1989): 213.
62. Ibid., 214.
63. Ibid., 214–15.
64. "Al-munaqashat," 159–62.
65. Ibid., 163–66.
66. Al-Taher, "Al-qawmi," 25–26.
67. Ibid., 26–27.
68. Shafiq al-Hout, "Azamat," 29–30.
69. Ibid., 30–31.
70. Samaha, "Moscow," 10–11.

7. Peace or Pax Americana?

1. Adel Ridha, 4855–56.
2. Hussein, *Souriya,* 265.
3. Haykal, *Harb,* 162.
4. 'Adel Ridha, *Qira'ah,* 374.
5. Haykal, *Harb,* 29–30, 224–25.
6. Ibid., 225–26, 293–97.
7. Ibid., 187–88, 291.
8. 'Adel Ridha, *Qira'ah,* 295, 489.

9. Baker, *The Politics of Diplomacy,* 115–17.
10. Ibid., 117–22.
11. Quandt, *Peace Process,* 386–94.
12. Baker, *The Politics of Diplomacy,* 427.
13. Quandt, *Peace Process,* 385.
14. Baker, *The Politics of Diplomacy,* 373–74.
15. Haykal, *Harb,* 465–66.
16. Khaled Muhammad Hussein, *Souriya,* 229.
17. Baker, *The Politics of Diplomacy,* 423.
18. Ibid.
19. Ibid., 447–48.
20. Ibid., 500–501.
21. Ibid., 507.
22. Haykal, *Harb,* 598.
23. Ibid., 592.
24. Quandt, *Peace Process,* 399–400, 403, 409.
25. Fayyadh, *Istratijiyat,* 9.
26. Ibid., 175–78.
27. Naddaf, *Nayef Hawatmah,* 196–99.
28. Ibid., 200, 206–7.
29. Ibid., 212–14.
30. Ibid., 218–21.
31. Ibid., 230.
32. Friedman, "Israel and PLO Ready," A7.
33. Gazit, "Al-Assad," 129–31.
34. Haberman, "For Golan Heights," 4.
35. Schmidt, "Backed by Key Arab Nations," A1.
36. Friedman, "The Assad Factor," A7.
37. Khaled Muhammad Hussein, *Souriya al-muʿassirah,* 257–62.
38. ʿAdel Ridha, *Qira'ah,* 494–95.
39. Ibid., 495–501.

8. The Search for a Unified Strategy

1. Bitterlin, *Hafiz al-Assad,* 377.
2. See Talhami, "From Palestinian Nationhood to Palestinian Nationalism," passim.
3. Peterson, "Why Palestinians Get Little Sympathy," 9.
4. Popular Democratic Front for the Liberation of Palestine, "Memorandum," 4.
5. Ibid., 3.

Bibliography

Syrian National Archives:

The Papers of Hassan al-Hakim
The Papers of Fawzi al-Qawuqji
The Papers of Hizb al-Shaʿb

Abaza, ʿIssam, and Hisham Shishakly. *Al-Julan: Tarikhiyyan wa atmaʿ al-ʿadow bashariyan wa idariyan jughrafiyan iqtisadiyan* (The Golan: Its history and the enemy's demographic, economic, geographic and administrative ambitions). Damascus: ʿIssam Abaza, 1975.

ʿAbd al-Mawlawi, Muhammad. *Al-inhiyar al-kabir: Asbab qiyam wa suqut wihdat Misr wa Souriya* (The great collapse: Causes of the rise and fall of the Egyptian-Syrian union). Beirut: Dar al-Maseerah, 1979.

ʿAbd al-Rahman, Ahmad, and Mahmoud Darweesh. "Hiwar maʿ Abu ʿAmmar: Hatha al-shaʿb yuʿti wa yafouq al-suʾal" (An interview with Abu ʿAmmar: This nation gives more than what is asked of it). *Filastin al-Thawrah*, Special commemorative issue, 1979.

Abu-Jaber, Kamel S. *The Arab Baʿth Socialist Party: History, Ideology, and Organization*. Syracuse, N.Y.: Syracuse University Press, 1966.

ʿAmmar, Abu. "Badaʾat al-thawrah al-haqiqiyah wa sanastamir" (The true revolution has begun, and we shall continue). *Filastin al-Thawrah*, 1979.

———. "Multazimouna waqf al-nar" (We are committed to the cease-fire). *Filastin al-Thawrah*, no. 486, December 3, 1983.

———. "Al-tabadul marhalah taleeha ithnatan" (The exchange is but one phase, to be followed by two more). *Filastin al-Thawrah*, no. 486, December 3, 1983.

Assad, Hafiz al-. "Al-nass al-kamil li-mashrouʿ dustur al-Jumhuriyah al-ʿArabiyah al-Souriyah al-matrouh ʿala al-istiftaʾ al-shaʿbi (The full text of the constitutional plan for the Arab Syrian Republic submitted for plebiscite). 1973.

ʿAzm, Khaled al-. *Muthakarat Khaled al-ʿAzm* (Memoirs of Khaled al-ʿAzm). Vols. 1–3. Beirut: Al-Dar al-Muttahidah lil-Nashr, 1973.

Baker, Hassan. Al-manthour al-maʾi lil-siraʿ al-ʿArabi al-Israʾili" (The water perspective on the Arab-Israeli conflict). *Al-Siyasah al-Duwaliyyah*, no. 104, April 1991.

Baker, James, III. *The Politics of Diplomacy: Revolution, War and Peace, 1989–1992*. New York: G. P. Putnam's Sons, 1995.

Bannerman, Graeme. "Saudi Arabia." In Haley and Snider, eds., *Lebanon in Crisis*, q.v.

Barakat, Halim. "The Social Context." In Haley and Snider, eds., *Lebanon in Crisis*, q.v.

Barout, Muhammad Jamal. *Harakat al-qawmiyeen al-'Arab: Al-nash'ah, al-tatawur, al-masa'ir* (The Arab Nationalist Movement: Its growth, development, and destiny). Damascus: Al-Markaz al-'Arabi lil-Dirasat al-Istrateejiyah, 1997.

Basily, Qostantin Mikhaelovich. *Souriya wa Lubnan taht al-hukm al-Turki min al-nahiyatayn al-siyasiyah wa al-tarikhiyah* (Syria and Lebanon under Turkish rule, from a political and historical perspective). Trans. Yasser Jaber. Beirut: Dar al-Hadatheh, 1988.

Bazzi, Naji "Abd al-Nabi. *Souriya, sira'al-istiqtab* (Syria, the struggle of polarization). Damascus: Dar ibn al-'Arabi, 1996.

Bitterlin, Lucien. *Hafiz al-Assad: Maseerat munadhel* (Hafiz al-Assad: The life story of a patriot). Trans. Elias Badawi. Damascus: Dar Tlas, 1994.

"Buyut faqirah wa hub li-'Arafat" (Poor homes and a love for Arafat). *Filastin al-Thawrah*, no. 486, December 3, 1983.

Center for Arab Unity Studies. *Dirasaat fi al-haraka al-taqadumiyah al-'Arabiyah* (Studies in the Arab progressive movement). Beirut: Center for Arab Unity Studies, 1987.

Cobban, Helena. *The Superpowers and the Syrian-Israeli Conflict*. New York: Praeger, 1991.

Cooley, John. "The Palestinians." In Haley and Snider, eds., *Lebanon in Crisis*, q.v.

Cowell, Alan. "Hurdle to Peace: Parting the Mideast's Waters." *New York Times*, October 10, 1993.

Darwaza, Muhammad 'Izzat. *Hawl al-haraka al-'Arabiyyah al-hadithah: Tarikh wa muthakarat wa ta'liqat* (On the modern Arab Nationalist Movement: A history and a memoir and commentary). Vol. 3. Sidon and Beirut: Al-Maktaba al-'Asriyah, 1959.

Dassouqi, Muhammad Kamal al-. "Thawrat Rashid 'Ali al-Kilani wa al-qadhiyah al-'Arabiyah" (Rashid 'Ali Kilani's revolt and the Arab question). *Al-Siyasah al-Duwaliyah*, no. 21, July 1970.

Dawisha, Adeed. "The Motives of Syria's Involvement in Lebanon." *Middle East Journal* 38, no. 2 (Spring 1984).

Democratic Front for the Liberation of Palestine. Memorandum on the Actual Situation of Palestinian Refugees. April 1, 1998.

"Al-dowrah al-rabi'ah 'ashrah lil majlis al-watani al-Filastini" (The 14th session of the Palestine National Council). *Filastin al-Thawrah*, 1979.

Embassy of the Syrian Arab Republic, Washington D.C. "The Golan Belongs to Syria." Unpublished report by Laura Drake, January 2, 1992.

———. "The Golan Heights: Fact and Fiction." Unpublished report. n.d.

Fansah, Bashir. *Al-nakbat wa al-mughamarat* (Catastrophes and adventures). Damascus: Dar Ya'rub, 1996.

Fayyadh, 'Ali. *Istratijiyat al-tafawudh fi al-tajribah al-Vietnamiyyah* (The strat-

egy of negotiations in the Vietnamese experience). Damascus: Dar Kan'an, 1992.
Friedman, Thomas. "The Assad Factor: Syria Makes its Influence Felt." *New York Times,* September 7, 1993.
———. "Israel and PLO Ready to Declare Joint Recognition." *New York Times,* September 1, 1993.
Gazit, Shlomo. "Al-Assad: The Price of Rejection." *Majallat al-Dirasat al-Filastiniyah* 16 (Fall 1993).
Ghouri, Emile al-. "Rad wa ta'leeq: Hadeeth Ahmad Shuqeiri fi *Akher Sa'ah*" (Comment and response to Ahmad Shuqeiri's interview in *Akher Sa'ah*). *Rasa'il Filastiniyah* (Beirut), no. 1, July 20, 1964.
"Ghusn al-zaitoun—wa bunduqiyat al-tha'ir" (The olive branch and the freedom fighter's gun). *Filastin al-Thawrah,* 1979.
Haberman, Clyde. "For Golan Heights Winery, Will It Be Stay or Go?" *New York Times,* November 2, 1993.
Haddad, Husni, and Salim Mujais. *Ba'l Haddad: Diraseh fi al-tarikh al-dini al-Souri* (The Ba'l Haddad: A study in Syrian religious history). Beirut: Dar Amwaj, 1993.
Haj Isma'il, Haider. *Tarikh al-hizb min khilal aalam Sa'adeh* (The history of the party through the passion of Sa'adeh). Beirut: Syrian Social National Party, 1989.
Haley, Edward, and Lewis W. Snider, eds. *Lebanon in Crisis: Participants and Issues.* Syracuse, N.Y.: Syracuse University Press, 1979.
Hamdan, Hamdan. *Akram al-Hourani: Rajul al-tarikh* (Akram Hourani: Man of destiny). Beirut: Bisan lil-Nashr wa al-Tawzee' wa al-'Ilam, 1996.
Hamma, Kheiri. *Al-murtafa'at al-'Arabiyah al-Souriyah al-muhtalah 'Al-Julan"* (The occupied Arab Syrian heights "The Golan"). Damascus: Hizb al-Ba'th al-Ishritaki—General Command, 1982.
Hassan, Bilal al-. "Min al-mukhayamat ila al-qimmah" (From the camps to the summit meeting). *Al-Youm al-Sabi',* no. 58, June 17, 1985.
Haykal, Muhammad Hassanein. *Harb al-Khaleej: Awham al-quwah wa al-nasr* (The Gulf War: The illusions of power and victory). Cairo: Mu'assassat al-Ahram, 1992.
———. *Li-Misr, la li-'Abd al-Nasser* (For Egypt, not for 'Abd al-Nasser). Beirut: Sharikat al-Matbou'at lil-Tawzee' wa al-Nashr, 1983.
———. *Salam al-awham: Al-mufawadhat al-sirriyah bayn al-'Arab wa al-Yahud* (The illusory peace: The secret negotiations between Arabs and Jews). Cairo: Dar al-Shuruq, 1996.
———. *Al-salam al-mustaheel wa al-dimuqratiyah al-gha'ibah* (The impossible peace and the absent democracy). Beirut: Sharikat al-Matbou'at lil-Tawzee' wa al-Nashr, 1986.
———. *Waqa'i tahqiq siyasi amam al-mudda'i al-ishtiraki* (Proceedings of a political investigation before the socialist prosecutor). Beirut: Sharikat al-Matbou'at lil-Tawzee' wa al-Nashr, 1986.

"Hiwar ma' Abu al-Luttof" (Dialogue with Farouq Qaddumi). *Filastin al-Thawrah*, 1979.

Hout, Shafiq al-. "Azamat al-harakah al-wataniyah al-Filastiniyah" (The crisis of the Palestinian National Movement). *Al Hadaf*, January 19, 1997.

———. *'Ishrouna 'aman fi munathamat al-tahrir al-Filastiniyah* (Twenty years with the Palestine Liberation Organization). Beirut: Dar al-Istiqlal, 1986.

"Al-hukumdar Khaddam yu'len al-harb 'ala mukhayamat Saida" (Commissar Khaddam declares war on the camps of Sidon). *Filastin al-Thawrah*, no. 569, August 3, 1985.

Husri, Khaldoun Sati', al-, ed. *Muthakarat Taha al-Hashimi* (Memoirs of Taha al-Hashimi). Vols. 1–2. Beirut: Dar al-Tali'a, 1978.

Hussein, Khaled Muhammad. *Souriya al-mu'assirah, 1963–1993* (Contemporary Syria, 1963–1993). Damascus: Dar Kan'an lil-Dirasat wa al-Nashr, 1996.

"Inter-Arab Relations." In Colin Legum, ed., *Middle East Contemporary Survey*, vol. 1. London and New York: Holmes and Meier Publishers, Inc., 1976–77.

"Itifaq bayn al-fasa'il al-ra'isiyah—Hawatmah: La badeel li-'Arafat" (An agreement among the principal factions—Hawatmah: No alternative to Arafat). *Al-Bayader al-Siyasi*, no. 90, February 25, 1984.

Iyad, Abu. "Fateh min al-fikrah ila al-wiladah ila al-fi'il" (Fateh from inception, to birth, to action). *Filastin al-Thawrah*, 1979.

Jabbour, George. *Al-fikr al-siyasi al-mu'asser fi Souriya* (Modern political thought in Syria). Beirut and Damascus: Al-Manarah, 1993.

Jihad, Abu. "Lam nakhruj min Lubnan" (We did not leave Lebanon). *Al-'Awdah*, no. 92, May 22, 1986.

"Kaifa wa limatha akhfaqat khutat Dimashq" (How and why did the Damascus plan fail). *Filastin al-Thawrah*, no. 563, June 22, 1985.

Kally, Elisha. *Al-miyah wa al-salam: Wujhat nathar Isra'iliyah* (Water and peace: An Israeli perspective). Trans. Randa Haider. Beirut: Institute for Palestine Studies, 1991.

Kayyali, Nizar al-. *Diraseh fi tarikh Souriya al-mu'asser, 1920–1950* (A study in Syria's modern history, 1920–1950). Damascus: Dar Tlas, 1997.

Khalidi, Rashid. "Behind the Fateh Rebellion." *MERIP Reports* 13, no. 119 (November–December 1983).

Kheir, Hani al-. *Adib al-Shishakly: Sahib al-inqilab al-thaleth fi Souriya* (Adib al-Shishakly: The man of the third coup in Syria). Damascus: Maktabat al-Sharq al-Jadid, 1995.

———. *Akram al-Hourani: Bayn al-tanaqulat al-siyasiyah wa al-inqilabat al-'askariyah* (Akram al-Hourani: Between political movements and military coups). Damascus: Matba'at al-Kateb al-'Arabi, 1996.

Khouli, Lutfi al-. "Mulahathat hawla al-thawrah al-Filastiniyah al-mu'assirah wa 'alaqatiha bi al-ahzab wa al-quwa al-taqadumiyah fi al-saheh al-'Arabiyah" (Remarks on the modern Palestinian revolution and its relationship to parties and progressive forces in the Arab arena). In *Dirasaat fi al-haraka al-*

taqadumiyah al-'Arabiyah (Studies on the Arab Progressive Movement). Beirut: Center for Arab Studies, 1987.

Khouri, Collette al-. *Awraq Faris al-Khouri* (The papers of Faris al-Khouri) Vol. 1. Damascus: Dar Tlas, 1989.

Lesch, David W. "The Saudi Role in the American-Syrian Crisis of 1957." *Middle East Policy* 1, no. 3 (1992).

Madani, Muhammad Nimer al-. *"Adnan al-Malki: Thalathat rasasat fi al-mal'ab al-baladi* ("Adnan al-Malki: Three bullets in the municipal stadium). Damascus: Al-Dar al-Hadeethah, 1996.

Maddy-Weitzman, Bruce. *The Crystallization of the Arab State System, 1945–1954*. Syracuse, N.Y.: Syracuse University Press, 1993.

"Mahdhar al-jalsah al-sirriyah li-majlis al-Jami'ah al-'Arabiyah" (Proceedings of the secret session of the Arab League Council). *Al-Youm al-Sabi'*, no. 59, June 24, 1985.

Mahfouth, Khadr al-'Ali. *Taht rayet al-Qawuqji* (Under Qawuqji's banner). Damascus: Matba'at Babil, 1938.

Mallouhi, 'Adnan al-. *Akram Hourani: 'Arrab al-inqilabat fi Souriya* (Akram Hourani: The midwife of coups in Syria). Damascus: Dar Dimashq, 1995.

Mardam Bayk, Salma. *Awraq Jameel Mardam Bayk: Istiqlal Souriya, 1939–1945* (The papers of Jameel Mardam Bayk: Syria's independence, 1939–1945). Beirut: Sharikat al-Matbou'at lil-Tawzee' wa al-Nashr, 1994.

Mattar, Fu'ad. *Hakim al-thawrah: Qissat hayat al-doctor George Habash* (The wiseman of the revolution: The life story of Dr. George Habash). London: High Light Publications, 1984.

"Mudawalat wa ajwa' al-Majlis al-Markazi al-Filastini: Lughah wahidah fi mukhatabat Dimashq" (The debates and the atmosphere of the Palestine Central Council: Damascus addressed in one language). *Filastin al-Thawrah*, no. 59, June 24, 1985.

Muhafathah, Muhammad Ahmad. *Imaret Sharq al-Urdun: Nash'atuha wa tatawurha fi rub'i qarn, 1921–1946* (Transjordan: Its rise and development during a quarter of a century, 1921–1946). Amman: Dar al-Furqan, 1990.

"Al-munaqashat" (Discussion following al-Khouli's article). In *Dirasaat fi al-haraka al-taqadumiyah al-'Arabiyah*. Beirut: Center for Arab Unity Studies, 1987.

Naddaf, 'Imad. *Nayef Hawatmah yatakalam* (Nayef Hawatmah speaks). Beirut and Damascus: Dar al-Manahel and Dar al-Kateb, 1996.

Nafi, Basheer M. "The Arabs and the Axis: 1933–1940." *Arab Studies Quarterly* 19, no. 2 (Spring 1997).

"Najah liqa' al-qimmah bayn 'Arafat wa Hussein" (Success of the summit meeting between Arafat and Hussein). *Al-Bayader al-Siyasi*, no. 91, March 3, 1984.

Nuwayhedh al-Hout, Bayan. *Al-sheikh al-mujahid 'Izz al-Din al-Qassam fi tarikh Filastin* (The patriot Sheikh 'Izz al-Din al-Qassam in Palestine's history). Beirut: Dar al-Istiqlal, 1987.

Owen, Jonathan. *Akram Hourani: Diraseh hawl al-siyaseh al-Souriya, 1943–1954* (Akram Hourani: A study in Syrian politics, 1943–1954). Trans. Wafa' Hourani. Homs: Dar al-Ma'aref, 1997.

"Palestinian Issues." *Middle East Contemporary Survey* 1 (1976–77).

"Palestinian Issues." *Middle East Contemporary Survey* 7 (1982–83).

"Palestinian Issues." *Middle East Contemporary Survey* 13 (1989).

"The Palestinians and the PLO." *Middle East Contemporary Survey* 10 (1986).

"The Palestinians and the PLO." *Middle East Contemporary Survey* 11 (1987).

Peterson, Scott. "Why Palestinians Get Little Sympathy from Lebanese Hosts." *Christian Science Monitor*, June 5, 1998.

"The PLO." *Middle East Contemporary Survey* 8 (1983–84).

"The PLO." *Middle East Contemporary Survey* 9 (1984–85).

"The PLO and the Intifada." *Middle East Contemporary Survey* 11 (1987).

"The PLO and the Intifada." *Middle East Contemporary Survey* 12 (1988).

"The PLO—Palestine Issues." *Middle East Contemporary Survey* 12 (1988).

"Qadiyat Filastin yumathiluha man nadhala bi 'ismiha" (The Palestine question should be represented by those who struggled in its name). *Al-Youm al-Sabi'*, no. 58, June 17, 1985.

Qarqout, Thouqan. *Tatawur al-harakah al-wataniyah fi Souriya, 1920–1939* (The development of the nationalist movement in Syria, 1920–1939). Damascus: Dar Tlas, 1989.

Qasimiyeh, Kheiriyeh. *Ahmad Shuqeiri: Za'iman Filastiniyan wa ra'idan 'Arabiyan* (Ahmad Shuqeiri: A Palestinian leader and an Arab pioneer). Kuwait: Committee to Commemorate Ahmad Shuqeiri, 1987.

———. *"Awni 'Abd al-Hadi: Awraq Khasseh* ('Awni 'Abd al-Hadi: Private papers). Beirut: Markaz al-Abhath, PLO, 1974.

———. *Muthakarat Muhsin al-Barazi, 1947–1949* (Memoirs of Muhsin al-Barazi, 1947–1949). Beirut: Al-Ruwaad lil-Nashr wa al-Tawzee', 1994.

"Al-qimmah al-Islamiiyah al-rabi'ah—'awdat Misr: Intisar akhar li-Abu 'Ammar" (The fourth Islamic summit—Egypt's return: Another victory for Abu-'Ammar). *Filastin al-Thawrah*, no. 493, January 28, 1984.

Quandt, William B. *Peace Process: American Diplomacy and the Arab-Israeli Conflict since 1967*. Berkeley: University of California Press, 1993.

"Rafdh al-tafweedh aw al-inabah aw al-musharakah" (Rejecting the Delegation of Authority or Joint Control). *Filastin al-Thawrah* 546 (February 23, 1985).

Ramadhan, 'abd al-'Atheem. "Al-diplomasiyah al-Misriyah athna' al-harb al-'alamiyah al-thaniyah" (Egyptian diplomacy during the Second World War). *Al-Siyasah al-Duwaliyah*, no. 22, October 1970.

Ridha, 'Adel. *Qira'eh fi fikr al-Assad* (A reading of Assad's thought). Cairo: Dar Akhbar al-Youm, 1993.

Ridha, 'Ali. *Souriya: Min al-istiqlal hata al-wihdah al-mubarakah* (Syria: From independence until the blessed union). Aleppo: Skeek Block lil al-tiba'eh, 1983.

Rokach, Livia. *Israel's Sacred Terrorism: A Study Based on Moshe Sharett's Personal Diary and Other Documents*. Belmont, Mass.: Association of Arab-American University Graduates, 1980.
Sa'adeh, Anton. *Fi al-mas'alah al-Filastiniyah* (Regarding the Palestine question). Beirut: Dar Fikr lil-Abhath wa al-Nashr, 1991.
———. *Al-muhadharat al-'ashr, 1948* (The ten lectures, 1948). N.p., n.d.
———. *Al-sira' al-fikri fi al-adab al-Souri, 1940* (The intellectual struggle in Syrian literature, 1949). Beirut: Syrian Social National Party, 1978.
Sadowski, Yahya M. "Cadres, Guns, and Money: The Eighth Regional Congress of the Syrian Ba'th." *MERIP Reports* 15, no. 6 (July–August 1985).
Sa'idi, Samir al-, ed. *Fursan al-'Uruba: Muthakarat al-shahid al-'aqeed al-rukn Salah al-Din al-Sabbagh* (Heroes of Arabism: The memoirs of the martyred Colonel Salah al-Din al-Sabbagh). Rabat: Tanet lil-Nashr, 1994.
Salem, Latifah Muhammad. *Al-hukm al-Misri fi al-Cham, 1831–1841* (Egyptian rule in Syria, 1831–1841). Cairo: Maktabat Madbuli, 1989.
Samaha, Joseph. "Moscow tunawe' 'ulaqatuha isti'dadan lil-shita' al-har" (Moscow varies its relationships in preparation for a warm winter). *Al-Youm al-Sabi'*, no. 25, October 29, 1984.
Samman, Nabeel al-. *Al-miyah wa salam al-Sharq al-Awsat* (Water resources and peace in the Middle East). N.p.: Nabeel al-Samman, n.d.
Sayegh, Rosemary. *Too Many Enemies: The Palestinian Experience in Lebanon*. London and New Jersey: Zed Press, 1994.
Sayel, Sa'd al-. Interview. "Taqyeem lil-'amal al-'askari al-Filastini dakhel wa kharej al-watan al-muhtal" (An evaluation of Palestinian military activity inside and outside the occupied homeland). *Filastin al-Thawrah*, 1979.
Schmidt, William E. "Backed by Key Arab Nations, Arafat Seeks to Conclude Pact." *New York Times*, September 7, 1993.
Seale, Patrick. *Assad: The Struggle for the Middle East*. Berkeley: University of California Press, 1990.
Sharif, Munir al-. *Al-Muslimoun al-'Alawiyoun, man hum? Wa ayna hum?* (The 'Alawite Muslims, who are they, and where are they?) Damascus: Al-Matba'at al-'Umoumiyah, 1960.
Shukri, Ibrahim. Interview. "Udwan Souri, la iqtital Filastini" (A Syrian aggression, not an inter-Palestinian war). *Filastin al-Thawrah*, no. 486, December 3, 1983.
Shuqeiri, Ahmad. *Mashrou' al-dowlah al-'Arabiyah al-muttahidah* (The project of the United Arab state). Beirut: Center for Palestine Studies, 1967.
Silverfarb, Daniel. *The Twilight of British Ascendency in the Middle East*. New York: St. Martin's Press, 1994.
Snider, Lewis W. "Inter-Arab Relations." In Haley and Snider, eds., *Lebanon in Crisis*, q.v.
———, et al. "Israel." In Haley and Snider, eds., *Lebanon in Crisis*, q.v.
Solh, Hilal al-. *Tarikh rajul wa qadhiyah: Riyadh al-Solh, 1894–1951* (The history of a man and a cause: Riyadh al-Solh, 1894–1951). Beirut: Hilal al-Solh, 1994.

Taher, Maher al-. "Al-qawmi wa al-watani fi al-nidhal al-Filastini" (The national and the regional in the Palestinian struggle). *Al-Hadaf,* January 19, 1997.

"Tahleel li-asbab al-khilaf bayn Fateh wa Souriya" (An analysis of the causes of the Fateh-Syrian dispute). *Filastin al-Thawrah,* no. 478, October 8, 1983.

Tal, Suhair Salti al-. *Harakat al-qawmiyeen al-'Arab wa in 'itafatha al-fikriyah* (The Arab Nationalist Movement and its ideological twists and turns). Beirut: Center for Arab Studies, 1996.

Talhami, Ghada. "From Palestinian Nationhood to Palestinian Nationalism." *Arab Studies Quarterly* 5, no. 4 (Fall 1986).

———. *Palestine and Egyptian National Identity.* New York: Praeger, 1992.

Tamir, Avraham. *A Soldier in Search of Peace.* New York: Harper and Row, 1988.

"Al-tanseeq qad yakoun al-nawah li-mawqef 'Arabi muwahad wa shamel" (Coordination may be the nucleus of a unified and comprehensive Arab position). *Al-Bayader al-Siyasi,* no. 90, February 25, 1984.

"Taqrir al-Ba'th: Ba'di al-toufan" (The Ba'th's first report: After me, the deluge). Editorial, *Filastin al-Thawrah,* no. 543, February 2, 1985.

Tlas, Mustafa. *Al-kifah al-musalah fi wajh al-tahadi al-Sahyouni* (The armed struggle faces the Zionist challenge). Damascus: Ministry of Defense, 1971.

"Al-Wafd al-Misri hamal risaleh min Abu 'Ammar li-sha'b Misr" (The Egyptian delegation carried a message from Abu 'Ammar to the Egyptian people). *Filastin al-Thawrah* 486 (December 3, 1983).

Wallach, Janet, and Wallach, John. *Arafat: In the Eye of the Beholder.* New York: Carol Publishing Group, 1990.

Yafee, Na'im al-. *Jamal Pasha al-saffah: Diraseh fi al-shakhsiyah wa al-tarikh* (Jamal Pasha the butcher: A study in character and history). Latakia: Dar al-Hiwar lil-Nashr wa al-Tawzee', 1993.

Zaitoun, 'Abd al-Wahab. *Min thawrat al-mujahid 'Izz al-Din al-Qassam ila thawrat abtal al-hijareh* (From the revolt of 'Izz al-Din al-Qassam to the revolt of the heroes of the stones). Damascus: Dar al-Ma'rifah, 1993.

Index

'Abbas, Muhammad, 141
Al-'Abbas, Abu, 116
Al-'Abboushi, Fahmi, 13
'Abd al-Hakim, 'Amir, 177
'Abd al-Rahman, Ahmad, 141
'Abd al-Shafi, Haidar, 201, 206–7
'Abd al-'Aziz, King, 19, 21, 32, 34–35
'Abd al-Baqi, Ahmad Hilmi, 33, 47, 59
'Abd al-Ghani, Qanout, 57
'Abd al-Hadi, Amin Bey, 5
'Abd al-Hadi, 'Awni, 6, 13, 14, 22
'Abd al-Hadi, Salim al-Ahmad, 5
'Abd al Hamid, Hayel, 137
'Abd al-Hamid, Sa'id, 21
'Abd al-Hamid, Sultan, 5
'Abd al-Ilah, 154
'Abd al-Karim, Ahmad, 57
'Abd al-Karim, Khalil, 5
'Abd al-Magid, Farid, 98
'Abd al-Majid, Shuman, 67
'Abd Rabbo, Yasser, 141
'Abd al-Rahman, Ahmad, 128
'Abduh, Imam Muhammad, 15
'Abdullah of Jordan, king/prince: assassination plot against, 49; conflict with Faisal over title to Iraq, 7–8; Egyptian criticism of, 36; Greater Syria scheme of, 21, 31, 39, 40; Jordanian dispute of 1947 and Syria, 32–33; pan-Arabism and, 155; Qawuqji and, 27–28
Abtal al-'Awdah (Heroes of the Return), 70, 179, 180
Abu al-'Abbas, 141
Abu al-Huda, Hassan Khaled, 9
Abu-Ghosh family, 3
Abu Kuwayk, Samih, 140
Abu Musa, 133, 143, 150, 152
Aden Accords, 139
Al-Afghani, Jamal al-Din, 15
'Aflaq, Michel, 39, 84–85, 163, 166, 169, 170

Al-'Ahd, 6
Al-Ahdab, 'Aziz, 114
Al-Ahmar, 'Abd Allah, 82
Al-Ahmar, 'Abdullah, 85
Ajami, Fouad, vii
Al-'Alami, Musa, 22
'Alawites, 11, 12, 144
Alexandretta, 159
Algeria, 64, 81, 133, 139, 193–94
Algiers Arab summit, 197, 198
Al-'Ali, Saleh, 15
Allon, Yigal, 53
'Aloubah, Muhammad 'Ali, 21, 30
'Alwan, Jasem, 64, 82, 93, 178
Amal: Fateh and, 144; Israel on, 122; Maronites and, 129; PLO and, 142, 143, 145, 146–47; support for, 143
'Amer, 'Ali 'Ali, 70
American University of Beirut, 170–71
Amin, Samir, viii
'Anabtawi, Salah, 174
Anglo-American Committee, 22
Anglo-Egyptian Treaty (1938), 169
ANM (Arab Nationalist Movement) (Harakat al-Qawmiyeen al-'Arab). See Arab Nationalist Movement
Ansar Committee for the Defense of Prisoners, 133
Anwar Pasha, 5
'Aqel, Sa'id, 156
Al-'Arab, Jabal, 27, 41–42
Arab Cooperation Council, 197
Arab Higher Committee, 22, 24, 31, 33–34, 62, 160
Al-'Arabi, Yousef, 86, 87
Arabian-American Oil Company (ARAMCO), 25, 90
Al-'Arabiyah al-Fatah, 5, 6, 9, 10, 14
Arab League of States, 128; 'Aleh 1947 meeting of, 26; Alexandria summit meeting, 67; Anshas 1946 meeting of,

Arab League of States—*continued*
  22; Ba'th Party and, 162; Cairo council 1945 meetings of, 22; charter signing, 22; Council of the, 148; Egypt membership in, 197, 216; emergency June 1985 meeting about Amal and Syria, 145–46; Jordan's support for, 67; Khartoum 1967 summit meeting of, 71–73, 75, 90, 188–89; meetings in 1964, 60; meetings in 1965, 58; military committee of, 26–27, 33; Nasser and, 55–56, 61, 74–75; PLO as member of, 186, 192; al-Qawuqji supporters and, 30; rejection of Johnston Water Plan, 55; responsibility to Palestinians, 147–48; Sa'adeh on, 158; self-description of, viii; Shuqeiri and, 59–60, 70, 75–76, 181; summit meeting of 1963, 55

Arab Liberation Movement (Harakat al-Tahrir al-'Arabi), 41

Arab Military Committee, 26–27, 33

Arab Nation, The: Nationalism and Class Struggles (Amin), viii

Arab Nationalism: A Critical Inquiry (Tibi), viii

Arab Nationalist Movement (Harakat al-Qawmiyeen al-'Arab) (ANM): AUB influences on, 170–71; Ba'thists and communists and, 63–64; Beirut meeting of December 1956, 176–77; break with Nasser, 179–80; building stage of, 174; Committee to Resist Peace with Israel and, 175; de-emphasis on term "party," 175–76; elite nature of early, 168–69; focus of, 167–68; intellectual phases of, 173–74; Iraq and, 176–77; Marxist-Leninist focus of, 180; membership of, 176; military and, 178; Nasser and, 93, 167–80, 176–80; origins of, 50, 168, 174–75; origins of ideology of armed struggle in, 171–72; Palestinian question versus Arab nationalism, 191; PFLP creation and, 91; post-1967 strategy, 179; reasons for emergence of, 167; Shuqeiri and, 180–83; Zureiq influences on, 170–71

Arab Socialist Labor Party (Hizb al-'Amal al-'Ishtiraki al-'Arabi), 180

Arab Socialist Movement, 97
Arab Socialist Party, 41, 163
Arab Socialist Union, 97
Arab summit meeting (1978), 106
Arafat, Yasser: at Arab summit of 1978, 106; Assad and, 127, 195–96; Assad's imprisonment of, 87–88; campaign to rebuild legitimacy, 138–39; on Camp David accords, 105–6; China trip of, 93; critics of, 113, 127, 137–38, 146, 150, 153, 206; diplomatic skills of, 216; early contact with Syria, 85–86; Egypt and, 136–41; election as chairman of PLO executive committee, 92; fear of attack by Assad, 127; Amin Gemayel and, 144, 145; Habash on ouster of, 139; infiltration of Golan, 87; Jordan and, 148–49; Lebanon withdrawal and, 123, 125–26; Madrid peace talks and, 206–7; mufti and, 64; Nasser and, 93; Oslo peace accords and, 207; on Palestinian-Syria connection, 105–6; PDFLP and, 206; PLO defections and, 128–29; PLO on Ba'thist pan-Arabism of, 110; PNC and, 137–38, 140–41; on post-Gulf War peace negotiations, 202, 203; prisoner exchanges and, 132–33; recruitment of guerrilla fighters by, 86; refugee camp war and, 141–42; relocation after withdrawal from Lebanon, 125; resignation from PNC executive committee, 137–38, 141; support for Saddam Hussein during Gulf War, 201; Syria and, 126–28, 195–96; Tripoli and, 131; and U.N. Resolution 242, acceptance by, 198; at U.N., 104–5, 185; "With No Boundaries," 136. *See also* PLO

ARAMCO (Arabian-American Oil Company), 25, 90

Areslan, 'Adel, 7

Argov, Shlomo, 122

Al-'Arisi, 'Abd al-Ghani, 5, 6

Al-Arsuzi, Zaki, 159

Al-'As, Sa'id, 18

Al-As'ad, As'ad, 107

Al-Ashmar, Sheikh Muhammad, 18

'Ashrawi, Hanan, 201, 202

Ashur (Assuria), 1

Al-Assad, Hafiz: Arafat and, 87–88, 127, 195–96; armed forces support for, 84; arms smuggling to Fateh, 64–65; assassinations allegedly involved in, 141; Baker on, 200; and Baker peace talks, pressure on, 201–2; Baʻth Military Committee and, 81; Baʻth Party and, 97; on comprehensive peace, 209, 210; coup of February 23, 1966, and, 84–85; coup of March 8, 1963, and, 83; criticism of PLO, 115, 124; definition of peace agreement, 209; failure in regard to PLO, 153; goals in confrontations with Israel, 100–101; imprisonment of, 81–82; knowledge of Israel's attack on Lebanon, 122; as minister of defense, 85, 88, 91, 100; October 1973 War and, 100–102, 109–10; Oslo peace accords and, 207–8; in Palestinian-Jordan war, 95–97; Palestinian policy of, 95–97, 114; on Palestinians and al-Ahdab "television coup," 114; pan-Arabism of, 151–52, 209; PLO criticism of, 96–97; PLO executive committee meeting with, 101–2; on PLO leadership, 129; pre-1967 war situation and, 88–89; reaction to Lebanese political divisions, 114–15; reaction to unilateral peace, 195–96; rise to power of, 80–85, 108–9; Soviet Union and, 106, 196–97; on Syria's involvement in Lebanon, 212; Syria's military capabilities and, 89–90
Al-Assad, Rifʻaat, 127, 138
Al-ʻAssali, Faisal, 37
ʻAssifa, 99, 111
Assuria (Ashur), 1
Al-Atassi, Hashem, 11–12, 39, 41, 44, 49, 163
Al-Atassi, Luʼay, 82, 83
Al-Din al-Atassi, Nur, 71, 85, 90, 96, 97
Al-Atrash, Mansour, 67
Al-Atrash, Muhammed, 43
Al-Atrash, Sultan Pasha, 18, 27
ʻAttallah, Ghazi, 128
ʻAttiyah, Hanafi, 17
Austin, Warren, 47
ʻAziz, Tareq, 107, 147
Al-ʻAzm, Khaled: on armistice lines, 36; arms acquisitions and, 34; in al-Atassi government, 39; Bandung Conference and, 48, 77; on Greater Syria scheme, 40; Hourani as minister of defense under, 40–41; law for foreign nationals appointments and, 49; on Nasserite unity plans, 58–59; Tapline agreement and, 35; on union of Egypt and Syria, 52
Al-ʻAzzam, ʻAbd al-Rahman, 30

Baddawi refugee camp, 128
Bader division, 125
Baghdad Pact, 50, 51
Baghdad summit meeting (1978), 106–7
Bakdash, Khaled, 52
Baker, James, 198–99, 200–202, 203, 205–6, 210
Al-Bakr, Hassan, 103
Balfour Declaration, 8, 10
Bandung Conference (1955), 48, 51, 76, 77
Barazi, Muhsin, 32, 37
Al-Barazi, Husni, 13
Basily, Qostantin Mickaelovich, 3–4
Al-Baʻth, 83, 104, 162. See also Baʻth Party
Baʻth Military Committee, 81
Baʻth Party, viii, 57; ANM and, 63–64; Arab League of States and, 162; Arab unity alternative approaches of, 164; attitude toward First Palestine War, 163; background influences on, 161; al-Baʻth, publication of, 83, 104, 162; Beirut conference in 1959, 81; Branch of Palestinian Action of, 166; Communist Party and, 177; division over separation from Egypt, 82–84; end of right wing of, 84–85; versus Fateh, 191; fifth meeting of 1962 regional congress, 83; Habash reaction to, 171; Lebanese, 143; Marxism and, 90; National Command Council of, 166; ninth emergency session, 78; opposition to Palestinian nationalism, 165; Palestinians and, 162; Palestinian view of, 148; pan-Arabism of, 161–67; people's war of liberation and, 164; PLO covenant and, 193; popular meetings of progressive Arab groups and,

Ba'th Party—*continued*
  164–65; promotion of people's war, 86; reaction to Syria-Iraq union, 40; renewal of membership of, 91–92; al-Shishakli and, 41; split in, 81, 97, 108; Ten Point Program and, 183; "The Proposed Palestinian Framework," 165–66
Al-Bayader al-Siyasi, 138
Baydhoun, Mustafa, 174
Begin, Menachem, 119
Beirut, siege of, 123
Ben Bella, Ahmad, 60
Ben Gurion, David, 56, 58
Benjedid, Chadli, 133
Biqaa' Valley, 119–20, 124, 128
Al-Bitar, Salah al-Din, 48, 57, 58, 81, 83, 85, 162, 163
Al-Bizreh, 'Afif, 50, 52
"Black September," 95
Bludan Arab conference (1937), 21, 22
Bludan Arab conference (1946), 22
Boumédienne, Houari, 106, 107
Bourguiba, al-Habib, 69, 125
Bourj al-Barajneh refugee camp, 142
Brezhnev, Leonid, 106
Britain: British-Iraqi treaty of 1930, 18; on Greater Syria scheme, 33; al-Hinnawi coup and, 39–40; mandate in Palestine, 163; mandate in Syria, 7; Palestine withdrawal plans of, 31; Palestinian uprisings against, 14–15, 17; prisoners of, 20
British-Iraqi treaty (1930), 18
Brown, George, 196
"Building for Peace" (Ross), 200
Bunche, Ralph, 36, 38, 54
Burns, Bill, 199
Burns, E. L., 53–54

Cairo agreement, 108, 149
Camp David accords, 105–8, 158, 187, 218
Casablanca Arab summit, 197
Cease-fire, in Lebanon, 123
Cedar Guards, 113
Central Committee for the Assistance of the Syrian Victims, 18
Central Committee of Fateh, 137
Central Committee of the Jihad, 18

Cham, 1, 2–3
Chamoun, Camille, 113, 118
China, 48, 69, 75, 93
Christians: emigration from Lebanon, 114–15; fighting in Lebanon, 118, 121; jihad and al-Qassam, 17–18; Maronite, 113, 129, 143
Christopher, Warren, 208
Churchill, Winston, 11
Collusion Across the Jordan (Shlaim), vii
Committee of Union and Progress (CUP), 4–5
Committee to Resist Peace with Israel, 174, 175
Communist party, 52, 63, 97, 177, 182
Copland, Miles, 37
Council of the Arab League, 148
Cuba, 128
CUP (Committee of Union and Progress), 4–5

Daghastani, Ghazi, 45
Dagher, As'ad, 13
Dalati, Zuheir, 67
Damascus, as pashalik of Ottoman Empire, 2–3
Darwaza, Al-Hakam, 174
Darwaza, 'Izzat, 13, 18, 26, 30
Al-Dawalibi, Ma'rouf, 44, 82
Dayan, Moshe, 43, 89, 119
"Death of Pan-Arabism, The" (Ajami), vii
Democratic Alliance, 139–40, 142
Democratic Front, 152
Democratic Party, 9
Dhahi, Jihad, 168–69
Al-Difaa', 14
Al-Din Zein, Farid, 36, 45
Dor, Gabriel, vii
Druze: clashes with Maronites, 129; establishment of state for, 11, 12; migration of, 89; Palestinian support for, 18; rebellions of, 3, 27, 41–42, 43; refugee camp war and, 143
Druze Progressive Socialist Party, 143

Eden, Anthony, 21
Egypt: abandonment of Syria, 105, 110; after Camp David accords, 196; al-

Za'im and Farouq meeting, 38; Anglo-Egyptian Treaty of 1938, 169; ANM and, 167–80; Arafat and, 136–41; break with Syria, 82–84; coordination with Syria, 50; criticism of 'Abdullah of Jordan, 36; disputes with PLO, 69; early rule of Syria, 2–3; first involvement in Palestine, 21; First Palestine War and, 31, 35–36; Hourani on separation of Syria and, 81; Iraq and, 35–36; Jordan and, 35–36, 88, 97–98; membership in Arab League of States, 197, 216; membership in ICO, 138; October 1973 War and, 102; Palestinian diplomatic initiatives and, 65; Palestinian revolution and, 93–94; PLO and, 69; PLO in peace plans and, 199; as PLO intermediary, 205; PLO militia relocation and, 125; policy toward Palestinians, 76–77; political relations with other Arab states, 56; reaction to Syria-Iraq union, 40; Saudi Arabia agreement with, 71–72; support of PLO, 67; Syria and, 45, 50, 88, 216; -Syria defense pact, 88; Syria's demands of, 61; -Syria economic pact, 51, 88; unity with Syria, 52–53, 57, 64, 74, 81–82. *See also* Nasser, Gamal Abdel

Egypt's Liberation (Nasser), 174
'Ein al-Hilwah refugee camp, 142
'Ein Jalut militia units, 125
Eisenhower Doctrine (1957), 50, 51
Eitan, Rafael, 119

Fadhel, 'Umar, 174
Fahd, King, 133, 201
Al-Fahoum, Khaled, 107, 124, 126, 128, 140, 152
Faisal, Prince, 5, 6, 7–8, 14, 19, 48, 49
Al-Faisal, Sa'ud, Prince, 131
Faisal I of Iraq, King, 177
Faisal of Saudi Arabia, King, 70, 71–72, 117
Faisal-Weizmann Agreement, 6
Falke Bernadotte plan, 33
Al-Farhan, Hamad, 174
Faris, Nabih Amin, 170
Farouq, King, 32, 33, 38

Fateh: after Lebanon withdrawal, 126; Amal and, 144; Arab sponsorship versus independence and, 214–15; versus Ba'th Party, 191; Central Committee of, 137; criticisms of, 186–87, 194, 204; failure of, 153; financial assets of, 87–88; independence of, 94; Jordan and, 214; lack of unity in, 92–93; in Lebanon, 98, 126; Madrid talks and, 205; media coverage of, 133–34; models of negotiation for, 204; movement outside of Syria, 86; Nasserite leanings of, 93, 214; origins of, 81; Palestinian opposition to, 143, 152; pan-Arabism and, viii, 150; PNC and, 116, 140; policy after battle of Karamah, 182; post-1967 war, 179; publications of, 126; reasons for leadership role of, 134–35; refugee camp war and, 144–45; renewal of contact with Gemayel government, 145; al-Sa'iqa and, 126, 134; Shuqeiri and, 64–65, 70, 180; Soviet Union and, 190; Syria and, 134, 135, 136; Syria's dislike of leadership of, 136, 138; Syria's support for early, 164, 182. *See also* PLO
Fawzi, Mahmoud, 55–56
Fertile Crescent project, 21, 38, 56
Filastin al-Thawrah, 126, 133, 151, 152
Fischer, Roger, 204
France: involvement in PLO's Lebanon withdrawal negotiations, 123; mandate in Syria, 7, 9, 10–13, 18–19; reaction to Syria-Iraq union, 40; support of PLO evacuation from Tripoli, 132; support of second Shishakli coup, 45; Sykes-Picot Agreement and, 10; Syrian assembly elections called by, 11–12; Syrian nationalism and, 19–20; treaty with Syria, 18
Frangieh, Suleiman, 113, 114, 115, 129
Free Nationalists, 118
Friedman, Thomas, 208
Front for the Liberation of Palestine (Jabhat Tahrir Filastin), 70, 179

Game of Nations, The: The Amorality of Power (Copland), 37
Gaza, 61, 217, 220

Gemayel, Amin, 129, 144, 145, 151
Gemayel, Bashir, 118, 119, 125
Gemayel, Pierre, 118
General Union of Palestinian Students, 81, 180
General Union of Palestinian Women, 180
Geneva Conference (1973), 103
Germany, 20, 27
Al-Ghanim, Walid, 163
Ghawsha, Samir, 140
Al-Ghoury, Emile, 22
Al-Ghussein, Jawid, 141
Al-Ghussein, Ya'qub, 22
Gidi pass, 102
Glubb Pasha, John B., 31, 49, 169, 174
Golan Heights: Egypt's abandonment of Syria over, 105; Israeli law and, 120; in October 1973, 102; as PLO infiltration point, 87; Syria's confrontation with Israel over, 89, 100, 208
Golan II, 208
Golden Square, 19, 20
Gorbachev, Mikhail, 196
Gouraud, Henri, 7, 11
Government of All Palestine (Hukumat 'Umum Falastin), 33, 34, 47, 165
Great Arab Revolt (1916), 177
Greater Syria scheme, 21–22, 31, 33, 39, 40, 162, 163
Greece, 132
Guardian, The, 145
Guerrilla warfare, 70, 78–80, 85–86, 87, 95, 109, 182. *See also* Amal; PLO
Gulf of 'Aqaba, 56, 70
Gulf War, 200–201, 202, 203, 210, 218–19

Haass, Richard, 200
Habash, George, 170, 174; on ANM, 177; Arab versus Palestinian nationalism, 191, 214; background of, 169; coups and involvement of, 178; Nasser and, 64, 93; on ouster of Arafat, 139; PFLP and, 63; reaction to Ba'th, 171; revolutionary group of, 49–50, 63, 64, 168
Habib, Philip, 120, 122, 123, 124, 151
Al-Hadaf, 126
Haddad, Sa'ad, 118
Haddad, 'Uthman Kamal, 20
Haddad, Wadi', 50, 174, 179
Al-Haffar, Lufti, 13
Al-Hafiz, Amin, 65, 67, 83–84
Haig, Alexander, 120
Al-Haj, Isma'il, 128
Hajjar, Bishop Gregorius, 17
Al-Hakim, Hassan, 41
Al-Halabi, Muhammad 'Ali, 107
Halal, Muhammad, 124
Hamdoun, al-Naqib Mustafa, 42–43, 57
Hammarskjöld, Dag, 55
Hamoudah, Yahya, 73
Al-Hamshari, Mahmoud, 100
Hanano, Ibrahim, 12, 15
Harakat al-Qawmiyeen al-'Arab. *See* Arab Nationalist Movement
Harakat Nassret al-Iraq (the Movement to Champion Iraq), 177
Al-Hariri, Ziad, 83
Hashem, Ibrahim, 8
Al-Hashimi, Taha, 8, 19, 20, 29
Al-Hashimi, Yassin, 19
Hashimites, 14, 21, 38, 41–42, 45
Al-Hassan, Bilal, 63
Al-Hassan, Hani, 183
Al-Hassan, Khaled, 117, 131, 183
Hassan Hamad, 5
Hassounah, 'Abd al-Khaleq, 59, 65
Hatoum, Saleem, 84, 85
Hawatmah, Nayef, 91, 92, 122, 123, 125, 132, 178, 179, 206
Haykal, Muhammad Hassanein, 51–52, 56–57, 94, 104, 122
Heroes of the Return (Abtal al-'Awdah), 70, 179, 180
Higher Military Council, 101
Hindi, Mahmoud, 26
Al-Hindi, Hani, 50, 64, 168, 169, 178
Al-Hindi, Mahmoud, 168
Hinnawi, Sami, 27, 39–40
History of the Arab Peoples, A (Hourani), viii
Hitti, Philip, 154
Hittin forces, 68, 76, 86
Hizb al-'Ahd, 6
Hizb al-'Amal al-'Ishtiraki al-'Arabi (Arab Socialist Labor Party), 180

Al-Hizb al-Ta'awuni al-Ishtiraki (Socialist Cooperative Party), 37
Hizb Filastin al-'Arabi, 170
Hizb al-Istiqlal, 9, 13, 14, 18, 24
Hizb al-Lamarkaziyah, 6, 9
Holst, Johan Jorgen, 207
Hourani, Akram: Arab Socialist Party and, 163; assassination plots against, 168, 177; in First Palestine War, 27; on Jordan River diversion, 57; military and, 46; as minister of defense under al-'Azm, 40–41; removal from power, 83; on separation of Egypt and Syria, 81; on union of Syria and Iraq, 39; al-Za'im coup and, 37–38
Hourani, Albert, viii
Al-Hout, Bayan Nuwayhedh, 18, 71, 72
Al-Hout, Shafiq, 98, 126, 149, 188–89
Howaidi, Amin, 167
Hukumat 'Umum Falastin (Government of All Palestine), 33, 34, 47, 165
Huleh Valley, 53
Al-Hurriyah, 126
Al-Husri, Sati', 14, 170, 171
Hussein, Saddam, 196, 197, 201
Husseini, Faisal, 205–6
Al-Husseini, 'Abd al-Qadir, 20, 29, 32
Al-Husseini, Amin, 17, 19, 24, 29–30, 32, 62. *See also* Mufti
Al-Husseini, Hamdi, 13
Al-Husseini, Ibrahim, 50
Al-Husseini, Jamal, 22
Hussein of Jordan, King, 61, 65, 68, 127, 148
Hussein of Mecca, Sherif, 5, 7

Ibrahim, Muhsin, 178, 179
Ibrahim Pasha, Syria empire building by, 1–2, 3
ICO (Islamic Conference Organization), 128, 137–38
Al-'Imleh, Abu-Khaled, 127
Independence Party. *See* Istiqlal Party
Intifada, 14, 183–84, 185, 217–18
IPC (Iraq Petroleum Company), 25
Iran, 20, 123, 139
Iran-Iraq War, 197, 216
Iraq, 139; 'Abdullah of Jordan's conflict with Faisal over title to, 7–8; ANM and, 176–77; Ba'th Party reaction to Syria-Iraq union, 40; British-Iraqi treaty of 1930, 18; Egypt and, 35–36; Faisal and Palestinians and, 14; Iran-Iraq War, 197, 216; Lebanon and, 123; Movement to Champion Iraq, 177; October 1973 war against Israel and, 101; oil pipelines, 25–26; Palestinian obstacles to Syrian nationalism, 20–21, 23, 163; potential invasion of Syria by, 43; al-Quwatli and, 20; revolt of al-Kaylani, 19–20; support for Palestinians during 1936 revolt, 18, 19; support for PLA, 68; -Syria agreements after First Palestine War, 38–39; Syria and, 44, 45, 118, 188; -Syria union, 40, 174–75; Turkish-Iraqi agreement of 1955, 50, 51
Iraqi-Syrian union, 174–75
Iraq Petroleum Company (IPC), 25, 90
Irbed, 96
'Ireqat, Sa'ib, 207
Al-Islah, 14
Islamic Conference, 216
Islamic conference (1931), 13
Islamic conference (1966), 70–71
Islamic Conference Organization (ICO), 128, 137–38
Islamic Unification Movement, 131
Israel: armistice agreement in First Palestine War, 46; armistice agreement with Syria, 35, 53; attack on Sumu', 68; attacks on Beirut and refugee camps, 122–23; border clashes with Syria, 50, 88; casualties in Lebanon, 130–31; confrontations with Syria, 43–44, 100–101, 121, 131; decline of pan-Arabism and creation of, vii; First Palestine War and, 31, 36; Golan Heights and, 89, 100, 120, 208; Jordan and, vii, 101; land expansion and Syria, 36; in Lebanon, 100, 118–30; on Lebanon and Syria, 111; massacre of Olympic athletes and, 99–100; missile crisis with Syria, 120; negotiators after Gulf War, 218; October 1973 War and, 101–4; "Palestinian Golan" designs of, 53–54; pan-Arabism and, 41–42; peace agreement with Syria,

Israel—*continued*
  211; peace plans of, 199, 201–2; peace treaty with Lebanon, 129; PLO and, 116–17, 120–22; PLO withdrawal from Lebanon and, 123–24; prisoner exchanges, 132–33; raids on camps, 100; raids on Syria, 54; raids on Syria and Lebanon, 100; reasons for peace agreement, 211; "red line" zone agreement, 119–20, 135; on repeal of Zionism-equals-racism statement, 203; response to al-Za'im coup, 38; settlers in demilitarized zones, 53; Syria intervention possible by, 43; -Syria missile crisis, 120; Syria reaction to recognition of, 47–48; threats to Syria over withdrawal from Lebanon, 124–25; as threat to entire Arab world, 186; U.N. and, 47–48, 53; water disputes with Syria, 54–58; withdrawal from Lebanon, 131
Israeli Council for Israeli-Palestinian Peace, 116
'Issa, Michel, 26
Istiqlal Party, 9, 13, 14, 18, 24
Italy, 20

Jaber, Haj Isma'il, 122
Jabhat Tahrir Filastin (Front for the Liberation of Palestine), 70
Al-Jabri, Ihsan, 41–42
Al-Jabri, Sa'ad al-Allah, 19
Al-Jabri, Sa'id al-Allah, 12
Jadid, Salah, 81, 83, 84, 85, 88, 89, 91
Al-Jamali, Fadhel, 44, 174–75
Jamal Pasha, Ahmad ("butcher of Syria"), 4–6
Jam'iyat al-Ikha' al-'Arabi, 4
Jardaneh, Nizar, 174
Jaysh al-Inqath (The Salvation Army), 26–27, 29, 31–32, 76
Al-Jaza'iri, 'Abd al-Qader, 4
Jerusalem, 72, 206
Jibril, Ahmad, 86, 87, 91, 116, 131, 133, 140
Jihad, 15, 17–18, 28
Jihad, Abu, 93
Jihad, Um, 87–88
Jinnah, Muhammad 'Ali, 29

Johnston, Eric, 54–55, 174
Johnston Plan, 55, 80–81, 174, 175
Jordan: Arafat and, 148–49; Assad during Palestinian-Jordan war, 95–97; Egypt and, 35–36, 88, 97–98; Fateh and, 182, 214; First Palestine War and, 31, 32–33; Greater Syria scheme and, 21–22; guerrilla activities in, 95–98; intifada and, 184; Israel and, vii, 101; at Madrid peace talks with PLO, 206; nationalist groups in, 174 (*see also* Arab Nationalist Movement); October 1973 war against Israel and, 101; Palestine policy of, 33–34; Palestinian armed struggle and, 94–98, 109; PLO creation and, 68; PLO militia relocation and, 125; PLO on, 108; PLO reconciliation with, 148–49; PNC and, 139–41, 148–49; radical Palestinian groups and, 63; relations with Israel, vii; support for Arab League of States, 67; Syria and, 33–34, 95–98, 105, 109, 118; Syria's demands of, 61; U.S. and, 95; war with Palestinians, 95–98, 109; West Bank and, 104. *See also* 'Abdullah of Jordan, King/Prince; Hussein of Jordan, King; Transjordan

Jordan River, 54–55, 57, 79
Jumblatt, Kamal, 113, 114
Jumblatt, Walid, 129
Al-Jundi, 'Abd al-Karim, 83, 84, 88, 90, 92

Kanafani, Ghassan, 63
Karamah, battle of, 94–95, 182, 215
Karamah, Rashid, 129, 131
Al-Karamah division, 99
Al-Karim, Sheikh Sa'id, 5
Kassis, Cherbel, 118
Kata'ib al-Fida' al-'Arabi, 49–50, 63, 168, 171, 177
Al-Kawakibi, 'Abd al-Rahman, 15
Al-Kaylani, Rashid 'Ali, 19, 20
Al-Kayyali, 'Abd al-Rahman, 12
Al-Kayyali, Fakher, 48
Kelly, John, 199
Khaddam, 'Abd al-Halim, 82, 85, 128, 131, 135, 206

Al-Khadhra, Subhi, 13, 26
Khalaf, Salah, 94, 123, 128–29, 137, 140, 183, 210
Al-Khalidi, Hussein, 22
Khalifa, Muhammad, 141
Khartoum summit, 71–73, 75, 90
Al-Khatib, Ahmad, 50, 114, 174, 175
Al-Khatib, Rouhi, 65
Al-Khouli, Lufti, 136, 166–67
Khouri, Iliya, 141
Al-Khouri, Faris: Arab League Charter and, 22; on Greater Syria, 163; imprisonment and torture by Jamal Pasha, 5; on Israel as a state, 47–48; mufti and, 77; on Pakistan support of Palestinians, 29; on People's Party and Syria unity, 12–13; as Syria's prime minister, 36
Al-Kifah al-musalah (Tlas), 78–80
Al-Kikhya, Rushdi, 40, 52
King-Crane commission, 6
Kishli, Muhammad, 179
Kissinger, Henry, 103, 106, 109, 115, 202–3, 210. *See also* United States
Kramer, Michael, 200
Kurtzer, Dan, 199
Al-Kutlah, 14
Kuwait, 67, 115
Kuwayk, Sami, 127
Al-Kuzbari, Ma'mun, 48

Labor Party, 136
Lake Huleh, 54
al-Lamarkaziyah, 6, 9
Larsen, Tirgi, 207
Lavon, Pinchas, 43
Lawrence of Arabia, 6
League of National Action, 171
League of Nations, 10
Lebanese National Democratic Front, 143
Lebanese National Movement, 113
Lebanon: battle of Tripoli and, 130–36; cease-fire in, 123; enlargement at expense of Syria, 11; Fateh and, 98, 126, 182; impact of PLO move to, 112–13; international media ignoring of, 149; Iraq and, 123; Israel fighting in, 100, 118–30; Israel's withdrawal, 131; long-term impact on PLO, 192; Palestinians and, 217; peace treaty with Israel, 129; PLO desire to return to, 142; PLO move into, 98–105; PLO moves to, 149; PLO remnants in, 219; PLO support for, 108; PLO withdrawal from, 123, 125–26, 188, 215; al-Sa'iqa and war in, 114, 116; siege of Beirut, and Syria, 124–25; Syria and, 110, 111, 112, 113–18, 122, 123, 130, 151, 212, 215; U.S. and, 121–22, 131
Liberal Party, 118
Libya, 97, 137

Al-Madhi, Mu'een, 13
Madrid peace talks, 201, 203, 206–7, 218
Al-Mahayni, Thabet, 174
Maher, 'Ali, 21
Mahmoud II, 1
Makhaibah dam, 57
Makhous, Ibrahim, 71, 73, 88, 90
Malik, Charles, 48
Al-Malki, 'Adnan, 27, 50, 80
Ma'louf, Shafiq, 156
Ma'na al-Nakba (Zureiq), 171
Mandates, 6–13, 18–19, 163
Mango, 'Ali, 174
Ma'oz, Moshe, vii
Mardam Bayk, Fu'ad, 35
Mardam Bayk, Jameel, 12, 20–21, 22, 34–35
Marines, U.S., attacks on, 131
Maronite Eighth Brigade, 143
Maronites, 113, 129, 143
Ma'rouf, Muhammad, 40
Maryoud, Hassan, 67
Maysaloun, battle of, 15
Meir, Golda, 60
Milhem, Muhammad, 141
Miller, Aaron, 199
Misr al-Fatah, 169
Missiles, 119–20, 151
Al-Mithaq al-Qawmi ("The National Covenant"), 185
Al-Mithaq al-Watani ("The Regional Charter"), 185
Mitla pass, 102
Mitterand, François, 132, 147
Miyah Miyah refugee camp, 142

Movement of Socialist Unionists, 97
Movement to Champion Iraq (Harakat Nassret al-Iraq), 177
Mubarak, Husni, 101, 136, 137, 183, 215
Mufti: Arab sponsorship and, 73; Arafat and, 64; First Palestine War and, 29–30; during First Palestine War and, 33, 45; flight to Iran, 20; al-Khouri and, 77; Nasser and, 62; origins of PLO and, 62; during 1936 Palestinian revolt, 19–20; pan-Arabism and, 18–19, 24; on people's war, 75–76; as political representative of Palestinians, 47; al-Qassam and, 17–18; relationship between Syrian leaders and, 77; support for Druze, 18; Syria and, 33, 77, 81; Syrian-Egyptian union and, 81
Muhammad 'Ali Pasha, 1–2
Muhammad Kurd 'Ali, 5
Muhsin, Zuhayr, 116, 117, 134, 135
Al-Muntada al-'Arabi, 5
Musa, Sa'id, 127
Muslim Brotherhood, 35, 40, 52–53, 76, 93, 161
Mustafa, Shaker, 67

Nablus uprising, 3
Al-Nadi al-Thaqafi al-Qawmi (National Cultural Club), 174
Nafouri, Amin, 57
Al-Nahaas, Mustafa, 21
Nahr al-Bared camp, 100, 128, 133
Al-Nakba, 166, 168
Nashashibi, Zuhdi, 138
Al-Nashashibi, Ragheb, 17, 22
Nassar, Fu'ad, 160
Nasser, Gamal Abdel: ANM and, 93, 176–80; Arab League Palestinian representation and, 61; at Arab League's September 1963 summit meeting, 55–56; on Arab summit meetings, 70–71; on armed struggle and Habash, 64, 93; at Bandung Conference, 48; creation of Middle East system and, 51–52; death of, 98–99; diversion of Jordan River and, 57; Egypt and PLO and, 69; Egyptian role in Jordanian crisis and, 97; *Egypt's Liberation,* 174; Fateh and, 93, 214; mufti Amin Husseini and, 62; on Palestinian appointment to Arab League of States, 74–75; on Palestinian liberation, 167; on pan-Arabism, 74; quasi-government for Palestinians and, 165; resignation of, 89; Yemeni civil war and, 71–72
Nasser al-Din, 'Ali, 171–73, 175
Nasser Muhammad, 'Ali, 106
National Alliance, 139
National Command Council, of Ba'th Party, 166
"National Covenant, The" (al-Mithaq al-Qawmi), 185
National Cultural Club (al-Nadi al-Thaqafi al-Qawmi), 174
Nationalism: Arab versus Palestinian, 191, 214; background of Palestinian, 154, 178–79; Ba'th Party's opposition to Palestinian, 165; characteristics of Palestinian, 190–91; definition of, 154–55; France and Syria, 19–20, 34; German theories of, 170; Iraqi and Palestinian obstacles to Syria, 20–21, 23, 163; versus Palestinian identity, 116, 216–17; al-Quwatli and, 155; Syria's nationalist bloc, 12–13; Syria's secret societies and, 4, 6, 8–9
Nationalist Party, 40, 161
"Nationalist Racial Philosophy" (Sa'adeh), 159
National Party, 52, 53
National Progressive Front, 97, 103
National Water Carrier, 55–56, 57–58
Non-Aligned Movement, 48
Al-Nuqrashi Pasha, Mahmoud Fahmi, 36, 62
Nushu' al-Umam (The Rise of Nations) (Sa'adeh), 156–58
Nusseibah, Hazem, 147
Nuwayhedh, 'Ajaj, 13

October 1973 War, 101–4, 109–10
Oil: Arab meetings on, 71; in First Palestine War, 34–35; Iraqi pipelines, 25–26; October 1973 War and, 104; Syria and issues of, 25–26, 34–35, 46, 162

Olympics, massacre of Israeli athletes at, 99–100
"Operation Pines," 121
Organization of Arab Palestine, 91
Organization of Lebanese Socialists, 179
Oslo peace accords, 188, 195, 207–8, 218, 220
'Othman, Amin, 169
Ottoman Empire: end of, 6–7; German officers in, 27; pashaliks of, 2–3; restoration of rule of, 3–4; Syria and, 2–3. *See also* Turkey

Palestine: Britain and, 14–15, 17, 31, 163; Egypt's first involvement in, 21; end of Ottoman empire and, 6–7; impact on Syria of loss of Arab, 213–14; Jordan policy toward, 33–34; as motivator for Syrian unity, 162; *nakba* and, 166, 168; national charter of 1919, 8; al-Qassam and fate of, 14–17; al-Qassam's contribution to, 17–18, 23; al-Qassam uprisings and, 15–16, 16–17; Sa'adeh insights into Arab approach to, 157–60; Shuqeiri on Arab issues versus, 49, 75–76; "Southern Syria" as name for, 8; Syria and fate of, 14–15, 23, 46; Tlas on, 79–80. *See also* Palestinians
Palestine Electric Works, 11
Palestine Liberation Army (PLA), 67–68, 86, 91, 180
Palestine Liberation Front, 86, 91, 129
Palestine Liberation Front General Command, 91
Palestine National Council (PNC): Arafat and, 137–38, 141; executive committee of, 140–41; Fateh and, 116, 140; membership of, 91, 116, 140; Shuqeiri and, 73
—meetings of: July 1968, 92; July 1971, 97; Cairo, twelfth session of, June 1974, 182–83; January 1979, 107–8, 110; February 1983, 189; November 1984, Jordan, 139–41, 148–49
Palestine National Fund, 67, 76, 140
Palestine National Salvation Front (PNSF), 142–43, 184
Palestine War, First: armistice agreement and, 35–36, 46; armistice critics and, 37; Ba'th Party's attitude toward, 163; Egypt and, 31, 35–36; inter-Arab dissension and intrigue during, 32–36; Iraq-Syria agreements after, 38–39; Israel and, 31, 36; Jordan and, 31, 32–33; military interventions during, 36–45; mufti and, 29–30; mufti during, 33, 45; obstacles to, 31–32; oil issues in, 34–35; Palestinians in Syria after, 49–50; Qawuqji and, 28–32; Saudi Arabia and, 31, 36; Shishakli and, 26–27; SSNP casualties in, 160; Syria's military preparedness for, 34; Syria's politics and army after, 37–45, 46; Syria–Saudi Arabia issues during, 34–35; Syria's contribution to, 26–27; U.N. and armistice talks after, 36
Palestinians: Arab attitude toward after October 1973 War, 104; Arab League of States, responsibility to, 147–48; Arab support for popular resistance of, 73; armed struggle issue and, 64, 93, 94–98, 171–72, 178–79, 193–94; Assad and, 95–97, 114; Ba'th Party and, 148, 162, 165–66; British and, 14–15, 17, 31, 163; communities of, 219–20; community and, 216–17; criticisms of, 58, 59, 80; dissolution of UAR and, 58; divisions among groups of, 93; Druze and, 18; dualism of responsibility among political groups of, 182; Egypt and, 65, 76–77, 93–94; establishment of army of, 67–68; fissures among, 85–92; government in exile, question of, 183, 184–85; as guerrilla fighters in Syria, 85–86, 87; guerrilla movement and, 78–80; Gulf War and, 200, 201; in high office in Syria, 49; identity issues, 116, 216–17; importance of revolt of 1936, 19; Iraq support during 1936 revolt, 18, 19; Lebanon and (*see* Lebanon); mufti and (*see* Mufti); Nasser and, 61, 74–75, 165, 167; nationalism and (*see* Nationalism); 1936 uprising and Syria, 18; opposition to Fateh, 143, 152; Pakistan's support for, 29; pan-Arabism and, 59, 110, 209; PLO and (*see* PLO); political parties of,

Palestinians—*continued*
14, 58, 59; post–Gulf War peace negotiations and, 202, 203; progressive Arab regimes co-optation of, 165–66; radical groups and Syria, 63–65; representation problem and Arab summit in Khartoum, 71–73, 188–89; revisionist views of, 188–89; revolt of 1936, 17, 18; Saudi support of, during 1936 revolt, 19; secret societies and, 13; separate versus comprehensive Arab solution and, 189–90, 191, 209; Shuqeiri and, 59–60; statehood declaration by, 184–85; statesmen and revolutionaries, 47–52; in Syria after First Palestine War, 49–50; Syria's early ties with, 22–23; U.N. and, 60; view of Syria, 148; war with Jordan, 95–98, 109; Zionists and, 216. *See also* Israel; PLO

Pan-Arabism: ʿAbdullah of Jordan and, 155; Assad on, 151–52, 209; of Baʿth Party, 161–67; connection with Islam, 154; Fateh and, viii, 150; Israel and, vii, 41–42; mufti on, 18–19, 24; Nasser on, 74; necessity for, 163; Palestinians and, 59, 110, 209; PFLP and, 74; Shishakli and, 46; Western scholarship on, vii–viii

Paris peace conference, 9–10

Paulet-Newcombe agreement, 9, 10–11

PDFLP. *See* Popular Democratic Front for the Liberation of Palestine

PDRY. *See* People's Democratic Republic of Yemen

"Peace for Galilee" operation, 122

Peel Commission on Palestine, 160

Peled, Mattiyahu, 54, 116

People's Democratic Republic of Yemen (PDRY), 139

People's Party, 35, 40, 41, 49, 52

People's Party (Hizb al-Shaʿb), 12–13

People's Republic of China, 69

Peres, Shimon, 207

Perlmutter, Amos, 202

PFLP. *See* Popular Front for the Liberation of Palestine

Phalangists, 113–114, 120, 121

PLA (Palestine Liberation Army), 67–68, 86, 91

PLO (Palestine Liberation Organization): achievements of, 153; Amal and, 142, 143, 145, 146–47; Arab sponsorship of, 61–62, 73, 93, 181; armed struggle versus diplomacy and, 193–94; ʿAssifa and, 99, 111; Beirut office of, 126; charter name changes, 187, 193; charter of, 65–66, 187, 193, 216; concessions, 197–98, 204, 205, 206, 210–11; contact with Israeli doves, 116–17; criticism of al-Assad, 96–97; criticisms of, 113, 115, 116–17, 123, 124, 146, 185–87, 204–5; defections from, 128–29; dispersal of troops of, 132; Egyptian support of, 215–16; evacuation from Tripoli and Syria, 131–32, 217; executive committee meeting of January 1984, 138–39; executive committee meeting with Assad, 101–2; factional unity issue and, 107–8; factions of, 127, 137; first phase of, 63–67; foreign policy of, 106; guerrilla groups and, 182; future of, 220; ideological tensions in, 182–83, 192–93; independence of, 92–98, 115–16, 183–84; Israel's plans to eject, 120–21; Jordan and, 108, 148–49; al-Karamah division, 99; lack of military preparedness, 122–23; Lebanese National Movement and, 113; massacre of Olympics athletes and, 99–100; media accounts of Tripoli siege and, 133–35; member groups of, 91–92; as member of Arab League of States, 186, 192; membership of, 180; militia relocation issues, 125; move into Lebanon, 98–105; Muhsin declared leader of, 135; October 1973 war strategies of, 101–2; origins of, 60–62, 165–66; in peace negotiations, 199; post-Lebanon withdrawal relations between Syria and, 126–27, 135–36; prisoner exchanges and, 132–33; al-Qastal division, 99; reaction to Sharon as Israel minister of defense, 120; recognition as Palestinian representative, 104, 111, 183, 187–88; refugees and, 126, 153; relations with Arab states, 68, 69; relocation in Syria, 125, 135–36; remnants of, in Lebanon, 219; resettlement in Tunisia, 132; revisionists and, 188–89; Saudi Arabia and, 117–18; second phase of, 67–74, 76; Shuqeiri and origins of, 180–83; Shuqeiri's influence on ideology of, 154; Soviet Union and, 69, 93, 123, 190; sullying of Syria, 151; supporters of, 104–5; Syria's attempted elimination of, 145; Syria's criticisms of, 186–87; Syria's failure to rein in, 152–53; Syria's infiltration of, 152; -Syria refugee camps war, 141–49; on Syria role in Beirut siege, 124–25; Syria's support for, 104–5; Ten Point Program, 183; ties with Syria, 99–100; ties with Western powers, 217–18; U.N. influence on, 111; U.N. Resolution 242, acceptance by, 198; -U.S. secret bargaining with after Gulf War, 218; -U.S. talks with, 200; withdrawal from Lebanon, 125–26, 188, 215; Yarmouk division, 99. *See also* Arafat, Yasser

PNC. *See* Palestine National Council

PNSF (Palestine National Salvation Front), 142–43, 184

Ponsot, Henri, 11–12

Popular Democratic Front for the Liberation of Palestine (PDFLP): Arafat and, 206; boycott of January 1984 PLO executive committee meeting, 138; creation of, 91; Democratic Alliance and, 139; militia of, 143; on Palestinian government in exile, 183; PLO and, 126, 129, 152; split from PFLP, 179

Popular Front for the Liberation of Palestine (PFLP): boycott of PLO January 1984 executive committee meeting, 138; creation of, 91; Habash and, 63; *Al-Hadaf* publication of, 126; Heroes of Return and origins of, 179; pan-Arabism and, 74; PLO and, 92, 129, 143, 152, 185; split in General Command, 116

Progressive Front, 121

"Proposed Palestinian Framework, The" (Mashrou' al-Kiyan al-Filistini), 165–66

Qaddafi, Mu'ammar, 97, 106, 197

Qaddumi, Farouq, 116, 141, 146–47, 184, 206

Al-Qadisiyah, 68

Al-Qahtaniyah, 6

Qasem, 'Abd al-Karim, 56, 64, 82

Al-Qassam, Sheikh 'Izz al-Din, 14–17, 75–76

Al-Qastal division, 99

Al-Qattan, 'Abd al-Muhsin, 91

Qawasmah, Fahed, 141

Al-Qawuqji, Fawzi, 18, 19, 45–46; Arab League supporters of, 30; background of, 27–28; First Palestine War of 1948 and, 28–32; nationalist views of, 28–29; obstacles to First Palestine War of 1948 and, 31–32; Quwatli and, 29, 30–31; as supporter of people's war, 75

Qays, Abu-'Adnan, 175

Qhadhiyat al-'Arab (The Arab Question) (Nasser al-Din), 173

Qiryat Shmona, 102

Al-Qleibi, al-Shadli, 107, 147–48

Quandt, William, 200, 203

Al-Qudsi, Nathem, 39, 58, 82

Quneitra, 104

Al-Quwatli, Shukri: First Palestine War of 1948 and, 29, 30–31; Iraq and, 20; King 'Abdullah and, 32–33; as member of nationalist bloc, 12; nationalism and, 155; Saudi Arabia and, 33; Shuqeiri and, 22, 77; Tapline agreement and, 35; torture by Jamal Pasha, 5; trip to Soviet Union, 51

Rabat summit, 104, 187–88

Rabin, Yitzak, 119, 199, 208

Al-Ra'ii, 174, 175

Al-Ra'i, 63

Rashaya al-Wadi camp, 100

Ras Shamra, 157

Al-Razaz, Munif, 84

Reagan administration, 120

Reagan plan, 148

"Red line" zone agreement, 119–20, 135

Refugees, 90–91, 113–14, 122, 126, 128, 141–49, 153, 175, 219–20

"Regional Charter, The" (al-Mithaq al-Watani), 185

Research Center for Palestine Studies, 67, 76

"Revenge, or Easing Shame" (Al-tha'r aw mahwi al-'aar) (Nasser al-Din), 172
Revolutionary Command Council, 83, 84, 85
Riadh, Mahmoud, 52, 107
Ridha, Muhammad Rashid, 15
Al-Rikabi, 'Ali Ridha, 9
Riyadh summit, 115–16
Rogers peace plan, 98
Ross, Dennis, 199, 200
Rutenberg, Pinchas, 11

Sa'adeh, Anton, 1, 39, 156–61
Al-Sab'awi, Younis, 168
Al-Sabbagh, Salah al-Din, 19
Sabra refugee camp, 125, 142, 143
Sacred Jihad, 29
Sadat, Anwar, 57, 102, 122, 183
Al-Sa'di, Sheikh Farhan, 17
Al-Sadr, Imam Musa, 100, 144
Safad uprising, 3
Al-Safir, 122
Safwat, Isma'il, 26
Sa'id, Fahmi, 19
Sa'id, Mustafa, 145
Sa'id, Riyadh, 140
Al-Sa'id, Hafiz, 5
Al-Sa'id, Nouri, 38, 49, 169
Al-Sa'iqa, 99; creation of, 91; Fateh and, 126, 134; Lebanon war and, 114, 116; opposition to Phalanigists, 113; PLO and, 138; post-1967 war, 179
Salamah, Sheikh Hassan, 32
Salem, Salah, 51
Salih, Nimr, 127
Salvation Army (Jaysh al-Inqath), 26–27, 29, 31–32, 76
San Remo agreement, 7, 13
Sarkis, Elias, 114, 124
Al-Sarraj, 'Abd al-Hamid, 177
Sartawi, 'Issam, 167
Saudi Arabia, 56, 201; agreement with Egypt, 71–72; disputes with PLO and Shuqeiri, 69; Fateh and, 182; First Palestine War and, 31, 34–35, 36; objections to PLO charter, 67; oil pipelines and, 25; Ottoman empire and, 27; PLO and, 117–18; PLO evacuation from Tripoli and, 131–32; PLO-Syria relations and, 128; Quwatli and, 33; reaction to Syria-Iraq union, 40; Riyadh summit and, 115–16; support for Palestinians during 1936 revolt, 19; support for PLO, 104–5
Al-Sayeh, Sheikh 'Abd al-Hamid, 140
Al-Sayel, Sa'ad, 99, 123
Al-Sayyid, Ahmad Lutfi, 159
Secret societies, 4, 6, 8–9, 13. See also specific societies
Sha'ath, Nabeel, 207
Shabab al-Tha'r (Youths of Revenge), 179
Sha'ban, Sheikh Sa'id, 131
Shabib, Kamel, 19
Shadhly, Sa'ad, 101
Shahbandar, 'Abd al-Rahman, 5
Shakour, Yousef, 89, 101
Shamir, Yitzhak, 199, 203
Al-Shara', Farouq, 146
Al-Sharabati, Ahmad, 31
Sharett, Moshe, 43–44
Sharm al-Sheikh, 70
Sharon, Ariel, 119, 120, 121–22
Shatila refugee camp, 125, 142
Al-Shawwa, 'Izz al-Din, 19, 30
Sherif Bey, 2
Shi'ites, 100, 131. See also Amal
Shishakli, Adib: assassination plots against, 49, 168, 169; Ba'th Party and, 41; coups of, 40–41, 44–45; on Druze rebellion, 42; First Palestine War and, 26–27; Hourani and, 40–41; pan-Arabism and, 46; Shuqeiri and, 48; U.S. attempts to restore power of, 44–45, 50
Shlaim, Avi, vii
Shqeir, Shawkat, 26
Shruru, Fadhl, 140
Shtura agreement (1977), 117, 118
Shufani, Elias, 140
Shukri, Ibrahim, 136, 137
Shuqeiri, Ahmad, 22, 48, 49; advantages of PLO charter, 65–66; after 1964 Arab summit meeting, 165; Arab League of States and, 59–60, 70, 75–76, 181; challenges to PLO project of, 63–74; coup against executive committee of PLO, 73; Fateh and, 64–65, 70, 180; ideology of PLO and contribution of, 154, 180–82,

216; Khartoum summit and, 71–73, 188–89; as leader of popular Palestinian effort, 59–60; legacies of, 76; on limitations of PLO charter, 66–67; main base of support for, 70–71; opposition to, 63–74; origins of PLO and, 180–83; on Palestine versus Arab issues, 49, 75–76; PLA and, 68; PNC and, 73; Quwatli and, 22, 77; radical underground opposition to, 63–65; removal from office of PLO, 92; Saudi Arabia's disputes with, 69; Shishakli and, 48; Syria's reaction to, 69–70; on territorial base for PLO, 60–61; Tunisia's disputes with PLO and, 69, 71; U.N. policy of, 75; weakness of PLO project of, 62

Shuraiqi, Muhammad, 32
Sidon refugee camps, 144–45
Sidqi, Baker, 19
Silo, Fawzi, 27, 41
Sixth Fleet, U.S., 45
Socialist Cooperative Party (al-Hizb al-Taʿawuni al-Ishtiraki), 37
Socialist Union party, 81
Al-Solh, Riadh, 5, 32
Al-Solh, Ridha, 5
Al-Solh, Sami, 48
Sourani, Jamal, 141
"Southern Syria," as name for Palestine, 8
Soviet-Syria economic agreement (1957), 50
Soviet Union: Assad and, 106, 196–97; Egypt and PLO and, 69; Fateh and, 190; Middle East policy of, 190; PLO and, 69, 93, 123, 190; PLO-Syria relations and, 128; refugee camp war and, 143; Syria and, 50, 51, 88, 130, 196–97; U.S. and, 130
SSNP (Syrian Social National Party), 143, 155–61
Sudan, 97
Suleiman, Hikmat, 19
Sumuʿ, 68
Supreme Muslim Council, 140, 160
Sweidani, Ahmed, 88
Sykes-Picot Agreement, 10
Syria: assembly elections in, 11–12; attacks on U.S. marines, 131; al-Bitar coup, 58; communism in, 52; on comprehensive peace agreement, 208–9; congress of 1920, 8; constitution of, 12, 82; coups, 40–41, 44–45, 82, 83, 84–85; creation of Arab kingdom of, 6–7; Egypt and (see Egypt); Fateh and (see Fateh); French mandate in, 10–13; Greater Syria scheme and (see Greater Syria scheme); Gulf War and, 200–201; Hamdoun coup, 42–43; al-Hinnawi coup, 39–40; impact of loss of Arab Palestine, 213–14 (see also Palestine); independence movement in, 12–13; international media on, 92, 132; international media on Lebanon war contributions, 123–24; Iraq and (see Iraq); Israel and (see Israel); Jordan and (see Jordan); June 1967 war and, 88–89; Khartoum summit and, 90; Lebanon and (see Lebanon); mandates and, 7–13, 18–19; military capabilities of, 89–90, 129–30; military support for guerrilla organizations, 87; missiles of, 130; mufti and, 33; nationalism in (see Nationalism); nationalist bloc in, 12–13; oil issues and, 25–26, 34–35, 46, 162; opposition to PNC meeting of November 1984, 139–40; origin of term for, 1, 6–7; origins of, 1–2; Oslo peace accords and, 207–8; Ottoman Empire and, 2–3; Palestinians and (see Palestinians); peace process and, 195–98; PLA and, 86, 91; post-Gulf War agreements and, 218–19; pre-1967 war situation, 88–89; reaction to PNC executive committee changes, 141; "red line" zone agreement, 119–20, 135; refugee problems of (see Refugees); regional defense pacts to control, 50–51; resumption of diplomatic relations with U.S., 103–4; Saʿadeh on ancient, 156–57; secret societies in, 4, 6, 8–9; separate peace agreement and, 208; Shishakli's first coup, 40–41; Shishakli's second coup, 44–45; Soviet Union and (see Soviet Union); Transjordan and, 27–28, 33–34; treaty with France, 18; unilateral peace and, 195–96; water disputes and, 54–58; al-Zaʿim coup, 36–38

Syrian-Egyptian defense pact, 88
Syrian-Egyptian economic pact, 51

Syrian Social National Party (SSNP), 143, 155–61
Syria under Assad (Ma'oz and Yaniv), vii

Al-Tagamu', 136
Al-Taher, Maher, 187
Al-Tal, Wasfi, 134
Tal al-Za'atar refugee camp massacre, 113–14
Tal'at Pasha, 4
Talee', Rasheed, 9
Ta'mari, Salah, 133
Al-Tamimi, Rafiq, 6
Tamir, Avraham, 104
Tapline Company, 25, 34–35, 36
Taqqadum (Progress) Party, 9
Tawfiq, Ahmad Pasha, 169
Tawfiq, Hussein, 50, 168, 169
Ten Point Program, 183
Al-Tha'r (Revenge), 174
Third World revolutions, 193–94
Tibi, Bassam, viii
Tlas, Mustafa: coups in Syria and, 84–85; Higher Military Council and, 101; on Jordan war, 96; *al-Kifah al-musalah*, 78–80; mediation in Jordan war and, 97; on 1967 war, 89; on Palestinian issue, 81; Palestinians and, 100; Syria's military and, 91; on Syria's union with Egypt, 82
Transjordan, 8–9, 19; Syria and, 27–28, 33–34; U.N. and, 33
Tripoli, 217; battle of, 130–36; as pashalik of Ottoman Empire, 2
Tunisia, 125, 132; disputes with PLO and Shuqeiri, 69, 71
Turkey, 11, 50, 51. *See also* Ottoman empire
Turkish-Iraqi agreement (1955), 50, 51

UAR. *See* United Arab Republic (UAR)
'Umran, Muhammad, 82
UNDOF (United Nations Disengagement Observer Force), 103
Unified Arab Military Command, 67, 68
Union of Kuwaiti Scholarship Students, 176
Union of Palestinian Writers, 180

United Arab Republic (UAR), 55, 56, 58, 64, 177, 178, 188
United Nations: Arab recognition of Israel and, 47–48; Arafat at, 104–5, 185; armistice talks after First Palestine War and, 36; influence on PLO, 111; Israel and, 47–48, 53; Palestinian representation at, 60; resolutions on Palestine question, 48; Shuqeiri policy toward, 75; Transjordan and, 33
—Security Council resolutions: 181, 184, 193; 242, 79, 90, 97–98, 101, 103, 123, 135, 184–85, 198, 209; 338, 103, 185, 209
United Nations Disengagement Observer Force (UNDOF), 103
United Nations High Commission for Refugees, 219
United Nations Relief and Works Agency (UNRWA), 175, 219–20
United Nations Security Council: Resolution III, 54; water issues and, 55–56
United Nations Special Committee on Palestine (UNSCOP), 26
United Nations Truce Supervision Organization (UNTSO), 53–54
United States: on Arab recognition of Israel, 47–48; Arafat and, 185; destabilization attempts on radical Arab regimes, 74; destabilization attempts on Syria governments, 50–51; on Israel plans to eject PLO from Lebanon, 121–22; Israel-Syria missile crisis and, 120; Jordan and, 95; in Lebanon, 131; peacemaking strategy of, 198–203; PLO foreign policy and, 106, 117; -PLO secret bargaining after Gulf War, 218; -PLO talks, 200; resumption of diplomatic relations with Syria, 103–4; Rogers peace plan, 98; Sadat on, 102; separate peace agreement and Syria, 208; Soviet Union and, 130; support for al-Za'im coup, 36–37; support for Shishakli, 44–45, 50; Syrian attacks on U.S. marines, 131. *See also* Kissinger, Henry
UNRWA (United Nations Relief and Works Agency), 175, 219–20

UNSCOP (United Nations Special Committee on Palestine), 26
UNTSO (United Nations Truce Supervision Organization), 53–54
Al'Urwah al-Wuthqa, 170, 174
'Usbat al-'Amal al-Qawmi, 170

Vietnam, 204–5, 218
Von Grobba, Fritz, 20
Von Horn, Carl, 53
Von Layser, [name?], 27
Von Papen, Franz, 20

Wafd Party, 21, 160, 169
Al-Wa'ii al-Qawmi (National Consciousness) (Zureiq), 170, 171
Al-Walid, Abu, 99
War of attrition, 89
Water issues, 10–11, 54–58
Al-Wazan, Shafiq, 123
Al-Wazir, Khalil, 87, 93, 128, 137, 141, 149–50, 183, 210
Weber, Max, 216
Weizman, Ezer, 119
West Bank, 61, 217, 220

"With No Boundaries" (Arafat), 136
World War II, 19–20

Ya'bad, battle of, 17
Yadin, Yigal, 119
Al-Yahya, 'Abd al-Razzaq, 141
al-Yamani, Abu-Maher, 141, 175
Yaniv, Avner, vii
Yarmouk division, 99
Yarmouk River, 55
Yemen, 71, 128, 179
Young Men's Muslim Association, 16
Youths of Revenge (Shabab al-Tha'r), 179

Za'een, Yousef, 85
Al-Za'im, Husni, 27, 36–38, 39
Al-Zarkali, Kheir al-Din, 13
Za'rour, Ahmad, 91
Zayyat, Mustafa, 174
Zhou Enlai, 48, 69, 93
Zionists, 9–10, 216. *See also* Israel
Zu'ayter, Akram, 13
Zu'ayter, Wa'il, 100
Zureiq, Qustantin, 170–71

Ghada Hashem Talhami is D. K. Pearsons Professor of Politics at Lake Forest College, Lake Forest, Illinois. She is the author of *Suakin and Massawa under Egyptian Rule, 1865–1885* (University Press of America, 1979); *Palestine and Egyptian National Identity* (Praeger, 1992); and *The Mobilization of Muslim Women in Egypt* (University Press of Florida, 1996).

www.ingramcontent.com/pod-product-compliance
Lightning Source LLC
Chambersburg PA
CBHW021343230426
43666CB00006B/390